# Communication Research

*Techniques, methods and applications*

First published 2001
Reprinted February 2006
Reprinted June 2006

© Juta & Co. Ltd 2002
PO Box 24309, Lansdowne 7779

ISBN 0 7021 5641 8

Design and layout: Catherine Crookes
Cover design: Catherine Crookes
Printed and bound by Formeset - Epping
Digital Imposition by Syreline Process

# Contents

Foreword 8

**Unit 1** **Quantitative and qualitative approaches to communication research** 15

Overview 15

Learning outcomes 16

1.1 Introduction 16

1.2 Different ways of knowing 17

1.3 A conceptual model of assumptions 20

1.4 Quantitative research approach 21

*Ontological assumptions 22   Theoretical assumptions 24*
*Epistemological and methodological assumptions 27*

Executive summary 29

1.5 Qualitative research approach 29

*Ontological assumptions 30   Theoretical assumptions 31*
*Epistemological and methodological assumptions 32*

Executive summary 34

1.6 Application of quantitative versus qualitative approaches 34

1.7 What about future research? 38

1.8 Summary 41

Self-evaluation and portfolio tasks 41

Assessment of learning outcomes 42

Suggested reading 43

**Unit 2** **Steps in the research process** 44

Overview 44

Learning outcomes 44

2.1 Introduction 45

2.2 Step 1: Identifying and analysing the problem 45

*Goals and objectives 48   Formulating the research problem,*
*subproblems and assumptions 51*

Executive summary 57

2.3 Step 2: Reviewing the literature 57

*Getting started 58   A critical review 60   Recording and summarising 63*

Executive summary 65

2.4 Step 3: Formulating hypotheses or research questions 66

*Concepts and constructs 66   Variables 70   Research questions 72*
*Hypotheses 73*

Executive summary 80

**2.5** Step 4: Selecting or developing the research design 81

*Who/what, where and when? 81    Characteristics of quantitative designs 82*
*Characteristics of qualitative designs 83    Threats to the validity of a*
*research design 84*

Executive summary 87

**2.6** Step 5: Writing a research proposal 88

*What is to be researched? 88    Why is the research study being done? 89*
*What are feasibility and ethical implications? 90    How is the research going*
*to be conducted 91*

Executive summary 92

**2.7** Step 6: Pre-testing the research design and collecting data 93

**2.8** Step 7: Analysing and interpreting data 93

**2.9** Step 8: Writing the research report 94

Executive summary 95

**2.10** Summary 95

Self-evaluation and portfolio tasks 96

Assessment of learning outcomes 97

Suggested reading 98


**UNIT 3** **DATA COLLECTION: SAMPLING, MEASURING, QUESTIONING**
**AND OBSERVING** **99**

Overview 99

Learning outcomes 99

**3.1** Introduction 100

**3.2** Sampling 100

*Accuracy of the sample drawn 101    Sampling error related to the*
*degree of confidence 104    Types of sampling  106*

Executive summary 115

Self-evaluation and portfolio tasks 116

**3.3** Measurement 117

*Principles and levels of measurement 117    The requirement of*
*reliability 121    The requirement of validity 124    Measurement scales 127*

Executive summary 132

Self-evaluation and portfolio tasks 133

**3.4** Collecting data by asking questions 134

*Problems experienced in the wording of questions and statements 134*
*Items in a self-administered questionnaire 137*
*Types of interview questions 143*

Executive summary 145

Self-evaluation and portfolio tasks 146

| | | |
|---|---|---|
| **3.5** | Collecting data by means of observations | 147 |
| | *Data-collection devices and techniques 147    Systematic observations 148* | |
| | *Ethnographic observations 151* | |
| | Executive summary | 153 |
| | Self-evaluation and portfolio tasks | 154 |
| **3.6** | Summary | 154 |
| | Assessment of learning outcomes | 155 |
| | Suggested reading | 158 |
| **UNIT 4** | **PROCEDURES FOLLOWED WHEN APPLYING A RESEARCH DESIGN** | |
| | **AND INTERPRETING RESEARCH DATA** | **159** |
| | Overview | 159 |
| | Learning outcomes | 160 |
| **4.1** | Introduction | 160 |
| **4.2** | Research conducted in controlled environments | 161 |
| | *Single-system research designs 162  Group designs 163* | |
| | *Control over the research environment 167* | |
| | Executive summary | 168 |
| | Self-evaluation and portfolio tasks | 169 |
| **4.3** | Conducting research in semi-controlled environments | 169 |
| | *Surveys 170    Compiling a self-administered questionnaire 172* | |
| | *Interviews 175  Focus groups 178  Problems related to implementation* | |
| | *procedures 182* | |
| | Executive summary | 184 |
| | Self-evaluation and portfolio task | 185 |
| **4.4** | Conducting research in natural environments | 185 |
| | *Field observations 186* | |
| | Executive summary | 190 |
| | Self-evaluation and portfolio task | 190 |
| **4.5** | What to do with the data, once collected | 191 |
| | *Content analysis 191    Analysis of verbal communication 197* | |
| | *Elementary descriptive statistics 200  Readability Ease test 206* | |
| | Executive summary | 209 |
| | Self-evaluation and portfolio tasks | 210 |
| **4.6** | Ethical issues | 211 |
| **4.7** | Summary | 212 |
| | Assessment of learning outcomes | 213 |
| | Suggested reading | 214 |

**Unit 5**  **Research of advertising, mass-media audiences and**
**mass-media efficiency**                                                    **216**
Overview                                                                        216
Learning outcomes                                                               217
5.1  Introduction                                                               217
5.2  Advertising message research                                               218
*Understanding consumers' behaviour 218    Message content 224*
*Message structure 230    Message effectiveness 231*
Executive summary                                                               239
Self-evaluation and portfolio tasks                                             239
5.3  Audience analyses of print and broadcast media                            241
*Audience profiles 241    Item-selection studies 242    Reader/non-reader*
*studies 243    Uses and gratifications studies 245    Typography and layout*
*research  247*
Executive summary                                                               247
Self-evaluation and portfolio tasks                                             248
5.4  Researching mass-media efficiency                                          248
*Reach, frequency and gross ratings points (GRPs) 248    Circulation 250*
*Ratings research 250    Non-ratings research 253*
Executive summary                                                               255
Self-evaluation and portfolio tasks                                             256
5.5  Summary                                                                    257
Assessment of learning outcomes                                                 258
Suggested reading                                                               259

**Unit 6**  **Organisational and development communication research**          **260**
Overview                                                                        260
Learning outcomes                                                               261
6.1  Introduction                                                               261
6.2  Environmental monitoring research                                          262
Executive summary                                                               264
Self-evaluation and portfolio task                                             264
6.3  Social audit                                                               265
*Organisational (corporate) climate 265    Substantive nature of an*
*organisation 266    Organisational and management structures 268*
Executive summary                                                               281
Self-evaluation and portfolio task                                             282
6.4  Researching participatory strategies                                       283
*Educational-therapeutic strategy 284    Behavioural change strategy 285*
*Supplementary employees strategy 287    A strategy of co-optation 288*
*A strategy of community empowerment 289*

Executive summary 291
Self-evaluation and portfolio task 292
**6.5** Participatory action research 293
*Orientation and research questions 293    RDP and intervention research 294*
*Participatory action research process 297    Our role(s) as researchers 301*
*Notes of caution 302*
Executive summary 303
Self-evaluation and portfolio task 303
**6.6** Public relations audit 304
*The research process in a PR audit 305*
Executive summary 312
Self-evaluation and portfolio tasks 313
**6.7** Communication audit 313
*Methods, techniques and measuring instruments 313    Applying a self-administered questionnaire 315    Findings of communication audits 317*
Executive summary 318
Self-evaluation and portfolio tasks 318
**6.8** Summary 319
Assessment of learning outcomes 320
Suggested reading 321
Unisa Library Communication Audit 322

**Unit 7    The research report** 341
Overview 341
Learning outcomes 341
**7.1** Introduction 341
**7.2** Thematic evaluation 342
*Problem criteria 343    Literature review and theoretical aspects 344*
**7.3** Methodological evaluation 345
*Research design 345    Collection of data 346    Analysis of data 349*
**7.4** Contextual evaluation 350
**7.5** Evaluation based on presentation criteria and credibility 352
Executive summary 359
**7.6** Summary 360
Self-evaluation and portfolio task 360
Assessment of learning outcomes 361
Suggested reading 362

Addendum A: Useful electronic addresses 363
Bibliography 370
Index 380

# Foreword

*Communication Research: Techniques, methods and applications* deals with both traditional (positivist) and qualitative research techniques and methods, such as participatory action research. The move towards a combination of research methods and techniques was prompted by a realisation over the years that communication research studies challenge us to explore and discover − and in some instances rediscover − the reasons for communication behaviour, effects and problems.

## Aim of this publication

Against the background of outcomes-based education, the teaching aim of this publication is to enable learners to achieve the following critical learning outcomes:

1.  **Research skills:**  Learners should be able to collect, analyse, organise and critically evaluate data relevant to communication research.
2.  **Problem-solving skills:**  Learners should be able to identify and solve communication problems through the application of appropriate research methods and techniques.
3.  **Communication skills:**  Learners should be able to plan, conduct and report on a pilot research study, using language skills in the written mode; and learners should be able to evaluate a research article according to scientific criteria.
4.  **Environmental literacy:**  Learners should be able to demonstrate knowledge of research involving the mass-communication media (content and audiences), and research programmes related to communication areas, such as organisational and development communication.
5.  **Developing macro vision:**  Learners should be able to demonstrate an understanding of the interdisciplinary nature of communication and of how communication research frequently involves other disciplines in the social sciences and the humanities, such as psychology, nursing, social work, education, criminology and sociology.

    The development of a macro vision therefore includes an understanding that communication research can make a positive contribution towards diverse needs and national priorities in the South African society, such as the promotion of democratisation and the Reconstruction and Development Programme (RDP).

6. **Self-responsibility skills**  Learners should be able to take responsibility for their own learning (self-teaching), at their own pace and to evaluate their own progress (self-evaluation). Learners are enabled to become life-long learners through the transference of research skills to other learning situations and different contexts. In order to promote the development of self-responsibility and writing skills as future researchers, learners are encouraged to write down their own examples and experiences that apply to their selected research projects, or as they apply to communication contexts that differ from examples presented in this publication.
7. **Individual values and skills**  Learners should become aware of:
    - communication research methods and techniques as learning skills;
    - communication research in areas, such as mass communication, organisational communication and development communication;
    - applying research skills in lifelong learning;
    - communication-related occupations;
    - their roles in promoting citizenship in today's multicultural information society;
    - the moral, ethical and legal requirements of scientific inquiry.

In order to achieve all of the above critical learning outcomes, each unit focuses on specific learning outcomes related to **knowledge, skills, competence** and **attitudes** or **orientations**, which are listed at the beginning of each unit.

## Presentation of content

**Unit 1** commences with a brief overview of the historical roots of communication research, which deals with theoretical and methodological assumptions that underlie quantitative (positivist) and qualitative (critical) approaches to communication research, as well as the need for a quanti-qualitative paradigm, are dealt with.

**Unit 2** deals with the procedures involved in the identification and analysis of a communication research problem; the analysis and evaluation of the planning of a research project or study; and with the steps to be followed when undertaking communication research.

**Unit 3** concentrates on data collection by means of sampling, measuring, questioning and observing. Whereas Unit 4 serves as an extension of Unit 3 by dealing with the selection and application of a particular research design, it also deals with what to do with the data once it has been collected – more specifically by conducting a content analysis, applying elementary descriptive statistics, and/or by applying a Readability Ease test.

In **Unit 5**, the above methods and techniques are applied, and additional methods and techniques are introduced for undertaking research of advertising, of mass-media audiences and of mass-media efficiency. In this unit the audience analyses and the evaluation of media efficiency deal with print and broadcasting media (radio and television).

The methods and techniques covered in Units 2–4 are also applied in **Unit 6**, in the contexts of organisational and development communication. This unit includes research that deals with environmental monitoring research, a social audit, participatory research strategies, a public relations (PR) audit and a communication audit.

The publication ends with **Unit 7**, which provides a framework of scientific criteria and guidelines that can be used when planning and writing a research report. These criteria can also be used when analysing and evaluating published research reports.

## Flexibility when reading this publication

It would probably make sense to read the units in sequence, because from Unit 2 onwards, the units progressively build on one another. However, because the units are presented separately, they can be read independently. For example, learners could start by reading Unit 7 to obtain an overview, because dealing with the writing and evaluation of a research report simultaneously functions as a synthesis or summary of the preceding units.

## To the readers

This book is specifically aimed at learners who study Communication for the BA or BBA degrees, or who study communication research as a part of diploma or certificate programmes, at the University of South Africa. However, learners, communication practitioners and researchers in fields of health, development, correctional services, education, or social work should find the application of techniques and methods in Units 5 and 6 particularly useful. These two units, with Unit 7, are the core units for the module 'Communication Research' prescribed for learners who major in Communication for a B-degree at the University of South Africa.

# Interactive approach and learning aids

An interactive approach has been followed in this publication, by adopting an informal writing style and by including several learning aids to encourage the reader's active involvement. The book contains seven interactive components and learning aids, the purposes of which are summarised below.

1. Each unit begins with an **overview** that briefly outlines the content of that unit.
2. Each overview is followed by a list of **learning outcomes**, which learners should aim to achieve by the end of that unit.
3. At the end of certain sections within the units and at the end of most units, an **executive summary** provides a synopsis of the key components of that section or of the unit as a whole.
4. Throughout the book, **marginal notes** highlight specific terms or phrases. These marginal notes fulfil two didactic purposes. First, they highlight the most important terms or phrases in each paragraph or page. Secondly, they provide a glossary of brief explanations of the meanings of the terms or phrases, as they relate to the context, discussions and application of communication research, as a subject; and as they relate to specific sections of this text, as a publication.
5. To accommodate different learning styles, three types of **self-evaluation** and **portfolio tasks** are included in each unit. First, some tasks are set that require learners as individuals to study-read the content of the unit. These tasks function as a form of evaluation of development of learners' individual values, as well as their research, problem-solving, communication and self-responsibility skills.

   Secondly, certain tasks encourage learners to work in groups. These tasks are included to facilitate group discussion with others (e.g. fellow-learners or professional communicators and researchers). These tasks are also aimed at developing environmental literacy and a macro vision. Thirdly, some of these tasks encourage learners to explore additional sources (e.g. community leaders, consumers, mass-media audiences, library resources, or the Internet) with the aim of strengthening their information retrieval skills and research skills.

   All the self-evaluation and portfolio tasks are ultimately aimed at encouraging learners to experience for themselves how research can make a contribution towards solving communication problems, irrespective of whether they deal with issues such as affirmative action, employment equity, reconstruction and development, and/or socio-economic upliftment.

The self-evaluation and portfolio tasks are linked to the learning outcomes formulated at the beginning of each unit. As many of these tasks involve practical research studies, learners are encouraged to do them with one or more of their fellow-learners. The benefit of such group work lies in the opportunity it provides learners to discuss, critically evaluate and motivate their answers and practical research endeavours. These tasks therefore enable learners to monitor their own progress, because they simultaneously function as an evaluation to determine whether learners have achieved the learning outcomes set for each unit.

Learners are also encouraged to open a file in which a personal record can be kept of the problems they investigated, procedures they followed to solve the problems, experiences involved, the end-results of each self-evaluation and portfolio task, and personal reflections on how their orientations changed over time. As portfolio tasks are problem-oriented, progressively constructing such a file provides learners with the opportunity to keep evidence of how they take responsibility for their own learning, which is not usually recorded. Such record-keeping activities can also improve learners' writing skills.

6. Towards the end of each unit, an **assessment guide** is included that can be used to evaluate the extent to which the learning outcomes have been achieved. This guide is presented in a tabulated form and consists of the following sections:
   - outcomes that are related to learners' knowledge, competence and orientations;
   - learners providing evidence of their performance;
   - examples of the minimum criteria that can be used (either by the learners themselves, or by teachers and examiners) to evaluate the evidence of performance; and
   - an evaluation of the performance, based on a five-point rating scale.

   Anyone who applies the minimum criteria suggested in this publication (for the assessment of the accomplishment of learning outcomes) is encouraged to add additional criteria, based on their personal circumstances and (research) experiences. This process would ideally give learners a sense of ownership of their self-evaluation and personal progress.

7. The publication also contains **extended sources** and **references** that can be consulted for additional information. In addition, Addendum A contains an alphabetical list of electronic addresses, and the Index provides page references of the most important key terms and phrases.

Each unit ends with a list of suggested reading, which provides further background material related to the issues dealt with in each unit; and, in certain instances, provide constructive guidelines when applying communication research in practice.

## Study guide

A study guide, written by the Department of Communication at the University of South Africa and published by UNISA Press, can also be consulted. Its teaching aim is twofold:

- to assist learners' understanding of basic research techniques and methods, and their application to solving communication problems; and
- to accomplish the seven critical learning outcomes listed above.

## Acknowledgements

This publication is a collaborative effort involving practitioners, academia from UNISA and other universities and technikons, professional researchers, past UNISA graduates, and present undergraduate and postgraduate students. For administrative assistance, I express my gratitude to Annelize Vermeulen, Marie-Hélène Bataille and Martha Malefo. In addition to inputs received, dating back to 1998, when the content was initially discussed in terms of an outcomes-based syllabus, this publication was made possible because of the copyright permission received, ideas, recommendations and, in certain instances, the critical reading done by: Charmaine Scriven, Lizelle van der Walt, Dr Elirea Bornman, Prof Magriet Pitout, Prof Rachel Barker, Lucas Oosthuizen, Jennifer Lemon, Stefan Sonderling, Prof Danie du Plessis, Prof Pieter Fourie, Beschara Karam, Katy Kahn, Prof Cornelius Plug, Zandi Lesame, Dawie Malan, Mpine Qakisa, Estelle Rossum, Marie van Heerden, David Wigston, Dr Daleen van Niekerk, Prof Sheila Steinberg, Marcia Wilson, Retha van Niekerk, Tamzin Lovell, Prof Ronél Rensburg, Elsa Thirion, Prof Sandra Marais, Tok Grobler, Dr Kathy Collins and Gisela van Rensburg. I am particularly indebted to Elize Terblanché for the diligence with which she acted as a critical reader and didactic advisor since I wrote the first drafts in 1999.

# In conclusion

With the explosion of information communications technology, the implementation of the Internet and e-commerce in corporate communication will continue to grow. These multi-channelled developments, in addition to traditional communication media, such as the telephone and fax, will continue to place new demands on the management of programmes that deal with clients' changing communication needs. These changes highlight the continuous need for both basic and applied research to determine how business capabilities and successes can be increased in this era of globalisation.

Despite the developments in various communication fields, a country such as South Africa still faces problems related to rapid urbanisation, poverty, education, social upliftment, and needs addressed by the Reconstruction and Development Programme (RDP). Although these problems and needs require multi-disciplinary initiatives, the communication specialist can and should play a central role.

Few learners who study communication in a graduate, diploma or certificate programme will become full-time or professional researchers. Nevertheless, as practitioners, they need the skills to evaluate and use research conducted and published by others; to initiate and be involved in effective communication interventions; and they need the skills to identify, investigate and solve communication and other social problems. The research techniques, methods and applications discussed in this publication can find pertinence in diverse communication fields, such as political and government communication; media studies; intercultural, development and health communication; information communications technology; and/or organisational and marketing communication.

I trust that this publication will benefit you, the reader, as a communication specialist, as a professional researcher, as a user of research findings, as a member of a mass-media audience, or as a participant and facilitator in problem-solving interventions in your workplace and community.

GM (TRUDIE) DU PLOOY
DECEMBER 2001

# Quantitative and qualitative approaches to communication research

*The whole of science is nothing more than the refinement of everyday thinking.*

ALBERT EINSTEIN 1879–1955

## Overview

Over the years, communication research has evolved through different phases. This is a result of innovations within the discipline, as well as experience and knowledge that has been incorporated from a range of other fields, such as psychology, sociology, linguistics and information science. As an introductory background, this unit deals with these historical roots, by considering different ways of acquiring knowledge, and the assumptions on which quantitative and qualitative approaches to communication research have been and are based.

We live in an age where most of the work force is engaged in either the production or the processing of information. It is therefore not unusual that communication research finds application in a variety of settings, including publishing, broadcasting, advertising and public relations, financial institutions and services, the manufacturing of consumer and industrial products, education, consulting agencies, government departments and non-profit organisations. Against this background, this unit compares quantitative and qualitative perspectives of organisational cultures, management functions and changes in organisational systems. It concludes by considering approaches to future research.

## Learning outcomes

By the end of this unit you should be able to demonstrate your understanding of:

- the different ways of knowing (by describing their characteristics);
- the assumptions on which the quantitative and qualitative approaches to communication research are based (by writing descriptive notes); and
- the implications that the above assumptions have for the selection of a research design (by making a motivated selection of an approach to research a particular communication problem).

## 1.1 Introduction

This unit traces some of the historical roots of communication research, by considering two approaches: **quantitative** and **qualitative** research. This brief and selective overview by no means represents a comprehensive or in-depth analysis. The issues, theories and research developments that are cited have been selected because they function as reference points for understanding current communication research methods and techniques, and can be used to guide future communication research.

**conceptual model:** a description of a system of ideas

The unit starts by considering the different ways in which we obtain knowledge. This is followed by a conceptual model of assumptions that offers criteria that facilitate the choices we make about research methods. These assumptions are then applied to the two research approaches. We also consider how some of these assumptions can form a basis for undertaking communication research in institutional settings characterised by changing organisational structures and functions. The unit ends with the argument that future communication research ought to consider a 'mixture' of approaches.

## 1.2  Different ways of knowing

Before considering the scientific method as a reliable way of acquiring knowledge, it is worth noting that there are other (non-scientific) ways in which we acquire knowledge.

The method of **tenacity** is a very unsophisticated way of finding answers to questions or solving problems. This method is based on the assertion that something is true (or false) simply because we believe it to be true (or false). For example, a person who tenaciously believes that violence portrayed in television programmes causes violent behaviour in children, will not be persuaded to believe otherwise, irrespective of the findings of research in this regard. In other words, what is believed to be good, bad, successful or unsuccessful in the past, will continue to be so in the future, even if it is idiosyncratic.

**idiosyncratic:**
a feeling, viewpoint or behaviour that is unconventional

Our parents, teachers, parliamentarians, medical doctors, religious leaders or elderly people in rural villages are examples of people whom we regard as knowledgeable. By turning to them for advice or to acquire more information, and by having faith in their knowledge, we make use of a method of **authority** to understand something. However, although a person may be acknowledged to be an authority in a particular area of knowledge, this does not mean that the correctness or truth of the knowledge cannot be questioned. According to Bless and Higson-Smith (1995:1-2), the mystical method is a variation of the authority method. This *way of knowing* can be illustrated by traditional healers, who are believed to have the ability to communicate the truth, which they obtain from supernatural forces. Nevertheless, the emphasis is on the source or communicator and not on the methods he or she uses to obtain information. The method of authority as a *way of knowing* is therefore based on our faith in the credibility of the communicator. This is often used in advertisements when a well-known personality (such as a sporting champion) endorses a particular product. Watt and Van den Berg (1995:10) argue that the authority method has an advantage over that of tenacity, because it would be more beneficial to rely on the testimony or advice of an expert, than to cling to a personal belief.

**a priori:**
before the fact

The third *way of knowing* is referred to as the a priori method, or the method of **reasonableness**. It involves making and accepting propositions or arguments because they are self-evident or stand to reason. The advantage of this method lies therein that if an argument is accepted as the truth, it must have withstood the evaluation of several people. It is not unusual for the a priori method to be used for knowledge development in disciplines such as philosophy and mathematics. What remains debatable is the question of who has the right or authority to define the meaning of *reasonableness*. For example, if the regulations of community radio stations are based on economic development, this could lead to logical and reasonable conclusions. However, these conclusions may be incorrect if the regulations are viewed from a different premise, such as the limiting or controlling of the free flow of information. The a priori method can therefore become problematic, because the criteria or assumptions a person uses to determine truth may be personally motivated and/or rejected by others.

The fourth *way of knowing* is the **scientific method**. Its basic characteristics or requirements distinguish it from the methods discussed above:

- **Science is empirical**  This characteristic means that researchers study that which can be perceived and classified or measured. The trustworthiness of the measurements will depend on the clarification (definition) of abstract concepts, propositions and relationships.
- **Science is cumulative and systematic**  One of the first steps of research is to review literature in order to benefit from and build (cumulatively) on past research. To be systematic, the methods used to perceive, experience and observe the real world must follow a logical order.
- **Science is objective**  This characteristic is aimed at eliminating subjective judgements by researchers. For example, rules for the classification of people's behaviour must be so explicitly defined that two or more independent observers will classify different patterns of behaviour in the same way. In other words, our internal beliefs, assumptions or theories must be supported by external evidence. However, because it is impossible to 'switch off' our personal attitudes, it would be more realistic to say that a scientific method should be intersubjective − that scientific 'truth' relies on the collective agreement of communication scholars' judgement.

- **Science is predictive**   Science relates the present to the future in two ways. Theories and hypotheses are formulated that predict a communication phenomenon, behaviour or event. These are tested to determine whether or not they are supported by what occurs in reality. Conversely, researchers search for order, patterns and consistencies among their findings to formulate theories or so-called laws.
- **Scientific research is public**   Science is a public enterprise, which means that the methods used, the sampling and data-gathering procedures, and the findings, must be freely available to other researchers.

    The public-ness of scientific research also makes provision for peer evaluation (especially in the academic sector) and the verification of research findings by other researchers. This characteristic is dealt with in greater detail in Unit 7, because it involves writing an explicit and objective report.

In response to the requirements of the scientific method, different **approaches** to communication research have evolved. However, because social and communication researchers do not concur on the use of terms to describe these different approaches, it is not unusual to find the following distinctions being made: applied versus basic research; survey versus non-survey research; experimental versus non-experimental research; dominant paradigm versus new paradigm; positivist versus critical approaches; naïve inquiry versus science (Oosthuizen 1996:1-25; Burger 1998:145-146; Watt and Van den Berg 1995:6-7; Drew, Hardman and Hart 1996:23-42).

**paradigm:**
a set of shared basic beliefs about how researchers view that which they study

The choice of terminology is often based on the perspective of the researcher. This will determine whether:

- the research involves manipulating or controlling a communication phenomenon (as in an experiment) versus communication research in a natural environment; and
- records involve numerical or verbal/descriptive types of data.

**experiment:**
an artificially controlled situation to study a phenomenon

Throughout this unit we have opted to differentiate between **quantitative** and **qualitative** approaches to communication research, to facilitate discussion, but with the acknowledgment that, in practice, methods from both approaches are often combined.

## 1.3 A conceptual model of assumptions

**assumptions:**
beliefs that are
unproven; neither
true nor false

Every research tradition is characterised by assumptions that guide researchers in the way in which they approach the phenomenon under investigation, their theoretical viewpoints and the selection of methods and techniques. Figure 1.1 is a conceptual model of assumptions based on a discussion by Smith (1988:299-318).

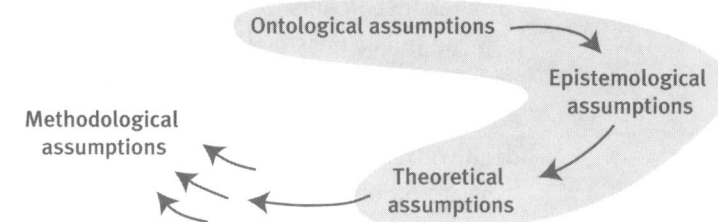

**FIGURE 1.1** Research paradigms – a conceptual model of assumptions (starting with ontological assumptions)

**ontology:**
assumptions
about the nature
of reality or
human existence

**Ontological assumptions** are based on the particular belief researchers hold regarding the nature of communication (as subject and phenomenon) to be investigated. In other words, these assumptions describe:

- the **nature** of human communication; and
- the **processes** involved when communication takes place.

The reality with which we are concerned is communication as a social phenomenon and any parts of that process (for example, communicators, media, messages, recipients, organisational settings, development purposes). The question that must be answered is: *What are our assumptions (as researchers) about the nature of these components and processes?*

**epistemology:**
the science of
knowledge

**Epistemological assumptions** offer answers to the question: *What are the appropriate ways in which to study communication (as subject and phenomenon)?*

**theory:**
a generalisation
that offers a par-
ticular explanation
of a phenomenon

**Theoretical assumptions** offer answers to the question: *What kinds of explanations are appropriate to communication (as subject and phenomenon)?*

**methodology:**
research strategy

**Methodological assumptions** offer answers to the question: *What research designs (methods used to collect, analyse and interpret data) are the most appropriate to investigate communication?*

These four categories of assumptions are interdependent. The way in which we view communication (reality) influences the ways we regard appropriate to study communication. These assumptions, in turn, influence the selection of a particular theoretical view to explain communication and collectively determine which research methods and techniques are applied.

Figure 1.2 illustrates that interdependence works both ways. The selected research methods influence theoretical views; research methods and theoretical views influence epistemological assumptions; and the three categories of assumptions affect our ontological assumptions.

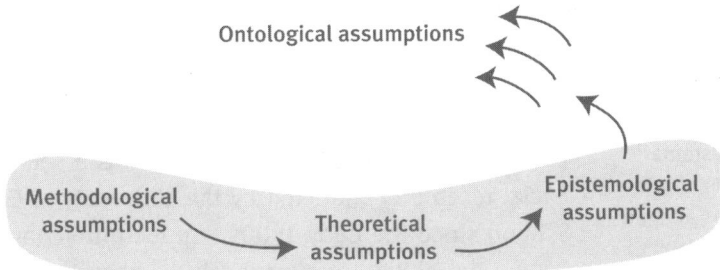

**FIGURE 1.2** Research paradigms – a conceptual model of assumptions (starting with methodological assumptions)

The relevance of these assumptions and their interrelatedness become more meaningful when applied to quantitative versus qualitative approaches to communication research.

## 1.4 Quantitative research approach

Quantitative research (also called positivist or empirical research) dates back to the seventeenth century in Europe, with Auguste Comte (1798-1857) being regarded as the true founder. Positivism is a philosophical system that restricts itself to data of experiences and rejects any form of speculation.

**1**

## 1.4.1 Ontological assumptions

Different views of the reality are linked to different views of communication, especially mass communication. In the late nineteenth and early twentieth centuries, social theorists, especially in Europe and North America, grappled with the changes accompanying industrialisation and urbanisation. Problems resulting from the change from rural to urban societies were economic and social, including crime, prostitution and isolation. At the time, the aim of quantitative research was to restore stability through the re-evaluation of social and moral values, using the methods of the natural sciences.

**industrialisation:** economic or social system characterised by manufacturing industries

Since the early twentieth century films, newspapers and other forms of popular culture, such as comics and magazines, were seen as having the potential to contribute to moral decline. World War I saw the use of the press and films in Europe and the USA for propaganda purposes. At the time it was argued that the mass media had the potency to **influence** and **manipulate** audiences.

**popular culture:** something shared and enjoyed by people in general; opposite of the so-called high culture

In Europe, and particularly in the USA, scientific (quantitative) research especially of the mass media was seen as a solution for social problems. Social research conducted by the University of Chicago (the Chicago School) since the early 1900s regarded the communication media as having the ability to re-establish the **moral unity** associated with earlier communities (by disseminating specific types of information) while simultaneously promoting **democracy** (by reflecting diverse opinions). Communication formed part of the sociological work of the Chicago School and the work of Robert Park, GH Mead, CH Cooley, Thomas Dewey and others (Hardt 1991).

**scientific research:** a systematic analysis of relationships and/or explanations of communication phenomena that can be quantified

During the first two decades of the twentieth century, the USA faced large-scale immigration from Europe. The mass media was regarded as having the potential to fulfil a positive function of fostering cohesion among individuals. Just as computers and telecommunications today are regarded as having the potential to promote universal enlightenment, so too were the establishment of mass-media institutions, such as radio in the 1920s and 1930s, regarded as fulfilling educational, informative and cultural functions. (At the same time, however, the media was blamed for its negative effects, notably linked to content in which violence, crime and sex were portrayed.)

Research findings in the 1950s (Katz and Lazarsfeld 1964) indicated that opinion leaders not only influenced people, but also the mass media. These findings resulted in a decrease in the number of views that regarded the mass media as having a strong or direct influence on audiences. This also meant that the ontology (view of reality) held by researchers was changing to that of the liberal pluralist view of society. According to this view, elites or ruling classes no longer controlled industrial societies. Instead, it emphasised 'the increasingly *diffused* distribution of power among and between a variety (or *plurality*) of constantly competing independent interest groups and elites' (O'Sullivan et al. 1996:230).

**liberal pluralist:**
a perspective that emphasises the differentiation and diversification of power structures and power relations

Although ideas around the concept **mass society** were raised towards the end of the nineteenth century, the term **mass communication** emerged only in the 1930s (Blumer 1939). The notion of (mass) society and mass-media recipients comprising isolated, defenceless individuals, gave way to a view of society made up of small groups, linked by networks of interpersonal ties and interdependencies (Oosthuizen 1996:8). In other words, mass-media audiences were protected from direct media influences due to their group affiliations.

The United States, the ideal model for a 'good' society in the 1940s and 1950s, represented the values of the *Western way of life* – a society that is:
- democratic (e.g. where free and fair elections take place);
- liberal (e.g. where freedom of speech is guaranteed);
- pluralistic (e.g. where differences of opinion are allowed); and
- orderly (e.g. peaceful).

The role of the mass media in promoting such a liberal democracy resulted in the functions it fulfilled being seen in a more positive light. The mass media:
- supplied diverse viewpoints that contributed to the free and open circulation of ideas; and
- monitored the ruling elites and government's performance.

**structural functionalism:**
the perspective of a phenomenon (e.g. the mass media) as a system with internal and external relations

In terms of structural functionalism, the mass media was regarded as a subsystem of society that provided continuity, integration, guidance and adaptation in society. Merton (1957) refined this almost idealistic view of the mass media being functional in creating and maintaining

equilibrium and consensus in society. He distinguished between manifest (intended) and latent (unintended) functions.

During the 1970s methodologies were still being borrowed from allied disciplines such as psychology and sociology. Meanings shared through communication were often treated as the starting points of research in order to draw conclusions about related consequences. Such a focus, however, failed to address the complexities inherent in human communication.

**modernisation:** urban societies characterised by mass production and capitalist economies

**post-modernisation:** culture that is transient, volatile, illogical, kaleidoscopic and appeals to sense instead of reason

The description given above of the ontological assumptions from a quantitative (positivist) perspective of communication is an oversimplification. More detailed discussions can be found in Gitlin (1978), Rogers (1986), Real (1989), DeFleur and Ball-Rokeach (1989), Hardt (1991) and McQuail (2000). It is evident, however, that ontological assumptions about communication (especially mass communication) have changed, as changes have occurred to the traditional agrarian society due to industrialisation, urbanisation, modernisation and postmodernisation.

## 1.4.2 Theoretical assumptions

This conceptual category identifies the assumptions on which theoretical explanations of communication are based. Communication as a science was founded on the bodies of theory and research in traditional disciplines, such as sociology and psychology, and more recently based on history, economics, literary studies and information science.

**information theory:** communication treated as a one-way process from communicator to recipient

Considering the norms and values with which the positivist approach viewed society (democratic, liberal, free, pluralistic and orderly), the research of mass-media content and its positive or harmful effects were, during the 1940s and 1950s, largely evaluated according to these norms. Lasswell (1948), a sociologist, was the first to describe the functions fulfilled by communication in the maintenance of society. His well known question 'Who says what to whom, through what channel and with what effect?' (McQuail 2000:52-53) regards mass communication as a process consisting of **linear sequences**. Another important theoretical development that guided media research in terms of a quantitative paradigm, was the **information theory** developed by Shannon and Weaver (1949). Their model was originally concerned with the technical efficiency of a communication channel and the interferences caused by noise. Although not initially applied to human communication, it offered a conceptual way of analysing human communication processes, particularly the effects of communication.

**stimulus-response:**
cause-and-effect

The **stimulus-response theory** (also called the magic-bullet theory or the hypodermic-needle theory) provided the initial conceptual framework whereby the mass media was regarded as all-powerful and had a direct effect on individuals and groups. This theoretical view of mass communication dates back to the 1930s and was most probably influenced by the power that propaganda supposedly had during World War I. This also represents the first phase of what is traditionally regarded as the *effects tradition* in media studies.

Early social scientists, including GH Mead, CH Cooley and Robert Park, did not view human communication as a cause-effect, linear process. If their views had been applied in a theoretical model to research communication, it would have treated communication as **human** and **social**, with the purpose of sharing meaning in an interactive manner. However, as McQuail (1996:44) points out, these alternative views of communication were not pursued, because the practical, quantitative research methods were assumed to be more relevant.

During the second phase of effects studies (in the 1940s), mass-media messages were thought to have been able to effectively transmit information. But they did not necessarily lead to changes in attitudes. Such views prompted:

- the questioning of earlier assumptions that the mass media had direct, unmediated effects; and
- the initiation of the view that mass media has limited effects.

**two-step flow model:**
mass-media messages disseminated in two stages

These views found support in research by Paul F Lazarsfeld and associates, who found that the mass media had limited influence on people's voting behaviour during election campaigns. The influence of informal and interpersonal communication gave rise to the **two-step flow model**. The importance of this theoretical model is that mass-media audiences were no longer deemed a mass of unconnected individuals. This implies that recognition was given to the notion that (theoretically) social relationships influenced how people received and relayed mass-media messages; and that the meaning of a message was not fixed, but could be interpreted (and relayed to others) differently.

The third phase of theories related to effects studies represent a distinct move away from the question *What do the media do to people?* to that of *What do people do with the media?* Emerging from the limited-effects view, the **uses and gratifications** approach is associated with the initial work of researchers such as Katz in the 1950s. They questioned the gratifications that mass-media audiences, such as radio soap-opera listeners, sought and obtained. The theoretical model was based on the assumption that, due to social and psychological differences, individuals' needs differ. This resulted in different uses of the mass media and, consequently, different levels of gratifications being obtained. Uses and gratifications theorists have, however, been criticised (notably by Elliot 1974 and Morley 1980) for taking for granted or ignoring the content and structure of mass-media texts.

**uses and gratifications:** the selection of and satisfactions recipients obtain from mass communication

In the United States, post-1970s, effects research started addressing more general issues, such as the long-term and indirect influence the mass media has in defining social reality. Mass media, as agencies of so-called ideological power, was partly based on the **agenda-setting theory**. According to this theory, the topics (viewpoints, symbols or questions) that the mass media selects, and the way in which the topics are presented, create the agenda about which audiences think and talk.

**agenda-setting theory:** mass media gives prominence to certain topics, issues or individuals

The theory represents two views about the influence of the mass media:
- that the audiences' views of reality are shaped by the mass media; and
- that issues being given priority by the mass media may not legitimately be so important in real life.

**cultivation theory:** people's beliefs and values are shaped by the selective view of society, conveyed by the mass media

When linked to George Gerbner's **cultivation theory** (Gerbner, Gross and Melody 1973), the mass media was regarded as having long-term influences on audiences' acquiring and sharing a particular worldview.

**worldview:** attitudes, beliefs, values or views of social reality characteristic of particular social groups

The theories used to explain communication in the quantitative (positivist) research tradition of the United States, have:
- made provision for other mediating factors, such as audiences' needs; yet
- essentially retained a cause-effect/influence conceptualisation of the process; and
- contributed to the development of research methodologies.

Methodological assumptions are (according to a quantitative approach) traditionally linked to a **deductive** form of theoretical reasoning. Deductive reasoning means that theories or conceptual models offer a premise that positivist researchers assume to be true. These assumptions (usually formulated as hypotheses) are researched (measured, compared, predicted or controlled), with the intention that they be verified.

**premise:**
assumption or proposition

## 1.4.3 Epistemological and methodological assumptions

The views of society and of the functions that the mass media could fulfil were based on assumptions that gave direction to theory building and the use of certain research designs. In this section we consider the assumptions that guide the way in which researchers acquire *knowledge* (epistemology), and the methodological assumptions that guide research designs.

Through the ages, people relied on numerous philosophers to explain the meaning of reality. By the mid-nineteenth century a need had developed to measure the validity of these theoretical views. At the time, scientists in sociology and psychology turned to the natural sciences (physics, chemistry and biology) for scientific methods that would enable them to obtain valid knowledge.

**validity:**
to approximate reality as closely as possible

By the end of the nineteenth century, these scientific methods dominated human sciences in the United States. At first, laboratory **experiments** were used to obtain reliable, valid knowledge of human behaviour. It became common practice to use statistical techniques to measure social realities. Paul Lazarsfeld and Carl Hovland, two of the founders of communication science in the United States, further popularised these scientific methods in the 1930s.

**reliable:**
to consistently obtain the same answer when researched at different times

In 1937, Lazarsfeld and his co-directors used **surveys** and **statistics** to research the effects of radio on society and to develop methods that could be used in **applied** research (to improve broadcasting in the United States). This project moved to the Bureau of Applied Social Research at the University of Columbia in 1939. Here it, together with other communication issues such as persuasive communication and

**applied research:**
research done with the purpose of understanding and solving practical problems

propaganda, was researched until after World War II. Using surveys, experiments and statistical analyses, the researchers became part of the mainstream of American sociological and social psychological research. During and after the war, communication researchers not only undertook applied research, but also wanted to develop methods that would enable them to formulate empirical generalisations. Addressing theoretical issues (such as political decision-making) and testing these issues empirically, meant that conceptual models (theories) to explain communication processes were also developed (**basic** research).

**basic research:**
research undertaken with the purpose of analysing theoretical relationships

The so-called *mass audience*, created by films, newspapers and radio, prompted research to measure the **reach** and **responses** of audiences. Research methods included the use of surveys, and describing audiences and their experiences in quantitative terms. In this context, 'quantitative' means that the raw data collected by means of questionnaires or observers' ratings is available in a numerical form.

**reach:**
number of people/households exposed to a mass-mediated message at least once during a specified period

Research included investigating the following:
- the intended effects of the mass media (e.g. persuasive effects of political campaigns);
- the unintended effects of the mass media (e.g. the effects of violent content on children); and
- aspects of the communication process that could contribute to understanding effects (e.g. content analyses of messages; a survey of the audiences' characteristics, such as their attitudes).

**numerical form:**
data expressed in numbers

Surveys, experiments and statistical analyses as research methods and techniques have been valued since the 1950s because they provide:
- reliable data of communication processes and states (e.g. attitudes) that could not be observed;
- data that could be generalised to a wider population; and
- answers about the so-called effects of the mass media.

For various reasons, these methods are still used for quantification and precise measurements. Although we now accept that mass communication does not have *magic bullet* effects, testing (null) hypotheses and finding no stimulus-response effects are still regarded as useful indicators in sectors such as marketing communication and advertising research.

**null hypotheses:**
no significant relationships exist between the variables being tested

> *EXECUTIVE SUMMARY:*
> **ASSUMPTIONS (QUANTITATIVE APPROACH)**
>
> Assumptions that guide researchers who apply a quantitative approach to communication research:
> - an objective and value-free reality exists that can be researched (ontology);
> - communication, as part of the social world, can be objectively measured (ontology and methodology);
> - the research process is essentially based on deductive reasoning (theory);
> - reality can be explained in terms of generalisations or universally valid laws (epistemology);
> - empirical observations, experience and/or experiments are the only source of real knowledge (epistemology);
> - methods that are objective can be developed to study reality (methodology);
> - hypotheses formulated about the nature of this reality (e.g. 'If X ... then Y') can be accepted or rejected, based on (objective) findings (methodology);
> - hypotheses can be used to predict and control that which is being studied (methodology); and
> - observations can be measured in quantitative terms (methodology).

# 1.5 Qualitative research approach

**ethnography:** field research, where data is collected by a researcher who participates with subjects over an extended period

Qualitative research has been assigned many different labels, such as field research, critical research, interpretative research, naturalism, ethnography, anti-positivist approach, an alternative approach, and constructivism. However, they all share a common focus: to interpret and construct the qualitative aspects of communication experiences. Let us consider the assumptions on which a qualitative approach is based.

## 1.5.1 Ontological assumptions

By the end of the nineteenth century, the changes brought about by industrialisation in countries such as Germany included political and economical inequalities. Philosophers' and politicians' criticisms of ideological power were mainly based on Karl Marx's (1818-1883) theory of historical materialism. **Materialism** regarded culture as dependent on the power and economic structure of a society. In terms of mass communication, this view assumed that those who control and/or own the media could select the ideas and ideology represented in the mass media.

Max Horkheimer, Theodor Adorno, Herbert Marcuse, Eric Fromm and Walter Benjamin were German intellectuals who founded the Frankfurt School in Frankfurt in 1923 (O'Sullivan et al. 1996:123). The School immigrated to the United States during the 1930s and was re-established in Frankfurt in 1953. In the United States, their analyses of the mass media (which they called the *culture industry*) were guided by the following views, namely that the mass media:

- **subverted** or **undermined** views that opposed the dominant capitalist class interests;
- produced and sold images, ideas and symbols as **commodities** (which meant that art and culture lost their intrinsic values and were considered in marketing terms, such as cost and demand);
- assisted the working masses to assimilate to a capitalist society, by providing escapism and producing a **false consciousness**.

**false consciousness:** myths or false impressions about power and dominance

The 1900s to the 1940s also saw researchers such as Malinowski, Margaret Mead and Radcliffe-Brown using ethnomethodology (or phenomenology) and ethnography to give **interpretative** descriptions of the experiences of small numbers of subjects (Denzin and Lincoln 1994:6-11). At that time, and especially after World War II, commerce and industry experienced an increase in internationalisation. Nation states were influenced by international trends in economic, political and security sectors, as well as environmental and health matters.

**ethnomethodology:** methods used to understand individuals' behaviour within the framework of their experiences

Modernists (between the 1940s and 1970s) argued that knowledge could be acquired by discovering reality *through the eyes of people who experience it.* The views held since the 1970s have argued that knowledge and truth about reality can only be constructed (not discovered).

**neo-:**
a new or revived form

**cultural studies:**
research that accounts for cultural practices and differences by investigating social relations and meanings

**feminist research:**
research that assumes women to be socially, economically and politically equal to men

This resulted in the further development of critical theory based on neo-positivism, neo-Marxism and materialism (De Vos 1998:245).

Since the mid-1980s and especially during the 1990s, communication researchers have continued to toil with the question: *How can we provide a qualitative, yet authentic, (re-)construction of subjects' communicative experiences?*

This meant revisiting requirements such as the reliability and validity of observations and generalisation of findings that are basic to quantitative (empirical) research.

Although no definitive answer has been found to the above question, it did contribute to the development of cultural studies, feminist research and participatory research. In the case of participatory research, researchers and the subjects being studied had to move closer to one another, to the extent of becoming co-researchers. The implications and dilemmas involved in participatory research are discussed in more practical terms in Units 4 and 6.

## 1.5.2 Theoretical assumptions

The Frankfurt School approached the mass media in a way that differed from that of the quantitative paradigm. As a result of the research done by the School, the process of mass communication was regarded as **oppressive** and **manipulative**.

During the 1930s, the theories of the scholars associated with the Frankfurt School were, among others, concerned with:
- analysing the nature of economic, political and cultural changes taking place at the time;
- analysing the consequences of these changes;
- exposing the contradictions on which class societies were based (which stood in the way of emancipation); and
- generating positive and progressive social development.

**emancipation:**
freedom from social class divisions

They were followed by C Wright Mills (1951 and 1956) and Marcuse (1964) who regarded mass-media institutions as **power elites** that wanted to bring about conformity in the economic and political sectors of society.

Two developments have emerged since the 1970s, mainly from Europe. Mass-media messages, especially news, have been analysed (decoded) in terms of the **ideological meanings** they contain. Secondly, notions of predictable mass-media effects were being denied. Instead, it was argued that messages were decoded and meanings constructed by the interests and social situation of recipients. According to these theoretical assumptions, messages that supported and legitimated power structures could be interpreted by recipients in an **oppositional** way.

Whereas the 1960s and 1970s saw research applied to test theories that had been constructed deductively (based on particular assumptions), the 1980s and 1990s saw the development of the grounded theory approach as a qualitative research method. According to this approach, research does not start with any theoretical perspective. Instead, research is used to create or develop theory, which can be supported or refuted, based on further data collection and analysis. A qualitative approach to communication research is thus primarily based on inductive reasoning. Research begins with questioning or observations and, on the basis of the latter, progresses to formulating (theoretical) propositions.

The following authors offer a more detailed discussion of the prerequisites and criteria of applicability when inductively constructing **grounded theory**: Strauss and Corbin (1990), Rubin and Babbie (1993), Denzin and Lincoln (1994) and De Vos (1998). As De Vos (1998:269) points out, grounded theory requires 'keeping a balance between creativity and science … [and a sensitivity that] … enables the analyst to see the research situations and their associated data in new ways, and to explore the data's potential for developing theory'.

## 1.5.3 Epistemological and methodological assumptions

If we regard communication as a process during which meaning is shared in different social contexts, then a quantitative approach is not adequate to research the **symbol systems** by means of which we communicate. Critical researchers were initially concerned about issues such as the subordination of the working class, but the period between the 1940s and 1970s became one of modernism.

During this time, qualitative research, rooted in anthropology and sociolinguistics, focused mainly on meaning, language and cultural experiences in social contexts. As this approach was concerned with understanding particular situations, rather than generalising findings, the methods used were primarily **case studies** and **in-depth analyses** (of interviews, recorded observations and documented communication). These methods included the use of techniques provided for by phenomenology and symbolic interactionism, as reflected in the work of Lofland (1971). Raw data collected by applying a more qualitative approach – for example, reports of in-depth interviews – are usually recorded in a non-numerical form.

**symbolic interactionism:** an approach that focuses on the meanings associated with symbols exchanged during communication

**non-numerical form:** data expressed in words

Since the 1970s, qualitative research has expanded into investigating culture, ethnographic studies of media use, issues related to ethnicity or gender; and cultural and economic domination (such as domination by First World producers of mass-mediated messages on Third World recipients).

From a postmodern feminist perspective, Mowrey (1995:277) argues:

*There are other truths … There are other ways of knowing besides reason, and other ways of defining reason. There are other selves that are subjects, and they must speak for themselves. They cannot be defined, explained, or absorbed into prearranged categories …*

According to McQuail (2000:49), the qualitative approach – or what he refers to as 'an alternative paradigm' – arose due to **criticism** of:

*… the linearity of the model of effect and its generally mechanistic character … the influence of market and military demands on research and the media; … the too rosy interpretations of research findings about media effects and audience motivations; …[t]he potentially dehumanizing effects of technology; … the excessively quantitative and individual-behaviourist methodologies; … [and the] neglect by communication research of vast areas of culture and human experience.*

**1**

> *EXECUTIVE SUMMARY:*
> **ASSUMPTIONS (QUALITATIVE APPROACH)**
>
> Assumptions that guide researchers who apply a qualitative approach to communication research:
> - reality is subjective (ontology);
> - insights into communication, as part of the social world, can be derived from the subjects' perspective (ontology and methodology);
> - the research process is essentially based on inductive reasoning, which is used to understand patterns in observations (theory);
> - reality can be described in terms of meanings that people attach to communication experiences (epistemology);
> - multiple sources of knowledge exist (e.g. values, experiences, cultures) and can be used to explore, interpret and understand a subjective world (epistemology);
> - qualitative themes and categories can be developed as methods to explore and describe meanings communicated in particular contexts (methodology);
> - research questions can guide the types of observations to be made, in order to understand a communication phenomenon (methodology); and
> - observations can be analysed thematically and holistically within contexts that consist of interrelationships (methodology).

# 1.6 Application of quantitative versus qualitative approaches

As we look to the future, we acknowledge the continued importance of researching interpersonal, small-group and mass-mediated communication, but anticipate that many communication research endeavours will focus on management communication. Such communication research encompasses communication in organisational and development contexts, as well as environmental monitoring research, social audits, public relations and communication audits (*see* Unit 6).

Ontological and epistemological assumptions about organisational settings are compared in Table 1.1 below. It includes assumptions about the nature of organisations (ontology) and assumptions that could guide the procedures we follow to acquire knowledge (epistemology).

**TABLE 1.1** Quantitative versus qualitative approaches to researching organisations

| QUANTITATIVE APPROACH | QUALITATIVE APPROACH |
|---|---|
| **Ontological assumptions about the organisational culture** | |
| The organisational culture is authoritarian. | The organisational culture is participatory. |
| Access to information leads to power. | Access to information leads to a shared responsibility and the development of knowledge competencies. |
| Perceptions are managed by the selective dissemination of information. | The dissemination of information is based on the principle of inclusivity. |
| Top management's authority and credibility are not questioned. | Top management's authority and credibility are questioned, unless it is transparent in matters such as budgeting, decision-making procedures, planning, and the formulation and application of policies. |
| Institutional control is centralised. | Institutional control is decentralised to subsystems, departments or sections in the organisation. |
| **Ontological assumptions about management's functions** | |
| Management's function is to reduce conflict. | Conflict is acknowledged and resolved by analysing relationships, and the strategies to be followed are collaboratively agreed to by the parties involved. |
| Management's function is to maintain order. | The maintenance of order is a joint responsibility of management and employees. |
| Management's function is to motivate employees by defining the goals of the organisation. | Management leads by example and provides an environment in which employees have access to information and in which they are free to question, discuss and participate in decisions that affect their work. |

| QUANTITATIVE APPROACH | QUALITATIVE APPROACH |
|---|---|
| **Ontological assumptions about changes in the system** | |
| An organisational system that changes causes conflict among the subgroups and individuals involved. | Subsystems are interdependent and changes are accommodated by the self-reliant abilities of individuals or subsystems in the organisation. This includes the empowerment of minority subgroups through knowledge, and taking on the shared responsibility of the outcomes of decisions taken. |
| Loss of control by management is regarded as a sign of inefficiency. | All stakeholders, through participation, trust and transparency, share responsibility. Change is not feared, but acknowledged as a core element in strategic planning. |
| **Epistemological assumptions** | |
| Variations are avoided. | Variations are seen as the roots of growth and development, and are not distrusted. Diversity and dialogue contribute to a more complete understanding of an organisation as a social environment. |
| The status quo is maintained by repeating previous models, programmes and research methods. | Renewal is sought on a continuous basis, allowing for the free flow of information, and resilience in the reformulation, testing and retesting of new models, programmes and research methods. |
| Operations are conducted in a deterministic manner and procedures are predictable. | Operations are conducted in a consultative manner and with recognition of the demands of the environment. Procedures are flexible and provide for participation. |
| The effectiveness of communication is researched by measuring predictions. | The effectiveness of communication is derived from interdependent relations among subgroups and individuals, and between the organisation and its external environment. Research is used as a vital tool to sensitise management and employees to potential conflict and changing needs. |
| Communication is meaningful when predicted outcomes (or effects) are realised. | Developing and maintaining relationships are more meaningful than predictable outcomes. A common (organisational) goal is pursued through collective support. |

| QUANTITATIVE APPROACH | QUALITATIVE APPROACH |
|---|---|
| **Epistemological assumptions (continued)** | |
| Problem-solving strategies are based on established procedures, policies and rules. Answers are sought by testing hypotheses and performance is evaluated in terms of strategic requirements. | Problem-solving strategies are guided by asking (research) questions that may not have been previously considered. Performance evaluation is seen as a creative opportunity that can be explored to meet changing organisational and individual needs. |
| To accommodate the above assumptions, the research design is selected with the goal of observing, testing, controlling, predicting and/or prescribing communication in quantitative terms. | To accommodate above assumptions, the research design is selected with the goal of exploring and interpreting communication in a qualitative and holistic manner. |

In comparing the qualitative and quantitative approaches, the quantitative approach to researching communication in organisational contexts can be criticised because:

- authority, control and accountability are formalised in an artificial division between top management and employees (as a result, top management and employees are alienated from one another);
- employees are not seen as self-motivated or creative individuals;
- change is (in a deterministic way) seen as the cause of conflict; and
- the rigid application of procedures, policies and rules can prevent an organisation from adapting to changes in the economic, social and/or political sectors of its external environment.

It is important to realise that, despite the differences in propositions and assumptions that underlie a quantitative versus a qualitative approach or views of the nature of organisations, in reality the approach applied will be directed by the research goal and objective. For example, if the goal is to obtain a broad overview of a particular organisation's communication channels, leadership styles and decision-making procedures, one would have to consider a more quantitative approach (e.g. using questionnaires). An analysis of employees' attitudes, perceptions and feelings would require a more qualitative approach (e.g. using in-depth interviews). These aspects are further discussed in Unit 2.

The challenges posed by conducting actual research is particularly relevant to researchers whose studies relate to organisations that function in a culture where reality is constructed by the World Wide Web and communication takes place mainly via electronic mail. According to Inayatullah (1998:236), the absence of face-to-face communication means that '[t]he assimilation and reflection as well as the intuition and the insight needed to make sense of intellectual and emotional data are lost'.

## 1.7 What about future research?

**globalisation:** internationalisation of ownership, production, distribution, transmission and reception

Globalisation has created the notion of an information society that has, during the past decade, brought about changes to postmodern societies. These changes, among others, include:

- an increase of the flow of information internationally;
- greater emphasis being placed on knowledge as a source of power;
- the growth of information as a source of wealth (e.g. information-based occupations);
- an increased dependence by subsystems in society (such as the financial sector) on information and communication technology, in order to function efficiently;
- an increase in free market and democratically elected political systems;
- the internationalisation of social life, including sport, politics, economics and mass-media entertainment;
- an increase in privatisation; and
- a decline in meaningful social ties (especially in the form of religious and family institutions).

Against this background, the qualitative approach to communication research should not be viewed as an alternative to the quantitative or positivist paradigm. Instead it should be treated as a complementary approach, especially when researching:

- advertising and mass-mediated communication (*see* Unit 5);
- the operational strategies of institutions, including their social responsibilities (*see* Unit 6); and
- issues related to reconstruction and development (*see* Unit 6).

Instead of choosing between the two paradigms, future communication research should continue to combine both quantitative and qualitative methods. Whereas the economic survival of media institutions and organisations in general may demand criteria, such as the generalisation of reliable (quantitative) findings, communication also involves abstract ideas and values that should be interpreted in ideological frameworks. The move away from studying communication in a so-called mass society, to studying communication in a so-called information society, including mass media and 'new' media (such as electronic mail and teleconferencing), requires a more pluralistic approach. Such an approach means that a particular research paradigm (a combination of different methods) is selected, because it is regarded as the most appropriate to the phenomenon being investigated at the time. Simultaneously, the approach should be flexible and remain subject to criticism and change.

Such an approach should, ideally, also make provision for a process of collective reflection. Collective reflection, as part of the research design, enables researchers and subjects participating in communication research to share their perceptions and experiences, thereby contributing to social transformation and development. (*See also* Unit 6.)

**triangulation:** using two or more theories, types of sampling, investigators, sources of data, and/or data-collection methods

The combination of two or more data-collection methods and reference to multiple sources of information to obtain data, are generally referred to as triangulation. De Vos (1998:359) and Johnson (1997:282-292) argue that, in addition to the use of two or more methods (e.g. a questionnaire survey followed by focus-group interviews) and multiple sources of data (e.g. a content analysis of an organisation's annual reports and interviews with top management), triangulation also applies to:

- the collection of data using different types of sampling;
- the analysis of the same data from two or more theoretical and conceptual perspectives (theory triangulation); and
- conducting observations or analysing data using more than one investigator (investigator triangulation).

Although triangulation may in practice result in the combination of a quantitative and a qualitative approach to communication research, the main reasons for applying it are to test theoretical assumptions in more than one way, and to increase the reliability and validity of observations, analyses and findings.

Contemporary ontological assumptions about communication can be summarised by stating that communication is:
● a purposive, complex, creative and developmental process; and
● a contextual phenomenon that takes place in a social, interactive reality, interrelated, amongst others, with physical, psychological, cultural and social contexts.

If current and future researchers accept these assumptions, any research design that attempts to decontextualise the communication phenomenon being researched must be avoided. Instead, future research designs should:
● acknowledge the human-ness of communication; and
● provide for changing contexts by adopting longitudinal (instead of cross-sectional) time dimensions.

(A longitudinal time dimension means that the research is conducted at different points over a long period of time, such as a few years. A cross-sectional time dimension means that the research is conducted at a single point in time, such as on one day or during one week.)

Human development, as part of the South African government's Reconstruction and Development Programme (RDP), requires communication scholars to analyse, initiate, adapt and manage change. Placing communication research at the centre of the human development agenda means that future research will require in-depth studies in order to provide action-oriented strategies and policies that will promote the efficient use of human resources.

A quantitative (positivist) paradigm is legitimised by objectifying the natural world in order to control (test or measure) it. This approach, according to which knowledge is based on rationality, has been criticised for denying other methods of acquiring knowledge (Bless and Higson-Smith 1995:1-3). As part of an ongoing response to the question: *What about future research?* we should take note of arguments by scholars such as Goduka (1999:26-35), who maintains that notions of objective methods and rationality should be broadened to include the diversity of views grounded in indigenous cultures and spiritual values.

# 1.8 Summary

The ways in which we acquire knowledge about a specific communication phenomenon is linked to assumptions that underlie different research processes and procedures. As reflected in Figures 1.1 and 1.2, and Table 1.1, these assumptions are interlinked and interdependent with the research methodology used. In other words, specific assumptions about reality influence theoretical explanations and knowledge constructions. These also determine which research design is used and eventually influence the interpretation of findings (in terms of reality).

The unit started by considering tenacity, authority, a priori and scientific enquiry as different ways of knowing. A conceptual model of ontological, epistemological, theoretical and methodological assumptions followed, and applied to quantitative and qualitative approaches. Applying some of these assumptions to organisational settings illustrated that different ways of looking at reality (ontology) and different ways of knowing (epistemology), influence the research design. The unit concluded with the argument that future communication research ought to consider a pluralistic approach that provides for the application of triangulation.

## *Self-evaluation and portfolio tasks*

1.1 A research study that is based on a quantitative approach will be based on ontological and theoretical assumptions, as well as a research design that differs from a study based on a qualitative approach. Write brief notes to describe these differences under the following headings:
- The view of reality and human behaviour.
- The goal or objective of the research.
- The form of reasoning usually used.
- The research design (the role of the researcher; how meaning is determined, how data is collected and interpreted).

1.2 You have been approached by your employer to research the effectiveness of communication within the organisation. Based on the epistemological and methodological assumptions discussed in this unit, which approach would you follow to conduct the research, and why?

Before continuing with Unit 2, you are encouraged to evaluate your achievement of the learning outcomes using the guide and the ratings below.

> **ASSESSMENT OF LEARNING OUTCOMES**
> Ratings for evaluation of performance:
> 5   very high (extremely good)
> 4   high (good)
> 3   medium (average)
> 2   low (poor)
> 1   very low (extremely poor)
> 0   evidence is absent

| Outcomes (knowledge, competence and orientations) *You should be able to demonstrate your understanding of:* | Evidence of performance | Examples of criteria used to evaluate evidence of performance | Evaluation of performance Ratings | | | | | |
|---|---|---|---|---|---|---|---|---|
| | | | 5 | 4 | 3 | 2 | 1 | 0 |
| The different ways of knowing | by describing their characteristics. | Characteristics that deal with assertions, sources, advantages and requirements of the ways of knowing are distinguished. | | | | | | |
| The assumptions on which the quantitative and qualitative approaches to communication research are based | by writing descriptive notes. | The differences between ontological, epistemological, theoretical and methodological assumptions of the two approaches are clear. | | | | | | |
| The implications that the above assumptions have for the selection of a research design | by making a motivated selection of an approach to research a particular communication problem. | The implications of the choice are described (motivated) in terms of whether the problem requires mainly quantitative measurement versus qualitative understanding, or a combination of both approaches. | | | | | | |

## SUGGESTED READING

De Vos, AS (ed). 1998. *Research at grass roots. A primer for the caring professions.* Pretoria: Van Schaik.

McQuail, D. 1996. *Mass communication theory: an introduction.* (3rd edition). London/Thousand Oaks, California: Sage.

McQuail, D. 2000. *McQuail's mass communication theory.* (4th edition). London: Sage.

Mouton, J. 1996. *Understanding social research.* Pretoria: Van Schaik.

Neuman, WL. 1997. *Social research methods: qualitative and quantitative approaches.* (3rd edition). Boston, Massachusetts: Allyn & Bacon.

O'Sullivan, T, Hartley, J, Saunders, D, Montgomery, M and Fiske, J. 1996. *Key concepts in communication and cultural studies.* (2nd edition). New York: Routledge.

Servaes, J. 1999. *Communication for development: one world, multiple cultures.* Cresskill, NJ: Hampton.

Watt, JH and Van den Berg, SA. 1995. *Research methods for communication science.* Needham Heights, Massachusetts: Allyn & Bacon.

Webster, JG and Phalen, PF. 1997. *The mass audience: rediscovering the dominant model.* Mahawa, NJ: Lawrence Erlbaum.

Winston, B. 1998. *Media, technology and society.* London: Routledge.

# Steps in the research process

*It is good to have an end to journey toward;*
*but it is the journey that matters in the end.*

URSULA K LE GUIN

## Overview

One of the basic characteristics or requirements of scientific research is that it is systematic – that the process of conducting research follows a logical order. This unit deals with the different steps of the research process with the focus mainly on identifying and analysing the research problem, reviewing literature, formulating hypotheses or research questions, selecting or developing the research design, and writing a research proposal.

## Learning outcomes

By the end of this unit you should be able to demonstrate your understanding of:

- the procedures involved in identifying and analysing a communication research problem (by formulating a research problem, subproblems, assumptions, a hypothesis(-es) and/or research questions in a logical manner);
- the analysis and evaluation of the planning of your own research project (by writing down formulations in a logical and systematic style, and by applying the ratings evaluations to decisions); and
- the steps followed in communication research (by describing each step in the research process with reference to key issues – particularly the first five steps).

## 2.1 Introduction

This unit focuses on the various procedures and/or steps in undertaking research. Although the steps are discussed in a particular order, they are not necessarily applied in a linear or chronological sequence. Sometimes activities undertaken and decisions made during one step overlap with the next step, and subsequent steps may force us to return to previous steps (for example, as a result of unanticipated difficulties or when circumstances change).

One of the critical learning outcomes that this publication aims to achieve is the development of problem-solving skills. This unit includes activities that form part of self-evaluation and portfolio tasks and should be treated as opportunities to become familiar with the different steps in conducting research. While working through the different steps in the sections below, you may want to consider undertaking a communication research project in an area that interests you.

A ratings evaluation is included at various points in this unit, which can be used to rate the meaningfulness, appropriateness and/or relevance of your formulations (as they apply to your chosen study).

Figure 2.1 on page 46 is a graphic summary of the steps that are discussed in this unit.

## 2.2 Step 1: Identifying and analysing the problem

According to Thomas (1984:142-143), two factors must be considered when identifying a human condition as problematic. Firstly, **norms** and **standards** that define certain behaviour or states of well-being as being appropriate should be identified. The identification can be based on professional codes of conduct, such as adhered to by journalists, teachers, psychologists, police officers or health workers, and/or based on agreement within a particular community. Secondly, the existing behaviour or conditions, as they apply to individuals or groups, should be compared with the standards to determine **discrepancies**.

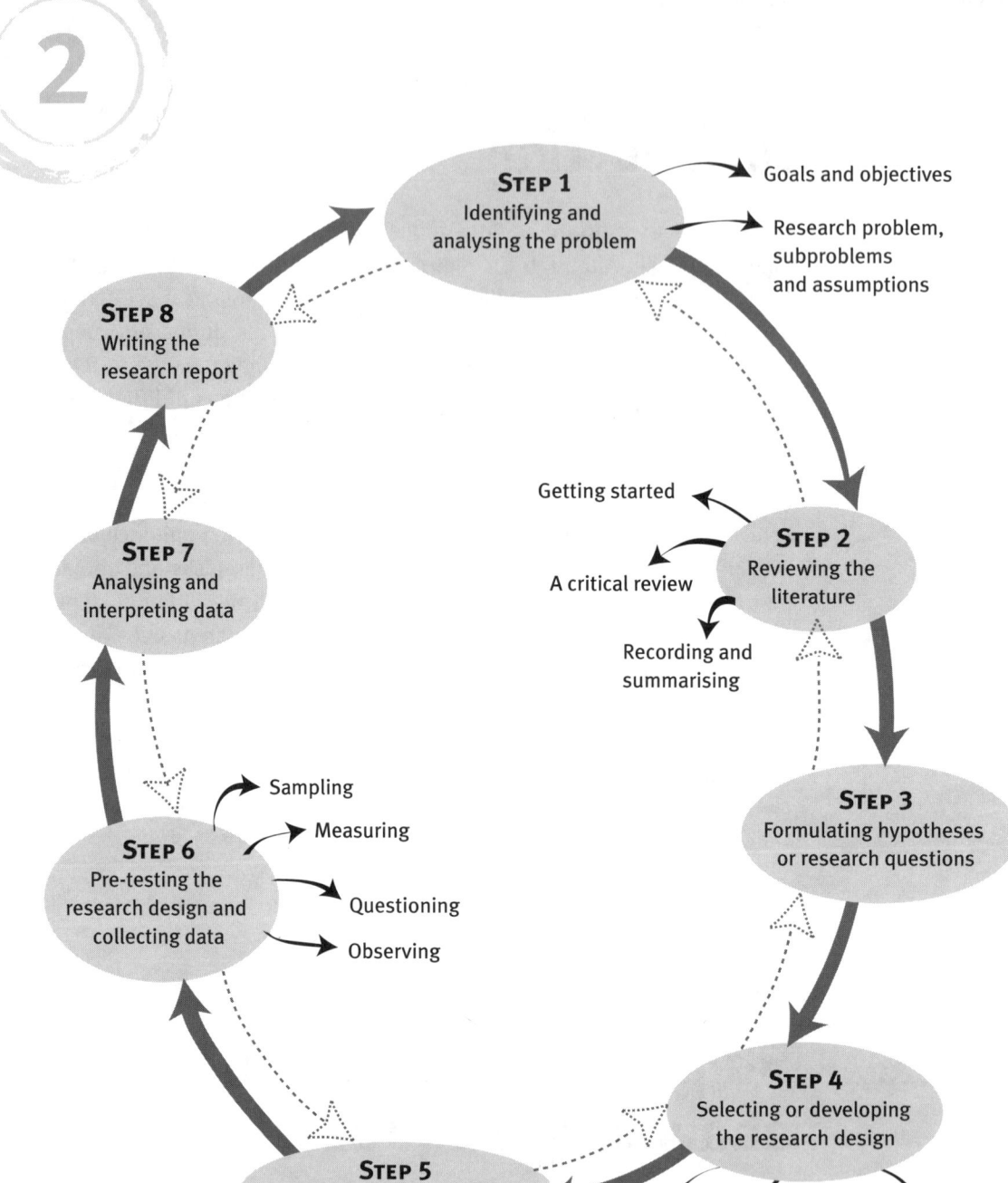

**FIGURE 2.1:** Steps in the research process

De Vos (1998:386) summarises this comparison: 'When the discrepancy between the standard and what is judged is sufficiently large, the behaviour or state of being is deemed to be a problem.'

It is important to note, however, that communication research in general, or the delineation of a specific research problem, is very often not prompted by a problematic human condition or communication behaviour that deviates from a norm or standard. Instead, communication research problems can have a variety of other **sources**:

- Our interests often motivate the choice of a particular topic to study (e.g. *A critical analysis of cultural meaning in music videos*). Although these interests may ignite the fire of wanting to do research, it requires a sustained curiosity, energy and commitment to keep that fire burning.
- A need in a particular community or wider society has become an increasingly important source of communication research (e.g. *The use of community radio in the Western Cape for educational purposes*).
- Literature and theories often stimulate investigation to verify their relevance in practice (e.g. *The role of opinion leaders in a multi-step flow model of television news dissemination in a specific community*). ·

**multi-step flow model:**
various number of relays in the flow of information from a mass medium to a large audience

**replication:**
research that reproduces a previous research study as an independent verification

- Previous research, when published, usually contains recommendations and questions that need further investigation. Previous research can also be used for the purpose of replication (e.g. *An evaluation of the role of interpersonal communication in the functioning of an academic library*). The advantage of replicating a study is that it increases the depth of research in a specific area.
- Communication practitioners and professionals often identify problems that not only have social relevance, but also need to be researched, because of their practical implications (e.g. *An analysis of how the Employment Equity Act, the Skills Development Act and Skills Development Levies Act affect specified business sectors*). In South Africa, over 130 new Acts of Parliament, covering more than 35 areas of legislation, have been promulgated since 1997. These can be fruitful sources of communication problems in areas such as telecommunications, organisational, educational, marketing, development (RDP), governmental, intercultural, political and health communication.

Once there is a clear indication of the source of the problem, we need to specify the **goals** as broad outcomes of the research and the **objectives** that collectively contribute to achieving the goals. It then becomes easier to formulate the research problem and to analyse it in terms of subproblems and assumptions.

## 2.2.1  Goals and objectives

Social scientists unfortunately do not agree on the use of and meanings conveyed by the concepts 'goals', 'aims', 'purposes', 'objectives' or 'outcomes' of research. For the sake of clarity, the following distinctions are made and used throughout this publication.

**goals:** basic research versus applied research

In this publication,**goals** are treated as synonymous with aims, purposes and overall outcomes. Two overall goals can be distinguished, namely basic research and applied research:

- The goal is pure or **basic communication research**, when a study investigates and develops theories to explain particular communication phenomena. In so doing, the knowledge base of communication as a science is expanded. Wimmer and Dominick (1997:12) also refer to basic research as 'academic sector research'.
- The goal is **applied communication research**, when a study investigates practical issues, often to find solutions for problems that can be applied in practice. Applied research is undertaken to explore solutions for communications problems; to describe and assess communication needs; to describe current policies and practices to make decisions for change; and to evaluate current practices.

**mutually exclusive:** placed in one and only one category

**Objectives** are not necessarily mutually exclusive. This means that a particular study can have more than one objective. Four objectives can be distinguished: exploratory, descriptive, explanatory and/or predictive objectives.

**Exploratory objectives** explore an unknown area of research that can be based on any one or more of the following: to obtain new insights as part of a pre-test or pilot test; to identify key concepts; to identify key stakeholders; to prioritise social needs; to identify consequences of communication problems; to develop hypotheses; to confirm assumptions; or to become familiar with unknown situations, conditions, policies and behaviours.

**research design:** method(s) and technique(s) used to collect, analyse and interpret data

Data replication and accuracy are not scientific criteria in these studies, because the research design is flexible to enable us to obtain an understanding of an unknown area of research. In addition to doing a literature survey, the methods normally used include personal and focus-group **interviews** (e.g. with practitioners or community leaders), **surveys** of larger populations (e.g. all the teachers in a province) and especially **case studies** (e.g. of specific organisations).

**Descriptive objectives** describe the characteristics of a phenomena, or relations between a number of variables, as accurately as possible. 'To describe' can be the objective in both quantitative and qualitative studies. For example, in qualitative research, the objective can be an in-depth description of a particular case study, such as illiteracy levels among street children. In quantitative research, the objective can be to give a description of the frequency with which a variable occurs, such as television viewing habits of a sample of families over a period of time.

A study with mainly descriptive objectives asks '*What is?*'. For example, *What is the illiteracy level among street children?* or *What are these families' viewing habits?*

However, when describing relations between variables, the objective is to investigate more than just 'what is'. The objective is to describe the degree to which two (or sometimes more than two) phenomena relate to one another or vary together. For example, the objective of such a study could be to describe the relationship between intelligence and literacy of street children, by asking: '*When children's intelligence varies, what happens to their levels of literacy?*' In this example both the intelligence and literacy scores of a group of street children would have to be recorded to determine whether and how these two variables are related for that particular group.

In addition to comparing variables within one group, descriptive objectives also investigate relationships by comparing different groups. For example, '*How do rural families' television viewing patterns compare with those of urban families?*'

The descriptions can be given in a **narrative** form, such as when describing the responses recorded during focus-group interviews (*see* Unit 4). The descriptions can be grouped according to a classification system, such as dividing potential consumers in advertising in a typology according to their values and lifestyles (*see* Unit 5).

**typology:**
a classification of things or people having common characteristics

Descriptions may also be based on **statistical analyses**, according to which variables are classified in frequency tables and systematically described – for example, with reference to arithmetic means, medians and cross-tabulations (*see* Unit 4).

**Explanatory objectives** indicate the direction of a cause-and-effect relationship between an independent variable (X) and a dependent variable (Y). (These variables are discussed in section 2.4.2.)

An explanatory study can be undertaken as **predictive** research. For example, when finding a positive relationship between the number of photographs on the front page of a newspaper (X) and an increase in the number of issues sold (Y), such findings can be used to predict that similar front pages will result in more issues being sold.

An explanatory study can also be undertaken as **evaluation** research. For example, having planned and implemented a new public relations campaign (X), its effectiveness in achieving specific goals (Y) can be researched. The two research methods normally used in explanatory research are based on **experimental** and **quasi-experimental** designs.

Although the formulation of the goal and the objectives of a research study appear to be a simple task, it has to be carefully examined and formulated to contribute to the planning of the research process. It is not unusual for a pilot study to start with exploratory objectives and find that, as the study develops, it needs to adapt to descriptive ('What is?') objectives. Similarly, a study may start with descriptive objectives but end up formulating and conducting research with cause-and-effect (explanatory) objectives.

Once the goal and objectives have been identified, we are faced with the task of formulating the research problem.

## 2.2.2  Formulating the research problem, subproblems and assumptions

The choice of investigating a research problem is often related to the researcher as an individual, to a particular institution and/or to a wider community or society. However, at least four criteria should to be met when selecting a problem area for research:

*relevancy:*
applicability

- **Relevancy**   The problem must be relevant to communication, irrespective of whether the goal is basic or applied research, and preferably also to society. Although the question of relevance may be arguable and a matter of degree, it's appropriateness has to be apparent or motivated in an unbiased manner.
- **Researchability**   Whether or not a problem area is researchable will depend on whether it merits scientific research. In other words, can the problem be resolved or probable solutions antici-pated by collecting evidence? *practically "doable"*
- **Feasibility**   The feasibility of investigating a problem area is normally dependent on the resources available. These resources include funds for expenses, the expertise of the researcher and other investigators (e.g. interviewers), access to data (including people as participants or respondents), the co-operation of the people involved, and time considerations. *Man - power + money -*
- **Ethical acceptability**   There are no fixed rules determining the extent to which the investigation of a research problem is ethically acceptable or unacceptable. However, if it has the potential of harming participants or exposing them to any form of risk (e.g. emotionally), the decision to undertake the research has to be informed by our social conscience. *not contravening any copywrite.*

### Guidelines for formulating a research problem

The following guidelines should be kept in mind when formulating a research problem:

1.  The problem can be formulated as an open-ended question. An open-ended question is one in which the content or nature of the answer or response is not specified. For example: '*What are the needs of managers in terms of international business communication?*

2. The open-ended question can be reformulated as a statement, in which one can refer to the method to be used. For example: *'Developing a course in international business communication for managers: a case study of ISCOR'.* In this example, *'case study'* indicates the method to be used and demarcates the extent of the problem by identifying one organisation.

3. When formulating the problem, one can also include an indication of the action or intervention that solving the problem would entail. In the above example *'Developing a course'* is the action. What is implied is that *'developing a course'* means 'developing and testing the effectiveness of a course'. Other examples of actions are:

   *Validation of a competency-based assessment of ...;*
   *An analysis of the role of conflict in ...;*
   *A qualitative evaluation of ...; and*
   *A comparative analysis of ....*

   It should be noted that not all research studies necessarily include an action or intervention. Where they are applicable, they should ideally be reflected in the problem formulation.

4. Dependent and independent variables should also be specified if they are to be researched. For example: *'An evaluation of the impact of telecommuting* (independent variable) *on quality of life* (dependent variable) *of teenagers living in major urban centres in KwaZulu-Natal'.*

   Stating these variables makes it unnecessary to state the method (one can assume that one of the experimental or quasi-experimental designs will be used). Furthermore, it becomes unnecessary to specify the action because we can read into the problem statement that it will entail a cause-and-effect investigation or an analysis.

As indicated in the introduction to this unit, we suggest you think of a communication research study that you would want to do while working through the different steps in this unit. The ratings evaluation on page 53 offers you the opportunity to formulate your own research problem and to rate its meaningfulness, appropriateness and/or relevance.

Each research problem should be analysed and broken down into related **subproblems** that can facilitate the solution of subsections or parts of the main problem.

## Subproblems

To identify subproblems relevant to the main research problem, those factors (or variables) that are relevant to the main problem need to be identified. The population parameters of people are discussed below, as examples of such factors, illustrating a practical way in which problems can be divided into subproblems.

**population parameters:** characteristics of the units of analysis that are relevant to the research

**units of analysis:** the smallest elements investigated

**target population:** the entire class or group of units, objects or subjects to which we want to generalise findings

If the unit of analysis involves **individuals** (subjects, respondents or participants), a list of all the demographic and sociographic variables (population parameters) that could apply to the specific target population can be made. These may include age, gender, educational level, income, years of employment, experience, living area and marital status. Depending on the area of specialisation in which the research study falls, other characteristics can be added, such as medical history (in health communication), or criminal record (in development communication).

If the unit of analysis consists of **groups** of people (e.g. married couples), many other variables can be added. These may include the duration of the relationship, the duration of the marriage, whether they have children, whether other family members share the home, recreational activities shared as a couple/family, how often they buy

newspapers, whether they have access to electricity, whether they have cell phones and access to the Internet, and the number of radio and television sets they own.

The meanings and other examples of the terms 'population', 'units of analysis' and 'population parameters' are further discussed in Unit 3, section 3.2. Having compiled a list of population parameters, **assumptions** about each variable can be noted.

## *Assumptions*

**assumption:**
a postulate,
hypothesis or
premise

The term 'assumption' can be used to refer to a postulate (a principle assumed to be true for the purpose of developing theory) or a hypothesis (a principle or statement of conclusion that is tested experimentally or by a series of observations).

However, the term 'assumption' is used in this discussion as a premise and as a tentative explanation or statement that is provisionally regarded as true (despite there being no proof). Irrespective of whether assumptions are based on personal experience or past research findings, they are used in this context to guide our reasoning in formulating arguments and to assist in identifying subproblems. For example:

**isiZulu:**
one of eleven
official languages
in South Africa

**M-Net:**
South Africa's
first subscription
television station

**Main problem** *Is it viable to introduce separate isiZulu television programmes on M-Net?*

**Assumption** (related to income as one of the population parameters) *Only isiZulu households that belong to the upper income bracket will respond positively towards such programmes, because of the additional payment required for an M-Net decoder.*

Similar assumptions can be made about other variables, such as age, urban versus rural habitats, or first languages used by current M-Net subscribers. Having written down all possible assumptions, these statements can be reformulated as **open-ended questions**. For example:

*How will income influence television viewers to subscribe to M-Net if isiZulu television programmes are introduced?*
or
*How will respondents in the upper income bracket respond to the introduction of isiZulu television programmes on M-Net?*

These open-ended questions can be treated as **subproblems**, with each one linked to a particular assumption (to be confirmed or rejected). If the research involves **other** units of analysis (e.g. the content of mass-media messages) the same procedure can be followed. Here, the population parameters will differ and not consist of demographic and sociographic characteristics. We illustrate these different population parameters by analysing the following *research problem*:

**Main problem** *How effective is marketing communication at UNISA?*

Various population parameters apply to this problem:
1. Different demographic and sociographic variables will apply to the different marketing publics, as clients, depending on whether they are alumni, present or potential students.
2. UNISA has unique characteristics as a distance, tertiary education institution, so the questions that need to be answered are:
   - What are these characteristics or properties?
   - Are these characteristics incorporated in the marketing of UNISA's courses and modular programmes?
   - How are these characteristics communicated in messages aimed at marketing UNISA?
3. Marketing communication implies the use of different media (e.g. calendars, pamphlets, press releases and advertisements). To get an overall picture, a content analysis would have to be done. Encoding characteristics differ, depending on the type of medium. Therefore, questions such as the following emerge:
   - How are the audiovisual codes (e.g. types of address, language, layout, typography, visuals, sound effects or music) used?
   - How do clients perceive the audiovisual codes?
   - What core messages are being marketed?
   - What persuasive techniques are used?

The diversity of these questions indicates that several *assumptions* can be formulated to function as pointers to the subproblems. Let us take the use of different media in the marketing campaign as an example:

**Assumption** *New students register at UNISA because the radio advertising campaign reached listeners living in rural areas.*

If the assumption is reformulated as *open-ended questions*:

- *Did new students, living in rural areas, register at UNISA because of the radio advertising campaign?*
- *Which media prompted new students to register at UNISA?*
- *Apart from the mass media, what other reasons prompted new students to register at UNISA?*

These open-ended questions can be treated as **subproblems**, with each one linked to a particular assumption (to be confirmed or rejected).

Based on the above examples and discussion, assumptions and subproblems appear to represent two sides of the same coin. As a result, we may find it unnecessary to formulate both. However, because an assumption can guide thinking and (as in the latter example) result in identifying more than one subproblem, it is a worthwhile exercise to do during the initial stages of research.

Reconsider the research problem you selected and divide the problem into subproblems and the assumptions on which these subproblems are based.

## EVALUATION

Write down your selected subproblems and assumptions and evaluate them using the following ratings scale. Ideally, the subproblems and assumptions should rate 2.

### The subproblems and assumptions

Rate 0   if the relationship between the main problem and the subproblems plus assumptions is unclear;

Rate 1   if the subproblems and assumptions are clearly stated, but are irrelevant or illogical in terms of the main problem;

Rate 2   if solving the subproblems and accepting/rejecting the assumptions will contribute to solving the main problem.

*Executive summary:*
**Step 1: Identifying and analysing the problem**

1 Sources of communication research problems/issues:
- norms, standards, codes of conduct;
- personal interests;
- a need in a community or society;
- literature and theories;
- previous research;
- communication practitioners and professionals.

2 Research goals:
- basic;
- applied.

3 Research objectives:
- exploratory;
- descriptive;
- explanatory.

4 Formulating the research problem:
- as an open-ended question;
- as a statement with proposed methods;
- as a statement with action;
- as a statement specifying variables.

5 Formulating subproblems:
- based on relevant factors;
- linked to assumptions;
- as open-ended questions;
- aimed at solving the main problem.

## 2.3 Step 2: Reviewing the literature

The second step in the research process involves the collection and synthesis of **existing** information relating to the research topic. The purpose of doing a literature survey is to find material related to the conceptual focus of the research problem. Such material can be in a published form (e.g. articles in professional journals) or in an unpublished form (e.g. dissertations and theses).

## 2.3.1 Getting started

A literature review usually begins by identifying what has been published on a particular topic. The most recent publications, especially articles in journals, often contain summaries and criticisms of earlier works, and usually list additional sources. Research reports, dissertations and theses often contain very useful summaries and critical evaluations of literature.

Researchers often start a literature review by consulting a few books, before searching for journal articles. Often the names of specific researchers and authors who have worked in a particular field appear repetitively in basic sources. These books also contain useful bibliographies that can guide the search for more specific sources. Although this (snowball searching) is a useful way to start a literature review, it may not lead the researcher to all the publications that could be pertinent to the research project.

**bibliography:**
a list of writings about a subject

Literature can be searched by **computer** or **manually**. To use a particular library's computer-based bibliographic processing system, requires a precise and complete description of the topic area, and terms that match the citations of its database. A manual search takes longer, but can provide access to sources, such as technical reports, doctoral theses and specific authors that may not be available via a computer search. Card catalogues (including authors, subject headings and publication titles), indexes (containing lists of books and articles about topics) and abstracts are three sources of reference in a manual search. Some libraries no longer offer a card-based manual search system. It is advisable to consult with a librarian, to become familiar with the procedure for undertaking a computer search and resources available via the Internet, and to get to know what other services the library offers.

**abstract:**
a brief summary of the main ideas of a book or article

Researchers often use the Web (or WWW) to visit websites maintained by colleges, universities, government agencies, companies or individuals. Using the Internet, access is obtained to a vast collection of documents stored on computers throughout the world, in the form of verbal texts, pictures, and sound and video clips. An alphabetical list of useful electronic addresses appears in **Addendum A** at the end of this book.

**WWW:**
World Wide Web; a part of the Internet

**website:**
a collection of web pages

The following general, practical guidelines may be followed when collecting information:

1. Identify the key words that describe the most relevant conceptual components of the research study. Consult encyclopaedias, text books, dictionaries and thesauruses, and examine the theory(-ies) that apply to the problem.
2. Using the key words carry out a literature search of the computer databases available at major libraries.
3. Consult journals that publish articles in the area of the study.
4. Consult the bibliographies of research articles, dissertations and theses, summaries, literary reviews and abstracts as secondary sources (and in so doing, identify primary sources of information and additional references).
5. If certain researchers and practitioners are known to be experts in a particular study area, contact them for additional source references, especially ones that may not have been published. This resource, daily newspapers and the Internet are particularly relevant if the problem area is of a current nature, such as the effects of new developments in the telecommunications industry.

Once the relevant literature has been located, it is important to determine whether the publications are primary, secondary or tertiary sources. A **primary source** provides primary data and includes autobiographies, letters, diaries, eyewitness accounts, political speeches recorded on an unedited video- or audiotape, information collected via a questionnaire or during an interview, or research results disseminated via the Web. A **secondary source** provides a secondary analysis of data found in primary sources, such as text books, biographies or a press report about a political speech. A **tertiary source** is further removed from the first-hand account of an event, because it contains an analysis of data found in secondary records, such as an article that uses press reports as sources.

**primary source:** first-hand account of an event

**secondary source:** second-hand account of an event

**tertiary source:** an account based on secondary data

Although tertiary and secondary sources provide valuable leads to primary sources, they should be **avoided**, because they may contain errors that could be perpetuated by depending on them alone. As a precaution, one should make every attempt to review literature representing primary sources of data. In addition, because of communication's multidisciplinary nature, one should investigate sources from other disciplines, such as health or sociology.

Secondary sources are useful for identifying the positions of scholars in other disciplines, and for determining whether there are conflicting points of view.

As the search progresses, two additional factors can be used to assess whether the information is relevant and applicable, namely the objectivity and the timeliness of the information.

**timeliness:**
currency or
prevalence

**objectivity:**
unbiasedness,
reliability and
validity

For example, research studies in certain fields, such as *development communication*, that were undertaken and published in the 1960s or 1970s are dated, because of the outdated theoretical assumptions on which they were based. Unless the information represents a classical work (e.g. by *Socrates*, as a basis for *persuasive communication*), any work older than five years needs to be critically evaluated to determine its timeliness. Objectivity can be evaluated by questioning whether the research was reliable and valid, if there are any signs of bias, and if the work has been scrutinised by peers, editors or examiners.

## 2.3.2 A critical review

A **review** of literature means a systematic and thorough survey of publications that are relevant to a research project. A **critical** review means that the publications are examined to determine their strengths and weaknesses. When doing a literature review our role is that of **critical reader**, not one of leisure. Many authors structure or organise their texts in a particular way. For example:

- each paragraph starts with a key statement and definitions of key concepts;
- the statements and definitions are elaborated on by dealing with related ideas or subcomponents; and
- the paragraph (or section) ends with examples illustrating the key concepts and/or subcomponents.

**structural labels:**
words that
describe the
organisation
of a text

'Key statement', 'definitions', 'subcomponents' and 'examples' are **structural labels** that can be written in the margin.

Here is an example of a research problem:

*A public relations audit of internal communication in a particular organisation*

'*Public relations audit*' refers to the **content**, and the structural label would be 'problem statement'.

Once we recognise that the author of a publication follows a particular (structural) writing style, we can use **labelling** to identify the sections that are relevant to the study. Making marginal notes helps the reader to remain focused and critical, and to identify relevant subsections easily. Other examples of structural labels include: 'key idea', 'assumptions', 'definitions', 'theoretical approach', 'repetition', 'examples', 'narration', 'quotations', 'illustrations', 'descriptions', 'statistics', 'method', 'findings', 'conclusions', 'limitations', and 'suggestions for future research'.

Researchers usually devise a critical reading procedure that is meaningful for them as individuals. Sections labelled 'examples' and 'narration' may constitute 'background information' to the area of research. Alternatively, we may want to refine 'method' as a label and differentiate between 'method to collect data' and 'method to analyse data'. We may want to expand on the labels given above, by adding other labels, such as 'sampling', 'validity tests' and 'reliability tests'.

Having identified the main research problem, the goal and objectives, and having considered possible subproblems and assumptions, it is essential that a critical review of publications is done to determine their strengths and weaknesses.

The **purpose** of a **literature review** is usually to answer these questions:
- What research has been done in a particular area? In other words, does the literature (e.g. an article) contain discussions about what is already known about the particular area of research and from which theoretical perspectives is the problem approached?
- What research methods have been used?
- What results have been generated?
- What was done with the results or findings?

As any research study progresses, the questions asked while reviewing the literature have to be continually revised and, if necessary, redefined. To identify information that is relevant to a particular study, we have to revisit our answers to these questions and write initial specifications or definitions for the concepts and variables in each answer. This will help to narrow the field of search, and these meanings can be adapted as

the research progresses. An error that must be avoided is defining the study too rigidly or too narrowly, so blocking information that may be valuable. Researchers need to ensure that they make provision for differing viewpoints or approaches to the problem that is being studied.

The following additional questions can guide critical reading. Although the word 'literature' is used, the questions are intended to include any source consulted, including talking to communication professionals, practitioners or other researchers.

- **Intellectual and research traditions** Can the literature provide access or guide us to historically original theorists and researchers that relate to or support the study?
- **Assumptions** Does the literature contain arguments or research findings that support the assumptions?
- **Research design** Are the data-collection and data-analysis methods valuable to the study? Can the study be replicated by using another population?
- **Definitions** should be drawn from literature to obtain consensus on the meanings of concepts and variables. When we reach the stage of formulating theoretical and operational definitions (*see* section 2.4.2) the literature review can be guided by these questions: Does the literature contain theoretical and/or operational definitions that we can use or adapt? Can alternative theories for understanding the problem be identified?
- Does the literature point to **shortcomings** or something that still has to be learned or investigated?
- Is the data **authentic**? In other words, is the literature based on sources or data that are genuine, such as first-hand accounts of participants involved in an event?
- Are both the author (source) and the data **credible**? For example, does the report show signs of bias, are articles refereed, and can the information be verified by checking other sources? Because research findings can be placed on the Internet without much restriction or peer evaluation, articles that appear in journals published by professional associations have more credibility, because scholars and researchers have refereed them. (The importance of peer evaluation is discussed in detail in Unit 7.)

**refereed:**
approved by someone whose judgement is authoritative and trustworthy

**peer evaluation:**
appraisal by other researchers and critics

These questions are general guidelines for researchers when analysing sources and data, and confirming their **authenticity** and credibility. The questions can be further refined when analysing particular media. For example, data in magazines and newspapers should be further analysed by considering the use of typography, layout, photography, headings and actual placement on a page. In the case of television, the use of different camera shots and angles, and the combination of different shots through editing, also have a direct influence on the meanings communicated.

## 2.3.3   Recording and summarising

It is not unusual for researchers to make notes on scraps of paper, only to regret it later when the notes are found to be incomplete or the sources can no longer be remembered. It is important to record the **bibliographic** information of every publication read, either on separate cards, or by entering these details directly on a computer file. Either form of record-keeping enables us to keep an alphabetical and chronological record of sources consulted. Bibliographic information should include the following:
- the complete name of the author(s);
- the date of publication;
- the complete title (and any subtitles) of the publication;
- the edition;
- the place of publication;
- the name of the publisher; and
- the access (or call) number of the library where the publication was obtained.

Additional information needs to be recorded for journal articles:
- the name of the journal;
- the volume and number of the edition; and
- the page numbers of the article.

When drawing information from the Internet, the details should include the name(s) of the author(s), year, titles, http (on-line address) and especially the date on which it was accessed. The date is important because such information may not be available on the Internet at a later stage.

A complete and correct list of all sources is an ethical requirement of research. It enables other researchers to verify and/or further study the sources consulted. One may also find that an author has written two

or more sources in the same year. If we fail to distinguish between the two publications (by adding an alphabetical letter at the end of the entry according to the alphabetical order of the titles, such as 2000a and 2000b) we would be unable to use or link direct quotations to a particular publication.

Before summarising publications, it is important to define what one is looking for. Table 2.1 is a suggested checklist for critical reading.

| TABLE 2.1 Checklist for critical reading | ✔ |
|---|---|
| 1. The nature of the communication problem | |
| 2. The goal of the research | |
| 3. Objectives | |
| 4. Hypotheses/research questions | |
| 5. Ethical implications | |
| 6. Theories, theoretical model | |
| 7. Definitions of concepts | |
| 8. Research design used | |
| 9. Sampling method and procedure | |
| 10. Data-collection method and procedures | |
| 11. Data-analysis method | |
| 12. Limitations | |

In the absence of 'fixed' rules, researchers usually devise their own systems of recording and summarising information. One way of doing it is to open a separate file for each of the 12 sections that appear on the checklist. The checklist can be expanded on to include aspects such as measuring scales used in past research. The content of each file can be further structured or subdivided to avoid plagiarism and (more importantly) to eventually review the content. Subdivisions may include:

**plagiarism:** using the thoughts and writings of others under the pretence of their being our own

- direct quotations, particularly definitions of concepts or specific hypotheses;
- a summary of the main points, without comments or criticism;
- new ideas or findings;
- other authors' criticisms of a publication;
- implications for communication theory or practice;
- questions related to the research problem, operational definitions and methodological criteria, such as reliability and validity.

## 2

It is worthwhile to continuously **compare** new summaries with previous notes. This will establish whether there is a degree of consensus among different scholars about the definition of key concepts and about theoretical approaches to a particular communication problem. If different theoretical approaches have been followed to investigate the same phenomenon, such a comparison can form the basis of our own literature review (as part of the research report).

**measuring instruments:** instruments (e.g. questionnaires or rating scales) used to assess events, objects, behaviours or characteristics according to certain rules

A comparison of the research designs and measuring instruments used in the past can help to determine whether a quantitative or qualitative research design would be the most suitable for a particular study. Previous studies often contain valid measuring instruments, and summaries of data against which our findings can be compared. Time and effort can be saved if a study as a whole, or the measuring instrument used, can be replicated.

To critically evaluate a single publication, or to compare several publications, is a skill that must be practised. Unit 7 contains further criteria for the evaluation process that can simultaneously improve our skills as critical readers.

---

*EXECUTIVE SUMMARY:*

**STEP 2: REVIEWING THE LITERATURE**

1 Identify what has been published in the topic area.
2 Distinguish between primary, secondary, tertiary sources.
3 Verify the objectivity, authenticity and credibility of the sources and data.
4 Do a critical review.
5 Write summaries and make comparisons.
6 Record bibliographic information.

---

## 2.4 Step 3: Formulating hypotheses or research questions

Concepts and variables are two elements in scientific research that are particularly important in formulating hypotheses and research questions.

### 2.4.1 Concepts and constructs

Concepts refer to symbols or words that represent abstract ideas and are the building blocks of theories. One of the characteristics shared by communication theories is that the concepts used are highly abstract (e.g. 'values', 'functions', 'effectiveness', 'motivation', 'persuasion') and often convey multiple meanings. That is why the meaning of a concept such as 'myth' will vary depending on whether it is defined from an anthropological, a literary or a semiotic perspective. If disparities in the meaning of a concept exist, it needs to be clarified and defined within a conceptual framework. Sources of conceptual frameworks are found in theories, theoretical models and typologies, which underline the interdependence of theory and research. This is why a literature survey is an integral part of the research process. Abstract concepts that are defined within the parameters of a particular conceptual framework are referred to as **constructs**.

**anthropology:** the study of humans, especially of their societies and customs

**semiotics:** the study of signs and symbols in language and pictorial communication

**construct:** concepts that are combined to describe a particular phenomenon

Whereas a **concept** provides a direct link between an abstraction (e.g. 'height') and reality (e.g. 'observing individuals who are short or tall'), a **construct** does not provide a direct link between the abstraction and observations. The latter is illustrated by the use of 'status', 'expertise' and 'objectivity', which are constructs (or abstract indicators) used to evaluate the 'credibility' of a communicator in persuasive communication.

To ascribe precise meanings to constructs involves the formulation of a theoretical definition and an operational definition. A **theoretical definition** explains the denotative and connotative meanings of a construct, in a logical and systematic manner. We need a theoretical definition of the verbal meaning(s) of constructs, so that others can understand our theory and to enable them to criticise and replicate our measurements and observations. The more abstract the construct, the more difficult the task of writing theoretical definitions. Accordingly, it is easier to obtain agreement on a theoretical definition of the construct 'age', than it is to define the meaning of 'social status'.

For example, suppose we ask a group of people to write down their explanation of the construct 'status'. The results may include:

- *a person who is wealthy, lives in a grand house and drives an expensive car;*
- *people who have the ability to fulfil important roles, such as politicians;*
- *a person with a university education;*
- *someone who dresses well and whose office contains expensive furniture;*
- *individuals who hold top management positions in a company's hierarchy;*
- *people in white-collar jobs, who do not do manual labour;*
- *groups who have power in sectors, such as finance;*
- *someone who is only accessible via a secretary or by making a prior appointment.*

The next step would be to combine these explanations – and any others found in published literature or used in previous research – into a verbal statement that defines the construct. Based on the above connotative meanings, the following definition can be formulated:

*'Status' is theoretically defined as the prestige, superiority, power, role-playing abilities and social class of an individual or group in different social contexts.*

**operationalisation:** the development of a measuring instrument to collect accurate data

Having formulated theoretical definitions of each construct, these definitions need to be re-examined and reformulated as **operational definitions**. This is done to enable us to observe or measure the constructs that apply in our research – a process that is also called operationalisation.

**functionalist:** a view of society and groups in society as integrated, harmonious and cohesive 'wholes'

Based on a functionalist conceptual framework, we can argue that status is a value judgement linked to a particular social context. For example, the status ascribed to an individual will differ depending on the social context in which we know him or her and in which he or she fulfils different roles – at work, at home or in a recreational context. In other words, a change in social context involves a change in the people involved in that context. This, in turn, may mean a change in the status of the individual. We argued that status conferral is a value judgement, which means that it does not necessarily correspond with people's personal perception of themselves. Because neither a value judgement, nor a construct can be directly observed:

**indirect measurement:** not directly observable (e.g. must be measured using scales)

- data has to be collected by means of indirect measurement; and/or (if possible)
- each abstract construct has to be broken down into concrete constructs that can be measured or observed directly.

Figure 2.2 illustrates how the construct 'status' can be broken down into levels of abstraction. The **abstract** constructs are measured indirectly and the more **concrete** constructs are measured directly (e.g. by establishing someone's income), or observed directly (e.g. the size of a person's office). We can then operationally define 'status' as being a combination of the constructs listed in the figure, and we can combine them to obtain an overall summary of an individual's status.

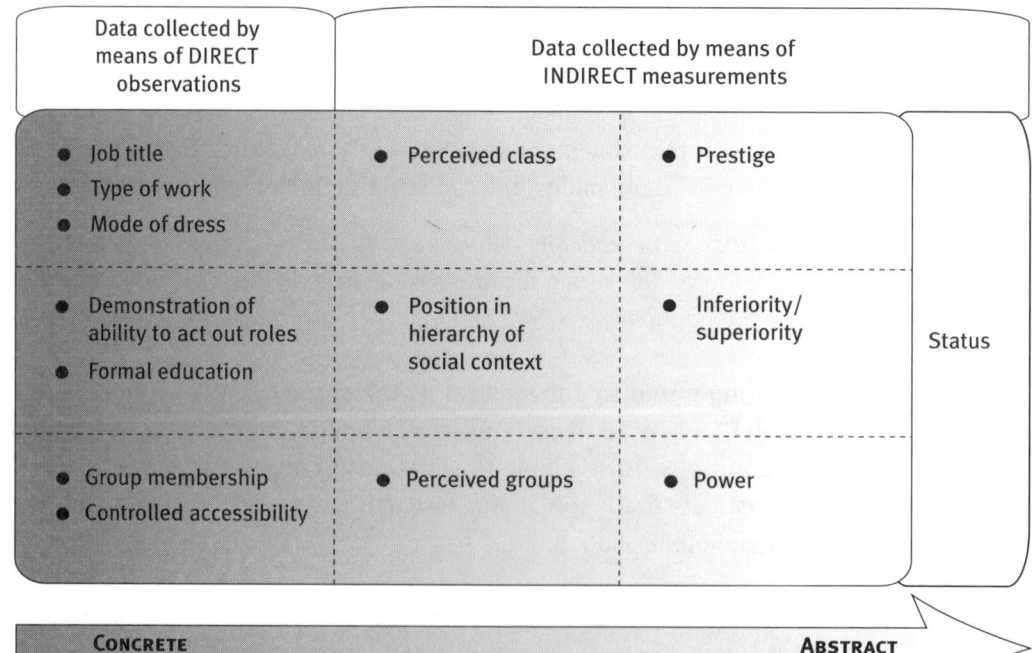

| Data collected by means of DIRECT observations | Data collected by means of INDIRECT measurements | | |
|---|---|---|---|
| • Job title<br>• Type of work<br>• Mode of dress | • Perceived class | • Prestige | |
| • Demonstration of ability to act out roles<br>• Formal education | • Position in hierarchy of social context | • Inferiority/superiority | Status |
| • Group membership<br>• Controlled accessibility | • Perceived groups | • Power | |

CONCRETE → ABSTRACT

**FIGURE 2.2:** Levels of abstraction in defining 'status' as a construct

Measuring instruments developed in a research study will depend on several factors, such as the actual nature of the problem and whether the methodological preference is qualitative or quantitative. For example, a physically disabled woman is appointed head of the human resources department in a company. After a period of time, we want to evaluate the degree of status she enjoys from her subordinates' perspectives. If a small group of people were involved, we would opt for a qualitative approach, using in-depth interviews. However, if we want to analyse how television confers status on and legitimises the authority of politicians, we can opt for a quantitative approach and undertake a content analysis of news programmes or conduct a viewer survey using an interview schedule or questionnaire. (These measuring instruments are further discussed in Unit 3.)

Irrespective of the measuring instrument used, it is important that the construct(s) be operationalised if we want to collect reliable data on a particular phenomenon (e.g. the status of a head of department). The techniques used for indirect measurement usually consist of a list of items representing the characteristics of the construct. These items are formulated as statements or questions, in the form of scales, a questionnaire or an interview schedule (*see* Units 3 and 4).

By administering these items in an interview or questionnaire, respondents' opinions of the construct are obtained (e.g. whether status is a characteristic of a person). The following statements are examples of characteristics denoted by status that can be used in the operationalisation of the construct:
- Prestige is associated with the division of labour.
- Inferiority and superiority are linked to the hierarchy of role positions in a specific context.
- The power of the individual is determined by group membership (e.g. the more elite the group, the greater the individual's power).
- Past events, the present context and future prospects determine the degree of prestige conferred on an individual or group.
- Society stratifies groups and individuals in perceived classes.
- Superiority is perceived as an individual's ability to act out roles.

These characteristics can be used to compile a list of items (statements and questions) that deal with aspects of status, without mentioning 'status' as a construct (*see* Unit 3, section 3.4.3 for an example).

Based on the above discussion and examples, we cannot refer to definitions as being 'true' or 'false' because they are delimited according to particular theories and models, which accommodate both connotative and denotative meanings. Instead, we should question whether a theoretical definition meets the requirements of **face validity**, and whether operational definitions meet the requirements of **measurement validity**. (The requirements of measurement validity are discussed in Unit 3.)

**face validity:** when a definition of a concept matches the observed reality

## 2.4.2 Variables

**variables:** characteristics that differ

The term **variable** refers to any aspect of an organism, or of the environment to which different values can be ascribed – for example, age, gender, income, educational level, the number of responses to a questionnaire survey, or political preferences. However, when conducting research, one must distinguish different ways in which variables are classified, in order to specify exactly what we want to observe or measure.

**dichotomous variable:** divided into two parts

**polytomic variable:** many parts

Variables can be classified according to the number of values they assume. Variables that can assume only one of two values are called **dichotomous variables**. For example, we are either employed or unemployed; either alive or dead; either pregnant or not pregnant; we cannot be something in between. **Polytomic variables** are variables that can assume a variety of values. For example, in order to measure subjects' political affiliation, we have to provide for a variety of political parties that are registered or recognised in a particular country. Different religious denominations are also an example of polytomic variables.

**discrete variable:** a variable that includes a fixed set of values

**continuous variable:** a variable that assumes a value over a range of values

A distinction can also be made between variables on the basis of whether or not they can be divided into subparts. In mass-media research a distinction is usually made between discrete and continuous variables. A **discrete** variable cannot be divided into subparts. For example, the number of television sets in a home is a discrete variable. Many variables researched in communication assume a spectrum (or continuum) of possible values, which are usually measured by means of a scale. These variables are called **continuous variables** and include a variety of constructs, such as anxiety, credibility and attitudes.

It is important to differentiate between a variable and the measurement of a variable (*see* Unit 3). For example, a television viewer's attitude towards racial conflict on the news can be regarded as a continuous variable. However, if the viewer's attitude is measured by counting his or her responses to a number of options in a questionnaire, these measures tend to be discrete. In other words, the distinction between discrete and continuous variables largely depends on how such variables are operationalised and/or measured.

Variables can also be described as **independent** or **dependent**. Research hypotheses usually contain independent, dependent and extraneous variables. The **independent** variable (X) is sometimes referred to as the treatment, experimental, causal or stimulus variable. The **dependent** variable (Y) is sometimes referred to as the criterion measure, the effect or the response. When distinguishing between independent and dependent variables, the objective is usually to measure the effect of (X) on (Y).

Independent and dependent variables apply to a cause-effect relationship (or stimulus-response relationship) between phenomena, events or actions. When conducting an experiment, the **independent** variable(s) are controlled and manipulated. The purpose of such control and/or manipulation is to isolate the actual factors (variables) that cause certain phenomena.

The situation does sometimes arise where we want to measure the influence of certain variables on other variables, but where we cannot control or manipulate the independent variables – for example, in investigating the influence of gender, age, educational level, income and language preference on consumer behaviour. These variables are usually examples of demographic characteristics, which vary among individuals, and are referred to as **characteristic variables, attribute variables** or **organismic variables**.

**extraneous:**
irrelevant

The last category of variables encompasses **extraneous variables**. These unwanted variables can be present in a variety of research settings and may influence research results. For example, income may be used as an independent variable (stimulus) to determine its association with television viewers' subscription to DStv (response). However, income becomes an extraneous variable if another factor

**DStv:**
digital satellite
television

(e.g. viewers' need to be able to watch direct broadcasts of World Cup rugby matches) is studied to determine its influence on viewers' subscription to DStv. Because income could have been a factor in viewers' decisions, it confuses the actual cause (the need – as independent variable) of the observed effect (the subscription – as dependent variable). **Intervening** and **confounding** variables are other names used to describe these unwanted variables.

After we have identified the constructs relevant to our research, formulated the theoretical and operational definitions of these constructs, and identified the type of variables to be measured, we are in a better position to decide whether we have to formulate research questions or hypotheses.

## 2.4.3 Research questions

Research questions (instead of hypotheses) are used in communication research for a variety of reasons. These include:
- when we are unsure about the extent or nature of the problem;
- when our objective is mainly exploratory;
- when we want to collect preliminary information about the problem;
- when our research design is qualitative; and/or
- when we want to collect more information about something in order to develop testable hypotheses.

The following are examples of research questions that can be formulated to investigate the subproblems discussed in section 2.2.2.

Research questions to investigate the introduction of isiZulu television programmes:
- *How does the respondents' income bracket influence their attitudes towards the introduction of isiZulu television programmes on M-Net?*
- In the case of respondents who supported the introduction of isiZulu television programmes on M-Net: *Is there a positive correlation between income brackets and gender groups?*

The inclusion of two or more research questions will have to be motivated. In the last example, we will have to motivate why a comparison between men and women in terms of income brackets is relevant to our research.

Research questions to investigate marketing communication at UNISA:

- *Did new students register at UNISA because they made personal contact with alumni?*
- *What prompted new students to register at UNISA?*

The first question investigates a relationship between two variables: whether *'contact with alumni'* caused *'new students to register at UNISA'*. However, research questions need not be limited to investigating relationships, which is illustrated by the second question. The fact that the second question is an open-ended question, in which no specific causal variable is investigated, indicates that we are unsure and want to explore all possible reasons for prompting the behaviour.

**circulation figures:**
total number of copies of newspapers or magazines sold and delivered to subscribers

Researching newspaper circulation figures, television viewers' programme preferences and policy-related studies, are examples of studies in which research questions would be used to obtain general indications of the phenomenon that we are investigating. (*See* Units 3, 4, 5 and 6 for more examples of research questions.)

## 2.4.4 Hypotheses

**hypothesis:**
a prediction of an outcome concerning the relationship between two or more variables

A **hypothesis** differs from a research question, in that it:

- is formulated in the form of a statement (not a question);
- predicts an outcome; and
- can be tested statistically.

Because hypotheses consist of statements that can be tested, they enable us to isolate very specific areas of communication to study and to quantify variables. These characteristics represent five important criteria that have to be met when formulating a hypothesis:

1. The hypothesis must be supported by **current knowledge** about the topic area, which again emphasises the importance of a literary review. If in mass communication it is accepted that news is disseminated via a multi-step flow, there is no point in formulating a hypothesis that suggests otherwise.

**operational:**
specifying procedures or patterns of behaviour to observe or measure a construct

2. The words used to represent constructs as variables must be **operational**, otherwise they cannot be included in a hypothesis. To test the following hypothesis, we would have to operationally define (in quantitative terms) the meanings of *'remembering'*, *'high frequency'* and *'low frequency'*:

*There is a significant difference between remembering radio advertisements for children who are exposed to low-frequency broadcasts and for children who are exposed to high-frequency broadcasts.*

3. A hypothesis has to be logically consistent.

   Logical consistency argues that if A = B and B = C, then A must also equal C.

   If a hypothesis, for example, suggests the following:

   *(A) Interpersonal contact between a company's public relations consultant and the editor of a newspaper implies*

   *(B) an informal relationship based on friendship, and that an informal relationship based on friendship means*

   *(C) the publication of only positive news about the company, then…*

   *(A) Interpersonal contact between a company's public relations consultant and the editor of a newspaper should also mean*

   *(C) the publication of only positive news about the company.*

4. In order to contribute to the development of communication knowledge, a hypothesis has to be **testable**.

   *The sales figures for Volkswagen sedan cars would have been higher if Toyota sedan cars were not sold in South Africa.*

   This hypothesis is not realistic because there is no way in which we can test whether more Volkswagen cars would have been sold in the absence of Toyota cars.

   *Films with an 18-year age restriction are ten times worse than films with no age restriction.*

   This hypothesis cannot be tested because we are unable to measure what is meant by '*worse*'. The hypothesis can only be tested if the construct 'worse' is operationally defined in specific detail, such as the use of abusive language or the types of violent acts being portrayed. The quantity '*ten times*' also creates a problem, because it suggests that for every ten violent acts in the age-restricted films, there will be one similar act in other films.

   *Children who watch too much television develop antisocial behaviour.*

   This hypothesis cannot be tested because we do not know what is meant by '*too much*' or what actions represent '*antisocial behaviour*'.

5. A hypothesis must be written as a concise or succinct statement.

   *The high degree of provincialism found in South Africa and the*

**testable:** examinable in order to determine truth or falsity

*differences in the lifestyles of people living in Western Cape versus those living in Gauteng, means that the appreciation index levels of regular viewers and non-regular viewers will differ for the same television programme.*

**appreciation index:**
an instrument that measures entertainment gratification derived by television viewers

The above statement is long-winded and adds to the vagueness of what is being hypothesised. It is not clear whether the appreciation index levels of regular viewers are being compared with non-regular viewers, or whether a comparison is being done of viewers living in different provinces.

## Types of hypotheses

Qualitative studies usually do not test hypotheses. However, tentative hypotheses can be formulated as guidelines, which can function as underlying assumptions. These can be disregarded once the rationale for a qualitative study has been established. When dealing with a particular institution or a subculture, it is useful to start by describing the properties of the system or population as in a case study or ethnography.

**case study:**
a method of research involving an in-depth study of a single unit (e.g. an organisation)

According to Watt and Van den Berg (1995:47-51), hypotheses can be classified and therefore worded in different ways:

- relationship hypotheses versus comparative hypotheses;
- directional hypotheses versus non-directional hypotheses; and
- research hypotheses versus null hypotheses.

To illustrate these differences, let us look at examples of hypotheses that can be formulated to investigate the subproblems discussed in 2.2.2.

A **relationship hypothesis** proposes the existence of a specific relationship between two variables and is measured by observing these.

*The income of subscribers and support for the introduction of isiZulu television programmes on M-Net are related.*

**covariance:**
differences in both variables that can be related to one another

To test for the probable truth (or falsity) of this relationship, we measure the variables in the individuals sampled, with the purpose of finding covariance. In other words, the majority of subjects in high-, average- and low-income groups should respond similarly:

- respondents with high income support the introduction of isiZulu programmes;
- respondents with average income are neutral or unsure about the
- introduction of isiZulu programmes; and
- respondents with low income do not support the introduction of isiZulu programmes.

While *'income'* as a variable allows us to think of *'more'* or *'less'* (or of *'high'*, *'average'* and *'low'*), we are sometimes faced with nominal variables that cannot be graded, such as gender. Here, a **comparative hypothesis** is the only option.

*Support for the introduction of isiZulu television programmes on M-Net is related to subscribers' gender.*

Because we cannot think of gender in terms of *'more'* or *'less'*, we test for the probable truth (or falsity) of this relationship by grouping individuals in two groups (male and female). We would anticipate different responses from the two groups.

The hypotheses stated above do not propose a positive or a negative relationship between the variables. They simply state the expectation or prediction that these variables are related, which make them examples of **non-directional hypotheses**.

If we were to predict how variables are related, we would formulate **directional hypotheses**, which in the following examples predict positive relations between high income and support for the programmes; and between male gender and support for the programmes.

*High-income subscribers and support for the introduction of isiZulu television programmes on M-Net are positively related.*

and ...

*Support for the introduction of isiZulu television programmes on M-Net is positively related to male gender subscribers.*

By writing a hypothesis in terms of a positive relation, we are predicting that there is a significant relationship between variables. This is usually called a **research hypothesis** ($H_1$). The logical opposite statement, called a **null hypothesis** ($H_0$), argues that there is no significant relationship between variables, or that the relationship being measured is one of chance. The null hypotheses of the above examples would therefore read:

*Subscribers' income and support for the introduction of isiZulu television programmes on M-Net are not related.*

and …

*Support for the introduction of isiZulu television programmes on M-Net is not related to subscribers' gender.*

According to Wimmer and Dominick (1997:231), stating the null hypothesis is redundant because each research hypothesis ($H_1$) has a logical alternative ($H_0$). Nevertheless, the null hypothesis is considered and important when we test hypotheses for statistical significance. Significance testing measures a difference or relationship that is beyond one that occurs by chance alone. In statistical analyses, the null hypothesis reflects the scepticism we have of our own hypotheses. In other words, when a statistical analysis indicates that the data does not support the null hypothesis, the latter is rejected and the research (alternative) hypothesis becomes relevant.

## *Types of relationship*

The distinction made between the research hypothesis and the null hypothesis indicates that two concepts can be related in different ways, depending on the nature of the relationships we want to research.

A **null relationship** (e.g. between income and time spent watching television) states that there is no relation between income and watching television, and that the one does not influence the other in any way. If we find that two groups of viewers from high- and low-income groups spend the same average number of hours watching television per day, we would conclude that television viewership and income are unrelated.

A **covariance relationship** states that a change in variable A is positively or negatively associated with a change in variable B. To determine whether the amount of time spent watching television is really associated with income, one would have to measure television viewership in relation to at least two levels of income. If there is a high level of viewership (that the average amount of time is more) in relation to high income, the relationship is positive. However, if we find a high level of viewership in relation to low income (or vice versa), the relationship is negative.

When measuring a covariance relationship, a change in one variable is **associated** with a change in another, and does not necessarily represent a cause-and-effect relation. We would be interested in determining whether two variables co-vary if we:

- are unsure about the relationships between variables;
- want to make future predictions that involve similar variables;
- are unable to explain why A should cause an effect on or a change in B;
- cannot propose a time order of B occurring as a result of A;
- need more information to formulate a cause-effect statement; and
- suspect that two variables change and are the effects of another common cause, such as an extraneous variable.

A **causal relationship** exists when a change in one variable (the cause) results in a change in another variable (the effect). However, other conditions also have to be met if we want to investigate **causality**.

- **Covariance** is a necessary condition, but insufficient to prove causality. By knowing people's income we can infer their television viewership. However, to prove such predictions requires statistical calculations.
- The two variables must be **spatially connected**. When we investigate a subject's income and average hours spent watching television, they are two concepts that exist at a given time and apply to a given respondent. This condition is usually met by the way we define the **unit of analysis** (such as an individual, group, organisation or mass-media message).
- **Temporal ordering** is the third requirement for causality. This means that the change in the cause (independent variable) has to take place before the change in the effect (dependent variable). This is a very interesting condition because the reverse may not apply. If the argument holds that high income causes viewers to watch more than the average number of hours of television daily, if a person's income increases, we should expect an increase in the number of hours he or she spends watching television. If a person's television viewership decreases (e.g. because of programming

changes), we would not expect a decrease in that person's income. If temporal ordering of the cause and effect does not occur or cannot be observed in real life, we may manipulate the relationship through an experimental design.

- A **plausible explanation** of why a cause can bring about a change in the effect needs to be written down as part of a theoretical definition of the relationship. If a likely reason cannot be found, one would rather consider a research hypothesis based on a covariance relationship (not a causal relationship).
- We could argue that people with high incomes have more leisure time, and therefore spend more time watching television. Although this statement provides a plausible explanation for the cause-effect relationship, we are not measuring leisure time, just as we are not measuring television channel preference.

Reconsider the research problem, subproblems and assumptions that you have chosen to investigate. Consider whether research questions or hypotheses are appropriate to investigate the problem and do the following ratings evaluation.

## EVALUATION

Write down the research questions or hypotheses that apply to your research problem and evaluate them using the following ratings scale. Ideally, the research questions or hypotheses should rate 2.

*The research questions*

**Rate 0** if the research questions fail to distinguish constructs and variables;

**Rate 1** if the research questions clearly indicate the constructs and variables to be researched;

**Rate 2** if the constructs and variables are logically linked to the issues formulated as subproblems and assumptions, and to the objectives of the study.

## *Evaluation (continued...)*

### The hypotheses

**Rate 0**  if the type(s) of hypotheses and relationships are unclear;

**Rate 1**  if the type(s) of hypotheses and relationships are clearly formulated and if they support current knowledge about the topic area, are concisely written, quantifiable, logically consistent and testable;

**Rate 2**  if the requirements for 'Rate 1' are met, in addition to testing the issues formulated as subproblems and assumptions, and the objectives of the study.

## *Executive summary:*
### Step 3: Formulating hypotheses or research questions

1 Elements:
   - concepts;
   - constructs;
   - theoretical definitions;
   - operational definitions.

2 Variables:
   - dichotomous;
   - polytomic;
   - continuous;
   - independent versus dependent;
   - characteristic;
   - extraneous (inter-vening/confounding).

3 Research questions asked depend on:
   - the nature of the problem;
   - the research goal and objectives;
   - the research design.

4 Criteria for formulating a hypothesis:
   - is based on current knowledge;
   - operational;
   - logical consistency;
   - testable;
   - a concise statement.

## 2.5    Step 4: Selecting or developing the research design

**mutually exclusive:** an analysis that can be placed in only one category or approach

A research design is a plan of how the research is going to be conducted, indicating who or what is involved, and where and when the study will take place.

As Units 4–6 deal with specific methodological research designs, we concentrate here mainly on quantitative and qualitative approaches (as overall approaches) to research designs. We argued in Unit 1 that the two approaches should not be seen as mutually exclusive and that, in reality, a research design often includes characteristics of both approaches. For example, a qualitative design can include quantitative characteristics, such as using several data recorders (not just one interpreter) to enhance the validity and reliability of data collection. This type of research design is generally called **triangulation**.

**triangulation:** using two or more theories, types of sampling, investigators, sources of data and/or data-collection methods

### 2.5.1    Who/what, where and when?

After distinguishing different types of variables, we should already have an idea of who or what we want to investigate. Nevertheless, it is advisable to clearly specify:
- the units of analysis (individuals, families, organisations or artefacts, such as newspapers or television programmes);

- the population and the type of sample to be drawn;
- the geographic area (e.g. in one city, province or country); and
- the time-dimension (cross-sectional or longitudinal).

These aspects are discussed in detail in Unit 3, because they are an integral to **collecting data**.

## 2.5.2 Characteristics of quantitative designs

A quantitative design is suitable when we want to count and/or measure variables.

The method of reasoning can be both inductive and deductive. **Inductive** reasoning begins with a literature review of primary sources, such as observations made by other researchers, which will guide the observations in our study. These observations are measured using an existing instrument (e.g. a Likert scale), or by designing a new one. However, quantitative designs are usually based on **deductive** reasoning, which begins with the formulation of hypotheses that identify the constructs, variables and relationships to be measured. This procedure also involves the formulation of operational definitions, which transform abstract concepts into constructs that can be observed and measured. For example, a behavioural or pragmatic (theoretical) model for effective interpersonal communication is used to explain specific behaviours that communicators and listeners should use to achieve intended outcomes.

By using this theoretical model as a conceptual framework to formulate hypotheses, abstract characteristics would need to be operationalised, such as confidence (plus shyness and anxiety); immediacy (conveying interest and attention); interaction management (verbal and nonverbal skills that contribute to exchanges during a conversation); the creation of impressions; and expressiveness (openness while talking and listening). Operational definitions would therefore have to define specific behaviours that do (or do not) demonstrate these characteristics.

The **objectives** of a quantitative design are to predict, describe and explain quantities, degrees and relationships, and to generalise from a sample to the population by collecting numerical data.

A variety of **methods** and techniques can be used to **collect** the **numerical data**, such as surveys, using self-administered question- naires, and experimental designs (*see* Units 3 and 4).

In a scale that measures attitudes, for example, the numerical data is based on the frequency with which subjects respond in a certain manner, say, 'agree' versus 'disagree'.

The **methods** used to **analyse data** obtained via quantitative design, include the use of numerous statistical techniques. The first step may be the use of descriptive statistics to describe and organise (summarise) vast amounts of data (*see* Unit 4). Inferential statistics are used to test hypotheses and to generalise findings from a sample to the population from which the sample was drawn.

## 2.5.3 Characteristics of qualitative designs

A qualitative design is appropriate when we intend examining the properties, values, needs or characteristics that distinguish individuals, groups, communities, organisations, events, settings or messages.

The method of reasoning is usually **inductive**. In other words, based on specific assumptions, one would start with observations and end with descriptions of what was observed, or continue to formulate a theory that explains what was observed. If questioning (instead of observing) were used, one would base the questions on assumptions and end with descriptions (summaries and interpretations) of the responses received. Since observations, questions and deductions are guided by assumptions, these have to be well established in the literature to avoid the risk of approaching observations based on subjective or faulty reasoning.

The **objectives** of a qualitative design are to explore areas where limited or no prior information exists and/or to describe behaviours, themes, trends, attitudes, needs or relations that are applicable to the units analysed.

**Methods** and techniques that can be used to **collect data** include participant observation and surveys, using open-ended questions in questionnaires or in interview schedules (*see* Units 3 and 4). If data is collected by observing people, the following categories should be kept in mind:

- the content of what people say (including literal and connotative meanings);
- external or physical signs (clothing, hairstyles, tattoos, etc.);
- kinesics (facial expressions, gestures, bodily postures);
- proxemics (signifying status and control in social interactions); and
- language behaviour (stuttering, slips of the tongue, silences, who speaks to whom, duration of speaking and paralanguage features).

The **method** used to **analyse data** obtained via a qualitative design usually centres on content analysis, which is a systematic analysis of written or verbal responses and audiovisual materials. For example, by analysing who sends the messages, the recipients, the media, and the intention and actual content of messages, we can identify and describe interpersonal communication patterns.

These observation descriptions can either be used to confirm established theories or, if prior information does not exist, they can be used to formulate new theoretical concepts representing the categories and relationships observed. A qualitative design can also go a step further, by doing a **comparative analysis** of the findings and the data from a previous study involving different groups or cultures. Such a comparison may offer possible explanations of similarities and differences found in two groups that, in turn, may prompt a new research study.

Qualitative designs are more flexible than quantitative designs. We may, for example, start with the objective of describing a particular phenomenon or event, but through the observation or questioning process, we may change the objective to a combination of a description and an interpretation (explanation).

## 2.5.4 Threats to the validity of a research design

The **internal** validity of a research design deals with the extent to which the design can account for all the factors that may affect the outcome of the hypotheses to be tested or the research questions to be answered. **External** validity refers to the extent to which conclusions can be generalised to the 'real world'. Factors that threaten the validity of a research design are influenced by the **time-dimension**, which can either be cross-sectional or longitudinal.

## Cross-sectional designs

**cross-sectional:**
at a single point
in time

Collecting data from a sample in a cross-sectional design means that the research is conducted in a short period, such as one day or a few weeks. The following factors contribute to **internal** validity:

- an accurate operationalisation of theoretical concepts, which means constructing reliable measuring instruments (*see* Unit 3);
- drawing a random sample of subjects or respondents (*see* Unit 3);
- the unobtrusiveness of the measuring instrument and/or the researcher's behaviour, so that neither the measurement nor the researcher disrupts, directs or intrudes on what is being researched;
- the effectiveness of manipulating the independent variable (especially in experimental research) to be assured that it produced an effect on the dependent variable.

**reliable:**
a measure
that gives the
same answer
when tested at
different times

**unobtrusiveness:**
not interfering or
meddling

When considering the **external** validity of a cross-sectional design, the following factors may contribute to external validity:

- drawing a representative sample from the population and not using volunteer or convenience samples (*see* Unit 3);
- conducting the research in real-world settings and not in artificial classroom or laboratory settings;
- avoiding multiple measurements or treatments of a single subject, thereby avoiding interference factors such as fatigue.

## Longitudinal designs

Longitudinal designs are used when we want to collect information at different points over a long period of time. This also provides for **changes** that may occur during that time.

There are three types of longitudinal design: a trend study, a cohort study and a panel study.

**accessible
population:**
the units of analy-
sis in the target
population to
which researchers
have access

In a **trend study**, different **random samples** are drawn from an accessible population over a period of time, such as once a month or annually. For example, if the study involves investigating readers' attitudes to a particular newspaper over a ten-year period, the units of analysis of the population of readers will change in this time.

In a **cohort study**, a **specific** accessible population is surveyed over a period of time – for example, investigating children's attitudes towards television programmes. The names of the accessible population would be listed and a sample would be drawn from this list at different times. This means that the sample will, by necessity, change.

In a **panel study**, a sample is drawn at the beginning of the study and the **same sample** is researched over a period of time. For example, having drawn a random sample of ten-year old children from an accessible population in a predetermined geographical area, we would survey the same sample when they are aged 11, and again when aged 12, etcetera. A panel study enables us to investigate changes that occur over time and the **reasons** for such changes.

The following factors influence the **interval** validity of longitudinal research designs:

- **History:** Social and personal changes that take place between measurements can produce unanticipated changes in the independent variable.
- **Maturation:** Given the time between measurements, adults and especially children, develop new abilities that are not produced by the independent variable.
- Subjects who know that they are involved in a research project may become sensitised by the measuring instrument when it is applied for the first time. This can **bias** their behaviour or attitudes towards the topic being investigated. If subjects become familiar with the experimental task or measuring instrument, learning takes place, which can affect subsequent performance or responses. These factors are generally referred to as the **reactivity** of subjects.
- If the measuring instrument does not meet the requirements of test-retest **reliability** (*see* Unit 3), different results will be obtained at different points in time.
- **Subject mortality:** If a study, especially a panel study, is extended over a long period, such as a few years, some individuals who were included in the original sample may be difficult or impossible to trace. Their exclusion in subsequent measurements may skew the results.
- Lengthy questionnaires and long periods of focused attention should be avoided because they can result in **subject fatigue**. The responses at the end of the process may differ from those at the beginning.

**bias:**
to influence, slant, prejudice, or improperly affect research data

**skew:**
departure from the norm

All of these factors, especially subject mortality, can simultaneously threaten the **external validity** of a longitudinal research design.

*EXECUTIVE SUMMARY:*
**SELECTING OR DEVELOPING THE RESEARCH DESIGN**

1   Characteristics of quantitative designs:
    - based on inductive and deductive reasoning;
    - descriptive and explanatory objectives;
    - methods used to collect numerical data;
    - statistical techniques are used to analyse data.
2   Characteristics of qualitative designs:
    - usually based on inductive reasoning;
    - exploratory and descriptive objectives;
    - methods used to collect qualitative data;
    - descriptive, in-depth techniques are used to analyse data.
3   Threats to the validity of a research design:
    - internal validity;
    - external validity;
    - cross-sectional research design;
    - longitudinal research design (trend, cohort, panel).

People often question at what point a research proposal should be written and what it should contain. Having identified and analysed the research problem and related variables, started a literature review, and selected a research design, one arrives at the point where attention should be given to writing a **research proposal**.

# 2.6 Step 5: Writing a research proposal

Various research methodology books in the social sciences have different frameworks that can be used when writing a research proposal. However, the actual headings used are not as important as answering the 'What?', 'Why?', 'How?', 'Who?', 'Where?' and 'When?' questions:

- What is to be researched?
- Why is the research study to be undertaken?
- What are the goal(s) and objectives(s)?
- What are the research questions or hypotheses?
- What are the ethical implications?
- How is the research going to be conducted?
- Who is involved?
- Where will the study take place?
- When will the research take place?

## 2.6.1 What is to be researched?

The opening paragraphs of a proposal should contain the following information:

- the area of study (e.g. marketing communication);
- the goal and objectives;
- the main problem, subproblems and assumptions;
- the research questions or hypotheses;
- in quantitative research: operational definitions of the most important constructs (to clarify whether data will be collected by observing, questioning or measuring);
- in qualitative research: the questions, processes, relationships or patterns to be discovered and/or developed.

The descriptions of the objectives (*see* section 2.2.1) can be guided by answering these questions:

- If the objective is exploratory: what is to be explored?
- If the objective is descriptive: who/what is to be described, when, where and, sometimes, why?
- If the objective is explanatory: what, who, when, where, how and

why does X (independent variable) affect the what, who, when, where and why of Y (dependent variable)?

When a study has more than one objective, they should be presented in order of importance or in chronological order. If a descriptive objective depends on undertaking an exploratory study, the latter should be described first.

**availability sample:** a sample of units of analysis drawn because they are accidentally or conveniently available

It is important to note that each objective can be investigated using a different research design and different methods. For instance, focus-group interviews can be conducted with an availability sample to test initial assumptions (exploratory objective), followed by a survey questionnaire of a representative sample of a specified population (descriptive objective).

## 2.6.2 Why is the research study being done?

The importance and relevance of the research study to communication, and its researchability, must be motivated. The following broad aspects offer some ideas on which we can elaborate, depending on the nature of the study:

- it must contribute to existing knowledge (in practice, policy and/or theory);
- if applicable to policy areas, it should make a contribution to new policy guidelines;
- it should be of practical relevance for communication practitioners;
- it could contribute to the development of research methods by applying existing methods in new or unique circumstances;
- it should contribute to information that can be used to solve real-world problems.

If funds or grants are received for the study, arguments as to how the proposed study will solve a problematic issue or will assist people, for example in terms of rural development, must be specified. Our motivation must, therefore contain a clear indication of who will ultimately benefit from the findings.

## 2.6.3 What are feasibility and ethical implications?

Although we may not have final answers at this stage on the finer details of the research design, or the procedures to be followed to collect information, it is wise to examine the ethical implications of the study. For instance, if the research proposal contains a problem that is too complex to be investigated in a specified time, or if the costs are beyond the individual or institution undertaking the study, these problems may create ethical problems at a later stage.

Questions that arise include:
- whether the main research problem, sampling procedures and research method are relevant and appropriate (e.g. is the data to be researched easily available and/or the subjects accessible?);
- whether investigating the research problem is practical and feasible (e.g. what are the costs in terms of money, time, space, equipment, computer programmes and co-operation that we may need from others, such as training interviewers?);
- whether our personal bias and subjectivity during observations or when interpreting data influence the development and application of measuring instruments and the treatment of the data;
- whether the study is subject to political, institutional or personal constraints;
- whether inaccurate and invalid findings are acknowledged when they are interpreted and reported.

When **people** are involved as subjects, respondents or participants, the proposal should specify how their human and civil rights will be protected, with reference to:
- the principle of 'do no harm' (not to cause physical discomfort, emotional stress, humiliation or embarrassment);
- obtaining informed consent (direct or substitute consent, especially where children are involved);
- ensuring their legal and cognitive competency;
- obtaining voluntary consent; and
- ensuring privacy (confidentiality and anonymity).

The importance of these ethical considerations at every stage of planning and implementing research can best be summarised by paraphrasing Bulmer (1982:1): our responsibilities are not only aimed at the ideals of objective truth and knowledge, but are especially concerned with the subjects of our research. The ethical issues relevant to a particular research study can be summarised by the truthful answers we give to these seven questions:

1. What are my motives as a researcher?
2. What means and/or procedures will I use?
3. How will I ensure that subjects are not harmed?
4. What is the legal and cognitive competency of the person who gives informed consent?
5. How will I ensure the privacy, confidentiality and anonymity of subjects?
6. What are the anticipated findings for the study?
7. What are the possible consequences of publishing these findings?

## 2.6.4 How is the research going to be conducted?

The theoretical approach(es) that have been, or will be, reviewed and the research design to be applied, need to be described.

In a quantitative study, one or more of the following **methods** is selected and must be motivated: a survey, one of the field research methods, content analysis, an experimental or a quasi-experimental design. The motivation of the selection must be related to the nature of the problem, objectives, population parameters, the geographic area and the time-dimension. In the final report, this motivation can also be linked to other more specific detail, such as the actual research questions or hypotheses that were investigated or tested. The research design should also include an indication (and motivation) of the probability or nonprobability **sampling** methods to be used (*see* Unit 3).

The **data-collection method** (observing, questioning, measuring, or a combination of these) also has to be briefly described. In a quantitative study it could read as follows:

*A self-administered questionnaire will be applied in a group administration to measure employees' needs for in-service training.*

In a qualitative study, it could read:

*A semi-structured questionnaire schedule will be used by a moderator in seven focus-group interviews, using a tape recorder to record verbal interactions.*

Qualitative studies make use of observations and questioning, such as in-depth or focus-group interviews, as data-collection methods – not (statistical) measurements. Because generalisation is one of the criticisms of qualitative studies, it is important that even during the proposal stage, there is an indication of how the data will be accurately collected and how the reliability of the processing and interpretations of the data are to be secured.

The method of **data analysis** must also be specified when formulating a research proposal. If, for example, inferential statistics and a computer are used to test hypotheses, this will influence prior steps and decisions (such as the scales used in the measuring instrument and the type and size of the sample drawn). In qualitative studies that involve open-ended questions or content analysis, descriptive data is usually analysed after developing a framework of categories and applying inter-coder reliability tests.

*EXECUTIVE SUMMARY:*
**STEP 5: WRITING A RESEARCH PROPOSAL**

1. What is to be researched?
2. Why is the research study being undertaken?
3. What are the goal(s) and objective(s)?
4. What are the research questions or hypotheses?
5. What are the ethical implications?
6. How is the research data to be collected?
7. Who is involved?
8. Where will the study take place?
9. When will the research take place?
10. How will the data be interpreted?

## 2.7 Step 6: Pre-testing the research design and collecting data

The collection of data can be based on **existing** information, such as doing a:
- literature survey (e.g. of primary sources available from libraries and on the Internet);
- quantitative content analysis (e.g. of television advertisements); or
- critical (qualitative) analysis (e.g. of policy documents).

**pilot test:**
a trial run
conducted on a
small scale

This step involves collecting existing or 'new' data, on the basis of which the research questions can be answered, hypotheses tested, objectives fulfilled and, ultimately, the problem solved. It is advisable to pre-test, or **pilot test** the method used to collect the data, to determine whether it is relevant and effective. Requirements, such as reliability and validity, which form part of a pilot test are discussed in Unit 3.

## 2.8 Step 7: Analysing and interpreting data

This is a crucial step in the research process, because the analysis and interpretation of data form the basis of conclusions and recommendations. They also influence whether or not recommendations will be implemented in a particular study. The methods used vary from the development of content analysis categories for descriptive data, to the use of descriptive statistics (to summarise and compare data). These methods are dealt with in greater detail in Unit 4.

## 2.9 Step 8: Writing the research report

The final step in the research process is to write a report that not only communicates findings, conclusions and recommendations, but also provides a logical and accurate record of the entire research process.

The format of the report will depend on why the research was initiated. In contract research, it may consist of a brief overview of the nature of the problem, the objectives of the study and the methods used, with greater emphasis and detailed information on the findings and recommendations. Very often, such research is also reported verbally (e.g. to the top management of an organisation), supported by visuals, such as graphic summaries.

A report of research initiated and/or supervised by academic institutions, usually follows a standard format. The following is an example based on a Master's dissertation, entitled 'Television audience ratings and programme appreciation in South Africa' (Hanekom 1990).

---

SUMMARY (ABSTRACT)

TABLE OF CONTENTS

LIST OF FIGURES

LIST OF TABLES

CHAPTER 1  The need for and background to this study

CHAPTER 2  An overview of the development of mass communication research with specific reference to the uses and gratifications approach

CHAPTER 3  The television audience

CHAPTER 4  Methodology

CHAPTER 5  Results of the study

CHAPTER 6  Interpretation and synthesis

SOURCES CONSULTED

APPENDIX A  English questionnaire

APPENDIX B  Afrikaans questionnaire

---

The format of the report not only depends on why the research was initiated, but also on the nature of the study. Reports for Master's and Doctoral research, for example, usually contain at least one chapter that deals with a review of related literature.

A number of criteria can be used as guidelines for planning and writing a research report. These criteria, which can also be used to critically evaluate other research reports, are dealt with in detail in Unit 7.

*EXECUTIVE SUMMARY*

Step 6: Pre-testing the research design and collecting data
(*See* Units 3, 4, 5 and 6).
Step 7: Analysing and interpreting data
(*See* Units 3, 4, 5 and 6).
Step 8: Writing the research report
(*See* Unit 7).

## 2.10 Summary

This unit dealt with the different steps that may be followed when conducting communication research. These steps should be treated as guidelines and not as fixed or prescribed.

The unit started with the identification and analysis of the main research problem, as well as the formulation of subproblems, assumptions, hypothesis(-es) and/or research questions. It considered how to start reviewing existing literature, what it means to do a critical review of such literature, and the importance of making summaries and recording bibliographical details. The selection of a research design dealt with the distinction between quantitative and qualitative research. The type of information that should be included in the formulation of a research proposal, received special attention in this unit.

The last three steps in the research process: pre-testing the research design and collecting data; analysing and interpreting data; and writing the research report, were mentioned only briefly as they are dealt with in greater detail in the units that follow.

## Self-evaluation and portfolio tasks

**2.1** You have been granted funds to study a communication problem of your choice. What will you study?

If you are unsure about what to study, describe three potential sources of communication problems that you could consult.

**2.2** Consider each of the following studies and decide on the units of analysis, the objective of the study, and if it is suited to a cross-sectional and/or one of the three longitudinal designs.
- An investigation to determine whether women, who were appointed six months ago, are experiencing communication problems in a specific organisation.
- A survey of television and radio broadcasters' views of the freedom of information (or lack thereof), measured annually between 2002 and 2007.
- An evaluation of the views of employees of the top 10 private companies in South Africa about the effectiveness of affirmative action in their organisations.
- An analysis of policy documents of the Department of Posts and Telecommunications to determine the provisions made for in-service training.

**2.3** Think of a communication research problem that you want to investigate and write a brief description to answer each of the following questions. Your answers should also contain an indication of why you regard the answer as relevant.
- What is the main research problem?
- What is the extent of the problem? For example, is it prevalent in one organisation, or in a section of the community, or would it entail researching a wider community?
- What are the subproblems and underlying assumptions?
- What is the goal and what is/are the objective(s)?
- What are the research questions or hypotheses?
- Which research design would be appropriate to investigate the main research problem?

Before continuing with Unit 3, you are encouraged to evaluate your achievement of the learning outcomes using the following guide.

## ASSESSMENT OF LEARNING OUTCOMES

Ratings for evaluation of performance:

5   very high (extremely good)

4   high (good)

3   medium (average)

2   low (poor)

1   very low (extremely poor)

0   evidence is absent

| Outcomes (knowledge, competence and orientations) *You should be able to demonstrate your understanding of:* | Evidence of performance | Examples of criteria used to evaluate evidence of performance | Evaluation of performance | | | | | |
|---|---|---|---|---|---|---|---|---|
| | | | Ratings | | | | | |
| | | | 5 | 4 | 3 | 2 | 1 | 0 |
| The procedures involved in identifying and analysing a communication research problem | by formulating a research problem, subproblems, assumptions, hypothesis(-es) and/or research questions in a logical manner. | The problem statement identifies issues, method(s) and, where applicable, actions, and meets the criteria of relevancy, researchability, feasibility and ethical acceptability.<br><br>Subproblems are based on relevant factors and are aimed at solving the main problem.<br><br>Assumptions, hypothesis(-es) and/or research questions are logically linked to goals, objectives and subproblems. | | | | | | |
| The analysis and evaluation of the planning of your research project | by writing down formulations. | Each decision taken during the planning stage is logically linked and systematically presented, and evaluated by means of a ratings scale. | | | | | | |

| Outcomes (knowledge, competence and orientations) *You should be able to demonstrate your understanding of:* | Evidence of performance | Examples of criteria used to evaluate evidence of performance | Evaluation of performance | | | | | |
|---|---|---|---|---|---|---|---|---|
| | | | Ratings | | | | | |
| | | | 5 | 4 | 3 | 2 | 1 | 0 |
| The steps followed in communication research | by describing each step in the research process. | Key issues (e.g. threats to the validity of the research design) that need to be considered during each step are explicitly described – particularly as they apply to the first five steps. | | | | | | |

## *SUGGESTED READING*

DePoy, E and Gitlin, LN. 1998. *Introduction to research: understanding and applying multiple strategies.* (2nd edition). St Louis, Mo: Mosby.

De Vos, AS (ed). 1998. *Research at grass roots. A primer for the caring professions.* Pretoria: Van Schaik.

Drew, CJ, Hardman, ML and Hart, AW. 1996. *Designing and conducting research; inquiry in education and social science.* (2nd edition). Needham Heights, Massachusetts: Allyn & Bacon.

Neuman, WL. 1997. *Social research methods: qualitative and quantitative approaches.* (3rd edition). Boston. Massachusetts: Allyn & Bacon.

Rosnow, RL and Rosenthal, R. 1999. B*eginning behavioral research. A conceptual primer.* (3rd edition). Upper Sadle River, NJ: Prentice Hall.

Terre Blanche, M and Durrheim, K (eds). 1999. *Research in practice: applied methods for the social sciences.* Cape Town: UCT Press.

# Data collection: sampling, measuring, questioning and observing

*Millions saw the apple fall, but Newton was*
*the one who asked why.*

BERNARD BARUCH

## Overview

If is often not practical, feasible or financially viable to investigate an entire population. In such a case, we are required to draw a sample. This unit starts with the different requirements that have to be met when drawing a sample, and the different types of samples that can be drawn, including their advantages and disadvantages. Thereafter the unit deals with different methods and techniques used to collect data. Using measurements and constructing scales are discussed, as well as the importance of measurements and scales meeting the reliability and validity requirements. Questioning and conducting systematic and ethnographic observations are considered as additional data-collection methods and techniques.

## Learning outcomes

By the end of this unit you should be able to make and communicate informed decisions when collecting data by:
- drawing a sample (by meeting sampling requirements and differentiating between types of samples);
- applying measurements (according to the principles and levels of measurement, by meeting reliability and validity requirements, and by constructing scales);

- formulating items for a questionnaire and an interview (in the form of questions and statements); and
- conducting observations (by compiling an observation schedule and devising coding categories).

# 3.1 Introduction

In Unit 2, steps 6 and 7 in the research process comprise pre-testing the research design and analysing data. A research design that is aimed at collecting quantifiable data often uses questioning and measuring as data-collection procedures. Observing and questioning are often used to collect qualitative data. This unit concentrates on the procedures for drawing a sample, applying measurements, constructing scales, formulating questions, and conducting observations to collect data.

# 3.2 Sampling

**population:**
all possible units of analysis

**representative:**
a subset of the population that reflects the population's features

**population parameters:**
nature, size and unique characteristics of the population

Sampling involves following a rigorous procedure when selecting units of analysis from a larger population. The term 'population' not only refers to people, but can also be defined as any group or aggregate of individuals, groups, organisations, social artefacts/objects, or social interactions and events. In order to collect accurate data about all the members of a population, we could question, analyse or investigate every member. This is called a **census**. However, due to constraints such as time, costs and geographic distances, a census in communication research is usually impractical. In quantitative research, a sample of the population must be drawn in such a way that it is **representative** of that population. The first step in selecting a particular type of sample is to define the **population parameters**. For example:

*All the prime-time television programmes broadcast on a daily basis, from January to June 2003, by all the South African television stations.*

This population (television programmes) has four population parameters in common: they are broadcast on a daily basis, during a particular time, during the specified six-month period, and by South African television stations.

Due to constraints such as time, cost and personnel, we may not always have access to the actual population to which we want to generalise findings. Therefore, before drawing a sample, we need to make a clear distinction between the **target** population – for example, all the readers of a particular newspaper – and the **accessible** population. When this occurs, we have to be realistic and define the accessible population to which we *are* able to generalise the findings, such as subscribers of a particular newspaper. The distinction between these two types of population has a serious implication for research, because the more narrowly the accessible population is defined, the more limited the generalisability of the findings.

**target population:** the actual population to which we want to generalise findings

**generalisability:** to infer that a finding applies to a wider group

**historical research:** collecting, classifying and analysing existing data

Sampling is not only applicable when generating or collecting new data, but is also relevant when conducting historical research. This is particularly important in terms of counteracting risks of error or bias that may be present in public records, private documents or mass-media messages. Bias can occur if the data that is collected is not authentic; if the eyewitness, author, recorder or the data are not credible; and/or if some records over a long period have been lost or damaged. (Other sources of existing data are discussed in Unit 2.)

A question that faces all researchers is:

*How can we determine that the sample actually represents the population parameters?*

This question can be answered by considering the **accuracy** with which the sample is drawn, the **level of confidence** and the amount of **sampling error** that will be tolerated.

## 3.2.1 Accuracy of the sample drawn

According to Stacks and Hocking (1992:180), three factors influence sample accuracy:
- the population parameters;
- the size of the sample; and
- the standard error of measurement.

A homogeneous population – one that shares several common characteristics (parameters) – will require a **smaller** sample size than a heterogeneous population. Depending on the **goal** and the

**objectives** of the research, if a population of people represents differences in socio-economic status, occupation, educational level, language preferences and geographic distribution of dwellings, then a larger sample would have to be drawn to accommodate these differences. For example, assuming a sample of 500 voters has been drawn and we want to cross-analyse gender (men versus women), political affiliation (ANC, IFP and other) and attitude change (experimental group versus control group), the increased size of the sample could be calculated as 2 x 3 x 2 x 500 = 6 000.

A method that can be used to estimate the accuracy of the sample is to calculate the **standard error**. This can be done in different ways, depending on the type of sample drawn. For the purpose of this unit, we briefly deal with a formula that is applied when drawing a **simple random sample**.

**standard error:** an estimation of the amount of error present in a sample

**simple random sample:** every unit in the population has an equal chance of being selected

$$s = \sqrt{\frac{P(1-P)}{n}}$$

s = standard error
$n$ = number of cases
$P$ = population parameters

**FIGURE 3.1:** Standard error calculation

Assume that we want to measure the differences in radio listening habits of men and women and that there is an accessible population of 10 000 listeners, of whom 2 000 are men and 8 000 are women. One of the population parameters ($P$), gender, is known. So $P$ is 0.80, which represents 80% women; and 1 - $P$ is 0.20, which represents 20% men.

If the sample size is 10 ($n$ = 10), the standard error is 0.126 or 12,6%, which is the square root of (0.8 x 0.2) ÷ 10. If the sample size is increased to 100 ($n$ = 100), the standard error is 0.04 or 4%. The standard error (12,6% versus 4%) reflects the extent to which the sample will correspond with the population. Its calculation is based on both the **size** of the sample to be drawn and our **knowledge** of the population parameters.

**normal curve:** bell-shaped curve

In order to interpret the difference between a standard error of 12,6% versus a standard error of 4%, we need to interpret these percentages against a normal curve (distribution), which is illustrated in Figure 3.2.

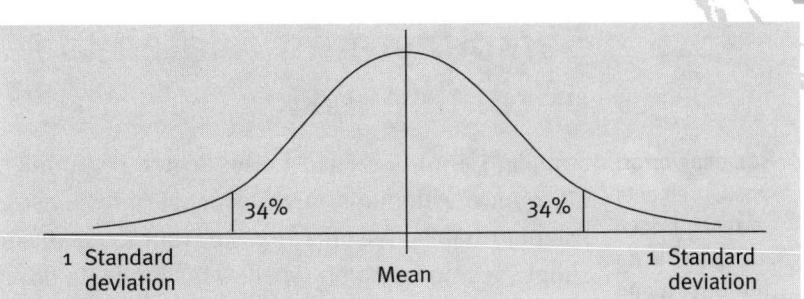

**FIGURE 3.2:** A normal distribution

According to Stacks and Hocking (1992:180), 'sixty-eight per cent of the samples we might choose will fall within one deviation away from the true parameter value'. In other words, with a sample of 10, we know in advance that 68% of the units of analysis might differ by up to 12,6% when compared with the population parameters. This could result in a skew distribution.

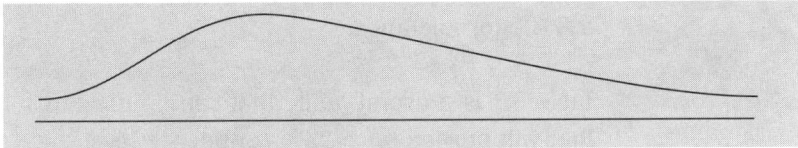

**FIGURE 3.3:** A skew distribution (sample = 10)

If we increase the sample to 100 units, we know that 68% of the units may differ by up to 4% when compared with the population parameters. By increasing the sample size, from 10 to 100, the distributions are less skew and begin to resemble a normal curve.

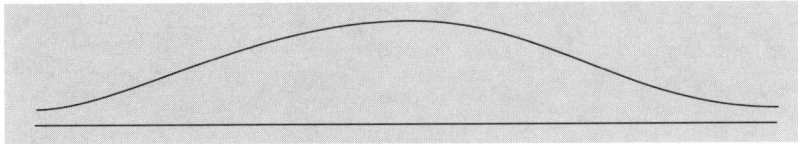

**FIGURE 3.4:** A less skew distribution (sample = 100)

Calculating the standard error enables us to predict how the normal curve or normal distribution will skew from the centre of the curve.

**systematic random sample:** selecting every nth unit from the sampling frame

In certain probability sampling procedures, such as drawing a **systematic random sample**, the degree of accuracy depends on whether or not a complete list of the units of analysis in the population is available. This list is called the **sampling frame**.

# 3

## 3.2.2 Sampling error related to the degree of confidence

**sampling error:** measurements taken from a sample that do not correspond with that which exists in the population

Sampling error is related to the degree of confidence that we can place on our findings, such as people's responses about their radio listening habits. Assume that we want to establish by means of a simple yes/no question whether respondents do or do not regularly listen to a particular radio station. This prompts the following question:

*How many units of analysis (people) do we need to include in the sample to be able to conclude with confidence that their responses are representative of the population?*

According to Babbie (1983:415-416), convention has established that we should aim for at least a 95% confidence level for any response. Assuming the population size is more than 50 000 radio listeners, a sample of 384 listeners would provide for a 95% confidence level and a 5% error tolerance.

Table 3.1 is a useful guide that can be used to select a sample size that will provide for a 95% confidence level.

| TABLE 3.1: Simple random sample sizes at 95% confidence level ||
|---|---|
| **POPULATION SIZE** | **SAMPLE SIZE** |
| Infinity | 384 |
| 500 000 | 384 |
| 100 000 | 383 |
| 50 000 | 381 |
| 10 000 | 370 |
| 5 000 | 357 |
| 3 000 | 341 |
| 2 000 | 322 |
| 1 000 | 278 |

(Meyer 1973:123).

Table 3.2 offers a shortcut to selecting a sample size and standard tolerated error. For example, if a 5% error is acceptable, but we want to increase the confidence level from 95% to 99%, the sample should be increased from 384 to 663.

**TABLE 3.2:** Simple random sample sizes with tolerated error at 95% and 99% confidence levels

| TOLERATED ERROR | CONFIDENCE | |
|:---:|:---:|:---:|
| | **95%** | **99%** |
| 1% | 9 604 | 16 587 |
| 2% | 2 401 | 4 147 |
| 3% | 1 067 | 1 843 |
| 4% | 600 | 1 037 |
| 5% | 384 | 663 |
| 6% | 267 | 461 |
| 7% | 196 | 339 |

(adapted from Hsia 1988:122)

**realised sample:**
the real sample on which findings are based

**response rate:**
proportion of sampled units that complete a survey

It is important that Table 3.1 and Table 3.2 be regarded as **guides** only. It is also important to recognise that the sample drawn is not always the **realised sample**. This is particularly relevant in survey research conducted by self-administered postal questionnaires, where the response rate is usually low. If we want a realised sample of 381 and anticipate a 10% response rate, the size of the sample drawn should increase to 3 810.

In addition to tolerable error, such as less than 5% (0.05) or over 95% confidence, the size and type of sample drawn must also meet two other requirements: **internal** and **external validity** (*see also* Unit 2). In experimental and field research, internal validity will be threatened if we confuse differences among individuals sampled for the groups with the effect of an experimental treatment. A way to avoid this threat is to select subjects or respondents **randomly**. Using convenience samples or people who volunteer, often results in a non-representative sample, which minimises the external validity of the sample. In other words, the findings are limited to the sample drawn and cannot be generalised to a wider population because the sample is not representative of the wider population.

**randomly:**
according to chance or haphazardly

An important principle basic to sampling is that the extent to which we can generalise findings from one study to people, conditions, times or settings that **differ** from those that prevail in a specific study (called **ecological generalisability**) will be determined by both the accuracy

**ecological fallacy:**
making assertions
about one sample
based on the
study of another
sample

and confidence with which the sample is drawn. Researchers using qualitative methods should especially be aware of the danger of basing assertions on **ecological fallacy**.

Given that different statistical procedures require different sample sizes and, because a single formula or method cannot be suggested for every research method or statistical procedure, it is essential to study further texts that deal with sampling procedures prior to undertaking actual research. Apart from considerations of accuracy and confidence, the size and type of sample drawn will depend on the research goal. Furthermore, the size of the sample will depend on the time dimension of the research, the costs involved, available personnel, the homogeneity of the population, subgroup comparisons and technical considerations, such as the use of a computer to code responses.

### 3.2.3 Types of sampling

Three sampling categories can be distinguished: **probability, quasi-probability** and **nonprobability** sampling (Stacks and Hocking 1992:176-188; Watt and Van den Berg 1995:83-108). These categories are based on meeting the following requirements, namely whether:

- every unit in the population has an equal and therefore probable ($p$) chance of being selected as part of the sample, ensuring that the sample will have the same parameters as the population;
- the researcher does not predict or control the random choice of units of analysis;
- a sampling frame can be compiled; and
- every possible combination of units can be drawn from the sampling frame, thereby eliminating bias that occurs when excluding certain units.

Probability samples meet these requirements, quasi-probability samples meet some of these requirements and nonprobability samples usually do not meet these requirements.

# Types of probability sample

Two types of sample are true representative samples: simple random sample and stratified (or known quota) sample.

A **simple random sample** is drawn when a sampling frame is available and each unit in the population has an equal chance of being selected. Two techniques can be used to draw such a sample: using a computer to create a sampling frame of random digit telephone numbers and/or by using a table of random numbers. The first technique is particularly useful when a sampling frame does not exist. Although some of the telephone numbers created by the computer may not work, those that do have an equal probable chance of being selected. The procedure followed is the same as when using a table of random numbers, which is described below.

**TABLE 3.3:** Examples of random numbers

| | | | | | | | |
|---|---|---|---|---|---|---|---|
| 087 | 163 | 079 | 196 | 033 | 164 | 200 | 033 |
| 252 | 194 | 081 | 221 | 107 | 045 | 144 | 255 |
| 174 | 021 | 185 | 170 | 064 | 019 | 248 | 093 |
| 146 | 157 | 061 | 139 | 023 | 178 | 213 | 191 |
| 119 | 181 | 174 | 038 | 221 | 209 | 001 | 118 |
| 227 | 134 | 005 | 111 | 037 | 098 | 123 | 179 |
| 216 | 011 | 183 | 158 | 259 | 117 | 051 | 182 |
| 199 | 056 | 004 | 217 | 077 | 014 | 210 | 095 |

For example, if we want to draw a simple random sample of the editorial cartoons published in the *Sunday Times* over a five-year period, we would number each cartoon from 000 to 260 (i.e. 5 years x 52 cartoons). Assuming we want to sample 10% of the population, we would select 26 numbers from a table of random numbers. Table 3.3 illustrates what a section of such a table may look like, but it should not be used for research purposes because it does not contain a sufficient number of digits to ensure randomness. Determine the starting point by selecting any number listed and then select the remaining 25 numbers by reading the numbers in the column below, or above; or in the rows to the left or right of the table, or by selecting 25 numbers at random. Assuming we decided to read down, having selected 081 as the starting point, the sample would include the cartoons numbered 81, 185, 61, 174, etcetera.

| SIMPLE RANDOM SAMPLING | |
|---|---|
| **ADVANTAGES OR STRENGTHS** | **DISADVANTAGES OR WEAKNESSES** |
| 1. Easy to draw if the population is small and a sampling frame exists. | 1. Time-consuming when the population is large, unless a computer is used to automatically draw the sample. |
| 2. The possibility of selection bias is eliminated. | 2. A list of population parameters has to be compiled. |
| 3. A representative sample can be obtained. | 3. If a sampling frame does not exist, the data-collection costs increase because each unit drawn has to be checked to determine whether it belongs to the population. |
| 4. External validity can be inferred. | |
| 5. A sample can be drawn via a computer. | |

A **stratified random sample** is drawn when we not only want to draw a representative sample, but also want to include subgroups in the sample in the same proportion as they occur in the population. Such subgroups are called **strata** or **known quotas**. A population can be divided into different strata, based on almost any characteristic or variable, such as different age groups, income groups, gender groups, religious groups and/or political groups.

Suppose we want to investigate the attitudes of the middle and top management personnel of the top ten financial institutions towards an affirmative-action programme. As gender may influence respondents' attitudes, we would want to ensure that the proportion of men and women in the sample is the same as in the population. The steps in the sampling procedure of this hypothetical example are as follows:

- We identify the population parameters of the target population and compile a sampling frame.
- We establish that the target population consists of 1 368 middle and top management personnel in the ten institutions, of whom 1 094 (80%) are men and 274 (20%) are women.
- Having decided on a 30% sample of the target population, we then randomly select 30% from each strata of the population, which results in 328 male personnel and 82 female personnel being selected for the sample.

Figure 3.5 illustrates a **proportionate** stratified sampling procedure, whereby the sizes of the strata sampled are based on their proportions in the population. According to Wimmer and Dominick (1997:68-69), **disproportionate** stratified sampling can be used when one stratum is seen to be particularly important. In such cases, we over-represent or oversample that stratum. Applied to the above example, we may be particularly interested in the attitudes of female personnel and, accordingly, increase the 20% sample to 60%. This over-representation will also enable us to subdivide the women into smaller groups or strata, according to their differences in age, period of employment, job description and section in which they are employed, or any other variables that we want to investigate. The application of a disproportionate stratified sample can also be justified when some strata are heterogeneous, proportionally too small to investigate, and/or too costly to investigate.

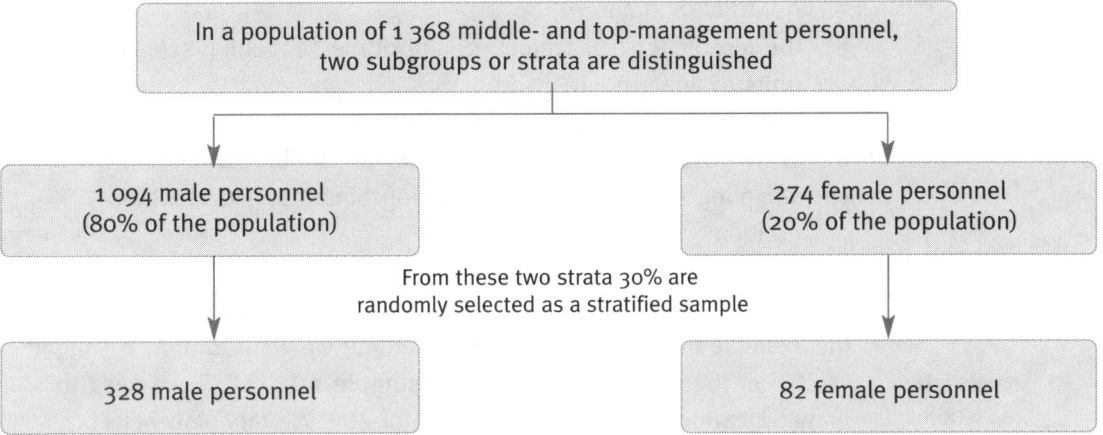

**FIGURE 3.5:** Selecting a (proportionate) stratified random sample

| STRATIFIED RANDOM SAMPLING | |
|---|---|
| **ADVANTAGES OR STRENGTHS** | **DISADVANTAGES OR WEAKNESSES** |
| 1. Easy to draw, if the population is small and a sampling frame exists. | 1. Time-consuming when the population is large, unless a computer is used to automatically draw the sample. |
| 2. The characteristics can be represented in the sample in the proportion they occur in the population, ensuring the representativeness of relevant variables. | 2. A list of population parameters has to be compiled as a sampling frame. |
| 3. Accuracy is increased because sampling bias is eliminated. | 3. If a sampling frame does not exist, data-collection costs increase because each unit drawn has to be checked to determine whether it belongs to the quota for a stratum. |
| 4. A sample can be drawn by means of a computer. | 4. Selected units may have to be rejected from the sample if the quota for a stratum is full. |
| 5. The sampling error is reduced. | |
| 6. The sample is drawn from homogeneous subgroups. | |

# Types of quasi-probability samples

A quasi-probability sample is similar to a probability sample, except that the **procedure** used to draw the sample differs and may contain some sample bias. A **systematic random sample**, a **multistage random sample** and a **cluster random sample** are three types of quasi-probability samples, and are used when drawing a true probability sample is unfeasible. When drawing **quasi-probability** samples:

- every unit in the population has an equal and therefore probable (*p*) chance of being selected as part of the sample – however, because of the systematic choice procedure used, the sample is *not* truly random;
- the researcher *can* predict or control the sequential selection of units of analysis;
- a sampling frame can be compiled; and
- every possible combination of units *cannot* be drawn from the sampling frame, thereby introducing bias that occurs when excluding certain units.

**sample rate:** also called sampling ratio; the proportion of units in the population selected for a sample

Drawing a **systematic random sample** can best be explained using the example of editorial cartoons. Assuming we want to draw a sample of 20% of the population, which is a **sample rate** of 1/5, we need to draw 52 cartoons from the population of 260. We randomly select a starting point, then systematically select every *n*th unit in the sampling frame. We could have randomly selected 21 as a starting point, and a **sampling interval** of 5. The sample will then be selected, starting with the cartoon numbered 21, and include every fifth cartoon (cartoon numbers 26, 32, 36, 41, etc.), until a sample of 52 has been drawn.

**sampling interval:** the distance between each unit selected for a sample

A simple formula for determining the sampling interval is:

$$\frac{\text{population size}}{\text{desired sample size}} = \text{sampling interval}$$

In the example, the sampling interval is 260 ÷ 52 = 5.

A simple formula for determining the sample rate or ratio is:

$$\frac{\text{sample size}}{\text{population size}} = \text{sample rate}$$

In the example, the sample ratio is 52 ÷ 260 = 0,2.

When drawing a systematic random sample, both the starting point and the interval can be selected at random. However, one must guard against sampling bias due to **periodicity**. For example, in a content analysis of television political news over a period of several months, the starting point is randomly selected as day 6 (Saturday) and the interval selected at random is 7. This means that the news programmes broadcast on every Saturday of each week are selected. Such a sample would be biased, because political news is not as frequently broadcast on Saturdays as on other days of the week.

**periodicity:**
the order in which units are arranged or located in the sampling frame

| SYSTEMATIC RANDOM SAMPLING | |
|---|---|
| **ADVANTAGES OR STRENGTHS** | **DISADVANTAGES OR WEAKNESSES** |
| 1. Easy to draw if the population is small and a sampling frame exists.<br>2. The selection procedure is generally inexpensive.<br>3. A representative sample can be obtained.<br>4. External validity can be inferred.<br>5. A sample can be drawn by means of a computer.<br>6. Increases the accuracy of selection (compared to simple random sampling). | 1. Time consuming when the population is large, unless a computer is used to automatically draw the sample.<br>2. A list of population parameters has to be compiled as a sampling frame.<br>3. Periodicity can bias the sample drawn. |

Communication research sometimes requires more than one sampling stage, especially when it is conducted on a national level, when the sampling frame either does not exist, or when it consists of a few million units of analysis. This is known as a **multistage random sample**. Samples are drawn from different sampling frames, which consist of large aggregates of the basic unit of analysis.

For example, we can draw a sample from a sampling frame of provinces or states in a country, followed by a sample of a district that consists of geographically demarcated sections or areas. During the next stage of sampling, individual blocks are randomly selected, and in the final stage, a convention such as *every seventh household from the southeastern corner* is used to sample individual households. During each of these stages, a simple random sample is drawn from a sampling frame of provinces, of districts, of areas, of blocks, of households and, eventually, of individual subjects. This sampling procedure is particularly suited to select units of analysis from well-defined geographic areas, which explains why it is also called an **area sample**.

The reason why multistage random sampling is treated as a quasi-probability sample is that it is not always possible to sample units from each of the sampling frames on an equal probability basis. For example, when sampling blocks in a neighbourhood, each block will, in all likelihood, have a different number of houses and population sizes. As a result, the sample drawn will be biased and, because of the different population sizes, it cannot be treated as a probable sample.

| MULTISTAGE RANDOM SAMPLE | |
| --- | --- |
| **ADVANTAGES OR STRENGTHS** | **DISADVANTAGES OR WEAKNESSES** |
| 1. Can be applied in complicated sampling situations.<br>2. Costs can be reduced if sampling frames are well-defined.<br>3. A sample can be drawn by means of a computer. | 1. Time consuming when the population is large, unless a computer is used to automatically draw the sample.<br>2. A list of population parameters has to be compiled as a sampling frame.<br>3. Sampling frames must consist of large aggregates of the basic unit of analysis.<br>4. Samples can be biased. |

A **cluster random sample** can be seen as a quasi-probability or a nonprobability sample, depending on how it is drawn. We have selected to categorise it as a quasi-probability sample because (as in the case of drawing a multistage random sample) there are possibilities for sampling bias in the procedure. The initial sampling step is similar to that of multistage sampling. A sample of groups or clusters is drawn, after which every unit in the selected clusters is included in the sample. In other words, the final sample is not a probability sample.

Suppose we want to establish how the employees of a national supermarket chain with 310 branches feel about in-service training programmes. Instead of visiting and surveying the 310 branches, we would allocate a number to each branch and, by using a table of random numbers, select 93 branches (30% of the population). The branches represent the clusters and all the workers at those branches constitute the sample.

Such a sample is biased, because employees at the other branches do not have an equal probability of being included in the sample.

| CLUSTER RANDOM SAMPLE | |
|---|---|
| **ADVANTAGES OR STRENGTHS** | **DISADVANTAGES OR WEAKNESSES** |
| 1. The costs of data collection are minimised.<br>2. A sample can be drawn by means of a computer.<br>3. Useful when clusters are well defined, such as organisations. | 1. A list of cluster population parameters has to be compiled as a sampling frame.<br>2. Samples can be biased.<br>3. Each unit of analysis has to be assigned to a specific cluster.<br>4. The clusters sampled may not be representative of the population. |

## *Types of nonprobability samples*

Drawing a nonprobability sample means that:

- every unit in the population does *not* have an equal and therefore probable *(p)* chance of being selected as part of the sample, implying that the sample will not necessarily have the same parameters as the population;
- in most cases, the researcher predicts or controls the choice of units of analysis;
- a sampling frame *cannot* be compiled;
- every possible combination of units *cannot* be drawn from the sampling frame, creating sampling bias; and
- the sample is *not* representative of the target population and therefore has no external validity.

**replication:**
repeating the
study using
a number of
similar samples

These characteristics also represent the **disadvantages** or **weaknesses** of nonprobability sampling. One way to counteract the possibility that the findings were a one-time occurrence is to apply replication, which is facilitated by describing the actual sample drawn in as much demographic and other detail as possible.

Despite the disadvantages, communication researchers sometimes find themselves in a position where it is difficult or impossible to draw a random (probable) sample. The following are examples where drawing a nonprobability sample could be considered:

- when conducting exploratory research, such as a pilot study;
- when pre-testing a measuring instrument, such as a questionnaire;
- when information about a small subgroup (and not a sample of a target population) is to be collected;
- when a sampling frame cannot be compiled;

- when the number of observations are difficult to obtain or are limited; and/or
- when the target population is small and drawing a non-random sample will include a large proportion of the population.

Communication scientists use different labels for nonprobability samples, but they are all descriptive of the procedures involved when drawing them. The four labels are: convenience, purposive, volunteer and snowball samples.

A **convenience sample** (sometimes called an **accidental**, an **available**, or an **opportunity** sample) is drawn from units of analysis that are conveniently available. When considering artefacts as units of analysis, these could include all the magazines on display in a shop, or all the radio phone-in programmes that are broadcast over a period of time. People on the street, people leaving a cinema, consumers in a shopping mall, children attending a particular school, as well as friends and neighbours, are other examples of such units of analysis. Researchers who conduct a snap-survey among people who happen to be available – for example, to evaluate opinions of a new product or advertisement – often refer to this type of sampling as a **dipstick** sample.

When drawing a **purposive** sample, a distinction can be made between a **known-group** sample and a **quota** sample. Previous knowledge of the populations and/or the objective of the study can result in a researcher using his or her judgement to select a sample. This is called a purposive known-group sample. According to Hsia (1988:132), such a sample can also be called a **judgement** sample. Suppose we want to investigate the influence of an unofficial power hierarchy on communication flow in an organisation. Because we have reason to believe that the management, three union representatives and the manager's secretary can provide the information needed, we select these individuals as a purposive (**known-group** or **judgement**) sample.

Where previous knowledge leads to a purposive sample being drawn that *can* guarantee the inclusion of certain population parameters, it would be termed a purposive quota sample.

Suppose we want to investigate the communication problems the aged (those who are 65 years or older) are experiencing in retirement homes and villages. According to an expert on the aged, members of the National Association for the Aged represent a cross-section of the target population. By selecting a percentage of these members, we would be drawing a **purposive quota** sample, and can ensure that groups and/or population parameters found in the target population are represented in the sample.

A **volunteer sample** consists of people such as students, readers or television viewers who volunteer to participate in a study. Apart from the disadvantages discussed above, this type of nonprobability sample should be used with caution, because volunteers often share characteristics related to approval-seeking needs, intelligence and education levels that are not found among non-volunteers. These, and other characteristics, such as occupational status, can increase the sampling bias and unrepresentativeness of population parameters.

A snowball that rolls down a hill gathers snow on its way. This description is an analogy for the nature and procedure used when drawing a **snowball sample**. For example, we may place an advertisement in a magazine, inviting readers to take part in a survey to determine their views about publishing nude photographs in a magazine to which children have easy access. We make telephonic contact with those readers who respond and enquire whether other family members could be interviewed as part of a larger (snowball) sample.

## EXECUTIVE SUMMARY:
### SAMPLING

1 Sampling requirements:
- representativeness;
- defining population parameters;
- target versus accessible populations;
- accuracy of the sample drawn;
- calculation of the standard error;
- level of confidence;
- internal validity; and
- external validity.

2 Types of sampling:
- Probability samples:
  - simple random sample;
  - stratified random sample.
- Quasi-probability samples:
  - systematic random sample;
  - multistage random sample;
  - cluster random sample.
- Nonprobability samples:
  - convenience sample;
  - purposive sample;
  - volunteer sample;
  - snowball sample.

## Self-evaluation and portfolio tasks

**3.1** What are the population parameters of the following populations?
- All the employees that represent middle and top management in the top three insurance firms in South Africa.
- All the buyers of *MOM* soap powder in KwaZulu-Natal.
- All the editorial cartoons published in the *Sunday Times* (an English Sunday newspaper).
- All the phone-in programmes broadcast by *Radio-fm*.

**3.2** Read the scenario below and indicate to which population the findings of this sample's responses can be generalised:
- Research problem: Which sections of the *Sunday World* are preferred by its readers and for what reasons?
- Target population: All current readers of the *Sunday World*.
- Accessible population: Readers who currently subscribe to the *Sunday World*.
- Sample drawn: Ten per cent of the readers who currently subscribe to the *Sunday World*.

**3.3** A target population of undergraduate students is grouped as follows:

| DEGREE | YEAR OF STUDY | | | TOTAL |
|---|---|---|---|---|
| | 1st | 2nd | 3rd | |
| BA | 5 500 | 3 000 | 2 500 | 11 000 |
| BCom | 2 000 | 2 000 | 1 500 | 5 500 |
| BSc | 1 500 | 1 500 | 500 | 3 500 |
| Total | 9 000 | 6 500 | 4 500 | 20 000 |

- Describe how to draw a simple random sample from this population with a 5% error and a 95% confidence level, and indicate the minimum size of the sample.

**3.4** Read the following studies and for each case indicate which type of sample you would draw and the steps you would follow to draw that sample:
- An analysis of the buying habits at all the major supermarkets in a province such as KwaZulu-Natal.
- A content analysis of advertisements published in a monthly magazine over a five-year period.
- A questionnaire has been designed as an instrument to measure users' levels of satisfaction with the services offered at an academic library. A pilot study has to be undertaken to test the questionnaire.

## 3.3 Measurement

One of the essential requirements of empirical communication research is that the information or data collected during a research study be scored accurately and consistently. This section deals with the four levels of measurement (nominal, ordinal, interval and ratio) and different methods that can be used to assess the reliability and validity of measurements. This is followed by a discussion of the procedures used during the development and scoring of Likert scales and semantic differential scales.

**measurement:**
assigning numerals to variables being studied

There are two reasons why the ways in which we identify and measure the variables during the planning stage of empirical research are important. First, sound and accurate data enable us to draw conclusions that are meaningful and credible. Secondly, errors in measurement (or less-than-accurate measurement) of variables can result in a bias against the eventual findings and conclusions.

The crucial questions to be asked are: *How do we collect data?*; and *How can we avoid measurement errors?*

These questions can be answered by distinguishing different levels of measurement and by considering the principles on which measurements are based.

## 3.3.1 Principles and levels of measurement

Variables that appear in a research hypothesis or research question are transformed into concrete indicators once a measuring instrument is designed.

**discrete variable:**
a variable that can be subdivided into a finite number of parts

Numerals refer to symbols such as 1, 2, 3, etcetera, which are used to distinguish subgroups of discrete variables and function as **qualitative** labels. For example, 1 can represent men and 2 can be used to represent women. The use of numerals here differs from the use of numerals that represent **quantitative** values (called numbers). Suppose a respondent answers 60 out of 100 questions correctly in response to a measure that tests his or her knowledge. The number 60 has a quantitative value that can be calculated as a percentage. The term 'numeral' must not

be confused with the term 'number'. To assign numerals to variables refers to **mapping** which, according to Smith (1988:42), is 'the systematic matching of a set of substantive concepts (the empirical indicators of variables) with a corresponding set of structural values (numerals)'.

Mapping procedures differ according to levels of measurement, because each level of measurement dictates the type of statistical formula that can be used to analyse the data. However, one rule that is critical in measurement is the **rule of correspondence.** If we want to measure the continuous variable 'friendliness' on a five-point scale, the appropriate rule of correspondence could be to assign:

**continuous variable:**
a variable that takes on any value in a range of values

- 1 to 'very friendly';
- 2 to 'moderately friendly';
- 3 to 'averagely friendly';
- 4 to 'moderately unfriendly'; and
- 5 to 'very unfriendly'.

In other words, we would *not* be following the rule of correspondence if we assign 4 to 'moderately friendly'.

**isomorphism:**
structural similarity

The measurement procedures must also adhere to the **reality isomorphism principle**, which means that the measurement scales must be structurally similar to that which we want to investigate. Suppose the values of a continuous variable such as 'persuasiveness' range from low to high. If we were to measure persuasiveness using discrete categories ('yes'/'no') we would *not* be adhering to the principle. Consequently, 'persuasiveness' cannot be accurately measured with such an instrument.

## Nominal level measurement

A nominal level of measurement involves allocating numerals to variables so that we can identify, name or label them. For example, television news items that deal with political topics could be labelled category 1 and television news items that do *not* deal with political topics could be labelled category 2. When comparing men with women, or readers with non-readers of a newspaper, or radio listeners with non-listeners, we are using a nominal level of measurement.

From these examples, it is clear that the nominal level of measurement is appropriate for measuring **discrete** variables.

The numerical system used for a nominal level measurement is adequate if it contains three characteristics (Smith 1988:43-44; Babbie 1990:128).

**exhaustive:** a category system that enables every unit of analysis to be placed in one of the categories

First, we must ensure that the subclasses or categories into which we divide a variable are **exhaustive**. For example, if we divide the variable *sources of advertisements* into the categories: *radio, television, newspapers* and *magazines*, our categories are *not* exhaustive. What about other sources, such as word of mouth, billboards, posters, advertisements screened in a cinema, or advertisements on buses?

**mutually exclusive:** a category system that ensures that a unit of analysis can be placed in one and only one category

Secondly, the categories must be **mutually exclusive**, which means that all members (e.g. respondents) of a sample must fall within one and only one category. For example, a respondent is **either** a *listener* or a *non-listener* of a specific radio station.

Thirdly, each category that represents the variable as a subclass must be labelled with a different numeral, so that we can differentiate the categories or subclasses. For example the variable sources of advertisements could be labelled: 1 = *radio*, 2 = *television*, 3 = *newspapers*, 4 = *magazines* and 5 = *other sources*. Depending on the objective of the study we may want to subdivide *other sources*, to differentiate between advertisements heard in taxies and advertisements distributed as knock-and-drop pamphlets (in which case each category must be labelled with a different numeral).

## Ordinal level measurement

**rank order:** variables are arranged in a particular order, e.g. from high to low

When using ordinal level measurement, rank order is used to determine the differences between variables. For example, when ranking the speeches made by three political speakers, 1 is used to label the best speech, 2 for the second-best speech, and 3 for the third-best speech. By using an ordinal level of measurement, we do not, however, measure the **extent** to which variables differ from one another. In other words, we do not know to what extent *category 1* speech differs from or is better than *category 3* speech.

The ordinal level of measurement **differs** from nominal measurement because the numerals used to label categories should follow the correspondence rule. For example, if we investigate the **importance** of

advertisement sources, we can use an ordinal level of measurement. We can assign the numerals in rank-ordered sequence, where 1 would be ranked *more important* than 2, and 2 would be ranked *more important* than 3, etcetera.

When using an ordinal level measurement, we must be aware of two characteristics. First, the numerals used to rank particular categories only reflect a ranking of each category in relation to the other categories. The political speech that respondents rank as 1, means that it is ranked as *the best speech* compared to the other two speeches – nothing more. Secondly, the distances or differences between each numeral used to rank the categories are **unequal**. The political speech ranked 1 may be excellent when compared to the speech ranked 2, whereas the speech ranked 2 may only be slightly better than the one ranked 3. Ordinal level measurement is appropriate for continuous variables, when the distance or difference between the values of the variables is unknown or anticipated to be unequal.

**continuous variable:**
a characteristic that can take on an ordered set of values e.g. from low to high

## *Interval level measurement*

Similar to ordinal scaling, when a variable is subdivided into categories in an interval level of measurement, these categories are rank-ordered in a sequence from low to high (or high to low). However, one of the main characteristics of an interval level measurement is that the **intervals** between the numbers must be of **equal** size. In other words, the numerals allocated to the categories represent the rank of each category (as in the case of ordinal measurement) *and* its relative value within the rank-ordered sequence. Achievements recorded in percentages, calendar days, duration counted in seconds and minutes, and sizes of printed messages measured with a ruler, are examples of variables measured on interval scales.

## *Ratio level measurement*

**absolute zero:**
a natural zero point

A ratio level measurement is similar to an interval level measurement, except that it includes what is called an **absolute zero**. In other words, when we allocate a numeral of 0 (zero), it indicates that the variable being measured is absent. Physical distance, mass, height, income, birth, and number of children in a family, and the number of cellular phones in a household, are examples of such variables.

When **choosing the level** of measurement, we should formulate the operational definitions of theoretical constructs at the highest possible level, which increases the sensitivity of the measurement and the use of statistics to test hypotheses. In other words, operational definitions should be formulated in such a way that we could use ratio or interval levels of measurements.

## 3.3.2 The requirement of reliability

Measurement reliability means that the measure must be stable and consistently produce the same measurements (or answers) over a period of time. Sources of unreliability can be found in the items (questions or statements) on a measure and/or can be introduced by the subjects being investigated.

Items on a measure may be inconsistent and diminish reliability because 'they are vague, confusing, or simply irrelevant to common concepts' (Reinard 1994:233). Similarly, subjects can contribute to the unreliability of a measure due to random errors, such as subject fatigue, emotional or health problems, memory fluctuations, environmental conditions, or familiarity with the type of measurement instrument used.

**random errors:** various factors that cause subjects to contribute to the unreliability of a measure

Six methods can be used to assess the reliability of a measure. Although they differ in the procedures used to collect the data, they have a common purpose: to compute or calculate the reliability coefficient. A reliability coefficient ranges from no reliability (0) to perfect reliability (1). However, we hardly ever read of a coefficient of 0 or 1 in communication research reports. Instead, coefficients consisting of decimal points such as 0.84, 0.91 or 0.79 are reported. The relation between the reliability coefficient and how good the measure is, is summarised below in Table 3.4.

**coefficient:** a correlation that measures the amount of coincidence or association between things

| **TABLE 3.4:** Interpretation of reliability coefficients | |
|---|---|
| **RELIABILITY OF** | **MEANS THAT THE CONSISTENCY OF THE MEASURE IS** |
| 0.9 or higher | extremely good |
| 0.80 - 0.89 | good |
| 0.70 - 0.79 | fair |

### Test-retest reliability

As the name indicates, test-retest reliability means that the same measure is administered twice to the same group of people, but on two different occasions, and the reliability is determined by comparing the consistency of the scores. The test-retest method is therefore concerned with measuring **stability** as one of the three components of reliability (Wimmer and Dominick 1997:53-57). This method is considered useful when the measure contains single items and/or items that combine factors that are independent of others on the same measure (Reinard 1994:235).

**stability:** the extent to which repeated administration of a measure provides the same results

There are some limitations to this method. As it involves two data collections, it tends to be time consuming. In addition, the possibility exists that respondents may repeat their responses during the second test because they remember how they responded during the first test. People may also change their views over a period of time. These two limitations can lower the reliability estimate.

### Alternate-forms reliability

A common pool of measurement items is divided among different forms – usually two – which are given to the same group of respondents. If the different forms show consistency, then it may be accepted that the scores for one form would be close to the scores for the alternate form. The alternate-forms method is therefore suited to assess the **equivalency** component of reliability. However, one of the problems experienced with this method is to be able to design two parallel versions of the same measuring instrument that measure precisely the same phenomenon.

**equivalency:** extent of agreement between two measuring instruments or two coders

### Split-half reliability

When this method is used, the measurement items are divided (split) into two parts. Each half is scored separately and the consistency checked between these two scores. The split-half method is also suited to assessing the **internal consistency** among items, as a third component of reliability. For example, in a questionnaire that consists of 60 items, we would not compare the responses to the first 30 items with the responses to the second 30 items, because respondents may have become tired towards the end. In this example, we would create

**internal consistency:** the extent to which all parts of the measuring instrument measure the same phenomenon

two halves by combining all the even-numbered items and scoring them as one test, versus all the uneven-numbered items as the other test. When this happens, we could refer to the method as 'odd-even reliability' (Reinard 1994:235).

**odd-even reliability:** internal consistency between odd- and even-numbered items

## *Item-to-total reliability*

Each item in a measurement is correlated with all the items in the measurement. This method is particularly useful when testing measures during a pilot study, because any one item that scores zero (0) when correlated with the other items, points to the likelihood that the item is testing something completely different from the other items, and that it should be deleted from the final measure.

## *Intercoder (or interjudge) reliability*

This method is usually applied in a content analysis to determine how reliable the interpretation (or coding) of communication content is, especially when two or more observers analyse the same content.

Content can vary and include messages communicated by the mass media, respondents' written responses to open-ended questions in a questionnaire, historical documents and/or notes made during observations or interviews. Intercoder reliability is therefore determined by calculating the average correlation among coders to determine the **equivalency** with which the measurement procedures, rules or categories (specified by the operational definitions) are applied by coders.

Although different statistical tests can be used, we tend to rely on one of the following in communication research: Cohen's *kappa* and Scott's *pi*. However, as both these methods involve intricate computation, they are not elaborated on in this unit. (Compare Cohen 1960; Scott 1955; Fleiss 1981 for the formulae and applications of these tests).

## *Computer programs*

Apart from the five reliability methods described above, two further statistical tools can be used if we have access to computer programs to calculate the reliability coefficients. When a measure contains items that can be scored as either *correct* or *incorrect*, the Kuder-Richardson formula 20 (abbreviated as *K-R 20*) can be used to measure reliability. If a measure contains items that measure respondents' perceptions, attitudes or ratings, Cronbach's *alpha coefficient* can be used.

As respondents' perceptions, attitudes or ratings do not reflect *correct* or *incorrect* options, Cronbach's alpha measures reliability by establishing the consistency with which respondents reacted to the items on the measure. Cronbach's alpha is a more sophisticated application of the split-halves method, because multiple pairs of subcategories are randomly selected from a measurement, and all these paired categories are correlated as an index of the internal consistency of the whole measuring instrument. (Compare Cronbach 1970; Ferguson 1971; and McCroskey 1982 for the formulae and applications of these statistical tools.)

The methods used to determine the reliability of a measurement, such as the reliability of a questionnaire, are determined by considering the stability and internal consistency (equivalency) of the measure. The importance of reliability can best be summarised as: 'Test unreliability creates instrumentation bias, a source of internal invalidity in an experiment' (Tuckman 1978:161). Measuring internal consistency does not guarantee that the measurement actually measures what we wanted to investigate.

## 3.3.3   The requirement of validity

When discussing validity in this section, we are concerned with measurement validity, which is *not* synonymous with internal and external validity of a research design (*see* Unit 2). Measurement validity deals with the degree to which the measurement we use actually measures what we intend or claim to have measured. By claiming that a measure is valid, we are implying that it is also reliable. In other words, a measure cannot be valid unless it is also reliable.

The methods that we can use to determine measurement validity represent an external form of evidence. In the words of Reinard (1994:240) 'validity is the consistency of a measure with some outside criterion or standard by which to judge the test'. A measurement's validity depends on how closely the operational definitions overlap with the theoretical definitions of the phenomena being measured. Although the four procedures or methods are discussed separately, we could combine some of them to give further support to the validity of a measurement.

## Face validity

Face validity – sometimes called **content validity** – is determined by that quality of an item or indicator judged to be a reasonable measure of a particular variable. If we want to evaluate the construct competence as a *political speaker*, and if the measuring instrument only assesses the effectiveness of the speaker's *verbal skills*, this measure lacks face (or content) validity because other factors, such as *nonverbal communication* and the *structuring of the speech*, which also contribute to the evaluation of competence, are not assessed.

The disadvantage of face validity is that our judgement as researchers could be biased and no other external evidence exists to support the assumption that the measurement or indicator is, in fact, valid. One way to minimise subjectivity is to use several experts to judge the measurement independently.

## Expert-jury validity

This method of validation is similar to that of face validity, except that several people regarded as experts on the subject matter, and not an individual, evaluate the merit of the measure. The same disadvantage, as described above, therefore applies. An expert jury is frequently used during pilot studies aimed at the development and improvement of a measuring instrument, such as a questionnaire.

## Criterion-based validity

When using criterion validity, we can apply one of two methods in which an outside criterion to evaluate the measure's validity can be applied: concurrent or predictive validity. In **concurrent validity** a new measurement is correlated with a measure of the same thing that has previously been validated.
**Predictive validity** is the degree to which a measure predicts known groups in which the phenomenon or construct that we are researching

must exist. If we design a measure to gauge successful advertisers, we could administer the measure to a group of advertisers known to be successful and another group known in advance to be unsuccessful. If the test distinguishes between the two groups, we can claim predictive validity and apply the measure to the sample we want to investigate.

A problem experienced with predictive validity is to determine the criteria against which we check the scores. For example, what constitutes *successful advertisers?* Are they *individuals* or *groups*? Is '*successful*' measured in terms of how many of their advertisements respondents can *recall*; or by how many of their products are actually *sold?*

## Construct validity

The assessment of the construct validity of a measuring instrument is a complex process that often involves both content-related evidence and criterion-related evidence. It 'involves relating a measuring instrument to some overall theoretic framework to ensure that the measurement is actually logically related to other concepts in the framework' (Wimmer and Dominick 1997:56).

Consider the construct *credibility* as it applies to a particular communicator, such as a politician. First, we must clearly define the variable being measured (e.g. credibility means that the politician is an authority in a particular area, such as finance). Secondly, hypotheses based on a theory underlying the variable need to be formulated. These hypotheses should state how a politician who has a *lot* of credibility will behave in a certain situation, compared to a politician who has *little* credibility.

Two examples of possible hypotheses are:
- *If a politician answers questions from a television interviewer without any hesitation, then we regard him or her as an authority.*
- *If a politician insists that a television interviewer provides possible questions in writing before the interview, we tend not to regard him or her as an authority.*

The third step involves testing these hypotheses, logically and statistically. As these statistical tests are beyond the scope of this unit, the following comments, related to the *credibility* of a politician, should suffice to illustrate the complexities involved. We defined *credibility* with reference to *authority* and hypothesised that to answer questions without hesitation is a valid measure of *authority*. However, the construct validity of a measurement should draw on the full theoretical definition of the construct.

In the example we need to answer several questions: Does this indicator measure the politician's ability to perform in front of a television camera instead of his or her expertise? What about the content of the replies? Furthermore, does the operational definition of the construct *credibility* with reference to *authority* provide for all the components logically linked to the construct? What about *dynamism, trustworthiness* or *honesty* and *consistency* as components of *credibility*?

## 3.3.4 Measurement scales

Scaling is concerned with the conceptualisation of the operational definition, to provide numerical measurement, which can involve one or more of the following:

- **counting** the frequency of an occurrence, such as the number of times employees have face-to-face communication with the manager during a week;
- **comparing** two units or groups, or changes that occur in one group, such as before and after an independent variable has been introduced in an experimental group;
- **ranking** quantitative characteristics of the unit of analysis, such as more or less violence in television programmes, longer or shorter duration of broadcast time, greater or lesser lengths of newspaper reports; and
- **ranking** qualitative characteristics of the unit of analysis, such as poor versus good.

Many communication research studies are aimed at measuring people's attitudes, perceptions or judgements, for which a number of measurement scales have been developed over the years. The most well-known are: Thurstone scales, Guttman scales, Likert scales, and semantic differential scales. We focus only on the last two scales, because the construction of both Thurstone scales and Guttman scales is labour-intensive and time consuming.

## Likert scales

When using a Likert scale, subjects as respondents are asked to **rate** a particular statement by selecting one of these responses: *strongly agree, agree; neutral, disagree,* or *strongly disagree.*

**neutral:** also sometimes called *uncertain, undecided,* or *neither agree nor disagree*

The procedure followed to construct a Likert scale involves three steps:

1. We compile a large number of both positive and negative statements about the topic (artefact, person, organisation or abstract concept) that we want to research.
2. We then undertake a pilot test by selecting a random sample of subjects who are asked to rate the statements (i.e. indicate their degree of agreement or disagreement with each statement). A five-point continuum is used during this rating test, although a 7-point scale can also be used. We score each statement about the research topic by distinguishing between positively worded and negatively worded items by following the procedure explained below (*see* Figure 3.6 and Figure 3.7).
3. We analyse the scores and select those statements for a final scale that clearly represent high scores (e.g. indicating strong agreement with positively worded statements) versus low scores (e.g. indicating strong disagreement with positively worded statements). An important aspect during this third step is that we must ensure that the statements selected as items for the final scale must be **representative** of the measure, for which factor analysis can be used.

**representative of the measure:** responses that agree with a respondent's overall score

**factor analysis:** a multivariate statistical procedure

*Instruction:*
*Place a tick ✓ next to the one choice that indicates your opinion.*

| All advertisements for tobacco products must be censored. | | |
|---|---|---|
| Choice | | (Score assigned) |
| | Strongly agree | (5) |
| | Agree | (4) |
| | Neutral | (3) |
| | Disagree | (2) |
| | Strongly disagree | (1) |

**Figure 3.6:** Example of a Likert scale item (positively worded)

The scores assigned, that appear between brackets next to each response, do **not** appear on an actual Likert scale item in a question-naire. In a **positively** worded item, such as shown in Figure 3.6, the scores are arranged from 5 (*strongly agree*) to 1 (*strongly disagree*). To maintain attitude measurement consistency, the scores are **reversed** for an item that evaluates a contradiction or opposition to a previously positively worded item. As illustrated in Figure 3.7 below, *strongly agree* is scored as 1 and *strongly disagree* is scored as 5, because we assume that respondents will strongly disagree with the statement.

*Instruction:*
*Place a tick ✓ next to the one choice that indicates your opinion.*

| Censorship on advertisements of tobacco products impedes freedom of speech. | | |
|---|---|---|
| **Choice** | | **(Score assigned)** |
| | Strongly agree | (1) |
| | Agree | (2) |
| | Neutral | (3) |
| | Disagree | (4) |
| | Strongly disagree | (5) |

**FIGURE 3.7:** Example of a Likert scale item that contradicts another positively worded item

A Likert scale therefore assesses the **degree** to which respondents agree or disagree with statements about a specific topic or issue.

Two advantages of using a Likert scale are the ease with which we can develop the scale and that **reliability** can be measured while collecting the data. However, if the **topic** being investigated changes, the items (statements) used on the Likert scale usually have to be composed anew. Another disadvantage is the possibility that a **total** score may hide specific details of a respondent's response.

semantic space:
the idea that
people tend to
evaluate things
along a spatial
continuum

## *Semantic differential scales*

The semantic differential scale – developed by Osgood, Suci and Tannenbaum (1957) – is based on the idea of **semantic space**. They also contend that people's evaluation occurs along three dimensions of meaning: activity, potency and evaluation. Considering the three dimensions of meaning, the bipolar adjectives that are frequently used for each dimension are illustrated in Figures 3.8, 3.9 and 3.10 below (*see* Stacks and Hocking 1992; Robinson and Shaver 1973).

| valuable | : ..... : ..... : ..... : ..... : ..... : ..... : ..... : | worthless |
| honest | : ..... : ..... : ..... : ..... : ..... : ..... : ..... : | dishonest |
| good | : ..... : ..... : ..... : ..... : ..... : ..... : ..... : | bad |

**FIGURE 3.8:** Semantic differential scales – evaluation dimension

| active | : ..... : ..... : ..... : ..... : ..... : ..... : ..... : | passive |
| sharp | : ..... : ..... : ..... : ..... : ..... : ..... : ..... : | dull |
| fast | : ..... : ..... : ..... : ..... : ..... : ..... : ..... : | slow |

**FIGURE 3.9:** Semantic differential scales – activity dimension

| large | : ..... : ..... : ..... : ..... : ..... : ..... : ..... : | small |
| heavy | : ..... : ..... : ..... : ..... : ..... : ..... : ..... : | light |
| strong | : ..... : ..... : ..... : ..... : ..... : ..... : ..... : | weak |

**FIGURE 3.10:** Semantic differential scales – potency dimension

In Figures 3.8, 3.9 and 3.10 all the positive adjectives (or items) are arranged on the left-hand side and all the negative items on the right-hand side of the scales. In an actual test, the order of the positive and negative adjectives would be **alternated** (as illustrated in Figure 3.11 on page 131), to prevent response bias.

Suppose we want to measure how employees feel about different communication channels and settings in organisational communication. We would place each channel, setting or other variable at the top of a series of 7-point scales, with bipolar adjectives on either side. Figure 3.11 is an example of a semantic differential scale.

(Note that this hypothetical example reflects only **one** of many communication experiences that could and would be listed in an investigation of how the employees feel.)

*Instruction:* Listed below are several pairs of adjectives. Place a tick ✓ on the line between each pair to indicate how you feel.

Soccer

dull      : ..... : ..... : ..... : ..... : ..... : ..... : ..... :      exciting

For example, if you feel that soccer is always dull, place a tick in the first space right next to the word 'dull'. If you feel that soccer is only slightly described by the word 'dull', place a tick in the second or third space. If the two words in a pair are equally descriptive of soccer, or if neither word applies, place a tick in the fourth (middle) space. If you feel that soccer is only slightly described by the word 'exciting', place a tick in the fifth or sixth space. If you feel that soccer is always exciting, place a tick in the seventh space, right next to the word 'exciting'.

Now rate each of the communication experiences that follow.

### Making decisions in a small-group setting

| | | | | | | | | |
|---|---|---|---|---|---|---|---|---|
| unfriendly | : ..... : ..... : ..... : ..... : ..... : ..... : ..... : | friendly |
| sociable | : ..... : ..... : ..... : ..... : ..... : ..... : ..... : | unsociable |
| bad | : ..... : ..... : ..... : ..... : ..... : ..... : ..... : | good |
| harmless | : ..... : ..... : ..... : ..... : ..... : ..... : ..... : | harmful |
| inferior | : ..... : ..... : ..... : ..... : ..... : ..... : ..... : | superior |
| easy | : ..... : ..... : ..... : ..... : ..... : ..... : ..... : | difficult |
| gloomy | : ..... : ..... : ..... : ..... : ..... : ..... : ..... : | joyful |

**FIGURE 3.11:** Example of a semantic differential scale

The scoring procedure for a semantic differential scale is done as follows. Scores from 1 to 7 are allocated for each of the seven open spaces on the scale, starting with 1 next to the negative side and progressing to 7 next to the positive side. Note that the series of numerals that connect each pair of adjectives (or characteristics) is an **ordinal** level of measurement. The scores of the different scales are then added to calculate a composite score for each respondent.

Assume that a respondent marked the spaces for the first three scales in Figure 3.11 as indicated below:

| | | | | | | | | |
|---|---|---|---|---|---|---|---|---|
| unfriendly | : ..... : ..... : ..... : ..... : ..... : ..... : ✓ : | friendly |
| sociable | : ..... : ✓ : ..... : ..... : ..... : ..... : ..... : | unsociable |
| bad | : ..... : ..... : ..... : ..... : ✓ : ..... : ..... : | good |

These items would be scored 7 (friendly), 6 (sociable) and 5 (good), which totals 18 (or an average of 6.0 out of 7).

Multiplying the number of scales that measure the same underlying dimension can increase measurement **reliability**. For this reason a statistical technique (factor analysis) should be performed during the pilot stage of developing a semantic differential scale, so that those scales measuring the same underlying dimension (or factor) can be combined to increase measurement reliability.

Both the Likert scale and the semantic differential scale can be used to investigate responses that range from favourable to unfavourable towards an artefact, an individual, a group, an organisation or a construct. However, the **evaluation** dimension is of particular interest in communication research, because by measuring respondents' **attitudes**, we are simultaneously dealing with predispositions of actual behaviour (favourably or unfavourably) towards the artefact, person or construct being investigated.

## *Executive summary:*
## Measurement

1 Principles and levels of measurement:
   - rule of correspondence;
   - reality isomorphism principle;
   - nominal level measurement;
   - ordinal level measurement;
   - interval level measurement;
   - ratio level measurement.

2 The requirement of reliability:
   - test-retest reliability;
   - alternate-forms reliability;
   - intercoder (or interjudge) reliability;
   - split-half reliability;
   - item-to-total reliability;
   - computer programs.

3 The requirement of validity:
   - face validity;
   - expert-jury validity;
   - criterion-based validity;
   - construct validity.

4 Scaling:
   - counting, comparing, ranking;
   - Likert scale;
   - semantic differential scale.

## Self-evaluation and portfolio tasks

**3.5** The following item appears in a questionnaire:

> Based on the Minister's speech today, how would you judge his knowledge of the new Constitution?

On a sheet of paper, apply mapping according to the rule of correspondence to the Minister's speech as an indicator of 'knowledge'. Arrange the following properties on a five-point scale: 'unsure', 'moderately adequate', 'very inadequate', 'moderately inadequate' and 'very adequate'.

**3.6** Which level of measurement – nominal, ordinal, interval or ratio – would you use to measure each of the following?
1. The duration of radio advertisements in seconds.
2. Preference for a certain political party.
3. The age of newspaper readers.
4. Topics given priority as news stories in newspapers.

**3.7** Which method(s) would you use to determine the **reliability** of a measurement, with the purpose of assessing each of the following characteristics?
1. stability;
2. internal consistency; and
3. equivalency.

**3.8** Which method(s) would you use to assess the **validity** of the measuring instrument you would want to use to measure each of the following?
1. A newspaper that has a vacancy and wants to measure applicants' abilities as proofreaders.
2. Voters' evaluation of the status held by leaders of different political parties.

## 3.4 Collecting data by asking questions

We conduct interviews or surveys by asking questions, and collecting self-report data or behavioural observation data. The unit of analysis is usually individual persons and we collect information that **describes** their abilities, opinions, attitudes, beliefs and/or their knowledge of a particular topic or issue. In cases where the units of analysis are artefacts, such as newspapers or policy documents, we combine survey research with content analysis. 'Asking questions' to collect data can be used in survey research (for example, in a questionnaire), in field research (for example, conducting focus-group interviews), in experimental research, and in observational research. These methods and procedures are discussed in Unit 4.

Irrespective of the circumstances in which questions are asked, we need to first consider the **problems** characteristic of questions and statements to which we invite a response from a subject.

**self-report data:** subjects provide their own information – for example, by keeping a diary or filling in a questionnaire

**subject:** person being researched; also called participant in field research and respondent in survey research

### 3.4.1 Problems experienced in the wording of questions and statements

The **wording** of self-administered questionnaires and interview schedules – as questions or statements – is a challenging task. This is especially the case when we consider the type of wording that we ought to **avoid**:

**Double-barrelled questions**: *Are you in favour of an annual increase in income and fringe benefits?*

Whenever the word 'or' or 'and' appears in a question or statement, this should be a warning sign that **two** questions have been formulated. Even if all the respondents answer 'yes', we would not know whether they chose 'increase in income' or 'increase in fringe benefits', or both.

**Questionable assumption**: *Do you prefer this newspaper with or without the property supplement?*

The presence of 'or' in this example means that it is another double-barrelled question. It also contains a false or questionable assumption that all respondents 'prefer' this newspaper.

**Loaded language**: *Do you prefer working flexitime given the advantages it represents?*

The justification to answer 'yes' has been **loaded** in this question. Any respondent who wishes to answer 'no' will be contradicting apparent advantages not mentioned in the question. A position for or against the issue must not be part of a question.

**Leading questions (or statements)**: *Do you agree with the majority of the employees who believe in flexitime?*

Loaded language can also result in a leading question being asked, which pressurises a respondent to **agree** and biases the response.

**Questions with one logical answer**: *Can the educational supplements of newspapers promote the acquisition of learning skills among learners?*

Loaded language and leading questions may also result in a question being formulated, to which only **one** logical answer can be given. A question that asks whether something can or might occur in the future has one logical answer − 'yes'.

**Presumptive questions**: *Have you stopped using drugs?*

These questions make it impossible for a respondent to give a fair answer. Irrespective of whether a respondent answers 'yes' or 'no' to this type of question, he or she faces a dilemma, especially if the use of drugs is illegal.

**Negative items**: *The public relations department should not increase the number of press releases about the company's activities.*

Negative questions or statements should be avoided, because respondents can easily misinterpret them. If a respondent were to answer 'yes' to this statement, we cannot be sure whether he or she read (or heard) the 'not' in the statement. In other words, we do not know whether the 'yes' means 'yes, increase', or 'yes, do not increase but decrease', or 'yes, do not increase but maintain the present number of press releases'.

**Incomplete questions (or statements):** *Do you think we should spend more money on health?*

This question forces the respondent to express an opinion based on incomplete information. The question remains: more on health than on what? Sports facilities, educational facilities, perhaps housing; or even more on which aspects of health?

**Vague agents of action:** Reconsidering the last example, who is 'we' – the national government or one of the provincial governments? The agent required to perform the action must be specified to avoid vague responses.

**Vague questions (or statements):** *What do you think of your local newspaper?*

Responses to a question that is vague or imprecise will not yield very useful information. If there were two or more local newspapers, we would not know to which one the responses apply. Even if there were only one such newspaper, it is not clear what we are investigating – the actuality, objectivity, newsworthiness, or the diversity of the content; or the pictures and layout; the cost – or something else?

**Lengthy questions (or statements):** *Should the fact that subordinates are questioning the status of shop stewards be rectified by the shop stewards after consultation with top management?*

A lengthy question, such as this example, obscures what we actually want respondents to think about and to respond to.

**Ambiguous language:** *How likely would you be to adopt protective measures against this issue?*

Expressions such as 'protective measures' and 'issue' are subject to more than one interpretation, especially if neither the question nor the questionnaire specifies whether the topic being investigated deals with, for example, increased inflation or the prevention of AIDS.

**Complex questions**: *Should serious Members of Parliament in South Africa be required to use several official languages?*

Before answering 'yes' or 'no' to the language issue in this question, the respondent would have to differentiate between 'serious' and 'non-serious' Members of Parliament. Adding the word 'serious' to the question makes it more complex, and may create the impression that the question applies to a small group of people − or so the respondent may think.

**Abbreviations**: *Should SOCCER focus its campaign on obtaining local support?*

Unless explanations are given of the abbreviations or acronyms, we cannot expect respondents to interpret them universally. *SOCCER*, in the South African context, can be interpreted as a very popular ball game or as an acronym for a political party that participated in the 1994 general election.

A respondent, without any interference from or the involvement of a researcher, fills in a self-administered questionnaire. A questionnaire can be used in controlled environments (e.g. when conducting an experiment), in semi-controlled environments (e.g. when doing field research) and in uncontrolled environments (e.g. when conducting a survey among respondents on a national basis).

## 3.4.2 Items in a self-administered questionnaire

Not all questionnaires consist of questions. Some consist of statements that require respondents to indicate the extent to which they agree or disagree with statements (e.g. when using Likert scales).

Although both questions and statements may be used in questionnaires, we should select one or the other to **minimise** the number of **different** instructions, such as to 'circle', 'cross', 'order', 'tick', 'check' or 'rank', that precede each question/statement. Different instructions can confuse respondents unnecessarily.

A distinction can also be made between **direct** and **indirect** questions. For example, instead of asking respondents (directly) to react to specific programmes broadcast on a particular community radio station, they could be asked (indirectly) to describe the quality of programmes broadcast on a particular radio station.

Questions can also be of a **specific** or **general** nature. Although general questions may be interpreted as less threatening by respondents, these can also yield vague responses. For example: *How do you feel about your work environment?*

In contrast, the following question addresses a very specific issue: *How do you feel about the fact that a computer constantly monitors your work output?*

In addition to general versus specific questions, and direct versus indirect questions, questionnaires usually contain closed- and open-ended questions. Although some of the following headings, such as closed-ended questions, contain the word 'questions', some of the illustrative examples may be statements.

An **open-ended question** allows respondents to answer the question in their own words. For example: *Which of the services offered by this library are most important to you?*

An open-ended question is particularly useful if we want to encourage respondents to express attitudes or opinions in their own words; and especially if we are unsure of the number of responses that may be elicited.

A **closed-ended question** contains a fixed number of answers, from which a respondent has to select one. For example:

| *(Select and tick one answer)* |
| **The services offered by this library are:** |
| ☐ superior |
| ☐ excellent |
| ☐ good |
| ☐ fair |
| ☐ poor |

An important requirement of a closed-ended question is that respondents must commonly understand the language and terms used. One disadvantage of using such a question is that the possible answers are limited to the number of categories included as options.

A **paired-comparison question** is similar to a closed-ended question, because a respondent has to select one of the given options. The **difference**, however, is that the respondent has to select one of **two** alternatives at a time. For example:

> **The library wants to extend its services. If you had to choose between the following two options, which one would you, as a library user, prefer? (Tick one answer)**
>
> ☐ longer opening hours    ☐ more computer terminals

A paired-comparison question is very useful if the two items (answers) that we wish to rate are expected to be close in desirability, and if it offers a practical solution when we have several options to rate, that make simple ranking difficult.

Babbie (1990:369) defines a **contingency question** as one 'that is to be asked of only some respondents, as determined by their responses to some other question'. The 'other' question referred to here is a **filter** question that is used to identify a subgroup from the respondents sampled. For example:

> 18.    Are you satisfied with the sources that you found during this visit to the library? (Tick one answer)
>
> ☐ Yes (If yes, please answer questions 19 to 24)
> ☐ No (If no, disregard questions 19 to 24 and go to question 25)

In the example, questions 19 to 24, which follow on from question 18, are contingency questions for respondents who replied 'yes' to 18 (the filter question). Contingency questions are particularly useful when we have differentiated between respondents to whom certain questions may not apply, especially near the beginning of a questionnaire.

A **ranking question** is similar to a closed-ended question, except that the purpose is to ask respondents to rank or rate a number of options.

> **Instruction:** Which of the following sources do you rely on most as your sources of news? Number your **most** important source as 1, your **second choice** number 2, and so on, until you number the **least** important source as 5.
>
> ☐ newspapers   ☐ radio   ☐ fellow workers
>
> ☐ television   ☐ magazines

The **priority** is of essence in a ranking question, such as first, second, third choice, and **not** the **degree** of differences between the options ranked.

An **inventory question** is similar to a closed-ended question, except that respondents have to list the options that apply to them personally.

> Which of the following newspapers report reliable information about political changes in South Africa? (Tick all the newspapers that you think apply.)
>
> | | | |
> |---|---|---|
> | ☐ Rapport | (1) | [4:1–9] |
> | ☐ Sunday Tribune | (2) | |
> | ☐ City Press | (3) | |
> | ☐ Sunday Times | (4) | |
> | ☐ Sowetan | (5) | |
> | ☐ Beeld | (6) | |
> | ☐ Burger | (7) | |
> | ☐ Metro | (8) | |
> | ☐ Other (fill in the name/s) | (9) | |

The items or categories listed in an inventory question are not mutually exclusive and should be fairly well-known to respondents. This type of question also makes provision for respondents with differing backgrounds. Not all respondents necessarily read all these newspapers and, by adding 'other' as an open-ended option, respondents who read other newspapers can add these to the list.

**Matrix questions** consist of a number of closed-ended questions, with each question's options scaled. Respondents are asked to select the option that reflects their attitude, opinion or judgement. The same scale is repeated for each question or statement, Likert scales being the most commonly used. For example:

| For each of the statements (31-34) circle one of the options to indicate how you feel. | | | | | | |
|---|---|---|---|---|---|---|
| **SA** = Strongly agree (with the statement) | | | | | | (1) |
| **A** = Agree (with the statement) | | | | | | (2) |
| **N** = Neither agree nor disagree (with the statement) | | | | | | (3) |
| **D** = Disagree (with the statement) | | | | | | (4) |
| **SD** = Strongly disagree (with the statement) | | | | | | (5) |
| 31. My supervisor is trustworthy. | **SA** | **A** | **N** | **D** | **SD** | [4:10] |
| 32. My supervisor is incompetent. | **SA** | **A** | **N** | **D** | **SD** | [4:11] |
| 33. My supervisor is stupid. | **SA** | **A** | **N** | **D** | **SD** | [4:12] |
| 34. My supervisor is supportive. | **SA** | **A** | **N** | **D** | **SD** | [4:13] |

Matrix questions enable us to use standard measurement scales, such as Likert scales, and to combine questions or statements that logically belong together. Let us assume that the above example is a section of a questionnaire that deals with organisational communication. Just as these questions deal with statements related to the *supervisor*, other questions dealing with, for example *subordinates*, *sending information*, *receiving information* or *channels of communication* can be grouped together.

In Unit 2 statements were given as examples of characteristics denoted by the concept *status*, that can be used in the operationalisation of the construct. When used in a measuring instrument, matrix questions (instructions and options) can be used to determine respondents' views about these statements:

| My supervisor enjoys prestige because s/he: |
|---|
| 61. is not a manual labourer |
| 62. fulfils a superior position in the company |
| 63. is a member of an elite group |
| 64. has the power to increase salaries |
| 65. shows an awareness of employees' daily needs |
| 66. will be fair when changes take place in future |
| 67. belongs to a high socio-economic class |
| 68. can effectively negotiate between conflicting parties |

The list of items on the previous page deal with aspects of *status*, without mentioning it as a construct.

**Multiple-choice questions** consist of closed-ended questions, in response to which respondents must select one option from a number of possible options. For example:

| Different age groups have different radio-listening preferences. Please indicate your age by putting a tick against one of the groups below. | |
| --- | --- |
| ☐ 19 or younger | ☐ 40-49 |
| ☐ 20-29 | ☐ 50-59 |
| ☐ 30-39 | ☐ 60 or older |

Multiple-choice questions are useful when we are able to group underlying units, such as age, language or employment categories, and especially when mutually exclusive categories (options) can be formulated. Multiple-choice questions are also very useful when combined with a scale, to measure an amount and/or the sensitivity to degrees of conviction.

An example of a multiple-choice question that measures **amount**:

| This is the amount of information I receive about how well I am doing my work: |
| --- |
| ☐ Enough |
| ☐ More than average |
| ☐ Average |
| ☐ Little |
| ☐ None |

An example of a multiple-choice question that measures **sensitivity to degrees of conviction**:

| I trust my immediate supervisor. |
| --- |
| ☐ Always |
| ☐ Most of the time |
| ☐ Sometimes |
| ☐ Seldom |
| ☐ Never |

In addition to the distinction made between telephonic and face-to-face interviews, interviews can also be structured, partially structured or unstructured. These are discussed in Unit 4. For the moment, it is worth noting the kind of unstructured questions that are often asked during interviews that are partially structured or unstructured.

## 3.4.3 Types of interview questions

**interview schedule:** a guide with instructions for the interviewer, questions to be asked and open space to record follow-up questions

An interview schedule that is used during interviews contains both open-ended and closed-ended questions and statements. However, the type of closed-ended question that can be asked during a personal or telephonic interview is limited. For example, to ask an inventory question with a long list of options is unsuitable because, by the time the interviewer reads the last option, the respondent may have forgotten those that appeared earlier on the list.

Unstructured questions in an interview schedule usually consist of open-ended questions, free-narration questions, role-playing questions and follow-up questions.

**Open-ended questions**: *What do you think is the best way to inform employees of the affirmative action programme that management has decided to introduce?*

The reason for asking an open-ended question in an interview is the same as when asking it in a self-administered questionnaire: to invite the respondent to answer in any way he or she may wish. Since open-ended questions do not have structured or specified **answers**, they can elicit underlying ideas, feelings, sentiments and suggestions that researchers may not even have considered.

**Free-narration questions**: *Tell me how you see the ideal affirmative action programme for this company?*

A free-narration question is another type of open-ended question, where the respondent is invited to tell his or her *own story.*

**Role-playing questions**: *If you were the director of this company, how would you inform employees of the new affirmative action programme?*

A role-playing question is similar to a free-narration question. It is also an open-ended question, but the difference is that the respondent is asked to fulfil or to play a particular role.

**Follow-up questions**: As the name suggests, follow-up questions **follow** either a structured or an unstructured question. They are typical in telephone and personal interviews because the interviewer asks a follow-up question in **response** to an answer or statement made by the respondent. Follow-up questions are particularly useful to clarify the response given by the respondent, to obtain an explanation for the response, or to elicit examples and/or to double-check a response.

For example, in response to the above role-playing question a respondent may answer: *I would arrange meetings on a departmental basis and inform employees in a face-to-face communication setting.*

An appropriate follow-up question could simply be: *Why?*

According to Reinard (1994:181), three strategies for follow-up questioning can be used: probing, mirror and climate questions. A **probing question** (as a follow-up question) aims to elicit more information about the respondent's attitudes, emotions or behaviour, by asking *When?, Where?, What?, How?* or *Why?*

A **mirror question** (as a follow-up question) repeats the respondent's response, either to obtain further information or for one or more of the purposes mentioned above. For example:

Question:        *Which type of television programme is your favourite?*
Answer:          *Soap operas.*
Mirror question: *Soap operas?*

A **climate question** (as a follow-up question) differs from probing and mirror questions, because it is not necessarily asked in response to a specific answer given by the respondent. Instead, a climate question is asked to determine how a respondent feels about the interview, especially if he or she seems unsure or unwilling to participate.

## *EXECUTIVE SUMMARY:*
## COLLECTING DATA BY ASKING QUESTIONS

1 Problems with wording questions/statements:
   - double-barrelled;
   - questionable assumption;
   - loaded language;
   - leading;
   - one logical answer;
   - presumptive;
   - negative;
   - incomplete;
   - vague agents of action;
   - vague formulation;
   - lengthy;
   - ambiguous;
   - complex;
   - abbreviations.

2 Items in a self-administered questionnaire:
   - open-ended questions;
   - closed-ended questions;
   - paired-comparison questions;
   - contingency questions;
   - ranking questions;
   - inventory questions;
   - matrix questions;
   - multiple-choice questions.

3 Unstructured questions asked during interviews:
   - open-ended questions;
   - free-narration questions;
   - role-playing questions;
   - follow-up questions.

## Self-evaluation and portfolio tasks

**3.9** The following questions contain wording that **will** create problems if used in a questionnaire. Identify the **problem** in each example and rewrite the question so that the problem can be **eliminated**.

1. Should we insist on meeting management regularly on a face-to-face basis, or continue with messages being communicated via memos?
2. Do you agree with the majority of union members that minimum wages must be increased?
3. Do M-Net programmes leave something to be desired?
4. Do you think that educational television programmes can improve children's language skills?
5. Do you think that new employees appointed in junior positions get their due in this company?
6. How long have you been employed in this company?
   - ☐ 1-5 years
   - ☐ 5-10 years
   - ☐ longer than 10 years
7. Who should be RSA's next President?
   - ☐ Thabo Mbeki
   - ☐ Kader Asmal
8. When not on duty, do you prefer to read a book or just watch television?
9. Where did you hear of the minister's resignation?

**3.10** What type of question or scaling is best suited to collect data about each of the following?

1. Employers' opinions about a new management policy that was recently instituted.
2. The reaction of those taxi drivers who regularly travel long distances between cities in a specific province, to a planned-for campaign to prohibit taxies from using freeways.
3. The 'best-liked' politician in a particular province.
4. The impressions of members of a political party about their current leader.
5. The demographic characteristics of viewers of a television soap opera such as *Egoli*.
6. The number of television sets in a specified number of households.

## 3.5 Collecting data by means of observations

Research that involves a face-to-face situation, between the researcher and the subject, necessitates observation and, in certain instances, participation on the part of the researcher. Observations can be made of observable behaviours and patterns of interpersonal communication, with reference to variables such as duration and frequency. Observations can also focus on the quality of certain communication behaviours, the kind of people involved, and socio-temporal contexts or settings. Observations can be used for a variety of research objectives, of which the following are examples:

- to explore an area during the preliminary stages of a research study, that can then be studied more fully by means of other methods, such as interviews;
- to supplement or confirm data previously collected in a survey or through interviews; and/or
- to facilitate the development and testing of particular theories.

From the examples, it becomes clear that observational research can be treated as a research method on its own, or (which often occurs in practice) it can be regarded as a research approach in which a combination of methods and techniques are used.

## 3.5.1 Data-collection devices and techniques

In addition to using questions, scales, self-administered questionnaires and interview schedules, researchers who want to collect information by means of observations can use different instruments, or even design their own. Providing informed consent is obtained from the subjects, **hardware** (mechanical or electronic devices) can be used, such as audiotape recorders, videotape recorders, stopwatches, infrared photography and one-way mirrors. Audio- and videotape recorders are particularly useful for collecting data in a natural setting, such as a hospital, for later analysis.

Data-collection devices that are often used in ratings research (*see* Unit 5) by radio and television broadcasters include electronic meters

(also called people meters) and diaries. When using electronic meters, the data is automatically collected and does not require the presence of a researcher (as observer). These devices are installed in sample households and automatically record when a radio or television set is switched on or off, and the selected station or channel.

**Software** includes paper-and-pencil instruments, such as the observer filling in interview or observation schedules, making (field) notes during or after the observations, or filling in a log or diary. When subjects are asked to keep a diary of the radio or television stations that they listen to or watch, they would also be asked to record the exact times and the number of people present. This specific example, however, does not involve the presence of an observer.

Three methodological aspects can be distinguished when collecting data via observations:
- techniques used to collect data;
- the different roles fulfilled by the researcher; and
- the procedures fo analysing and interpreting the data.

**construction:**
the developing, compiling or composing of items for a new scale

In this section, we concentrate on the techniques used to collect data; the other two aspects are dealt with in Unit 4. Although observational research can be distinguished on the basis of the three methodo-logical aspects noted above, for the moment we will distinguish between **systematic** observations and **ethnographic** observations. These directly influence the way in which data are collected, including the selection and construction of measuring instruments.

## 3.5.2 Systematic observations

**standardised observation schedule:**
a pre-structured form on which observations are recorded as ticks, numbers or icons

The objectives of systematic observations are rooted in quantitative (positivist) research, where operational definitions of concepts are made as precise as possible in order to measure observable human behaviour accurately and objectively. The collection of quantitative data requires that a standardised observation schedule be compiled before the observations take place. Such an observation schedule contains a checklist of the behaviours of interest, divided into categories that observers use to code their observations. The process of defining the variables, as well as observational categories and procedures, must be clearly specified before observation, and they will vary depending on the objectives of the study and the particular behaviour to be observed.

Table 3.5 illustrates an example of an observation schedule to collect quantitative data about the verbal communication of a chairperson in a meeting. In this case, the objective of the observation is to record the frequency with which the chairperson initiates and responds to communication.

| **TABLE 3.5:** An observation schedule: initiation-response behaviour | |
| --- | --- |
| Frequency with which the chair-person **initiates** discussion of a new topic | Frequency with which the chairperson **responds** to questions, comments, and requests from the meeting |
| ✓✓✓✓ ✓✓✓✓ ✓✓✓✓ ✓✓✓✓ ✓✓✓✓ ✓✓✓✓ ✓✓✓✓ ✓✓✓✓ ✓✓✓✓ ✓✓✓✓ ✓✓✓✓ | ✓✓✓✓ ✓✓✓✓ ✓✓✓✓ ✓✓ |

The actual categories used depend on the behaviour to be observed and the objectives. Assuming the objective is to research the leadership role fulfilled by a chairperson, the 'response' category can be subdivided, based on past research and both theoretical and operational definitions of the construct 'leadership'. Table 3.6 contains hypothetical examples of such categories.

| **TABLE 3.6:** An observation schedule: initiation-response behaviour and categories for response behaviour | |
| --- | --- |
| Frequency with which the chairperson **initiates** discussion of a new topic | Frequency with which the chairperson **responds** to questions, comments, and requests from the meeting |
| ✓✓✓✓ ✓✓✓✓ ✓✓✓✓ ✓✓✓✓ ✓✓✓✓ ✓✓✓✓ ✓✓✓✓ ✓✓✓✓ ✓✓✓✓ ✓✓✓✓ ✓✓✓✓ | 1. Praise or encouragement ✓✓ |
| | 2. Acceptance, with clarification and direction ✓✓✓ |
| | 3. Questions, with the intent that the meeting responds ✓✓✓✓ ✓✓ |
| | 4. Criticism, with the intent to justify authority ✓✓✓ |
| | 5. No verbal response ✓✓ |

It is important to note that the numerals do not represent a scale. They classify a particular kind of response and the enumeration can either be done using ticks (as in the example above) or by writing the numerals in chronological order. Such a chronological record may, for example, reflect a tendency for a chairperson to start a meeting with positive responses and, as the meeting progresses, the responses may become negative or nonexistent. *See* Table 3.7 for such an example.

**TABLE 3.7:** An observation schedule: categories and chronological order of response behaviour

| DURATION OF MEETING | ORDER OF CHAIRPERSON'S RESPONSES |
|---|---|
| 09:00-09:14.59 | 1; 1; 2; 2; 3; 2; 3 |
| 09:15-09:30.59 | 4; 3; 5; 3; 3; 4 |
| 09:31-09:44.59 | 3; 4; 3 |
| 09:45-10:00 | 5 |

**KEY (CATEGORIES):**

1  Praise or encouragement
2  Acceptance, with clarification and directions
3  Questions, with the intent that the meeting responds
4  Criticism, with the intent to justify authority
5  No verbal response

In addition to being chronologically linked to duration, the record of responses observed can also be linked to topics on the agenda.

Generally, systematic observations are preferred when the reliability of the study is important. Two or more observers can observe the same behaviours using the same observation schedule. Their observations are therefore structured and data, once recorded, can be compared (*see* section 3.3.2). Systematic observations can also be conducted over longitudinal time dimensions, involving different types of subjects and different situations, using the same observation schedule.

**subjects:**
also called participants or informants in field research

The importance of pilot testing the observation schedule, to ensure that the categories are both mutually exclusive and exhaustive, cannot be emphasised enough. When reconsidering the categories for responses in Tables 3.6 and 3.7, you will find that these are not exhaustive, because the concept 'responses' can be further subdivided. The chairperson:

- interrupts another speaker;
- provides verifiable information;
- provides subjective opinion;
- provides suggestions;
- requests for information;
- requests an opinion; or
- requests suggestion(s).

Depending on the objective of the study, these responses can be refined by including categories that record whether the chairperson responds to requests from the meeting with refusal, or with a counter argument, and/or whether those present in the meeting openly discuss requests.

In above examples, individual **people** are the units of analysis. Systematic observations can also be made using **messages** as the unit of analysis. A content analysis of the amount of space devoted to different political parties in specific newspapers over the period of a year is one such example. **Historical** or **respective** studies also use systematic observations. In this case, researchers do not manipulate the independent variable because the variables (messages) have their values fixed sometime in the past.

Whereas systematic observations require the formulation of specific hypotheses or research questions, formulating operational definitions and devising categories for an observation schedule, there are instances when we rely on natural processes to provide qualitative information. These observations are discussed in the next section.

## 3.5.3 Ethnographic observations

Ethnography has its roots in anthropology and is a qualitative approach to in-depth studies of ways of life, beliefs, formal and informal relationships, communication behaviours, ideologies and many other dimensions of a particular culture or group of people. This approach emphasises that, to understand human communication, we need to study the ideas, attitudes, motives and behaviour from the point of view of the subjects in natural situations.

As ethnographic observations are unstructured, note-taking is usually used to record observations. Writing notes during observations is not encouraged, because it may influence the subjects' behaviour and/or supplant the observing. Instead, notes have to be made as soon as possible after the observation and must be systematically classified to enable analysis of the observations.

The classification or indexing scheme is usually developed as the study progresses. For example, when conducting audience ethnographic observations, categories of verbal and nonverbal communication can be devised after observing a family watching television, while we write notes based on our observations, and/or the categories can be based on listening to audiotaped recordings of the television programme and family members' conversations.

Table 3.8 contains three examples of how the same observation of verbal communication can be indexed differently.

| INDEX<br>(Examples of written notes, based on ethnographic observations of verbal communication) | MEANING OF THE INDEX | SUBJECT SPEAKING |
|---|---|---|
| 'Knowing that I am part of the decision-making team is important to me.' | The quotation marks indicate that this is a direct quotation. | John |
| Making decisions in a group setting is important for him. | The absence of quotation marks indicates that we have noted what we remember, or the phrase represents a paraphrase. | John |
| [Team work is valued.] | A phrase between square brackets indicates that we record our impressions. | John |

**TABLE 3.8:** Different ways to index the same verbal observation

Instead of using quotation marks and square brackets, other markings and icons can be used. Table 3.9 illustrates an indexing scheme designed to record observations of nonverbal behaviour.

## 3

**TABLE 3.9:** Examples of indexing nonverbal communication

| NONVERBAL COMMUNICATION | KEY |
|---|---|
| Shows tension | |
| Appears relaxed | |
| Over dramatises | |
| Appears positive | |
| Appears unmoved or neutral | |
| Appears negative | |

Observers have to do an enormous amount of data collection (and subsequent retrieval) by hand, which underlines the importance of accumulating observations in an orderly manner and keeping a systematic record. Irrespective of the style or format used, basic information, such as the time, date, place and any other information related to the behaviour or event observed should be recorded. Additional categories can be devised as the study progresses, to record as much as possible about the physical, social and temporal context in which the behaviour took place. Such details are useful for later analysis, especially the assessment of reactivity and a critical reflection of the methodological procedures followed.

**reactivity:** a subject's response to changes in the context and/or in reaction to other subjects

### EXECUTIVE SUMMARY:
### COLLECTING DATA BY MEANS OF OBSERVATIONS

1  Data-collection devices and techniques:
   - hardware (e.g. videotape);
   - software (e.g. pencil and paper).

2  Systematic observations:
   - quantitative data (frequency, duration).

3  Ethnographic observations:
   - qualitative data (from subjects' perspective).

## Self-evaluation and portfolio tasks

**3.11** Think of a communication situation to which you have easy access and in which you want to use systematic observations to collect quantitative data. Think of categories into which the behaviour or communication interaction can be divided and devise an observation schedule. Conduct an observation (e.g. for 30 minutes) and record your observations. Evaluate your performance by:
- noting any problems you experienced while making the observations; and
- evaluating the appropriateness of the categories in your observation schedule.

**3.12** Think of a communication situation to which you have easy access and in which you want to use ethnographic observations to collect qualitative data, from the perspective of the subjects. Think of the types of behaviour or communication interactions on which you want to concentrate. Conduct an observation (e.g. for 30 minutes) and record your observations. Evaluate your performance by:
- noting any problems you experienced while making the observations and especially recording your observations in this way;
- describing what the data conveyed about the perspective of the subjects that you observed; and
- indicating whether your observations should be followed-up with a full-scale study.

# 3.6 Summary

A basic understanding of the four **levels of measurement** (nominal, ordinal, interval and ratio) is important because they convey different amounts of information and because some types of statistical techniques or procedures are inappropriate for the different scales. Nominal scales label and group data as frequencies and percentages. Ordinal scales use numerals to indicate the ranking of data. The numerals used in interval scales represent equal intervals on a continuum and the characteristics of ratio scales include all of the above, plus a true zero point.

Various methods can be used to assess the consistency or **reliability** of a measurement. The methods described in this unit are test-retest reliability, alternate-forms reliability, split-half reliability, item-to-total reliability and intercoder reliability. When assessing whether an instrument accurately reflects that which it is intended to measure, we can defend its relative **validity** on the basis of face validity, expert-jury validity, criterion validity, predictive validity, concurrent validity and/or construct validity.

Of the many types of measurement **scales** and items that are used in communication research, we selectively dealt with Likert scales and semantic differential scales. The discussion of measurement in communication research in this unit is, of necessity, brief and incomplete. Before developing measurement scales and undertaking pilot studies to test such scales, we would have to do further consultations, including studying literature that deals specifically with topics such as the development of tests for evaluation purposes and statistical techniques with computer applications that are used to measure the reliability and validity of such measures.

When collecting data by asking **questions**, we concentrated on the problems that can be experienced in wording questions, the types of questions asked in self-administered questionnaires, and unstructured questions asked during interviews.

We ended this unit by looking at the collection of data by means of systematic versus ethnographic **observations**.

Before continuing with Unit 4, you are encouraged to evaluate your achievement of the learning outcomes using the following guide.

## *ASSESSMENT OF LEARNING OUTCOMES*

Ratings for evaluation of performance:
5   very high (extremely good)
4   high (good)
3   medium (average)
2   low (poor)
1   very low (extremely poor)
0   evidence is absent

| Outcomes (knowledge, competence and orientations) *You should be able to make and communicate informed decisions when collecting data by:* | Evidence of performance | Examples of criteria used to evaluate evidence of performance | Evaluation of performance | | | | | |
|---|---|---|---|---|---|---|---|---|
| | | | Ratings | | | | | |
| | | | 5 | 4 | 3 | 2 | 1 | 0 |
| Drawing a sample | by meeting sampling requirements and differentiating between types of samples. | Requirements: representativeness, population parameters, target versus accessible populations, accuracy, standard error, level of confidence, internal and external validity.<br><br>Appropriate selection of probability, quasi-probability and/or nonprobability sample. | | | | | | |
| Applying measurements | according to the principles and levels of measure-ment; by meeting reliability and validity require-ments; and by constructing scales. | Principles: rule of correspondence, reality isomorphism, categories are mutually exclusive and exhaustive.<br><br>Levels of measurement: nominal, ordinal, interval, ratio.<br><br>Reliability: test-retest, alternate-forms; inter-coder, split-half, item-to-total, computer programs.<br><br>Validity: face, expert-jury, criterion-based, costruct.<br><br>Scaling: counting, comparing, ranking; Likert scales; semantic differential scales. | | | | | | |

| Outcomes (knowledge, competence and orientations) *You should be able to make and communicate informed decisions when collecting data by:* | Evidence of performance | Examples of criteria used to evaluate evidence of performance | Evaluation of performance | | | | | |
|---|---|---|---|---|---|---|---|---|
| | | | Ratings | | | | | |
| | | | 5 | 4 | 3 | 2 | 1 | 0 |
| Formulating items for a questionnaire and an interview | in the form of questions and statements. | Avoidance of the following problems: double-barrelled questions, questionable assumptions, loaded language, leading, one logical answer, presumptive, negative, incomplete, vague agents of action, vague formulation, lengthy, ambiguous, complex, abbreviations. The appropriate use of items: open-ended, closed-ended, paired-comparison, contingency, ranking, inventory, matrix, multiple-choice, free-narration, role-playing, follow-up. | | | | | | |
| Conducting observations | by compiling an observation schedule and devising coding categories. | Categories are guided by objectives, are based on operational definitions, are mutually exclusive and are exhaustive. | | | | | | |

## *SUGGESTED READING*

Babbie, ER. 1995. *The practice of social research.* (7th edition). Belmont, California: Wadsworth.

Davies, CA. 1999. *Reflexive ethnography: a guide to researching selves and others.* London: Routledge.

DePoy, E and Gitlin, LN. 1998. *Introduction to research: understanding and applying multiple strategies.* (2nd edition). St Louis, Mo: Mosby.

De Vos, AS (ed). 1998. *Research at grass roots. A primer for the caring professions.* Pretoria: Van Schaik.

Drew, CJ, Hardman, ML and Hart AW. 1996. *Designing and conducting research; inquiry in education and social science.* (2nd edition). Needham Heights, Massachusetts: Allyn & Bacon.

Hsia, HJ. 1988. *Mass communications research methods: a step-by-step approach.* Hillsdale, NJ: Lawrence Erlbaum.

Neuman, WL. 1997. *Social research methods: qualitative and quantitative approaches.* (3rd edition). Boston, Massachusetts: Allyn & Bacon.

Rosnow, RL and Rosenthal, R. 1999. *Beginning behavioral research. A conceptual primer.* (3rd edition). Upper Sadle River, NJ: Prentice Hall.

Stacks, DW and Hocking, JE. 1992. *Essentials of communication research,* New York, NY: HarperCollins.

Terre Blanche, M and Durrheim, K (eds). 1999. *Research in practice: applied methods for the social sciences.* Cape Town: UCT Press.

# Procedures followed when applying a research design and interpreting research data

*The key to everything is patience. You get the chicken by hatching the egg ... not by smashing it.*

ARNOLD GLASOW

## Overview

This unit is a continuation of the data-collection phase while conducting research. While reading it, keep in mind the data-collection methods and techniques discussed in Unit 3. This unit first concentrates on collecting information or data in different environments, by distinguishing between so-called controlled environments (usually associated with experimental research); semi-controlled environments (such as when conducting a survey), and natural environments (such as field research). Having dealt with the advantages, limitations and implications of selecting one or more of the methods and techniques involved in conducting research in these environments, the second half of the unit selectively focuses what to do with the data. The latter includes content analysis, the use of elementary descriptive statistics and the application of a Readability Ease test. The unit ends with ethical issues that must be considered when coding and interpreting data.

**4**

## Learning outcomes

By the end of this unit, you should be able to demonstrate your understanding of:

- how to collect research data (by selecting and applying a particular research design); and
- what to do with the data once it has been collected (by conducting a content analysis, applying elementary descriptive statistics, and/or applying a Readability Ease test).

## 4.1 Introduction

In Unit 3 we emphasised that the appropriate levels of measurement and scales for a research study's objective must be determined by their reliability and validity. We also dealt with asking questions and conducting observations when collecting data. Unit 3 is an essential introduction to this unit, in which we consider two questions:

- What procedures need to be followed when collecting data? (and)
- What do we do with the data once it has been collected?

Traditionally, the following methods are distinguished in communication research: historical research, survey research, field research, content analysis and experimental research. As each of these methods can be further divided into different categories, such as quasi-experimental designs, 'true' experimental designs and factorial experimental designs, a detailed discussion of the procedures followed when applying these methods (and their variations) are beyond the scope of this book. Instead, we selectively deal with some of these methods by focusing on the most widely used procedures.

In Unit 2 we pointed out that communication researchers do not assign the same meanings to terms such as 'goal', 'aim', 'purpose' or 'objective' of a study. The same applies to the use of these terms: 'design', 'method', 'technique' and 'measuring instrument'. For example, we refer to content analysis as a method, yet it could also be called a measuring procedure, and even an interpretation procedure. We have not attempted to clarify the meanings of these terms in exact definitions. Instead, we emphasise that terms are used differently and that their meanings depend on the context in which they are used.

The following three examples illustrate this: In one case field research is regarded as a method to collect data and the interviewer, together with an interview schedule, are treated as the measuring instruments. In another case, interviews are regarded as a method to collect data, and the different types of questions as techniques.

Wimmer and Dominick (1997:455-461), refer to focus-group interviews as a 'methodology', an 'approach' and a 'research tool'. From these brief comments, it becomes clear that certain terms (e.g. method versus technique) are used interchangeably, depending on the context.

In view of the above comments, we purposefully avoid structuring this unit by using the five 'methods' mentioned above as headings, because procedures followed in one method (e.g. content analysis) overlap with another (e.g. classifying field notes in field research).

We need to keep the following in mind when considering the procedures for collecting data:

- the sampling and data-collection processes and how they influence requirements, such as validity;
- whether the research problem concerns the past, present or future;
- the setting or environment (e.g. laboratory or natural setting); and
- the extent to which we control the environment in which the research is conducted.

Many of these factors have been addressed in previous units. Although we selectively 're-visit' some of them in this unit, the **setting** and the extent to which we **control** the research environment are used to structure the next three sections.

## 4.2 Research conducted in controlled environments

Research conducted in controlled environments has its methodological roots in the **quantitative** or positivist approach to research. The objectives must be stated in terms of variables that have been operationally defined, so that the outcome of an intervention can be measured.

Control is an important part of experimental designs, which usually take place in laboratory-type conditions. This control includes the manipulation of the independent variable and the random assignment of subjects to an experimental group or a control group. As experiments are usually based on a hypothesis that contains a prediction of future changes or effects, they are based on a future orientation.

## 4.2.1 Single-system research designs

**single system:** an individual, couple, family, group, organisation, community, culture, situation, problem or process

A single-system design – also called a **case study** – involves the observation and in-depth analysis of a single system. These designs are useful during the early stages of research as they may suggest hypotheses or research questions that can be tested. No blueprint exists of the procedures that should to be followed when conducting a case study. Instead, the designs are **flexible** and often **responsive** to the demands and circumstances of the research problem.

A case study is guided to obtain a specific desired outcome (rather than to test a causal hypothesis), by answering an **evaluative** research question such as:

*Did the teachers' communication skills improve during the course of the training programme?*

With individuals, the desired outcome (objective) could be a change in a subject's life style (e.g. to apply safe sex); with groups, it could be to improve their communication skills; and with community practice, it could be to create employment opportunities. A single-system design is applicable when we look for what is special and different, such as what characterises the community and its values, or what distinguishes the case or group. Measurements of outcomes are normally based on one or more of the following:

- self-report measurements (e.g. questionnaires);
- interviews; and/or
- observations.

The application of these techniques and methods indicates that a case study is often selected when conducting field observations, with the objective of collecting qualitative information. Single-system designs need not be based on a future orientation, but can – initially – focus on investigating and describing present conditions, behaviours or attitudes.

Some researchers treat a case study as a type of experiment. However, it is not a true experiment, because there is no comparison or control group. Because the results of case studies could be due to subjects' reaction to the measurement, the research setting and other threats to internal and external validity (*see* Unit 2), such findings cannot be generalised to a wider population. In fact, when such threats to internal and external validity do apply to a particular case study, this also means that it cannot be replicated.

Nevertheless, case studies, are often selected because of the following **advantages**:

**Gestalt:**
a whole

- A case study enables a researcher to build a Gestalt about the single system, based on various data sources.
- A case study is useful to investigate people's experiences of making adjustments, such as those being made in South African organisations on the basis of affirmative action and employment equity regulations.

**development:**
in the context of a single-system design, this focus is called a case history

- A case study can be used to describe processes of development, such as speech development in children, or the improvement of teachers' communication skills after a series of training sessions.
- Case studies are flexible in that the researcher can structure the design according to the available money, time and subjects, and the social setting.

This last advantage is probably the most important of a single-system design, because it can be planned to accommodate the distinctive nature of the research problem and objective of the study.

We have elected to categorise case studies in so-called 'controlled' environments, mainly because of the control the researcher has over determining the parameters and extent of the design. When compared with conducting a **survey**, the distinguishing feature of a case study is the **intensity** and **depth** of information collected.

## 4.2.2    Group designs

Experimental research based on a group design involves manipulating the independent variable or variables, and is conducted in a controlled environment or setting. As indicated in section 4.1, many different designs can be distinguished. However, we focus on the following three designs, because they are the most basic and widely used:

- pre-test-post-test control-group design;
- post-test-only control-group design; and
- factorial design.

Table 4.1 contains letters of the alphabet that are used as notation for experimental research designs.

| TABLE 4.1: Notation for experimental research designs | |
| --- | --- |
| $R$ | Random sample from a population and random assignment (or selection) of units of analysis to a group. |
| $O_1$ | The first measurement of the dependent variable (or effect). |
| $X$ | The independent variable (cause or stimulus). |
| $O_2$ | The second measurement of the dependent variable (or effect) |

**pre-post test design:**
an abbreviation for pre-test-post-test control-group design

**post-test-only design:**
an abbreviation for post-test-only control-group design

**absence:**
in experimental research: the control group receives no manipulation

**covariance:**
a statistical analysis to compensate for differences between groups

**randomisation:**
a process of assigning individuals to experimental and control groups, so that the groups are equivalent

**Pre-post test designs** and **post-test-only** designs provide a control (or comparison) group. The control group's and experimental group's experiences are identical, except that they are exposed to different levels of the (manipulated) independent variable. These levels can be a different type of manipulation or the level of absence.

The objective of these designs is to look for changes in the dependent variable and, more specifically, **comparative differences** between the experimental group and the control group. In other words, both groups are exposed to the same conditions, **except** for the effects produced by the different levels of the independent variable. If the hypothesis is to test a covariance between the independent and dependent variable (*see* Unit 2), then the covariance can be tested statistically.

| TABLE 4.2: Notation for the pre-post test design | | | | |
| --- | --- | --- | --- | --- |
| $R$: | $O_1$ | $X$ | $O_2$ | (experimental group) |
| $R$: | $O_1$ | | $O_2$ | control group) |

Subjects are randomly assigned to experimental and control groups, and if the two groups score similarly during the pre-manipulation measurement, we can be confident of randomisation (an important requirement when conducting experiments).

The **pre-post test design** enables us to compare the following groups:
- before-and-after comparisons within the experimental group;
- before-and-after comparisons within the control group;
- before-and-after comparisons between the experimental and control groups.

The treatment, or independent variable, is given to the experimental group after the pre-test ($O_1$) and before the post-test ($O_2$). The absence of $X$ for the control group means that the treatment is not given to the group. Table 4.3 summarises a hypothetical example of results that illustrate the use of a pre-post test design.

**TABLE 4.3:** Subjects' outcomes per experimental versus control group

| Group | Pre-test ($O_1$) | Post-test ($O_2$) | Difference ($O_1 - O_2$) |
|---|---|---|---|
| Experimental | 30 | 58 | - 28 |
| Control | 31 | 33 | - 2 |

**equivalence:** equal in terms of the variables that are important to the study

The pre-test shows that the results for the experimental group and the control group are very similar, which indicates their equivalence. For example, both groups are asked to rate (using a Likert scale) the degree to which they would support a political party. Almost the same percentages (30% and 31%) rate very strong support for the party. The experimental group is exposed to a number of videotaped speeches made by the leader of the party over a period of time, as independent variable (or treatment), after which 58% of the group rated very strong support for the party – a difference of 28%. As the control group was not exposed to the videotapes ($X$), we would not expect their post-test results to differ appreciably.

A **post-test-only design** differs from a pre-post test design in the absence of a pre-manipulation measurement of the control group.

**TABLE 4.4:** Notation for the post-test-only design

| R: | | X | $O_1$ | (experimental group) |
|---|---|---|---|---|
| R: | | | $O_1$ | (control group) |

The post-test-only design only provides for a comparison of the experimental group and the control group after the manipulation of the independent variable ($X$). As illustrated in Table 4.4, the control group is unexposed to $X$. Suppose our objective is to test the effects of a television advertisement on consumers' intention to buy a perfume. We would follow this procedure:

- Randomly select two groups of consumers.
- The experimental group is exposed to the television advertisement and takes the post-test.
- The control group is not exposed to the advertisement and takes the same post-test.

In the absence of a pre-test, the equivalence of the experimental and control groups cannot be confirmed. Nevertheless, $R$ enhances equivalence. This design is often used when it is not possible to conduct a pre-test, or in situations were a pre-test is expected to have a strong influence on the post-test results.

The situation sometimes arises where we want to test two or more independent variables ($X_1, X_2, X_3, X_4, X_5,$ ... etc.) and not a single independent variable. There are many different designs that involve multiple independent variables. We deal with the most common one: **factorial designs**.

In the post-test-only design, the independent variable was either present or absent. Assume that the marketing team of the perfume company wants to determine whether another factor (e.g. smelling the perfume) will have a different effect on consumers' intention to buy the perfume, compared with the television advertisement. Table 4.5 summarises the construction of such a factorial design.

**TABLE 4.5:** A factorial design with two independent variables

|  | No sample of perfume | ($X_2$) Sample of perfume |
|---|---|---|
| Not exposed to television advertisement | Group 1<br>(Control group)<br>Measure intention to buy. | Group 2<br>(Experimental group)<br>Measure intention to buy. |
| Exposed to television advertisement ($X_1$) | Group 3<br>(Experimental group)<br>Measure intention to buy. | Group 4<br>(Experimental group)<br>Measure intention to buy. |

The example in Table 4.5 contains four groups – each receiving a different combination of levels of the independent variables:

- Group 1 serves as control group, because it is not exposed to the television advertisement and it does not get to sample (smell-test) the perfume. The marketing team can regard this group's intention to buy the perfume as an indication of consumers' average purchasing behaviour (in the absence of an advertisement and actually smell-testing the perfume).
- Group 2 (experimental group) is not exposed to the television advertisement, but it does get to sample the perfume.
- Group 3 (experimental group) is exposed to the television advertisement, but does not get to sample the perfume.
- Group 4 (experimental group) is exposed to both the television advertisement and to sampling the perfume.

If we decided to use a pre-post test design, the notation would read:

| Group 1: | R: | $O_1$ | | | $O_2$ |
|----------|-----|-------|-------|-------|-------|
| Group 2: | R: | $O_1$ | $X_2$ | | $O_2$ |
| Group 3: | R: | $O_1$ | | $X_1$ | $O_2$ |
| Group 4: | R: | $O_1$ | $X_1$ | $X_2$ | $O_2$ |

Covariance (statistical tests) can be used to differentiate the effects of:

- $X_1$ (the television advertisement) on Groups 3 and 4, which should not be present in Groups 1 and 2; and
- $X_2$ (a sample of the perfume) on Groups 2 and 4, which should not be present in Groups 1 and 3.

A factorial design therefore enables us to investigate the effect an independent variable has on a dependent variable, and to investigate the interactional effects of more than one independent variable on one or more dependent variables.

## 4.2.3  Control over the research environment

If a research problem requires data to be collected in controlled environments, the design that is selected should be suitable and reflect both the conceptual and empirical basis for the change hypothesised. (Other applications of these designs are included in Unit 5.)

It would only make sense to select an experimental design if we can control the threats to internal and external validity. One of the advantages of an experimental design is its **internal** validity, because of the control a researcher can place on extraneous variables. Threats to validity, such as maturation and reactivity, were discussed in Unit 2. The following are **controls** that apply specifically to experimental designs:

- Ensuring that groups are **equivalent**. The similarity can be obtained either by randomisation or by matching. Randomisation occurs when each individual in the population has an equal chance of being assigned either to the experimental group or to the control group. Whereas matching takes place on the basis of characteristics such as gender, age, socio-economic status, or educational level, one subject is assigned to the experimental group, and a subject with matching characteristics is assigned to the control group.

**matching:** assigning subjects to experimental and control groups based on similar characteristics, for example, gender and age

- Ensuring that **conditions** are **similar** for both the control group and the experimental group, except for the different level of the independent variable.

- Ensuring that the **conditions** of the experiment are representative of conditions in the **natural** world (which is often not possible). For example, conducting tasting tests of breakfast cereals in an artificial setting, such as a company's research laboratory, differs from the situations in which we usually have breakfast. Every effort should be made to arrange the research setting in such a way that it simulates conditions in the real world. Depending on the nature of the experiment, such arrangements may include the physical setting, seating arrangements, materials used and even the time of the day.

External validity will be further enhanced if an experiment is repeated several times, in a longitudinal time dimension.

### *EXECUTIVE SUMMARY:*
### RESEARCH IN CONTROLLED ENVIRONMENTS

1. Single-system designs.
2. Group designs:
   - Pre-test-post-test control-group designs;
   - Post-test-only control-group designs;
   - Factorial designs.
3. Control over the research environment.

The research designs outlined above are the simplest and concentrate on the manipulation of the independent variable. A number of different designs are available to meet the specialised needs of communication researchers. For further information about these designs, refer to the suggested reading list at the end of this unit.

## 4.3 Conducting research in semi-controlled environments

Research in which the independent variable can be manipulated, but in which the setting is not necessarily controlled, usually involves the use of surveys and interviews. The reason for grouping these methods under the heading 'semi-controlled environments' is because varying levels of control can be applied. For example, a researcher may control the measuring instrument (e.g. the design of a self-administered questionnaire), but not the responses of the people who fill in the questionnaire.

**contemporary population:** individuals who are currently alive and can be questioned

When conducting a survey or interviews, we collect data from a contemporary population. Although the research design is a present orientation, features of the present can be combined with the past and the future. Subjects can be asked to recall past behaviour, and they can be asked their opinions to predict (hypothetical) future behaviour.

## 4.3.1   Surveys

A survey enables us to collect large amounts of data about variables, such as people's lifestyles, attitudes, demographics and motives. Such data collection is relatively inexpensive, may occur in realistic settings, and is not necessarily limited by geographic boundaries.

The types of surveys are generally classified as: mail surveys, computer-administered surveys, group-administered surveys, telephone surveys and personal (or face-to-face) surveys. The most important differences of these types of surveys are summarised in Table 4.6.

### *Mail surveys and computer-administered surveys*

**self-administered
questionnaire:**
a questionnaire
that respondents
fill in on their own

In a mail survey, a self-administered questionnaire is sent to individuals in the sample, which they fill in and return by a given date. A technologically more advanced version of mail surveys is to send respondents computer disks that contain a self-administered questionnaire (DBM survey), which they complete on their personal computers.

**DBM survey:**
disk-by-mail
survey

These two types of survey differ from the others in that there is no direct contact between the researcher and the respondents. Consequently, no opportunity exists to clarify questions or queries that a respondent may have, the respondent cannot be encouraged or convinced to cooperate, and no follow-up questions may be asked. The use of a self-administered questionnaire also implies that certain individuals in the sample may not be able to answer the questions, either due to unfamiliarity with the language used in the questionnaire, or illiteracy. In addition to the characteristics summarised in Table 4.6, a mail survey enables us to reach respondents whom we might not be able to visit personally or contact via telephone.

### *Group-administered surveys*

In a group-administered survey, questions are administered directly to a sample of individuals as a group, during one session. The term 'questions' refers to a self-administered questionnaire, or verbal questions-and-answers, which may include respondents' evaluations of audio or audiovisual material. The locality of a group-administered survey varies from a school hall to a natural (field) setting, depending on the objective of the study and the sampling procedure used.

**TABLE 4.6:** Characteristics of different types of surveys

| TYPE OF SURVEY | STRENGTHS | LIMITATIONS |
|---|---|---|
| Mail | <ul><li>Low cost per respondent.</li><li>Large sample can be drawn.</li><li>Wide areas can be covered.</li><li>Responses can be standardised.</li><li>Best method for sensitive topics.</li></ul> | <ul><li>Low response rate.</li><li>Error by respondents.</li><li>Not always a representative sample.</li><li>Data-collection time is long.</li><li>Cannot ask follow-up questions.</li></ul> |
| Computer-administered | <ul><li>Comparative costs are medium.</li><li>High response rate.</li><li>Automatic data collection and entry.</li></ul> | <ul><li>Difficult to draw a representative sample.</li><li>Respondents must have a computer.</li><li>Cannot ask follow-up questions.</li></ul> |
| Group-administered | <ul><li>Comparative costs are low.</li><li>High response rate.</li><li>Data-collection time is short.</li><li>Responses can be standardised.</li><li>Researcher can answer questions from respondents.</li></ul> | <ul><li>Cannot draw a representative sample.</li><li>Cannot ask follow-up questions.</li><li>Respondents are not anonymous (but responses can be kept anonymous and confidential).</li></ul> |
| Telephone | <ul><li>Comparative costs are medium.</li><li>High response rate.</li><li>Data-collection time is short.</li><li>Researcher can answer questions from respondents.</li><li>Researcher can ask follow-up questions.</li><li>Respondents do not have to be literate.</li></ul> | <ul><li>Easier to draw a sample, but is not necessarily representative.</li><li>Time can limit the interview.</li><li>Respondents are not anonymous (but responses can be kept anonymous and confidential).</li></ul> |
| Personal | <ul><li>Medium response rate.</li><li>Rapport between researcher and respondents can be established.</li><li>Researcher can answer questions from respondents.</li><li>Researcher can ask follow-up questions.</li><li>Respondents do not have to be literate.</li></ul> | <ul><li>Difficult to draw a representative sample.</li><li>Comparative costs are high.</li><li>Data-collection time is long.</li><li>Difficult to standardise responses.</li><li>Respondents are not anonymous (but responses can be kept anonymous and confidential).</li></ul> |

In addition to the characteristics listed in Table 4.6, this type of survey enables the researcher to explain the objective of the survey and to answer any questions that may arise. The main disadvantage is that we cannot easily draw a sample that represents a diverse population, to assemble at one place, at the same time, which can result in drawing a convenience sample.

### Telephone surveys

During a telephone survey, the researcher (usually a panel of interviewers) directly addresses questions to the respondent over the telephone. In addition to the speed with which data can be collected, the fact that respondents do not have much time to think about their answers can increase the control over and accuracy of responses. In addition to the characteristics listed in Table 4.6, a major disadvantage of telephone surveys is that the sample is limited to respondents who have access to a telephone. When compared with personal interviews, an added disadvantage is that interviewers cannot observe a respondent's nonverbal behaviour.

### Personal surveys

**aided-recall techniques:** respondents are shown something (e.g. an advertisement) that might help them to remember

Face-to-face interviews are conducted with a respondent during a personal interview, either at the respondent's home or work, or in a field location. Unlike the other survey methods, personal interviews have a specific advantage in that a respondent can be motivated to participate. In addition to asking questions, other visual and measurement aids can be used, such as photographs, videotapes, a sample magazine layout, or product packaging mock-ups. Aided-recall technique applications are further discussed in Unit 5 and Unit 6.

## 4.3.2 Compiling a self-administered questionnaire

Collecting data via a self-administered questionnaire (by mail or by computer) means that the researcher is not present. When designing such a questionnaire, we have to give careful attention to wording the items, and the types of items formulated, (*see* Unit 3), including the formatting and pre-coding of the questionnaire.

## *Formatting the questionnaire*

The first page of a self-administered questionnaire must contain an **introduction**. This often takes the form of an introductory letter that identifies the sponsor, institution or person who is undertaking the survey, and is aimed at persuading the respondent to fill in and return the questionnaire by a specified date. Returning the questionnaire must be made as easy as possible – for example, by enclosing a stamped, self-addressed envelope. According to Wimmer and Dominick (1997:146) we should keep these six principles in mind when writing a successful introduction: it 'should be short, realistically worded, nonthreatening, serious, neutral, and pleasant, but firm'. Apart from stressing the importance of the survey, the introduction must also give respondents the assurance of confidentiality and anonymity.

The ethical requirement of obtaining informed consent from respondents before collecting data is virtually impossible. Therefore, the introductory letter should include information about voluntary participation and that if a respondent returns a completed questionnaire, this will be taken as an indication of informed consent. In this sense, the introductory letter fulfils the same functions as a **debriefing interview** (*see* section 4.4.1).

The **order** in which the questions and statements are arranged in a questionnaire could influence individual responses and the findings of a survey. It is therefore important that we develop and maintain a level of sensitivity to the problem, especially if the question order is a particular issue. In the absence of *golden rules* to solve this potential problem, the following three general guidelines can be followed when structuring the format:

**funnel pattern:** in a questionnaire: start with general questions, followed by specific questions

**warm-up questions:** general questions that serve as introduction to the topic

- **Use a logical sequence.** One example of a logical sequence is to use a **funnel pattern**. Questions about respondents' exposure to mass media in general can be followed by detailed questions about a specific medium, such as television, followed by more specific questions about genres or individual programme types. By using a funnel pattern, the more general questions simultaneously function as warm-up questions for the more detailed ones that follow. Asking the questions in a logical order also means that a question about, for example, how much time a respondent spends listening to a radio station, must *follow* (and not precede) a question to determine *whether* he or she actually listens to the station.

**inverted funnel pattern:**
start with specific questions, followed by general questions

- Another logical sequence, called an **inverted** funnel pattern, is based on the argument 'that specific questions are easier to answer and therefore more motivating for respondents' (Smith 1988:228). Apart from encouraging respondents to respond, the inverted funnel pattern is also useful when general questions are too broad to obtain meaningful answers.

- **Group questions on similar topics.** Concern about the possibility that a respondent will repeat similar views towards an issue (reflecting earlier answers) may tempt us to randomise items (i.e. **not** group them together). Babbie (1990:141) warns against this practice, arguing that randomising items 'will probably strike respondents as chaotic and worthless … [and] … they will have difficulty answering … since they must continually switch their attention from one topic to another'. A possible solution to ordering questions lies in applying an alternative-forms reliability test. By doing this, we can determine whether the grouping of questions that dealt with similar topics had an effect on the responses.

**alternative-forms reliability tests:**
compiling and pre-testing two versions of the same questionnaire

- **Ask demographic characteristics at the end.** Two reasons are offered for asking details, such as age, home ownership, occupation, marital status and gender at the end of a questionnaire. Being faced with such questions at the beginning of a questionnaire may result in it heading straight into a wastepaper basket. The respondent will regard it as yet another routine survey. Secondly, a respondent may become tired towards the end of a questionnaire and not fill in the last page. The general guideline is therefore that, unless these characteristics are **essential** to a survey, ask them at the end of a self-administered questionnaire. Research for advertising and mass-media research, such as planning a new series of television programmes, are examples of studies in which respondents' demographic details are essential.

Irrespective of the combination of questions and statements used, or the types of questions asked, and/or whether a funnel or inverted funnel pattern is used, it is best to run a pilot test or trial survey.

**pilot test:**
research on a small scale, prior to the main study (e.g. to test the measuring instrument)

Test the instructions and actual items on a pilot sample of between 40 and 50 respondents selected from the accessible population. During this test and revision stage, it is also worthwhile to consider using an expert-jury panel or a focus-group interview.

### Pre-coding the questionnaire

**pre-coding:**
numerals, as data-
processing codes,
that represent
possible options
are placed in the
right-hand margin

Pre-coding a self-administered questionnaire is an important part of compiling a questionnaire, because it facilitates the eventual analysis and processing of data via tabulation or using a statistical package. **Closed-ended** items are easier to pre-code, because of the fixed number of options. For example, in the inventory question in Unit 3, section 3.4.2, the [4:1−9] means that the responses will be entered on line or card 4, in columns 1 to 9, and such pre-coding demonstrates that we make provision for a respondent to tick all nine options.

In the matrix question in Unit 3, section 3.4.2, we pre-coded items 31, 32, 33 and 34 separately. In other words, if a respondent selects '*strongly agree*' as a response to item 31, then the numeral (1) will be entered on line 4, column 10. If a respondent selects '*strongly disagree*', numeral (5) will be entered on line 4, column 10. Numerical codes can be manually entered and then scanned or typed into a computer program.

**scanned:**
read

Pre-coding **open-ended** questions is difficult because written responses have to be examined and classified in categories by a trained coder, after the questionnaire has been returned. This procedure is discussed below in section 4.5. Since the number of categories is not necessarily known in advance, sufficient columns must be pre-coded or allocated, such as [4:00−99] − making provision for 99 different categories. If we know in advance that an open-ended item will be coded into *positive suggestions*, *neutral responses*, *negative opinions* and *no responses*, then we need only make provision for four columns.

## 4.3.3 Interviews

An interview is a transitory relationship between an interviewer and an interviewee. It is transitory in terms of its duration and the question-and-answer type of conversational exchange. The responses to interviews are recorded by the interviewer ticking off a checklist, making notes, and/or using an audio- or videotape. An **interview schedule** or **interview guide** used during a telephone or personal interview contains both open-ended and closed-ended items. The order in which questions are to be asked during a telephone or personal interview is also an important part of structuring an interview because this can:

- influence the pace and amount of time required to complete the interview;
- bias respondents to give a particular answer, especially if prior questions have brought an issue to their attention of which they were previously unaware; and
- contribute to a respondent losing interest or becoming bored with the interview.

**throw-away questions:** questions that are not coded or analysed

To counteract the fatigue or boredom factor and to keep respondents' interest, it is useful to include some throw-away questions. For example, *What is your favourite hobby?* could function as a break (and a throw-away question) during an interview with children to determine their reading habits.

Based on the types of questions asked, and the extent to which the interviewer interacts with a respondent, we can distinguish three types of interviews: structured interviews, partially structured interviews and unstructured interviews.

## Structured and standardised interviews

An **interview guide** or **interview schedule** is compiled with two sets of instructions. One set of instructions is compiled for the interviewer showing him or her how to proceed during the interview. This is not read to the respondent. For example, the interview schedule could contain the following instruction:

*If the respondent answers* **yes** *(to above question) ask the following:...*

**standardised:** using the same wording during each interview

The second set of instructions (questions) can be read verbatim, from the beginning to the end of the interview. In a structured interview, standardised questions are asked in a predetermined order, with minimal interaction between the interviewer and the respondent.

The **advantages** of using standardised questions and scales in a structured interview are:
- Structured questions require the interviewer simply to cross or check one of the answers and need no written notes.
- The procedure is standardised, which makes the task of tabulating, coding, transcribing and analysing the responses easier.
- Less time is used for the administration of the survey as a whole.

**paired-comparison technique:** subjects assess two options and select one

A paired-comparison technique is a particularly useful variation of the types of closed-ended questions discussed in Unit 3. For example, if we had to ask respondents to rank 20 advertisements based on their credibility, this may be a difficult – if not impossible – task. Instead, we can present respondents with two advertisements at a time, of which they have to rate one as being more credible. By repeating the paired comparison with all 20 advertisements, we can rank the 20 advertisements in order of credibility by counting the number of times each one was selected by the respondent.

Having had several practice rounds of conducting an interview to deal with any contingencies that might occur, the following are additional guidelines worth following when asking questions during a **structured** interview (Stacks and Hocking 1992:191-195):

- use the questions in the interview schedule;
- use the exact wording of the questions;
- ask every question in the order they appear in the questionnaire;
- repeat the questions a respondent misunderstands or misinterprets.

In addition to controlling the question order and limiting the research problem to be investigated, the researcher can control the setting in which the interview is conducted, and the demographic characteristics of both the interviewers and sampled interviewees.

## *Partially structured interviews*

The interview schedule for a partially structured interview also contains standardised questions and/or a list of topics. However, the interviewer is free to deviate and ask follow-up or probing questions based on the respondent's replies – especially if the replies are unclear or incomplete. This type of interview provides the interviewer with latitude to move in unanticipated directions, which is why it is used in **focus-group** interviews. Unlike a structured interview, the interviewer interacts with the respondent.

**focus-group interviews:** interviews conducted with a group of between six and twelve people

## *Unstructured interviews*

Although we acknowledge that an interview cannot be entirely unstructured, we differentiate it from the other two on the basis of the role fulfilled by the interviewer and the objective of such an interview.

During an unstructured interview, the role of the interviewer is to create an atmosphere of trust and to encourage the respondent to talk about a particular (broad) topic. Although this is a time-consuming process, it allows the interviewer to discover the respondent's ideas, views, suggestions and queries.

One of the main objectives of using an unstructured interview is to obtain insight and depth into the topic being investigated, and to allow the respondent more freedom in responding in his or her own words. In such cases, the objective is usually exploratory. Projective techniques (*see also* Unit 5) are adaptations of unstructured interviews.

**projective techniques:** interview techniques in which respondents project their own ideas or viewpoints – for example, to complete a narrative

Despite the above advantages, it is very difficult to quantify responses that differ both in types of topic dealt with and in the magnitude of emotions expressed. The main disadvantage of an unstructured interview and/or using mainly open-ended questions is that the interviewer has to somehow record everything that has been said.

Contrary to the absence of an interviewer when we use a self-administered questionnaire in a mail survey, the interviewer is **present** when we conduct an interview over the telephone or in a face-to-face setting. The extent to which assistants are trained as interviewers, will have a direct influence on **how** the data is collected and on the ultimate findings.

Given that focus-group interviews are frequently used in communication research – especially in field research – we deal with its procedures in more detail below.

## 4.3.4  Focus groups

Interviews conducted in small groups (focus-group interviews) can include different interviewing techniques and can take place in different settings. This type of interviewing has become popular in recent years, because it provides data that is rich in ideas and provides opinions and attitudes from the subjects' point of view. Depending on the objective of the research study, focus-group interviews can be combined with in-depth interviews, observations, surveys and even experimental designs.

The usefulness of a focus-group interview is demonstrated by the variety of research **objectives** to which it can be applied, such as:

- gathering data on a specific research problem (e.g. to determine the contributions made by non-governmental organisations to reconstruction and development programmes);
- testing a previously formulated research question or hypothesis;
- formulating new research questions or hypotheses on the basis of unanticipated responses;
- pilot-testing a new product (e.g. a new perfume);
- testing the validity of a measuring instrument, by using the group as an expert jury;
- identifying problems that audience members have with existing television programme schedules, or the content of a specific radio station, or the content of a particular newspaper;
- probing the effectiveness of advertising (or any other particular genre, such as news reportage) in one of the mass media;
- probing and solving problems in organisational communication;
- seeking input from community leaders in development communication;
- probing the effects of an advertising campaign by a political party, prior to and after a particular election; and/or
- determining mass-media audiences' attitudes, perceptions, frames of reference and behaviour (viewing, reading, listening) patterns.

## Procedures followed in focus groups

**moderator:**
term used for an interviewer, leader or facilitator of a focus group

The **procedures** followed are summarised in general terms. First, the researcher, as moderator, delineates the research topic or problem in general terms (e.g. *What perceptions do the employees in a specific organisation hold regarding management?)*, or in specific terms *(e.g. … perceptions of management's position regarding affirmative action; … regarding the workplace as a learning environment; … regarding the redress of blacks, women and disabled people through education).*

**moderator guide:**
topics and questions that direct discussions in a focus group

These topics and issues are used as a **moderator guide**. If questions are formulated in advance, they are usually open-ended to facilitate responses from the respondents' point of view. A moderator is, however, not restricted to the moderator guide and, as a critical listener, would ask follow-up questions when respondents raise relevant points.

Secondly, a group of between six and twelve people are **sampled**, usually based on a combination of a purposeful sample and a convenience sample. Depending on the objective of the research study, we would purposefully sample the subjects in such a way that they have shared some common experience, so that the interview focuses on the effects of the experience from the subjects' perspective. To determine the composition of a focus group, the objective, main problem, subproblems, assumptions and research question(s) should be used to guide the identification of the population parameters of the sampled group. We should, nevertheless, always question whether it is advisable to combine men and women, or people from different age groups, or members from the same family, or people with different life styles, or people with different first-language preferences in one focus group. A group representing diverse interests or characteristics is likely to contribute to conflict and division, rather than complimentary discussions. Although convenience and purposeful samples limit the external validity of the findings, they are often used because of the costs involved. It is also advisable to recruit more than twelve people to obtain a realised sample of between six and twelve people.

**realised sample:**
in focus groups, the subjects who actually attend

**screener:**
a questionnaire used to select individuals to attend a focus group

The use of a screener is important if we want to ensure that the individuals who are identified and recruited for the focus group match the desired population parameters (age, gender, knowledge of the topic, etc.). Once the sample has been drawn, subjects have to be **briefed** about the objective and duration of the interview (usually two or three hours), so that they can fill in informed-consent forms, and so that payment for their participation can be negotiated. If the research requires a record of respondents' demographic characteristics, a pre-group questionnaire can be compiled and filled in by respondents.

**informed consent:**
subjects have a full understanding of the implications of the study and agree to participate

**pre-group questionnaire:**
a questionnaire that respondents fill in before the focus group

Thirdly, the group meets at an interview location with comfortable surroundings, which is equipped with recording equipment, such as a one-way mirror, a video camera and/or an audiotape recorder. As an introduction, the moderator usually explains: the objective of the focus group, that there are no correct or incorrect answers, that their viewpoints are apt to differ, and that they are free to speak without being prompted. If a video recording is not used, it is advisable that respondents identify themselves (by mentioning a number or name) when they speak, to facilitate the identification when transcripts of the audiotaped conversations are coded and interpreted.

The success of the focus group depends on a number of factors:

- the date, day and time when it is conducted;
- the nature of the locality or setting;
- the way in which the moderator creates a relaxing atmosphere and allows the conversation to flow naturally;
- the way in which the moderator listens to responses, guides the discussion and promotes interaction between members to cover the topics or issues previously delineated;
- the way in which the moderator exercises self-control, avoids expressing personal viewpoints and avoids commenting on responses from the respondents;
- the way in which the moderator fulfils a regulatory role if the group members include so-called experts that dominate the discussion, or people that ramble on without coming to the point, or people who are shy;
- the gender, age, appearance and verbal language style of the moderator and/or
- the demographic and other characteristics of the respondents or participants.

The last step involves the **transcript** of the group's discussion, a content **analysis** by two or more coders, and drawing **conclusions**. The following are useful sources to consult for details and practical guidelines on conducting focus groups: Krueger (1994), Pitout (1996), Stewart and Shamdasani (1990), Wimmer and Dominick (1997), and Collins (1999).

Irrespective of the objective, it is important to note that focus groups are used to collect **qualitative** (not quantitative) data. (*See* Unit 3 for the use of questioning and observations to collect qualitative data.)

## *Sources of error*

In addition to external or situational factors (e.g. seating arrangements, noise, lighting) that can introduce sources of error, the personal style of the group members can affect the process of conducting a focus group. The following **measurement errors** can be attributed to respondents:

- error due to **social factors** (e.g. to convey a favourable impression to the moderator or other group members; due to the lack of anonymity; and the presence or absence of peers);

- error due to **compliance**, which occurs when a respondent agrees with statements irrespective of their content; and
- error due to **deviation**, which occurs when a respondent has a tendency to give unusual or atypical responses.

A number of **control procedures** can be followed to minimise errors created by respondents' personal styles. In section 4.3.3, we mentioned the use of 'throw-away' questions. In a similar way, socially neutral questions or topics can be introduced to counteract atypical responses. Ways in which to minimise compliance or the effect of social factors include developing rapport with respondents, stimulating interest in the topics, spending time getting acquainted and reducing anxiety.

**rapport:**
companionship

Co-operation and increased motivation may be obtained by selecting a setting that is conducive to the topic and population parameters (e.g. conducting interviews with husbands separate from wives when the topic deals with marriage). Another control procedure would be to conceal the true objective of the focus group, keeping in mind the ethical implications and the importance of conducting a debriefing interview.

## 4.3.5 Problems related to implementation procedures

When conducting a survey and/or interviews, we are investigating people's attitudes, feelings, knowledge or views. The **validity** of these methods can be minimised due to several factors, the first of which could be grouped together and called extraneous factors. For example, during group administrations and focus-group interviews, extraneous factors such as other people's presence may cause respondents to respond differently than they might have done during a personal (individual) interview. The characteristics and behaviour of the data collector, interviewer or moderator can also influence a respondent to react to the person conducting the interview, rather than focusing on what is being asked. In a telephone interview, such characteristics include the data collector's tone of voice, rude interruptions, speaking indistinctly or speaking with a marked accent. These characteristics, in addition to the interviewer's or moderator's appearance and dress, also apply in personal interviews, group administrations and focus groups.

**extraneous
factors:**
external or
additional
variables that
influence the
research process

In the application of DBM surveys, Wimmer and Dominick (1997:159) raise three questions regarding their reliability and validity: 'Who actually completes the surveys? Are responses more or less as accurate as those provided to interviewers or in typical mail interviews? How does the novelty of the approach affect respondents?'

One of the major problems experienced in survey research, is that of total non-response. This could be due to refusal to be interviewed telephonically or personally, refusal to fill in and/or return a questionnaire, not being at home when an interviewer calls, or not attending a focus group (which could be due to a variety of personal reasons). Non-response can also occur in the form of item non-response – for example, when a respondent omits to answer all the questions on a self-administered questionnaire. Although we may have paid particular attention to sampling procedures and pre-testing the questionnaire, moderator guide or interview schedule, a total non-response will jeopardise **accuracy** and the **confidence level** of the findings (*see* Unit 3).

**total non-response:** no response is received from a subject

**item non-response:** some information is not collected or obtained from each subject

**Inter-interviewer variability** can also create a problem, especially in unstructured interviews. This is because different interviewers may differ in the way they obtain and maintain rapport with respondents, the way in which they project a credible image, the way in which they respond to answers, and the way in which they record responses.

**inter-interviewer variability:** using more than one interviewer in a study

Although some degree of efficiency can be obtained when an interview context is structured, the limitation of **time** is an integral part of conducting interviews. An interviewer can undertake more interviews in a day if a tape recording is used. However, it is estimated that it takes up to nine hours to effectively transcribe an hour of recorded interview material.

**transcribe:** to reproduce taped speech exactly in written or typed form

Against the background of these potential problems, the following general guidelines are worth considering when planning and implementing **survey** research or when conducting **interviews** (Hsia 1988:150-151; Wimmer and Dominick 1997:162-163; Fraenkel and Wallen 1993:356-358):

1. Relate the questions to the objective and research question (or hypothesis) of the study. For example, if details about a respondent's age or religious affiliation are not important demographic characteristics, these should not be asked.

2. Formulate questions that are neutral, direct, clear and unambiguous, keeping in mind all the problems that the actual wording of questions can cause (see Unit 3).
3. Try to make the conditions under which the questionnaire is administered, or the interview conducted, as similar as possible for each person in the sample.
4. Use structured questions as much as possible, to facilitate subsequent coding and analysis.
5. Train interviewers for personal and telephone interviews, and moderators for focus-group interviews, how to ask structured and unstructured questions, and especially how to formulate follow-up questions.
6. Pre-test the questions, the structure (and, in the case of a printed questionnaire, the format, layout and pre-coding) and where necessary revise, change and/or remove questions that are irrelevant, vague or superfluous.
7. Pre-test the time it takes to conduct the interview or to fill in the questionnaire.
8. Obtain a full record (e.g. by means of a tape recording) of respondents' answers.

---

## *EXECUTIVE SUMMARY:*
## CONDUCTING RESEARCH IN SEMI-CONTROLLED ENVIRONMENTS

1 Surveys:
   - Mail surveys;
   - Computer-administered surveys;
   - Group-administered surveys;
   - Telephone surveys;
   - Personal surveys.

2 Compiling a self-administered questionnaire:
   - Formatting the questionnaire;
   - Pre-coding the questionnaire.

3 Interviews:
   - Structured and standardised interviews;
   - Partially structured interviews;
   - Unstructured interviews.

4 Focus groups.

5 Problems related to implementation procedures.

---

### Self-evaluation and portfolio task

4.3  You have been approached by the principal of a primary school in your community to investigate the following problem:

*Some learners are not performing as expected when comparing their poor examination results with their IQ and aptitude tests. The principal suspects that these poor performances can be ascribed to learners' home circumstances and poor communication between parents and children. Parents have agreed to become involved in a research study.*

Select one of the following data-collection methods or techniques, and describe the steps you would follow when preparing to investigate the problem:
- mail survey;
- group-administered survey;
- telephone survey;
- personal survey (interviews);
- computer-administered survey;
- focus groups.

## 4.4 Conducting research in natural environments

Research conducted in natural environments involves a researcher fulfilling the role of observer and, in certain cases, as an observer and participant simultaneously. The external validity of observational designs is usually high, because the variables being observed behave or operate normally and without researcher intervention. In contrast, the internal validity of observational designs is usually low, because:
- the researcher does not systematically manipulate an independent (causal) variable; and
- observations are usually conducted in the field, which means that the researcher cannot control extraneous variables.

**Historical** research, involving content analysis, can also be categorised as taking place in natural environments, because the researcher cannot manipulate variables that have taken place in the past. However, when discussing natural environments, we focus on what is generally referred to as **field** research.

Field research takes place in realistic and natural settings that are not controlled by a researcher. This is why subjects who are available (e.g. at a shopping centre) are usually included in such studies. The use of an availability sample questions the representativeness of the sample, and the extent to which it differs from the general population. In addition to sampling bias, subject mortality is a threat to the external validity of field research (*see* Unit 2). Despite these two threats, the fact that we do not control or manipulate the environment means that the subjects are not prone to reactive effects of the setting.

**subject mortality:**
in field research:
people decline
further
participation

One way in which the threat to external validity can be minimised is to make use of a **field experiment**, such as a post-test-only control-group design. This type of design is often used to test two appeals in an advertisement (*see also* Unit 5). Two groups are randomly selected from a target population, and each one is exposed to a different version of the message. The extent to which they respond positively towards future hypothetical purchasing behaviour is measured. Buying habits are complex forms of behaviours, which are not necessarily the result of exposure to one advertisement. Therefore, such field tests can, at best, measure hypothetical behaviour such as: *Next time you shop, how likely are you to buy this product?*

By introducing some form of control based on sampling and manipulating the independent variable, controlling the threat to external validity means that the research is no longer conducted in a natural setting. Therefore, other threats to validity that are typical of conducting research in controlled environments may also apply (*see* section 4.2).

## 4.4.1 Field observations

In Unit 3, a distinction was made between collecting data via systematic observations and ethnographic observations. The roles that a researcher (as observer) fulfils, depends on the observational method used, the objective of the study and the nature of the setting. These roles are summarised in Table 4.7.

**complete observer:**
also called on-looker observation

Collecting data as a **complete observer** minimises subject reactivity if it is conducted as covert observations. Data-collection devices include hidden cameras, microphones, a one-way mirror, video- and audio-tapes. Not interacting with subjects enables the researcher to

**covert observation:**
subjects are unaware of being observed

concentrate on what is being observed or to discuss observations with a co-observer during the collection process. However, not interacting with subjects also prevents the researcher from collecting in-depth information that explains subjects' behaviour, which is why this role is often used in systematic observations, using an observation schedule (*see* Unit 3). Another limitation of the observer remaining separate from the group being observed, is the difficulty (if not impossibility) for the observer to obtain access in natural settings.

| TABLE 4.7: Roles fulfilled by a researcher as an observer | |
| --- | --- |
| **TYPE OF ROLE WHEN CONDUCTING OBSERVATIONS** | **NATURE OF THE RESEARCHER'S ROLE** |
| Complete observer | Is detached and objective. |
| Observer (as participant) | Participates marginally, but maintains role as researcher. |
| Participant (as observer) | Participates as a member of the group while making observations. |
| Complete participant | Is totally involved (as participant). |

In contrast to complete observations, the remaining three roles are generally called **participant observation** because the researcher becomes involved as a participant. The degree of participation varies from marginal to complete.

When fulfilling the **observer-as-participant** role, the researcher interacts with subjects, but does not take on a role as a group member. The researcher comes to the group or setting as an outside investigator and is regarded by group members as 'the person is present because she is writing a book about ...', or 'the person is present because he is interested in ...'. As the group is aware of the observer's participation, it lends itself to sampling different times, events, and subjects systematically, and is an example of overt observation. Such participation also enables the observer to obtain a more complete view of the group being observed.

**overt observation:** subjects are aware of being observed

Researchers who conduct ethnographic observations, tend to take on the **participant-as-observer** role, in which they live or work together with the group and experience events from the perspective of the

group members. Being a participant can promote building trust and rapport between the researcher and the group, which, in turn, can minimise reactivity on the part of the group. This is a time-consuming process, during which the researcher has to establish new and sometimes problematic participant roles that need to be balanced with the role of observer. Acceptance by the group is not assured, because members know that they are being observed. This awareness can also create the so-called Hawthorne effect, because members of the group know that they are being observed.

**Hawthorne effects:** subjects behave atypically because they are aware that they are being researched

**Complete participant** observations can take place **overtly**. For example, when a public relations officer researches internal communication in an organisation, the members of the organisation know that they are participating in the research. Alternatively, complete participant observations can take place **covertly**. For example, by joining an institution or a group as a new member, the researcher's role or intentions are not known. The role of complete participant has two advantages:

- it can be done covertly, which eliminates reactivity on the part of the subjects; and
- it facilitates the researcher obtaining overt and therefore approved access to certain groups or settings, or − if done covertly − obtaining access to groups or settings to which the researcher could otherwise be denied.

However, as in the case of participant (as observer), being a complete participant creates the possibility of role conflict or identity conflict (between being both a participant and an observer).

Although the above discussion categorises the roles in four types, it is important to note that, especially in ethnographic observations, roles can change during the course of the observations.

**debriefing:** explaining in person or in writing what a study is about and offering additional feedback to subjects

It is generally accepted practice to interview subjects after a study has taken place, during which they are informed about the objectives of the research, given additional information and asked for feedback. These **debriefing interviews** are required of all ethical research, especially if subjects were unaware of being observed. In such cases, informed consent to use the data must also be secured (e.g. by obtaining signed consent forms from subjects). Participants' consent cannot be coerced and they have a right to know what is going to be done with the results, and any possible problems that may result from their participation.

Whatever information is collected during such a debriefing session must also be included in the research report. We have to report not only the number of observations that were made, but also what sampling procedure was used, how access was secured, together with demographic detail, such as the number of people, ages, gender and the duration, dates and times of the observations.

## *Sources of error*

Just as measurement errors have to be minimised by conducting relia- bility and validity tests for measuring instruments, the following errors can also occur due to the reactions of **observers**:

- A **halo effect** occurs when one pleasant (or unpleasant) charac- teristic or action influences the observer's general impression. For example, an observer may have a very favourable impression about the person being observed, because the latter holds a doctoral degree. This favourable impression then 'colours' the observations of the person, which should have been objective and unbiased.
- An **error of leniency** occurs when the observer's rating is too high or is always too favourable.
- An **error of central tendency** occurs when the observer ignores extreme (positive/negative) positions.
- An **error of severity** occurs when the observer's rating is too low or is always unfavourable. This error can also occur in conjunction with or due to a halo effect. For example, if an observer holds a negative attitude towards people who are HIV-positive, that negative attitude could influence unbiased observations of a person who is known to be HIV-positive – even an innocent baby.
- A **contrast error** occurs when the observer evaluates others as being opposite to him-/herself, with reference to a specific characteristic or view point – for example, related to political or religious affiliations.

**pilot tests:**
in observations:
training observers
through
rehearsals

Errors caused by observers' reactions can be minimised by training observers, by conducting pilot tests, and by using more than one

**4**

reflexivity:
continual
monitoring
of the research
process

observer. Techniques, such as reflexivity, triangulation and respondent validation can also be applied to minimise errors. Triangulation can involve checking observations with other sources of data, such as interview data or data collected at different times, settings or from different subjects.

Respondent validation can be undertaken by discussing the observations with the respondents, to check whether the observations correspond with their experience. Alternatively, subjects can be asked to give a written account of their experiences and perceptions. In this way, the researcher also obtains additional information about the perceptions, thoughts or motives of the subjects.

A more detailed application of participatory research (called participatory action research) is discussed in Unit 6, in the contexts of organisational and development communication research.

---

*EXECUTIVE SUMMARY:*
**CONDUCTING RESEARCH IN NATURAL ENVIRONMENTS**

1  Field experiments.

2  Field observations (different forms):
   - Complete observer (covert);
   - Observer-as-participant (overt);
   - Participant-as-observer (overt);
   - Complete participant (overt/covert).

3  Sources of error.

---

Because human behaviour is multidimensional, it is preferable to use more than one method of data collection. The ideal would be to use both observations (e.g. rating of behaviour based on observations) and self-report measures (e.g. self-administered questionnaires).

However, research conducted via observations takes place in settings that are not controlled by the researcher, and in some cases, the independent variable is measured because of natural manipulations. For example, when observing the interaction between health workers and patients in a hospital over a period of time, some patients will become better, whereas others' health will deteriorate. These natural changes cannot be controlled, but can understandably influence patients' interpersonal communication with the health workers.

# 4.5 What to do with the data once collected

In this section, we concentrate on **content analysis** (including the calculation of a **Readability Ease** test) and an introduction to elementary **descriptive statistics**.

## 4.5.1 Content analysis

Content analysis is used in various types of communication research, such as the analysis of mass-media content, transcripts of group discussions, or in organisational communication: the analysis of memos, electronic mail, transcripts of meetings and policy documents.

A common use of content analysis is to record the frequency with which certain symbols or themes appear in messages.

Content analysts have, in the past, used the following **units of analysis**:
- **physical units**, such as the medium of communication (e.g. radio), the number of pages, size and space in print media, time duration in broadcast media, audiovisual codes used in film and television, and nonverbal codes in interpersonal communication;
- **syntactic units**, such as paragraphs, sentences, phrases, clauses or words;
- **thematic units**, which are repeating patterns of propositions or ideas related to issues such as sex, violence, AIDS, equality, gender, or stereotyping based on age, race and disability;
- **propositional units**, such as questions, answers, statements, assertions or arguments.

The requirements of scientific research also apply to quantitative content analysis:

- The specified procedures followed must be **systematic**.
- The criteria or rules used to categorise the content of the text must be impartial and unbiased, to ensure **objectivity** and **validity**. Specified criteria not only enable critics to evaluate the conclusions reached, but also allow subsequent researchers to replicate the study.
- The content must be **quantified** in some manner, usually as numeral values or percentage frequencies.
- The meaning of these proportions or percentages has to be interpreted in the **context** in which the research problem originated.

All the requirements, except the last one, were discussed in Unit 1. To illustrate the importance of a contextual interpretation, let us take an example of employees who keep daily diaries of their communication experiences at work (as part of a communication audit of an organisation; *see* Unit 6).

**internal public:** employees in an organisational setting

The objective of the research is to monitor what effect the introduction of flexitime has on the communication between members of the internal public. A content analysis could reveal that the word conflict (or synonyms for the term) makes up 20% of the total number of words before the introduction of flexitime and 60% of the total number of words after the introduction of flexitime. This indicates that flexitime could be one of the reasons that contributed to an increase in dissension among employees.

The example illustrates an important point that should be kept in mind when doing a content analysis: although content analysis deals with the analysis of **messages**, the interpretation of findings can be 'shifted' to the people's communication behaviour. If messages are compared in terms of the communicator (e.g. to determine mainly who sends messages), such comparison can determine whether it was a single communicator over a longitudinal period of time, a single communicator in different situations, a single communicator but different recipients, or messages received from two or more communicators. Although such interpretations can be deduced, the emphasis and focus remains on analysing the content of the messages as units of analysis.

Some content analyses can be performed by a computer program – for example, scanning messages in a computer text file and summarising the number of times a word or phrase appears. Computers are frequently used to do Readability Ease tests of printed documents. The majority of analyses, however, involve work done by hand and the judgement of an analyst or coder.

The process for conducting a content analysis closely follows the steps discussed in Unit 2 and is therefore not repeated here. However, two steps normally create stumbling blocks, especially for junior researchers, when applying content analysis: sampling, and categorising and coding the data.

## Sampling

Based on the discussion in Unit 3, if we do not analyse all the collected data, we should aim to draw a random sample. However, this is not always possible as the sampling procedure is usually based on the characteristics of the content. Suppose we want to investigate how men and women are portrayed in children's television programmes. *'All children's television programmes'* broadcast on several channels, which make up the population, could result in a population of a few thousand programmes. To draw a representative sample of a homogeneous subgroup, we would have to consider many population parameters. These are just a few: the genre of programmes (for example, formal educational versus non-formal educational), the age of the targeted audience, dates broadcast, on which television stations they are broadcast, production techniques (for example, animated versus live characters), etcetera. Although random sampling is applied, further processes of stratification and drawing proportionate samples from each stratum need to be used. These were discussed in Unit 3.

## Coding or tallying the data

Unit 3 contains examples of observation schedules that were developed for recording observations. A similar type of coding or tally sheet is developed when analysing content. Content **categories** are variables that take on some value when applied in an analysis. They must meet the same requirements as nominal variables – of being mutually exclusive and exhaustive.

**array:**
a list of data ranked from lowest to highest

The first step is to compile a tally sheet to allocate the data to specific categories. Table 3.6, in Unit 3, contains an example of such a tally sheet, which assists the coder to organise the data as a visual summary. Data has to be arranged in a concise and logical order, or as an array.

The next step is to count the number of cases that belong to each category, with the frequency designated as *f*. The frequency is an indication of how often a particular characteristic occurred, such as the number of times the chairperson initiated communication during a meeting. In **qualitative** studies and studies based on nominal levels of measurement, a frequency count is the only quantitative type of data that can be obtained. In addition to constructing an array and counting frequencies, in **quantitative** studies that involve continuous variables (for example age), a frequency distribution can also be constructed.

**frequency distribution:**
the spread of certain characteristics across different categories

For example, to construct a frequency distribution for all men aged 20 and above, we have to construct categories that are mutually exclusive and exhaustive, such as 20-29; 30-39; 40-49, etcetera. The class is the category and the interval is the standard size of each category − for example, 10 years. Frequency distributions in which class intervals are used, can be used to analyse interval data, which can be illustrated in the form of a table, a pie chart, a bar chart or a histogram.

**histogram:**
also called a frequency distribution graph

The coding procedure depends on the level of measurement (nominal, ordinal, interval, ratio) that content categories take on. However, there are generally two scoring procedures: counting and scaling.

**contingency table:**
a four-cell table, displaying two variables in two categories simultaneously

**SPSS-X:**
Statistical Package for the Social Sciences

- **Counting** is appropriate when nominal categories are used, such as *true-false* or *present-absent.* Counting enables us to generate a contingency table and to use cross-tabulation. Cross-tabulation analysis is widely used in advertising and mass-media research, especially since the development of computer programs such as SPSS-X. Although nominal coding is a quick and a straight-forward coding procedure, it does not provide information about the frequency with which content categories occur. Counting the frequency with which a category occurs, using a ratio level of measurement, gives an indication of the relative importance of each category. Table 4.8 illustrates a hypothetical content analysis of the frequency with which photographs of spokespersons repre-senting two political parties have appeared in two Sunday newspapers over a period of a year.

**TABLE 4.8:** An example of a contingency table

| | | CATEGORY: PHOTOGRAPH OF POLITICAL SPOKESPERSON | | |
|---|---|---|---|---|
| | | PARTY A | PARTY B | TOTAL |
| CATEGORY: NEWSPAPER | Sunday News | 27 | 81 | 108 |
| | Sunday Week | 65 | 12 | 77 |
| | Total | 92 | 93 | |

- **Scale scoring** means that each category is assigned a rank or numerical weight (e.g. on a negative-positive scale) by a respondent in an interview or the coder(s) doing the analysis. The average across all respondents/coders are calculated for each category. The advantage of using scale scoring is that the **intensity** and the **valence** of each category can be coded. For example, each photograph of spokespersons for the two political parties can be coded using a three-point scale.

**valence:**
an evaluative
direction – for
example, negative

| 1 | 2 | 3 |
|---|---|---|
| Inferior | Neutral | Superior |

Although scale coding provides more (qualitative) information, the categories have to be defined as concretely as possible, and preferably pre-tested to ensure coder reliability. In the above example, coders could be trained to identify examples of and apply the scale as follows:

| 1. | Inferior | Above eye-level camera shot of the spokesperson |
|---|---|---|
| 2. | Neutral | On eye-level camera shot of the spokesperson |
| 3. | Superior | Below eye-level camera shot of the spokesperson |

Thereafter data from the nominal categories can be presented visually in the form of tables and graphs. In addition to frequency counts, **qualitative** data can be further summarised, based on the recorded tally sheet, as ratios and proportions. We refer to Table 3.5, in Unit 3, to illustrate the latter:

- The **ratio** equals the frequency of A divided by the frequency of B, multiplied by 100 to remove fractions or partials. In Table 3.5, the chairperson initiated the discussion 55 times and responded 17 times. By dividing the number of responses by the number of initiations, multiplied by 100, we have a ratio of 31 responses for every 100 initiations.

- A **proportion** consists of the relation in the size of one category to that of another, which is usually expressed as a percentage. According to Table 3.5, the chairperson communicated a total of 72 times (55 + 17). To calculate the proportion of responses, divide 17 by the total. The proportion of responses from the chairperson would therefore be 23,6%.

## Pre-coded versus post-coded categories

The purpose of a coding scheme is to convert the content (e.g. of a television programme) or responses to questionnaires and interviews into analysable data. When **pre-coded** categories are used, these will be the function of the research problem, the hypotheses or research questions of the study and the nature of the content. (*See* tables 3.6-3.9 in Unit 3, and tables 4.9-4.12 in this unit for examples.) In cases where a content analysis is done of responses to open-ended questions, or of recordings made during observations, these responses have to be coded before they can be allocated to a scale, ranked or counted.

**pre-coded categories:** categories that are defined prior to collecting data

**post-coding:** compiling coding categories after the data has been collected

**intercoder reliability:** two coders code all the data and their judgements are averaged to obtain final coding scores

**edit:** in this context: to delete

The categories used in **post-coding** has to be guided by the nature of the content, the research problem and the hypothesis(-es) or research question(s). Post-coding involves the following procedures: free responses are recorded (e.g. on audiotape), transcribed and only coded thereafter. Such transcripts make it possible to use a second or third coder to establish intercoder reliability (*see* Unit 3). The latter not only applies to transcribed data, but also to videotape recordings. If paralinguistic features are relevant to the analysis (such as the pitch and volume of people's speech) coders could be given the actual audio recording in addition to the transcription. We may be tempted to edit or ignore incomplete sentences, poor grammar or expressions that do not make obvious sense. However, such editing should be avoided, because it may hamper the true impression of how people communicate. Just as the reliability of measurements is raised in Unit 3, the reliability of **coding judgements** is also an issue when conducting a content analysis. If, for example, an interviewer or observer codes or summarises responses during an interview or observation, there is no way to check the **reliability** because there is no tape-based record of the responses.

### Coder training

Just as the training of interviewers and moderators is essential for conducting interviews, the training of coders is also essential to ensure the reliability of a content analysis. Coders should be given detailed definitions and descriptions of the content categories and instructions on how to carry out the coding. They should then analyse a representative sample of the content that they will ultimately analyse, after which an intercoder-reliability test of each content category should be done.

This test not only identifies poor coders, who can be eliminated or retrained, but also simultaneously identifies poorly defined categories or categories that are vague. For example, while testing the above three categories of coding spokesperson photographs, coders may find that additional categories have to be formulated to differentiate between a camera shot taken from the front and a profile shot (taken from the side) – because these shots can convey different meanings.

## 4.5.2  Analysis of verbal communication

Verbal communication, or narrative discourse, may serve informational, persuasive or entertaining functions. Five levels of analyses can be distinguished when describing and interpreting verbal communication:

- A **presentational** analysis of mediated communication. Such analyses can include an investigation of the application of auditory codes used in television, such as different types of address in advertisements.

**stylistic variations:** in terms of verbal language, also called register variations

- An analysis of the **stylistic** aspects of the language used. Stylistic variations often reveal the degree of formality of an occasion, the age, social status and/or occupation of the speaker. For example, if a pregnant woman loses her baby accidentally, it is not unusual for it to be referred to as a *miscarriage*; whereas if the pregnancy were ended voluntarily, this would be called *abortion*. In medical terms, what we called a *miscarriage* would be termed an *abortion*, and what we call *abortion* would be referred to as a *termination*.
- A **structural** analysis of how the message is organised.
- A **thematic** analysis, which consists of a description of the main ideas in messages.
- An **interactional** analysis of how people use messages in different settings.

For illustrative purposes we focus on the structural, thematic and interactional levels of analysis, to demonstrate how verbal (spoken) data can be categorised and coded. Table 4.9 represents categories that can be used in the analysis of interactions between two or more people (adapted from Reinhard 1994:146-149). The categories consist of an adjacency pair, which is created by one person initiating communication and another responding. This is an example of **contiguous analysis**, because our objective is to determine what type of message **follows** immediately after another message.

**adjacency pair:**
two messages
that are
connected

**contiguous:**
adjoining

**TABLE 4.9:** Contiguous analysis: an example of two adjacency pairs in interpersonal communication

| FIRST ADJACENCY PAIR | | SECOND ADJACENCY PAIR | |
|---|---|---|---|
| First person | Second person | First person | Second person |
| Asks a question to confirm a previous statement | Confirms previous statement | Gives an opinion – disapproval | Gives resistance by criticising the opinion |

The type of analysis illustrated in Table 4.9 can also be applied to interpersonal communication between characters in films, to a caller's dialogue with a host during a radio phone-in programme, to a televised interview with a political spokesperson, and even to communication between *Madam & Eve* as printed cartoon characters.

Tables 4.10 and 4.11 contain examples of categories that can be used in coding or tally sheets when analysing interactions in the workplace, where the task dimension of communication somehow needs to be balanced with the socio-emotional dimension. Other examples of interaction analysis can be found in Hawes (1972); Bales and Cohen (1979); and Fisher and Drexel (1983).

The objective of interactional analysis is not to evaluate whether the communication is *good* or *bad*, *effective* or *ineffective*. Instead, the objective is to describe how people use messages in different settings, such as during work-related meetings. With people fulfilling different roles (e.g. husband and wife, employer and employee), these analyses can bring us closer to understanding the nature of relationships between people, how people affect one another and, if patterns occur, even how people control one another.

**TABLE 4.10:** Contiguous analysis of the task dimension of communication

| TASK DIMENSION OF COMMUNICATION | | | |
|---|---|---|---|
| **Problem, task or issue** | **Types of questions asked** | | **Types of answers (or ways of starting a communication)** |
| Orientation | Asks for information (orientation, repetition, clarification, confirmation) | → ← | Gives information (orientation, repeats, clarifies, confirms) |
| Evaluation | Asks for an opinion (evaluation, analysis, emotive response) | → ← | Gives opinion (evaluates, analyses, expresses feeling) |
| Control | Asks for direction (suggests ways of action) | → ← | Gives direction (implying acknowledgment of the autonomy of the other) |

**TABLE 4.11:** Contiguous analysis of the social-emotional dimension of communication

| SOCIAL-EMOTIONAL DIMENSION OF COMMUNICATION (WHEN GIVING INFORMATION, OPINION OR DIRECTION) | | | |
|---|---|---|---|
| **Problem, task or issue** | **Positive responses** | | **Negative responses** |
| Decision-making | Agrees (consents, approves, obeys, shows passive acceptance) | → ← | Disagrees (disapproves, disobeys, shows passive rejection – e.g. by withholding help) |
| Tension-management | Releases tension (jokes, laughs, smiles) | → ← | Shows tension (tone of voice, kinesics, phonemics; withdraws) |
| Integration | Gives co-operation (gives reward, offers assistance, raises the other's status) | → ← | Gives resistance (asserts self, defends self, lowers the other's status) |

Although interactional analysis enables us to describe the communication between people, and to observe relationships between relational categories and other variables, such as age or gender, this method – as in the case of content analysis in general – cannot be used to draw valid conclusions about cause-and-effect relationships.

Table 4.12 illustrates categories that can be used when the objective is to analyse the consequential structure of messages and how people's responses are either supportive, serve as an extension, are non-supportive or confine an initial message.

| **TABLE 4.12:** Contiguous analysis of the consequential structure of messages | | |
|---|---|---|
| **FIRST PERSON SPEAKING** | **SECOND PERSON SPEAKING (IN RESPONSE TO THE FIRST PERSON)** | **FIRST OR THIRD PERSON SPEAKING (IN RESPONSE TO THE SECOND PERSON)** |
| One of the following:<br><br>● **Prescriptive:** warning, command, argument, statement<br><br>● **Negotiation:** invitation, apology, promise, request, question, suggestion | One of the following:<br><br>● **Supportive:** confirmation of initial message format – a 'one-down' message; submitting to opinion of the other<br><br>● **Extension** of initial message format – a 'one-across' message, neither agreeing nor disagreeing with the other; or repeating the same message<br><br>● **Nonsupportive:** disapproval of initial message format – a 'one-up' message; asserting own views or dominating the other<br><br>● **Confinement** of initial message format – no reaction; or termination of communication | One of the following:<br><br>● **Supportive:** confirmation of initial message format – a 'one-down' message; submitting to opinion of the other<br><br>● **Extension** of initial message format – a 'one-across' message, neither agreeing nor disagreeing with the other; or repeating the same message<br><br>● **Nonsupportive:** disapproval of initial message format – a 'one-up' message; asserting own views or dominating the other<br><br>● **Confinement** of initial message format – no reaction; or termination of communication |

These four tables illustrate that the kind of categories to be included in the tally or observation sheets can be adapted according to the objective of the study, the type of observation to be conducted and/or the type of content or data to be analysed.

## 4.5.3 Elementary descriptive statistics

Once the data has been coded in categories, it is analysed by reporting elementary descriptive statistics in the form of frequency tables. The analysis of photographs of political spokespersons indicated in Table 4.8 will read as follows:

**TABLE 4.13:** An example of a frequency table

| | PHOTOGRAPHS OF SPOKESPERSONS OF POLITICAL PARTIES A AND B | | |
|---|---|---|---|
| | | N | % |
| *Sunday News* | Party A | 27 | 25,0 |
| | Party B | 81 | 75,0 |
| | Total | 108 | 100 |
| *Sunday Week* | Party A | 65 | 84,4 |
| | Party B | 12 | 15,6 |
| | Total | 77 | 100 |

As can be seen in Table 4.13 the *Sunday News* published 59,4% more photographs of the spokesperson from Party B than *Sunday Week* (75% − 15,6% = 59,4%). Conversely, *Sunday Week* published exactly the same percentage more photographs of the spokesperson from Party A (84,4% − 25% = 59,4%).

Content analyses are particularly useful as descriptions of communication trends. However, they do not enable us to draw cause-effect conclusions. In the above example, we can only conclude that *Sunday Week* favours publishing photographs of the spokesperson from Party A, but we do not know what the effect of these photographs was on the readers; nor do we know the nature of the press reports that accompanied the photographs. A second disadvantage lies in the lack of external validity. We cannot generalise the percentages to other newspapers or to other political parties.

Once the content analysis has been completed and frequencies or trends summarised, quantitative data can be presented in tabulated form or in graphs. In the case of **qualitative** data, interpretations are normally in narrative form and not tested statistically. Although writing the research report is dealt with in Unit 7, it is worth noting that, when interpreting and describing qualitative data, three types of **narrative** can be used:

● **Confessional narratives** consist of descriptions by the researcher recounting the series of events that took place during fieldwork or observations, until certain conclusions could be reached. Although such a description may contain a wealth of in-depth information,

it is essentially a subjective account (almost like a personal diary) of the research study, and would generally not be highly regarded in a scientific community.

- **Impressionistic narratives** contain references to so-called factual data, but these are coloured by the interviewer's, observer's or coder's impressions. In other words, these interpretations and descriptions may include prejudice and bias on the part of the researcher (and should therefore be avoided).
- **Realist narratives** are preferred because they are written in a third-person type of address – in an impersonal, detached, neutral and objective way. The focus in these narratives is on interpreting and reporting conclusions on the basis of the data collected – not the researcher's personal experiences or impressions.

**third-person type of address:** uses references to 'he', 'she', 'it', 'they', 'the respondents', 'the participants', 'the subjects' *(not* 'I', 'me', 'my', 'us', 'we' or 'our')

When **quantitative data** (e.g. based on a nominal level of measurement) is analysed, the coded data can be analysed according to statistical tests. Table 4.14 contains some basic statistical notations that are used in this section.

| **TABLE 4.14:** Some basic statistical notations | |
|---|---|
| $X$ | any score in a series of scores |
| $\bar{X}$ | the mean (pronounced X-bar) |
| $\Sigma$ | the sum |
| $N$ | the total number of scores |
| $R$ | range |
| $f$ | frequency |

Data analysis (in **quantitative** research) that includes the use of statistical techniques usually involves two categories: statistics for **descriptive** purposes and statistics for **inferential** purposes. Descriptive statistics make it possible to provide a summary of certain characteristics of the units of analysis, such as annual income, age or educational level. Inferential statistics can be used to draw inferences beyond behavioural descriptions. According to Watt and Van den Berg (1995:383-391) selecting the appropriate statistical test depends on many variables, including:

- The level of measurement of the independent variable and of the dependent variable. Different statistical tests are used when these

variables are nominal, ordinal, interval or ratio.
- The number of independent variables that covary with the dependent variable. Bivariate statistical tests are used when only one independent variable is involved. Multivariate statistical tests are required if more than one variable is involved.
- The type of hypothesis that is formulated and has to be tested (comparative versus relationship hypotheses), together with the research design used.
- Whether the study involves comparing two populations, or comparing a sample with a population, or whether comparisons are made between two or more samples.

Statistics are used to show a probability or significance level and to infer causality between independent and dependent variables. However, statistical significance cannot establish causal relations. Such relations have to be an integral part of the research design and research questions asked or the hypotheses formulated.

As the choices of the most appropriate statistical tests and the mathematical computations are beyond the scope of this publication, we deal only with the most elementary descriptive statistics. For additional guidance in the selection of the most suitable statistical tests, refer to the suggested reading at the end of this unit.

Quantitative data can be described by two descriptive measures: the measure of central tendency and the measure of variance. The most typical value calculated for all units of analysis is the **central tendency**. This refers to the general trend of the numbers (or scores) in terms of their middle (central) value. For example, once all the ages of respondents are listed, the array constructed and the data summarised, the mode (the age most frequently found in the sample), the mean (the average age of the sample), and the median (the middle age in the sample) can be determined.

**mode:**
the most frequent score in a set of scores

The formula for calculating the mean is:

**mean:**
the average value in a set of scores

$$\bar{X} = \frac{\Sigma X}{N}$$

**median:**
the middle score in a set of scores

Table 4.15 summarises the appropriate use of these three measures of central tendency, based on a discussion by Seaman (1987:343-345).

**TABLE 4.15:** Measures of central tendency

| LEVEL OF MEASUREMENT USED | THE BEST MEASURE OF CENTRAL TENDENCY |
|---|---|
| Nominal | Mode (the most frequent score) |
| Ordinal | Median (the middle score) |
| Equal intervals/ratio and scores that are reasonably symmetrical | Mean (average) |
| Equal intervals/ratio, but the scores are skewed | Median (the middle score) |

**skewed:** scores that are asymmetrical or distorted

The reason why the median should be calculated (and not the mean) in the case where scores are skewed is that extreme or erratic scores would be given improper weight. For example, the average monthly incomes of five households are summarised in Table 4.16.

**TABLE 4.16:** Data arranged in a data array

| AVERAGE MONTHLY INCOME |
|---|
| R7 000,00 |
| R7 000,00 |
| R7 000,00 |
| R6 000,00 |
| R1 000,00 |

The mean is calculated by adding all the incomes and dividing this total by five (the number of scores), which is R5 600,00. Note that the one low income (R1 000,00) has pulled the mean income far lower than it would have been if the scores (monthly incomes) were symmetrical.

When calculating the **median**, which is the middle score that divides the scores in two equal parts, we first have to arrange the scores in rank order, from lowest to highest or vice versa. Once the scores, cases or observations have been arranged in rank order, the median can also be regarded as the **visual centre** of the distribution. In the above example, the median is R7 000,00, which conveys a different picture when compared with the mean. Note that the middle score is the median when the total number of scores is uneven (e.g. 5), whereas it would lie between the two middle scores when the total number of scores is even.

The value of the **mode** is the most easily determined once a frequency distribution has been compiled.

| **TABLE 4.17:** Data arranged in a frequency distribution | |
|---|---|
| **AVERAGE MONTHLY INCOME** | f |
| R7 000,00 | 3 |
| R6 000,00 | 1 |
| R1 000,00 | 1 |
| | N = 5 |

**unimodal distribution:** one point in the distribution where the frequency is highest

The data in Table 4.17 are examples of a **unimodal distribution** of the scores, because the highest value (3) is associated with one point on the distribution, namely R7 000,00. The mode is useful when we have scores that contain extreme variations. However, in cases where bimodal and trimodal distributions are found, the mode has little significance. In the above example, the distribution would have been bimodal if three of the other incomes were the same.

**bimodal:** two modes

When conducting experimental research, it is important to remember that if changes in an experimental group occur because of the statistical regression to the mean, and not because of the independent variable, they need to be controlled to prevent a threat to internal validity. For example, school children are selected on the basis of having obtained extremely low marks in a recent examination. They are provided with the treatment (e.g. watching a series of educational television programmes) and subsequently show some improvement. Such improvement may have been expected, given the tendency to move (regress) to the mean (or average), and not necessarily due to the television programmes. Assigning individuals randomly to control groups, for comparative purposes, can control regression to the mean.

**dispersion:** diversity

When examining **variation**, we are dealing with the dispersion of observations, or how they are distributed among many categories or values. The total range and standard deviation are two measures of variation.

**total range:** the difference between the smallest and largest observations

The **total range** is the simplest measure of dispersion because, by subtracting the lowest score ($X_{lo}$) from the highest score ($X_{hi}$), it enables us to get a rough idea of the scope of the observations.

Although the total range does give information beyond the central tendency, it does not convey the fluctuations that may occur within a set of scores. The formula used to calculate the range is:

$$R = X_{hi} - X_{lo}$$

The **standard deviation** involves a more complicated computational procedure to calculate the degree to which scores deviate or are scattered from the mean. 'Standard' refers to the extent to which a group average is spread around the mean. 'Deviation' is an indication of how much the spread of scores deviates from the mean.

As indicated above, various statistical techniques exist that can be used when analysing and comparing quantitative data. However, to do justice to the intricacies involved in these tests is beyond the scope of the publication.

We end this section with the application of one type of Readability Ease (RE) test and deal with it separately because the procedures followed differ from those described above. In fact, this RE test represents a combination of doing a content analysis and using a mathematical formula.

## 4.5.4 Readability Ease test

**readability:**
the ease with which a printed text is read and understood

The readability of a printed text depends on various factors, including:
- the use of headings and subheadings that summarise the essence of the content that follows;
- the use of colour or different typefaces to emphasise important points;
- the abstractness, variety and length or words used;
- the nature of sentence construction, especially the length of sentences; and/or
- the human interest, such as words used to describe people.

**SMOG:**
Simple Measure Of Gobbledygook

The Fog index, SMOG Grading, and Cloze technique are examples of formulas that have been developed to measure the readability of a printed text. Borcherds et al. (1991:237-243), and Du Toit, Heese and Orr (1995:282-284) can be consulted for illustrations of these techniques, and other techniques, such as the UNISA Fog Index. However, according to Wimmer and Dominick (1997:281) the **Flesch**

**Readability Ease** (RE) is still the best known formula to objectively measure the readability of (English) texts.

A RE (content) analysis is not only of interest to journalists writing for a target audience, but is important for any communicator who communicates in writing or print and who wants to increase the ease with which a printed text is read and understood.

Although computer programs are available to calculate the Flesch RE of a text, it can also be done 'by hand' following these steps:

- Draw a random sample of a section of the text that contains 100 words.
- Count the total number of syllables in these 100 words *(wl)*. Syllables that are not sounded separately (e.g. 'charged') are counted as a word with one syllable. A word such as 'employed' is counted as two syllables, because we do not pronounce 'em/ploy/ed' as three syllables. In contrast, a word such as 'supported' would be counted as three syllables, because the '-ed' is pronounced separately: 'sup/port/ed'.
- Calculate the average number of words per sentence *(sl)* by dividing the number of words by the number of sentences. Contractions and hyphenated words are counted as one word. Clauses that are separated by colons and semicolons are counted as separate sentences.
- Apply the following equation:

$$RE = 206{,}835 - (0{,}846 \times wl) - (1{,}015 \times sl)$$

This means that:
- the number of syllables is multiplied by 0,846;
- the average length of the sentences is multiplied by 1,015; and that
- both multiplications are subtracted from 206,835.

The score should fall between 0 and 100 and the RE can be interpreted using Table 4.18 as an estimate indication of the readability ease of the text.

**TABLE 4.18:** Readability Ease scores

| RE SCORE | READABILITY EASE OF ENGLISH TEXTS | MINIMUM EDUCATION REQUIRED BY THE READER |
|----------|-----------------------------------|------------------------------------------|
| 0 - 30 | Very difficult | Tertiary (e.g. degree) |
| 30 - 50 | Difficult | Tertiary |
| 50 - 60 | Fairly difficult | Grade 12 |
| 60 - 70 | Standard | Grades 9 or 10 |
| 70 - 90 | Fairly easy | Be literate |
| 90 - 100 | Very easy | Be literate |

Measurement of the readability ease concentrates on an analysis of the **text**. However, the RE score has to be interpreted keeping in mind the educational levels of the target audience, which varies from country to country. 'Standard' (RE 60-70) would apply to those readers who have completed Grades 9 or 10 (previously Standards 8 and 9 in South Africa). According to the 1996 census, 43,5% of the South African population aged 20 years and older, has either not received any formal education or has completed only primary education. Some 33,9% have completed some secondary education. Therefore, we can conclude that a text with a RE score of between 60 and 70 would be read with ease by only approximately 22,6% of the South African population aged 20 years or older (Statistics South Africa 1999:41).

**TABLE 4.19:** Calculating a Flesch Readability Ease (RE) score

Assuming we have drawn a sample of 108 words arranged in 10 sentences, with the first 100 words containing 150 syllables. Then:

$$wl = 150$$
$$sl = 108 \div 10 = 10,8$$

The RE equation would then be calculated as follows:

$$206,835 - (0,846 \times 150 \; wl) - (1,015 \times 10,8 \; sl)$$
$$\underline{206,835 - 126,9 - 10,96}$$
$$\mathbf{68,97}$$

As this RE score falls in the 'standard' category, readers who have completed a Grade 10 or a higher educational level should read the text with ease.

If a text is not of a scientific, technical or academic nature and the RE score is below 60, communicators can increase the RE by doing the following:

- use words with fewer syllables (e.g. *on* instead of *upon*; *weaken* instead of *deteriorate*; *use* instead of *employ* or *utilise*);
- use concrete, rather than abstract words;
- write short sentences;
- use punctuation to break sentences into units;
- expand difficult concepts by means of analogies or examples;
- use discourse markers to prepare the reader for what follows (words such as *because, whereas, nevertheless, since, while* and *therefore*);
- keep in mind the educational level, prior knowledge, needs and interests of the readers as a target audience.

Most computer programs contain language and vocabulary tests that can be applied to the typed copy. For example, WordPerfect has a RE score test that, in a matter of seconds, provides an analysis of English verbal texts by giving the following information: syllable counts, word counts, sentence counts, passive voice (the percentage of finite verb phrases used); sentence complexity; and vocabulary complexity.

Once changes have been made to a text that rates below 60, follow-up tests can (and should) be done to determine whether the Readability Ease has increased. Although the dependent variable being tested is Readability Ease, it can be linked to testing the cognitive dimension of the impact of a message (e.g. of a printed advertisement on a consumer). The cognitive and other dimensions of impact are further discussed in Unit 5.

---

### EXECUTIVE SUMMARY:
### WHAT TO DO WITH THE DATA ONCE COLLECTED

1 Content analysis:
  - Sampling;
  - Coding or tallying the data;
  - Pre-coded versus post-coded categories;
  - Coder training.

2 Analysis of verbal (spoken) communication.

3 Elementary descriptive statistics.

4 Readability Ease test.

---

## Self-evaluation and portfolio tasks

**4.5** You have been approached to undertake a qualitative content analysis of fictional television programmes to determine how frequently crime is broadcast. While watching television, make notes of the types of crimes that are broadcast, and on the basis of your own experiences and exposure to other mass-media messages related to crime, compile a tally or coding sheet of categories that you would use as coder. Ensure that your categories are mutually exclusive and exhaustive.

Pilot test you coding sheet by coding the number of times your categories occur during one evening and make additions if your list is not exhaustive.

**4.6** Read the following scenario and calculate the mean, the median and the mode. Which measure of central tendency would you regard to be most suitable for the data?

A self-administered questionnaire contains a five-point scaled item in which 21 employees are asked to rank the efficiency of an organisation's management. Each of the five options are assigned a numeral:

Excellent (1)
Good (2)
Fair (3)
Poor (4)
Extremely poor (5)

The 21 respondents' rankings are as follows:

1;
2; 2;
3;3;3;3;3;3;
4;4;4;4;4;4;4;4;4;4;4;
5;

$N = 72$

**4.7** Read the scenario on the next page, and calculate the mean and the total range for each group. Explain why knowing the total range can be a better indicator of the nature of data than calculating the mean.

Sixteen households are asked to keep a daily diary of the number of hours that anyone in the household watches television over a period of a month. The households are sampled to represent eight urban households and eight rural households. The number of hours recorded in the diaries is listed below.

| NUMBER OF HOURS WATCHING TELEVISION DURING ONE MONTH | |
| --- | --- |
| Rural households | Urban households |
| $X$ | $X$ |
| 79 | 56 |
| 101 | 42 |
| 51 | 51 |
| 49 | 49 |
| 4 | 59 |
| 41 | 48 |
| 14 | 43 |
| 61 | 52 |
| $N = 400$ | $N = 400$ |

**4.8** Select a printed text (e.g. a newspaper, a policy document, a newsletter from your local council, a book published for children, or this publication) and calculate the Flesch Readability Ease (RE) score and interpret the Readability Ease by consulting Table 4.18.
- In your opinion, is the Readability Ease estimated for the text suitable for the minimum educational level required by the intended readers?
- What measures would you advise the author of this text to take to increase the Readability Ease of similar documents?

## 4.6 Ethical issues

Traditionally, the areas of ethical concern in communication research deal with matters such as privacy, confidentiality, and institutional or professional control. These concerns have been addressed in previous units, such as Unit 2, section 2.6.3. Of specific concern in this unit, is that, while collecting and interpreting data, we are challenged to maintain a level of integrity based on two principles:
- to use a research design (methods and techniques) suited to the objectives and nature of the research problem; and

- to not knowingly imply greater confidence or significance than the data warrants.

These principles imply that the exact procedures used to collect data, including preceding explanations and instructions, which may have influenced a subject, must be reported, and that the data collected is scored accurately and consistently. The second principle specifically means that steps must be taken to assure the reliability and validity of the measurements used, prior to and during their administration in an actual study, and afterwards, when coding and interpreting the data.

Ethical issues that apply to interpreting and reporting data are again raised in Unit 7.

## 4.7  Summary

This unit dealt with procedures to be followed when conducting research in controlled environments, in semi-controlled environments and in natural environments, and what to do with this data.

Controlled environments are usually linked to experimental research, because of the control a researcher places on external variables that could influence the outcome of the test. We differentiated between single-system designs (a case study) and group designs. Under the heading of group designs, we dealt with pre-test-post-test control-group designs, post-test-only control-group designs and factorial designs.

Research in semi-controlled environments usually involves doing a survey and/or conducting interviews. We dealt with the advantages, limitations and applications of mail surveys, computer-administered surveys, group-administered surveys, telephone surveys, personal surveys, and different types of interviews. These interviews were cate-gorised as structured, partially-structured and unstructured. Thereafter we gave greater attention to focus-group interviews, because they are flexible and are applied in current research involving a variety of research objectives. We also dealt with the formatting and pre-coding of a questionnaire, and how to deal with problems that are generally related to implementing surveys and/or interviews.

By conducting research in a natural environment, such as when doing field research, we usually make use of observations to collect data and, in certain instances, combine our role as observer with that of participant in whatever setting or event is being observed. We emphasised the importance of conducting debriefing interviews and gave suggestions for how errors caused by the reactions of observers can be controlled.

Data, once collected, has to be analysed. Such a content analysis involves defining the unit of analysis, considering whether the data will be sampled and, if so, which sampling technique is appropriate to the population parameters. Categories used for the coding or tallying of the data can be pre-coded or post-coded. The unit contained several examples of pre-coded categories that can be used in the analysis of verbal (spoken) communication. Depending on the level of measurements used (nominal, ordinal, interval or ratio) the data can be counted (as frequencies) or scored by being allocated to an evaluative scale.

Thereafter we described how measures of central tendency and variation, as examples of elementary descriptive statistics, can be used to analyse and report quantitative data, and how different narratives can be distinguished, when reporting qualitative data. The unit ended with the application of a Readability Ease test of English printed texts, and ethical issues that apply when coding and interpreting data.

In the next two units, we concentrate on the application of these methods and techniques in a variety of specialisation areas.

Before continuing with Unit 5, you are encouraged to evaluate your achievement of the learning outcomes using the following guide.

### ASSESSMENT OF LEARNING OUTCOMES

Ratings for evaluation of performance:
5   very high (extremely good)
4   high (good)
3   medium (average)
2   low (poor)
1   very low (extremely poor)
0   evidence is absent

**4**

| Outcomes (knowledge, competence and orientations) *You should be able to demonstrate your understanding of:* | Evidence of performance | Examples of criteria used to evaluate evidence of performance | Evaluation of performance Ratings | | | | | |
|---|---|---|---|---|---|---|---|---|
| | | | 5 | 4 | 3 | 2 | 1 | 0 |
| Collecting research data | by selecting and applying a particular research design. | Selection of controlled, semi-controlled or natural environments, plus selection of specific data-collection technique(s), and method(s) are appropriate to the objective of the study, the research problem, subproblems, hypotheses or research questions, population parameters and nature of the data to be collected. | | | | | | |
| Knowing what to do with the data, once it has been collected | by conducting a content analysis, applying elementary descriptive statistics, and/or applying a Readability Ease test. | Selection and formulation of sampling, coding data, categories, and selection of descriptive statistics or RE test are motivated in terms of the objective of the study and nature of the data collected. | | | | | | |

## SUGGESTED READING

Baily, A. 1996. *A guide to field research.* Thousand Oaks, California: Pine Forge.

Bless, C and Kathuria, R. 1993. *Fundamentals of social statistics. An African perspective.* Wetton, Cape Town: Juta.

Davies, CA. 1999. *Reflexive ethnography: a guide to researching selves and others.* London: Routledge.

Deacon, D, Pickering, M, Golding, P and Murdock, G. 1999. *Researching communications. A practical guide to methods in media and cultural analysis*. London: Arnold.

DePoy, E and Gitlin, LN. 1998. *Introduction to research: understanding and applying multiple strategies*. (2nd edition). St Louis, Mo: Mosby.

Hammersley, M. 1998. *Reading ethnographic research: a critical guide*. London: Longman.

Howell, DC. 1995. *Fundamental statistics for the behavioural sciences*. (3rd edition). Belmont, California: Duxbury.

Marshall, C and Rossman, GB. 1989. *Designing qualitative research*. Newbury Park, California: Sage.

Stewart, DW and Shamdasani, PN. 1990. *Focus groups. Theory and practice*. Newbury Park, California: Sage.

Wimmer, RD and Dominick, JR. 1997. *Mass media research: an introduction*. (5th edition). Belmont, California: Wadsworth.

# Research of advertising, mass-media audiences and mass-media efficiency

*The true way goes over a rope, which is not stretched at any great height but just above the ground.*

FRANZ KAFKA

## Overview

South Africa has become part of a global economy, which means that advertising and mass-media industries have to compete with one another at regional, national and international levels. Whether the purpose is to promote a product through an advertising campaign, provide for readers' cognitive needs for information via the print media, or present audiences with opportunities for escapism, diversion and entertainment through radio and television programmes, one question remains central: *How can we develop a long-term relationship with our customers (and still show a profit)?* 'Profit' is used here in the widest sense to include the effective use of communication media for non-monetary purposes, such as the promotion of education and social development.

This unit concentrates on the practical application of various research methods and techniques to investigate the content, structure and effectiveness of advertisements. It also investigates audiences and the efficiency of print media and the electronic media. However, the sections in this unit are not necessarily media-specific. For example, the question: *What are the values, needs and behaviours of our customers or audiences?* is not limited to one particular mass medium or communication content. Therefore, the applications of research methods and techniques in this unit are thematically directed by the research goal and objectives of different research studies.

## Learning outcomes

By the end of this unit, you should be able to demonstrate your understanding and ability to:

- conduct advertising message research;
- undertake audience analyses of print and broadcast media; and
- research mass-media efficiency

by selecting appropriate research

methods or techniques and by conducting pilot studies.

# 5.1  Introduction

Having dealt with the need for a quanti-qualitative paradigm (in Unit 1), the methods, techniques and so-called 'tools' used to collect and analyse data (in Units 2 to 4), this unit concentrates specifically on the practical application of communication research. The unit starts by investigating advertising message research. The latter research requires an understanding of several variables, such as consumers' behaviours, values and lifestyles, plus the cognitive, affective and conative dimensions of persuasive effects. Apart from the research methods and techniques dealt with in Units 2, 3 and 4, additional methods and techniques are applied to research the content, structure and effectiveness of advertisements.

There is also a section dealing with audience analyses of print and broadcast media. Audience research includes the application of field, survey and experimental research. When applied to audiences (readers) of the print media, such research also deals with item-selection studies, and research related to typography and layout. When applied to audiences of both the print and broadcast media, such research involves audience profiles (demographics, psychographics and lifestyles), reader/non-reader studies, and uses and gratifications studies.

This unit concludes with the methods and techniques used to research mass-media efficiency. Such efficiency is determined by measuring aspects such as the reach, frequency, gross ratings points, circulation, ratings and non-ratings research.

The examples discussed, and the self-evaluation and portfolio tasks set in this unit are aimed at enhancing an awareness of the relevance of research in the mass media and aim to develop your:

- problem-solving skills and self-responsibility skills;
- media-literacy skills;
- awareness of the relevance of communication research in diverse settings related to mass communication; and
- understanding of the importance of a cultural and aesthetic understanding of the mass-mediated society in which we live.

## 5.2 Advertising message research

In this section, we focus on **message research** that can be applied in advertising. Message research can also be used in evaluating the messages that are disseminated by means of print media, radio and television, and messages used in a public relations campaign (*see* Unit 6).

Although reference is specifically made to advertising, the methods and techniques can also be applied to researching the mass media and public relations campaigns. We are essentially concerned with three aspects of messages: their **content**, their **structure** and their **effectiveness**. These aspects are dealt with against the background of understanding users' and consumers' behaviour, and research methods, such as **content analysis, field research, survey research** and **experimental research**, are commonly used.

### 5.2.1 Understanding consumers' behaviour

Researchers who want to determine why people buy specific products or brands, or why people prefer certain services to others, are essentially concerned with understanding consumers' behaviour. (Although the term 'consumers' is used in this unit, in some cases they may be 'users' of particular products or services.)

**pluralistic:** consisting of several differences, for example languages and cultures

A society such as South Africa, which is pluralistic, consists of a variety of subcultures or subgroups that share values, customs and traditions, that can directly influence preferences for certain foods, clothing and accepted roles for men and women. The fact that South Africa has eleven official languages, illustrates the diversities to be found among different subgroups, the presence of which advertisers, as well as mass-media producers and managers, should not ignore.

In South Africa, the role and status of blacks, women and disabled people have changed dramatically since 1994. By obtaining higher-level positions, lifestyle changes will continue to take place, which, in turn, can be expected to influence the basic selection of commodities and the consumption patterns (including the use of the mass media) of these subgroups. For example, working women will experience a lack of free time as one of the changes to which they have to adapt, which can influence their habitual purchasing behaviour. Alert researchers would undertake research to determine what timesaving, product-saving or service-saving innovations the mass media and advertisers could introduce. (For example, some of the larger cities in South Africa already have daily door-to-door delivery services for products such as milk, bread and even pet food.)

**market segmentation:** to divide the consumers in the mass market into homogeneous subgroups

Researching market segmentation is a difficult task, because it is difficult to link specific purchasing behaviour with particular consumer variables, such as age, gender or income. Other variables, such as occupation, educational level, social status and membership of social groups, are also relevant when researching the use of the mass media, consumer-product behaviour and the adoption of new ideas.

**multivariable:** involving many variations or alternatives

A multivariable system needs to be devised to enable researchers to predict consumer behaviour more accurately. The following is an example of such a system that distinguishes three broad groups of consumers, based on people's values and lifestyles.

1. **Consumers who are driven by physiological needs** buy for survival, either because they are aged or poor, and not because of impulse or choice. Their consumer behaviour is essentially based on the satisfaction of physiological motives, such as hunger and thirst, which are essential for survival.

**mass market:** unspecified number of consumers

2. **Consumers who are concerned with what others think of them** represent a diverse group that includes the so-called mass market. These consumers can be conservative and traditionalist; or ambitious and emulate those who are successful and rich; or achievers,

whose lifestyles are characterised by comfort, status and efficiency. The consumer behaviour of the mass market is essentially based on the satisfaction of social motives, which may be affectional (the need for meaningful relations with others), or ego boosting (the need to enhance their own personality).

3. **Consumers who value inner growth** are individualistic, tend to be artistic, and because their concerns include social responsibility, their lifestyles tend to revolve around conservation and healing.

**formative research:** continuous measurement of effectiveness during the planning stages

The above multivariable system is based on the argument that **formative research** to develop advertising themes and creating advertisements, would be more realistic and effective if consumers belonged to one of these three groups and their values and lifestyles could be described in finer detail.

We also need to consider whether the target market for a **new** product or service belongs to one of the groups described below. Extensive research has been done (e.g. Rogers 1962; 1986 and 1993) on how people initially become familiar and eventually accept new products or services. Although these groups are usually linked to the introduction of innovations in development research, they are also useful when researching consumers.

1. **Innovators** are willing to try out new ideas, even if some risk is involved.

2. The **early adopters** are careful and successful innovators, who are often used as reference by people wanting to know more about an innovation.

3. The **early majority** usually deliberates before actually adopting an innovation and are important to legitimise an innovation.

4. The **late majority** is cautious and adopts an innovation once the public has accepted it.

**laggards:** people who lag or trail behind

5. **Laggards** tend to live in the past and are suspicious of innovation and those who want to introduce it. If and by the time they do accept an innovation, it may already have been replaced by another.

These groupings are based on an **innovation adoption model** that represents certain stages that a consumer has to pass through before adopting a new product or service. These stages are: creating awareness and interest among consumers, enabling them to evaluate the product or service and to test it for a trial period. After the trial period, the product or service is either rejected or adopted. According to this model, the adoption of a product or service follows these steps:

awareness ➡ interest ➡ evaluation ➡ trial ➡ adoption.

Like individuals, certain mass media and well-known institution, can be used as **opinion leaders**. Opinion leaders can be defined as individuals or institutions that influence the flow or multiplication of a message and/or the value or worthiness attached to the message. This influence is achieved by giving advice, testimonials or by sharing ideas, attitudes and/or information with others. Well-known celebrities, artists and sporting heroes are often used to support a brand of clothing, or a health drink. Opinion leadership is an informal type of leadership, which is earned and maintained by the leader's competence (or competence as perceived by followers) and social accessibility. This enables them to promote a new idea, but also to actively oppose a new idea. According to Rogers and Shoemaker (1971:35) opinion leaders:

- 'are more exposed to all forms of external communication,
- are more cosmopolite,
- have higher social status, and
- are more innovative'.

As part of the formative research strategy, it is equally important to identify individuals or institutions who serve as models for others and to use them as innovators or early adapters. The identification of opinion leaders can be done by means of a consumer **survey** aimed at answering the following research questions:

1. *To whom, or to which institution do they (or might they hypothetically) go for advice and information about a particular topic (for example, financial investment advice)?*

   As the identification of opinion leaders is based on the majority of responses, the survey results will be most valid if all, or the **majority** of the members of a **population** are surveyed. For instance, if an insurance firm has a million customers, survey results based on a hundred customers' responses would not be valid.

2.  *Whom or which institutions do they regard as the leaders in a particular community or social system, with regard to a particular topic (for example, to get connected to the Internet)?*

    In this case, use can be made of a **purposive sample** of individuals who are knowledgeable about patterns of behaviour and influence in the social system, such as politicians, educators, community leaders and communication professionals. Based on their opinions, we can extend the survey to include other individuals and groups via **snowball sampling**.

3.  *To what degree do they perceive themselves to be opinion leaders on a particular topic (for example, in marketing red meat)?*

    In this survey, use can be made of **self-reporting techniques**, by asking questions such as:

    *In your opinion, do people come to you rather than other people for advice about marketing red meat?*

    Although self-reporting techniques depend on the accuracy with which respondents can identify their self-images and report on the perceptions of their own opinion leadership, they also enable us to identify others who are regarded as opinion leaders. If a respondent answers in the negative to the above question, it can function as a **filter question**, after which the following **contingency question** can be asked:

    *Whom would you approach for advice about marketing red meat?*

**marketing research:**
collection and analysis of data about people's needs, attitudes, motivations, behaviours, etcetera, in social, economic and political contexts

Communication researchers who focus on measuring the underlying **motives** that initiate consumer behaviour, are concerned with a psychological approach to studying human behaviour. In addition to motivation, this approach acknowledges that our behaviour is also influenced by cognition and learning.

Marketing research can investigate consumers' drives, urges or wishes, by linking research questions and/or hypotheses to the relationships that arise between the basic components of a communication process (communicator, medium, recipient), situated in a societal setting.

The following four areas of research questions were adapted from Russell and Verrill (1986:377), and from Patti and Moriarty (1990:15-35):

1. *Which **consumers** buy what they do, where, when, how and why?*
   These research questions enable researchers to study the behaviour of consumers and are aimed at the culmination of exchanges between them as recipients and communicators (e.g. advertisers, manufacturers, producers).
2. *Which **dealers** produce, promote, price and/or distribute what they do, where, when, how and why?*
   These research questions enable researchers to study the behaviour of dealers and are aimed at the culmination of exchanges between them and consumers or users (as recipients).
3. *Which types of **institutions** (such as dealers, producers or importers) develop what to facilitate exchanges, when, where, how and why?*
   These research questions enable researchers to study the institutional frameworks (e.g. advertising agencies) involved in the culmination of exchanges between dealers and consumers.
4. *Which kind of **behaviours** (of consumers, dealers and institutions) have what kind of effects on society, when, where, how and why?*

Irrespective of whether our research focus is on one or all of the above research areas, survey results that predict consumer behaviour based on people's **motives** have to be treated with scepticism. The reasons for this statement are found in the following tendencies that result in **bias**:

**bias:** systematic error due to not being neutral or objective

- It is difficult to link motives with behaviour because people do not necessarily understand what motivates them to behave in a certain manner, such as why they select a particular restaurant for a meal.

**motivational intervention:** a message that stimulates a wish, desire or drive, which causes a person to behave in a certain way

- Two people who are exposed to the same stimulus or motivational intervention can respond differently. For example, an advertisement for a funeral policy will evoke different responses from a terminally ill patient, from a newly married couple, from someone who has recently lost a loved one, and/or from someone living below the poverty line.
- The reasons people give for buying certain products or using certain services can be unrelated to the real reasons for such behaviour. This is particularly applicable if products serve as symbols of who we think we are (promoting our self-image) or promoting the different social roles that we fulfil. For example, a student buys a cellular phone on credit, because it is the 'in thing' to do in his or her peer group, not because he or she needs the facilities.
- An investigation of the effects of behaviours (of consumers, dealers and institutions) on society requires longitudinal research. During

**longitudinal
research:**
collecting data
at different points
over a long period
of time

such time circumstances can change, which makes it almost impossible to verify causal links between when, where, how or why certain messages had certain effects. Variables such as history, maturation, reliability, bias, mortality and fatigue, influence the internal validity of longitudinal research (*see* Unit 2).

Against the background of understanding consumers' behaviour, we now deal with researching advertising message **content**, **structure** and **effectiveness** in the next three sections.

# Message content

## 5.2.2

**globalisation:**
internationalisa-
tion of ownership,
production,
distribution,
transmission and
reception

**applied research:**
research that aims
to solve a practical
problem, rather
than to theorise

**copy testing:**
research to
determine the
most effective
way of structuring
a message

**campaign:**
organised series
of purposeful
communication
activities, includ-
ing mass commu-
nication, directed
at a specific goal

Advertising is expensive and, with increased competition due to globalisation, institutions have turned to message research as one of the basic management tools. The goal of this research is that of **applied research**, which aims to answer specific research questions (e.g. *Should our company stress its social redress policy that focuses on equity in a publicity campaign?* or *Should this product be promoted by a young teenager or a mature adult?*)

When we research the **content** of advertising messages, we apply what is traditionally referred to in the industry as **copy testing** (Wimmer and Dominick 1997:314-315). The term is misleading, because it suggests that only the verbal copy in an advertisement or mass-mediated message is evaluated. In reality, the so-called copy will depend on the medium. For example, in the case of a printed advertisement, codes such as word content, typography, font, layout, size, illustrations, photo-graphs, colour and use of white space can be researched. (Copy testing should not be confused with *copy measurement*, which refers to the quantitative measurement of a printed copy in centimetres, and the measurement of broadcast copy, such as news, in seconds.)

Copy testing takes place at every stage of an advertising campaign, from before the campaign starts, during the planning and structuring stage, and finally to determine its effectiveness. The identification of the primary appeal is crucial in any advertising and marketing campaign, which can be researched using three techniques: **focus-group interviews**, **motivational research** and **concept testing**. (An **appeal** can be defined as a statement that addresses people's desires, problems and goals, offers solutions for these problems and a means to obtain their goals.)

The nature, procedures, advantages and limitations of **focus-group interviews** were dealt with in Unit 4 and are not repeated here. When applied in researching advertising and marketing campaigns, we are evaluating the attributes, problems, strengths and weaknesses of a product or service from the consumers' point of view. Because targeted current or prospective consumers are selected for these interviews, and because the researcher or moderator does not predetermine answers, the value of focus-group interviews lies in that a variety of positive and negative responses can be elicited. Such research will also reiterate the fact that the needs and motivations of consumers differ. For example, when evaluating the products and services of a car rental firm, business people (whose firms pay for car rental) may be more concerned about the status symbolism, the mechanical and electrical reliability of the car, and the convenience of cars being available at airports. However, people who spend their own money on a rented car will very likely be more concerned with the costs involved.

**Motivational research** is based on an assumption that consumers' behaviour is motivated by emotions (of which they may be unaware). Historically, this kind of research has its roots in the psychoanalytic techniques of Sigmund Freud. A researcher can use the following techniques:

- unstructured and open-ended interviews (conducted individually or in focus groups);
- responses are recorded and transcribed verbatim; and
- the transcribed responses are analysed by means of a content analysis, with the specific objective of identifying motivational statements that can be turned into a unique advertising or marketing appeal.

**verbatim:**
written in exactly
the same words

The following are examples of listeners' responses, which serve as testimonials about the music broadcast by a new community radio station, and can be used as motivational statements:

**testimonials:**
credible
assertions
that endorse a
product or service

- *'... our unique cultural identity is promoted ...'*
- *'... the music creates economic opportunities for the local industry ...'*
- *'... for the first time, historical imbalances of the type of music broadcast, are being redressed ...'*
- *'... the creative and musical skills of local artists are recognised and encouraged ...'*

**Concept testing**   During the initial stages of a promotional campaign, a creative concept has to be formulated, which consists of a description of the advertising idea and primary appeal behind the product or service. To arrive at such a creative concept, several statements (and sometimes rough visual layouts) are placed on separate cards and given to potential consumers. They are then asked to arrange the various concepts (cards) in rank order.

**rank order:**
reorganise in a hierarchy, e.g. from the first to the last choice

The following are examples of appeals (creative concepts) that a technikon, university or college for adult distance education could use in concept testing its advertising campaign among prospective students:

- Our qualifications are recognised worldwide.
- With our qualifications, you can increase your income.
- You have a wide choice of professional degrees.
- Your can enrol and communicate with lecturers via the Internet.
- We offer business, computer, technical and vocational qualifications.

One of the limitations of concept testing is that respondents can only rank those concepts or appeals presented to them. In the above example, concepts such the costs involved, the availability of credit facilities and bursaries, the duration (one-year versus six-month courses), or the flexibility of when examinations take place, are not mentioned and therefore cannot be ranked. To minimise this limitation, we should follow up concept testing with personal interviews or focus-group interviews to establish whether other creative concepts should have been included. If so, the test needs to be repeated with the additional creative concepts included. Follow-up interviews can also be used to collect **diagnostic data**. In other words, the researcher can obtain explanations from respondents as to why they ranked the creative concepts in a particular order.

**diagnostic data:**
information that identifies causes of certain phenomena, such as people's behaviour

As researchers, we are not necessarily trained as advertising copy-writers, so it is useful to briefly consider the characteristic elements of a verbalised or visualised copy of an advertisement.

## Characteristic elements of advertisements

The following nine categories are characteristic elements of advertisements that can be used as guidelines for both the formulation and research of creative concepts:

**benefit:**
additional gain
or advantage

1. Advertisements should promise a (new or existing) benefit for the consumer or user. For example:
*'For the technologist and career expert of tomorrow'* (Technikon Free State).
*'Computers are the future – we make sure they're your future too!'* (College Campus)

**curiosity:**
a desire to
understand
something rare
or strange

2. If a new or existing benefit is not promised, the copy should provoke curiosity. For example:
*'Where do you want to go today?'* (Microsoft)
*'Alcohol is good for you'* (Toyota – to advertise support for a newly introduced petrol-alcohol blend)

**amplification:**
exaggeration and
elaboration, e.g.
by adding detail

3. The copy should contain an amplification of the product/service and/or its benefits, if these are not obvious. For example, the following is an extract of a printed advertisement for the Professional Training Centre at INSCAPE Design College:

*You benefit from:*
- *Individualised tuition: six in a class*
- *Dedicated design-qualified lecturer*
- *International quality: Approved Training Partner*
- *Industry-savvy: strong market contacts*
- *Design-savvy: links to 3-year Graphics course*
- *Commitment: training Corel since 1989*

(*Beeld* 1999a:7)

Amplification is often a necessity when persuading consumers to buy very expensive products, or products that are technically complex, or computers or equipment used in particular sectors, such as agriculture, forestry and fishing, mining and manufacturing.

**claims:**
assertions about
a service or pro-
duct supported
by data

4. Advertisements that contain claims must also contain proof to support such claims, either by relying on the credibility of the communicator (ethos), or by using an emotional appeal (pathos), and/or a logical argument (logos).

For example: Under the headline *'Mabelline creates a whole new kind of natural'* (this is the claim), the copy continues: *'True Illusion Makeup. It's a whole new makeup. A look that's flawless yet makeup free'*. The advertisement continues to explain how Micro-Mesh technology makes the makeup truly different. Proof of the

'true illusion' is provided by a woman's face, which (apart from the lipstick) reflects no indication that she is wearing makeup.

Notice how the name (Mabelline) is used above as part of the creative concept and how, in the following example, the name of the makeup is mirrored by the word 'maybe':

*'Maybe she's born with it. Maybe it's Maybelline'*
(Maybelline – New York).

In the above example, a celebrity endorses the makeup as a testimonial. Proof can also take the form(s) of:

- a warranty (for example, for a refrigerator);
- money-back guarantees (for example, mail order products);
- demonstrations (for example, of stain removers);
- approval from an accredited source (for example, *'Whiskas, the world's most preferred cat food. Developed with leading nutritionists and veterinarians of WALTHAM, the world's leading authority on pet care and nutrition'*);
- offers for a trial period (for example, book clubs); or
- emphasising the manufacturer's or dealer's reputation (for example, *'You pay less at Clicks'*).

5. The copy could also indicate what action the consumer or user is invited to take (if necessary). For example:
   - *'Call us today!!'* (Home Study College);
   - *' ... contact your Metropolitan branch or broker, or call toll-free ...'* (Metropolitan Life);
   - *'Simply complete the order form below and mail it together with your cheque/postal order to ... '* (Natruslim).

   These invitations are normally placed at the end of an advertisement, which closes the message on an active (rather than passive) note.

6. If the product or service has a brand name (e.g. Coca-Cola), this must obviously be included in the advertisement and is usually repeated verbally and/or visually (pictorially).

7. If the product or service is not targeted to the public in general, the appeals used must be identifiable by the prospective consumer or user. For example: *'Calling all students'* is very general, when compared with *'Calling all school-leavers'*, which gives a clearer indication of prospective clients.

**identifiable:**
recognisable and
enabling people
to associate
with it

**slogan:**
a motto,
catchword,
catch-phrase, or
(in radio or TV)
a jingle

**corporate
identity:**
the distinctive-
ness of an organi-
sation, usually
communicated
visually

8.  Not all advertisements need a slogan, but products that are repeat-
    edly purchased need hard-sell slogans that change with each
    campaign. Institutions and political parties often decide on one
    slogan that is repeatedly used to establish a corporate identity.
    Points 1 and 3 above contain examples of institutional slogans
    related to educational institutions, to which the following examples
    can be added:
    *'Increase your earning power with an INTEC Qualification'*
    (INTEC College);
    *'Knowledge is power'* (CTU Training Solutions);
    *'University of the future'* (October 6 University, Egypt);
    *'Training the nation by Distance Education'* (Home Study College);
    *'Building your career wherever you are'* (Technikon SA);
    *'Your future starts here'* (Peninsula Technikon);
    *'Katleho ya Setjaba ke Thuto − The success of the nation lies in
    education'* (Vaal Triangle Technikon);
    *'We train tomorrow's leaders today'* (Border Technikon);
    *'Specialisation in application'* (Technikon Pretoria);
    *'Technology works better by degrees'* (Port Elizabeth Technikon).

**factual
approach:**
rational
communication
which is logical,
descriptive
and/or scientific

**emotional
approach:**
communication
that expresses
and/or excites
feelings

9.  Advertisers know that clients have diverse needs and they are
    forced to communicate their persuasive messages in imaginative
    ways. Two broad approaches can, however, be distinguished: a
    factual and an emotional approach. A factual (or straightforward)
    approach makes strong claims about products and often uses
    demonstrations by experts in white coats. For example, a soap
    powder's colour-safe bleaching power (the claim) is demonstrated
    and *'clinically tested'* in a laboratory-type setting. However, according
    to an emotional approach, people's minds can be reached by
    appealing to their emotions. Nevertheless, even when aiming to
    convey facts about ideas, places, services or products, the chances
    are these facts will increase sales when they are presented in
    imaginative ways. For example, instead of saying *'We offer you a
    24-hour service',* Vodacom uses the phrase: *'You're always in touch'.*
    Or, instead of saying *'Use the Internet to buy property'* Auction
    Alliance, says *'Now bid for a house, with a mouse'.*

    Advertisements that deal with health, financial security, legal
    coverage and funeral schemes usually contain examples that
    begin with an emotional approach and end with factual copy.

For example, Hollard Direct Solutions begin their advertisement of a Hollard Burial Solution with the question '*When your parents pass away, whose funeral will it be?*' and end the advertisement with factual details of the burial plan and an application form.

## 5.2.3   Message structure

Once the content of an advertisement has been established, research has to be undertaken to establish the most effective way to structure the message. This can be done by either doing **formative research** (during the planning stages), and/or to test the advertisement in its completed form (known as **summative research**).

**summative research:**
a retroactive evaluation of a communication message, as a whole, after its completion

During both formative and summative research, our focus can be on either testing the various codes, known as **element research**, or testing the advertisement as a whole.

**element research:**
analysis of specific communication codes, for example, camera shots in television

The following are examples of research methods that can be used when conducting both formative and summative research:

- **Ratings research**: Several versions of the same advertisement are prepared, with one code having been altered, such as different typefaces in printed advertisements, or different types of background music in a radio advertisement. Two or more groups then rate these different versions. In this ratings research, the dependent variable being tested is mainly liking/disliking the advertisement (the affective dimension of impact). (Ratings research is discussed below in section 5.4.3.)

**affective:**
concerned with emotions

- **Readability Ease tests**: Various Readability Ease tests exist that can be applied as a content analysis of a printed text to measure whether readers understand and find it interesting. (The Flesch Readability Ease test was discussed in Unit 4.)

- In the case of radio and television advertisements, a rough cut can be made of the final version, using inexpensive portable equipment and amateur actors. Because of the production costs involved, a **storyboard** may be more suitable to test the most important scenes and dialogue or commentary. Involvement (affective dimension) and recognition (cognitive dimension) can be tested as dependent variables in this example, in addition to those dependent variables mentioned in the above two examples.

**storyboard:**
drawings or photographs that visualise key points of view in a progressive manner

**cognitive:**
mental phenomena, such as perception, memory and thinking

In South Africa, the Advertising Standards Authority is the body responsible for regulating advertising content. Despite the fact that the advertising industry has this self-regulatory body, audiences of the broadcasting media in South Africa have, according to past broadcasting policy documents (South Africa 1997:no page), found advertisements that have the following values embedded to be offensive: gender, racial and religious stereotypes, the portrayal of violence, sexism, advertisements aimed at children, and advertisements for alcohol. In view of the above finding, research as a **pilot test** of the structure and design of advertisements that address social values, is particularly important.

**pilot test:**
a study conducted on a small scale as a trial run

## 5.2.4 Message effectiveness

*How effective is our advertising? Are our investments paying off?* These are examples of questions that advertising departments or agencies ask. Before considering research methods that can be applied to provide answers to these questions, two factors must be taken into account when evaluating the effectiveness of advertising: **advertising goals** and the **dimensions of persuasive effects** that the campaign aims to achieve.

### Advertising goals

When considering the main **goals** of advertisers, we may assume that they are to increase sales (profits) and to increase their share in a specific market. From an organisational point of view, these are not advertising goals, but rather **marketing** goals. In contrast, **advertising** goals must define specifically what an institution expects to achieve. Such a definition should identify a specific effect, to be accomplished among a particular audience (consumers), to a specified degree and within a demarcated period of time. For example, a manufacturer introduces a new vitamin-enriched margarine, with the marketing goal of increasing its share of the margarine market from five to ten per cent. This addresses the general public or mass audience as marketing target. However, the advertising goal could be set as increasing the number of women (living in rural settlements in Northern Province) who identify (recognise) this margarine as one that is vitamin enriched, in six months' time. The latter group is therefore identified as a particular market segment.

**marketing:**
a management process that identifies, anticipates and satisfies profitability

**market segment:**
groups of users or consumers with similar needs and who can be reached by similar media

The promotion of a product or service usually follows these steps:

unawareness ➡ awareness ➡ comprehension ➡ conviction ➡ action.

These steps are an adaptation of the classic **AIDA** formula developed in the 1890s by St Elmo Lewis, which identifies four stages: catching a consumer's **a**ttention, stimulating a consumer's **i**nterest, and a **d**esire and finally resulting in **a**ction (Patti and Moriarty 1990:9). Action refers specifically to buying and using the product or service in question.

In addition to the traditional AIDA model and the innovation adoption model (discussed in section 5.2.1) two other models for setting and researching advertising goals have evolved over the years. According to the **hierarchy of effects model**, consumers pass through a hierarchy of:

awareness ➡ knowledge ➡ liking ➡ preference ➡ conviction ➡ purchase.

According to this model, these series of steps and effects take place longitudinally, over a period of time.

The **information processing model** also assumes that a consumer passes through steps that are similar to the hierarchy of effects model. The steps are:

presentation ➡ attention ➡ comprehension ➡ yielding ➡ retention ➡ behaviour.

As this model treats consumers as information processors, it adds a step not found in the other models: retention. This model emphasises the importance of recipients not only understanding the persuasive message, but remembering the information when making a purchasing decision at a later stage.

Advertising goals can be aimed at any one or more of the above steps. In the margarine example, the goal is achieving awareness and comprehension, and the effectiveness will have to be researched in terms of 'awareness' and 'comprehension'.

It must be noted that, although researchers may find the measurement of 'awareness', 'comprehension', 'conviction' and 'action' as acceptable measuring criteria, some researchers still prefer to use 'sales' as the most valid measuring criterion to determine advertising effectiveness.

## 5

This being despite the argument that the effectiveness of an advertisement can also be influenced by other factors in the communication marketing mix, such as product development, packaging, sizes, varieties, slogans, brand names, pricing, distribution and service.

**marketing mix:**
categories of factors and choices, usually based on the four Ps: product, price, place and promotion

Other advertising goals can also be distinguished – for example, to compete with a rival and draw customers or clients away from that rival, or to change the image of an institution, or to secure the continued support of current customers. It becomes clear that, before the desired effects of an advertisement can be tested, the goals of the advertisement or campaign have to be defined.

## Dimensions of persuasive effects

Three **dimensions of persuasive effects**, which a campaign aims to achieve, can be distinguished: cognitive, affective and conative (Leckenby and Wedding 1982; Wimmer and Dominick 1997:315-322; Belch and Belch 1998:144-163).

**post-test-only design:**
an experiment in which subjects (respondents) are not exposed to a pre-test

**The cognitive dimension** is usually tested by means of a post-test-only design (*see* Unit 4.) The following are examples of research questions, techniques and methods that can be used to investigate this dimension.

- Research question: *Which part of the advertisement attracts subjects' initial attention?*
  A physiological eye-tracking technique can be used to record the movements of subjects' eyes as they scan a printed or graphic advertisement. The sections of the advertisement that attract initial **attention** are established by analysing the path that subjects' eyes follow. The elements that can be tested include the product,

**logo:**
badge or emblem; an abbreviation for logotype

  service, headline, brand name, logo, slogan and/or the positioning of a model in a visual advertisement.
- Research questions: *Which advertisement is the best at catching subjects' attention? And why?* Various methods and techniques, such as interviews, survey research or focus-group interviews can be used. For example, subjects are exposed to several advertisements that advertise the same product and they are asked the above two questions.

In the above examples, **attention** is the dependent variable being tested.

- Testing for **comprehension** is another important dependent variable when evaluating the cognitive dimension of effectiveness. If, for example, television viewers interpret young babies in nappies as a nappy advertisement, instead of an advertisement for an insurance firm, such miscomprehension will obviously have serious effects on the success of the advertising campaign. New advertisements developed for any of the mass media are usually tested with focus groups, guided by open-ended questions such as *Which product (or service) is being advertised?*

- Subjects' awareness and recognition of an advertisement, as well as exposure to and recall of advertisements, are four additional dependent variables that can be tested. Testing for a change from **unawareness** to **awareness** is particularly important in product advertising (such as the example of the vitamin-enriched margarine), as well as in institutional campaigns (such as those conducted by financial and insurance companies). The reason for the latter is that there is little value in subjects being exposed to an advertisement and remaining unaware of what is being advertised, or being unable to remember the name of the product or service. This involves a pre-advertising test (to determine whether people can identify the product or institution) followed by a recall and identification test a few months after the introduction of the campaign.

**pre-advertising test:** research conducted prior to introducing an advertisement or a campaign

In the case of printed advertisements, **aided-recall** techniques are often used to test **recognition, exposure** and **recall**. For example, subjects are given a list of advertisements and asked to identify those that appeared in a particular magazine. Or subjects are given a general group of products, such as fruit juices, and asked whether they can remember an advertisement for a specific brand name. In the case of radio and television advertisements, survey research via telephonic interviews is also an appropriate data-collection method.

The following are examples of open-ended questions that can be asked about printed advertisements in which the **aided-recall** technique is applied:
1. *What does this advertisement tell you about the service?*
2. *What does the written message tell you about the service?*
3. *What does the picture tell you about the service?*

Content analyses (*see* Unit 4) are done of the responses and the results are summarised in, for example, favourable, neutral and unfavourable categories.

- When using **unaided-recall** techniques, by asking open-ended questions such as *Have you recently seen or heard an interesting advertisement for a fruit juice?*, the chances are that we will not elicit responses that apply to a particular brand. However, if subjects do indicate awareness, recognition or exposure, and if they actually recall the brand being tested, these responses will underscore the effectiveness of the advertisement.

**blind test:** the brand name of a product is concealed and its identification by consumers measured

- A **blind test** is another useful technique to test the effectiveness of advertisements, especially branded products. If subjects can identify the brand (e.g. by tasting a specific cool drink), or if they can differentiate between a branded product and other rival products (e.g. by tasting several different cool drinks), this provides a measure of the effectiveness of branding.

The techniques and examples described above are essentially post-test-only designs and the following categories are useful when coding subjects' statements and responses to questions:

- non-readers (subjects who do not remember having, read, seen or heard the advertisement);

**readers:** a collective term that includes readers, viewers and listeners

- associated readers (subjects who have read, seen or heard the advertisement, who are familiar with the brand name and/or who can associate with the product or service); and
- read-all readers (subjects who have read, seen or heard the entire advertisement and who can remember specific details of the advertisement).

**The affective dimension** focuses on consumers' feelings and can include testing subjects' involvement, the extend to which they like or dislike an advertisement, and their attitude change towards a product or service due to exposure to an advertisement. In other words, involvement, likes/dislikes and attitude change are the dependent variables in these tests.

The following are examples of research techniques and methods that can be used to evaluate the affective dimension of persuasive effects:

- **Survey research**, and especially semantic differential scales and rating scales (*see* Unit 3), are most frequently used to measure attitudes and attitudinal change. This process involves three steps:
  1. the measurement of subjects' attitudes before being exposed to an advertisement;
  2. their exposure to the advertisement, or series of advertisements; and
  3. measuring the same subjects' attitude after exposure.

  To test for a **change of attitude**, as in the case of awareness testing, implies that the findings of the remeasurement are compared with a corresponding survey after a series of advertisements have been run, to determine:
  1. whether attitudes have changed; and
  2. whether the degree of change is strong enough to cause consumers to buy the product or use the service.

**one-group pre-test-post-test design:**
one group of subjects is measured before and after exposure to an independent variable, and the measurements are compared

- A one-group pre-test-post-test **experimental** design, as a form of **forced exposure**, can also be used to determine the relative effectiveness of a single advertisement. This design is often preferred because of the difficulties involved in controlling subjects' exposure to a specific advertisement. It involves an evaluation and comparison of the responses of one experimental group of subjects before $(O_1)$ and after $(O_2)$ exposure to a stimulus $(X)$. For example, a group of teenagers is given a list of different flavours and brand names of potato chips and asked to rank their order of preference. They are invited to watch a popular film on television, during which one specific brand and flavour of potato chips is advertised. After the viewing session, the teenagers are again asked to rank their preferences. The relative effectiveness of the television advertisement is determined by comparing pre-viewing preferences, with post-viewing preferences. This method can be repeated with other groups whose demographic characteristics differ. This method can also be used when visiting subjects at home, and using advertisements for potato chips published in a magazine or newspaper as the intervening variable. These experiments are used to evaluate consumers' preferences, and changes in attitude and can be implemented to different markets before introducing an advertising campaign.

**intervening variable:**
a variable that is the effect of one variable and the cause of another variable

**PEAC:**
Program Evaluation Analysis Computer

- Tests can also be conducted in a **group administration** (*see* Unit 3), using a PEAC system. This method originated in the United States in 1978, to test the appeal of televised segments, sequences and scenes, for example divided into intervals of five or fewer seconds (Mielke and Chen 1983:42-43). This hand-held microcomputer has five buttons that range from *feel very positive* to *feel very negative* which each subject presses while listening to a radio advertisement, or watching a filmed or televised advertisement. Other measurement scales from which the respondents can select include:

| Too slow | | or | Clear | | or | Interesting |
|---|---|---|---|---|---|---|
| Just right | | | Uncertain | | | Don't know |
| Too fast | | | Not clear | | | Not interesting |

As a measuring instrument, or technique, this technological rating device has several advantages: it is convenient and can test groups of people simultaneously, responses can be monitored from moment to moment, feedback is immediate, and subjects' responses remain confidential and anonymous. Data collected by means of a PEAC system also has high internal validity. However, it does require quick responses from subjects and, once they have pressed certain buttons during the advertisement, they cannot change their minds.

**internal validity:** results reflect the measurement of expected conditions, rather than extraneous variables

**projective tests:** subjects respond freely to complete a story or picture

- To obtain greater insight into subjects' feelings, **projective tests** can also be used. Subjects are given an open-ended narrative or story that deals with the product or service being advertised, and they are requested to complete the story. When young children are involved, they can be asked to draw a picture that involves the product or service. In this test an unconscious transfer of subjects' individual impressions and feelings are made to completing the story or drawing the picture. This test functions as a form of self-disclosure, because it is based on the premise that subjects' responses will be an indication of their self-images and world view.

**The conative dimension** of measuring message effectiveness is concerned with two categories of consumer behaviour: to measure subjects' **predisposition** to buy a product or to subscribe to a service, and to measure subjects' **actual behaviour** as consumers. The methods and techniques used to research predisposition and/or actual behaviour include questioning, Likert scales and direct response – or actual sales.

- **Questioning** (face-to-face, telephonic or via questionnaire) is normally used in both cases. In the first case, subjects' predispositions are measured prior to the introduction of the advertisement (or campaign) and the same subjects' predispositions are measured thereafter. The following are examples of open-ended questions that can be asked:

*If you had to buy margarine, which brand would you buy? If this brand were out of stock, would you buy any other margarine?*

**post-campaign questions:** questions asked only after the campaign has run to measure the dependent variable(s)

Post-campaign questions can also be included to establish whether the campaign had negative effects on subjects' predisposition and actual behaviour. For example:

*Is there a brand margarine that you would not buy?*

A **Likert scale** (discussed in Unit 3) is particularly useful for testing subjects' predispositions and how their buying preferences and behaviour change during and after a campaign. Such a scale is represented in the following example:

| | |
|---|---|
| ☐ | I'll definitely buy this margarine |
| ☐ | I'll probably buy this margarine sometime |
| ☐ | I don't know whether I'll buy this margarine |
| ☐ | I'll probably never buy this margarine |
| ☐ | I'll never buy this margarine |

**Internet:** telecommunication links between computers, allowing two-way communication

- Subjects' **direct response** – for example, to coupons inserted in the print media, by phoning a toll-free number for more information or to place an order via the Internet – and actual sales is, however, a more reliable method of post-testing the effectiveness of an advertising campaign. These responses can also be verified by comparing pre- and post-campaign audits of stores' actual sales data.

## EXECUTIVE SUMMARY: ADVERTISING MESSAGE RESEARCH

1 Research requires an under-standing of:
- users' and consumers' behaviours, values and lifestyles;
- the role of opinion leaders;
- characteristic elements of advertisements;
- advertising goals;
- the cognitive, affective and conative dimensions of persuasive effects.

2 General research methods or techniques used:
- content analysis;
- field research;
- survey research;
- experimental research.

3 Specific methods or techniques used to research message **content**:
- focus-group interviews;
- motivational research;
- concept testing.

4 Specific methods or techniques used to research message **structure**:
- element research;
- formative research;
- summative research;
- ratings research;
- Readability Ease tests;
- pilot tests.

5 Specific methods or techniques used to research message **effectiveness**:
- pre-advertising tests;
- aided-recall techniques;
- unaided-recall techniques;
- blind test;
- PEAC;
- projective tests.

## Self-evaluation and portfolio tasks

5.1 View television advertisements during prime time on seven consecutive evenings, and judge whether or not the women (or blacks) who appear in the advertisements are portrayed in roles that were previously reserved for men (or whites).

5.2 How would the interpretation of an advertisement of a new household product (e.g. to clean carpets) differ among the five groups of adopters described in section 5.2.1?

5.3 What is the role of an opinion leader in an advertisement?

**5.4** You want to apply motivational research to prepare the message content of an advertisement for a product or service. Briefly describe your selected product (or service). Formulate your research questions or hypotheses, and ten questions that can be asked in an unstructured, open-ended interview. Draw a purposive sample of five individuals who are potential consumers. Follow the steps described in section 5.2.2 and write down the motivational statements that could be used in an advertising appeal.

**5.5** Why must traditional demographic research for the purpose of market segmentation be extended to include consumer lifestyle research?

**5.6** Why is it difficult to predict consumer behaviour, based on motives?

**5.7** Find and describe an example of a current advertisement that illustrates the use of an opinion leader.

**5.8** What was the last product that you bought that cost more than R1 000? What were your reasons (motivations) for buying the product? Did your family, friends, the salespersons or advertising play a role in your purchasing behaviour?

**5.9** You have been commissioned to conduct a concept test for a new cellular phone. Identify your target market (in terms of demographics and lifestyles). Compile five statements that represent creative concepts. Approach ten people who represent your target market and ask them to rank the concepts according to their preferences. After the concept testing, conduct interviews with your respondents and determine whether you should have included other concepts.

**5.10** Select advertisements (e.g. printed in your local newspaper) that:
- promise a (new or existing) benefit for the consumer or user;
- provoke curiosity;
- contain an amplification of the product/service and its benefit;
- contain claims and proof to support such claims;
- indicate what action the consumer or user is invited to take;
- has a brand name that is repeated verbally and/or visually ;
- contain appeals that give a clear indication of the prospective clients targeted;
- contain slogans;
- use a factual approach;
- use an emotional approach.

## 5.3 Audience analyses of print and broadcast media

Research by print and media industries is usually oriented towards practical application, especially media that rely on advertisements for financial survival. In this section, we consider different methods and techniques that can be used to analyse the audiences of these mass media.

### 5.3.1 Audience profiles

The term 'audience' – as used here – refers to magazine and newspaper readers, radio listeners and television viewers. Researching an audience's **profile** simply means that the demographic characteristics of a particular group (such as the readers of a particular publication) are summarised. For example, in the telecommunications sector, Singh (1998:49) differentiates among the following user groups: 'urban residential; rural users; small/medium-sized businesses; large users (e.g. banks); government administrations; public/private social delivery systems; and exporters'.

Despite sharing similar demographic characteristics, individual audience members may differ in terms of their attitudes and interests (psychographics), as well as their lifestyles. Therefore, providing management (editors, producers or advertisers) with a multidimensional profile of specific audiences will be of greater use when undertaking any of the following:
- launching a new publication;
- introducing a new programme;
- changing current content;
- changing layout or programme scheduling;
- preparing advertisements; and/or
- selling advertising space or airtime.

**AIO:**
an acronym for 'activities', 'interests' and 'opinions'

In order to obtain such a multidimensional profile, a **survey** is conducted among the members of a particular audience, using **AIO measures.** By giving respondents a battery of **attitudinal statements**, with a Likert scale that measures their degree of agreement or disagreement with the statements, we are able to cluster the respondents. For example, respondents who agree with the following statements, could be labelled 'traditionalists':

*A woman's place is in the home.*
*Children should be seen, not heard.*

Respondents who agree with the following statements could be labelled 'progressive':

*Women and men are equal.*
*Sex outside of marriage is acceptable.*

In addition to statements, a battery of **questions** can be compiled to determine:
- how members of the audience spend their time (activities at work and during leisure time); and
- what their interests are.

By grouping respondents who share similar activities, interests and opinions, the audience can be segmented into smaller and more specific lifestyle groups (called **lifestyle segmentation**). Whereas research that deals with **audience profiles** can be applied to both the print media and the broadcast media, the type of audience analysis dealt with in the next section, deals specifically with readers of print media, such as newspapers and magazines.

## 5.3.2   Item-selection studies

The second type of audience studies, called **item-selection** studies, applies more specifically to readers of print media. As the objective of such studies is to describe who reads specific sections of a publication, the unit of analysis is usually specific articles or reports (such as a front-page story), or content categories (such as entertainment, finance or crime). Although surveys, with self-administered **questionnaires** and **telephonic** interviews can be used to collect readers' responses, the ideal (although costly) method is **face-to-face interviews**. These interviews enable us to use **aided-recall** techniques (*see* section 5.2.4).

Respondents are given an entire publication and asked to recall which article or reports they have read, or specific articles or reports are pre-selected. In both cases, respondents can also be asked to identify (mark with coloured pens) which sections they have read. In so doing, a distinction can be made among, but not limited to, the following categories:

- reading the headlines only;
- reading a section of the report;
- reading the caption of a photograph;
- reading the report as a whole.

Variations in the length of reports and different types of content can then be correlated with respondents' psychographics and lifestyle characteristics.

## 5.3.3 Reader/non-reader studies

The term 'readers' is used collectively to refer to readers of print media, as well as radio listeners and television viewers. **Reader/non-reader** research is the third type of audience study. **Surveys** (face-to-face, telephonic or by means of self-administered questionnaires) are conducted with the objective of establishing who does and who does not 'read' a particular medium (such as a specific newspaper).

Once non-readers have been identified, we attempt to:

- describe them with reference to their demographic and lifestyle characteristics (such as the elderly, with a low income and illiterate); and
- obtain reasons why certain respondents are non-readers (by using open-ended questions).

However, the number of subjects or respondents categorised as non-readers is dependent on *how* non-readers are identified (operationally defined). If a three-options scale *(very often, sometimes, never)* is used together with the following question, the chances are that very few respondents would answer *never.*

*When do you read newspapers?*

Whereas, many more respondents can be expected to answer 'no' (and be classified as non-readers), in response to the following question:

*Did you read a newspaper today?*

**readership:**
number of people
who actually read
a publication

**Readership** studies are of particular importance in the advertising sector and are based on the premise that each edition of a publication is read by more than one person.

**AMPS:**
All Media
and Products
Survey

According to the Government Communication and Information System (1999:478), South African daily newspapers are read by 4,6 million adults, weekly newspapers by 8,6 million adults, and magazines by 8,8 million adults. In South Africa, AMPS has, since 1975, provided one of the world's largest multi-product and media surveys on an annual basis – including the estimated readership of publications. (An update of the latest figures is obtainable via the Internet address http://www.saarf.co.za)

Unaided-recall, aided-recall and recognition are three of the techniques normally used in readership surveys. The following are examples of questions asked during an **unaided-recall** test:

*Have you read a newspaper during the past week?*
(If the response is 'yes')
*Can you name the newspaper(s)?*

Once the publication is named (e.g. *Sunday Times*) specific questions about the content of the publication can be asked, such as:

*Which of the three sections in* Business Times *do you prefer to read? Why?*
*Did you read the last edition of the* Sunday Times *magazine?*
(If the response is 'yes')
*Which part of the last* Sunday Times *magazine did you read?*

**response bias:**
errors due to
individual
responses not
being truthful

It must be noted that reliability of unaided-recall techniques is open to question, because of response bias, such as trying to please or impress the interviewer, or the difficulty that the average reader has to remember the specific contents of a publication.

**masked recall:**
identifying a
publication, of
which the name
is concealed

The procedure followed when using **aided-recall** techniques is similar to the procedure discussed in section 5.2.4 (message effectiveness).

A variation of this technique, called **'masked recall'** (Wimmer and Dominick 1997:324), can also be used. In this procedure, the name of the newspaper or magazine is covered and subjects are asked if they can identify the publication, whether or not they have read the last publication and (if affirmative) if they can remember any of the contents. In order to verify the accuracy of the subjects' memory, applying a **recognition** technique can extend this procedure. This involves giving a copy of the particular publication to those respondents who remember having read it, with some phoney items included. Respondents who claim to have read these phoney items are then excluded from the audience calculation.

Research that distinguishes between readers and non-readers enables media managers to establish whether the content of the mass medium, the costs involved, accessibility, preference for other leisure-time activities or preference for another mass medium, are among the variables that contribute to respondents being non-readers.

In addition to the analysis of audience profiles, item-selection studies, and reader/non-reader studies, audience research can also deal with questions about why audiences select certain media and media content, and what satisfaction they obtain from mass-media communication. These research questions are dealt with in the next section.

## 5.3.4    Uses and gratifications studies

The uses and gratifications approach to audience analysis, is based on two assumptions:
- that media experiences can best be explained from the perspective of the audience members; and
- that the selection of a particular mass medium and content is a conscious, active and motivated choice made by audience members.

**Survey** research, using self-administered questionnaires, is usually undertaken, in which respondents indicate the degree to which they agree/disagree with a list of statements of the reasons why they have selected a particular medium and content.

These reasons are diverse and vary from seeking information to escaping from personal problems. McQuail (2000:388), for example, distinguishes among these four categories of media-person interactions: 'diversion; … personal relationships; … personal identity; … [and] surveillance'.

It would therefore be advisable, when listing possible reasons, to distinguish:

- possible gratifications that the audience may seek (which offer reasons why certain media and content are used and others are avoided); (e.g. *I prefer to watch* Egoli, *rather than* The Bold and the Beautiful *because the story deals with South African situations*) versus
- possible gratifications (satisfactions) that the audience perceives to have obtained (which offers reasons for an increase or decrease in circulation, sales or ratings); (e.g. *Watching* Egoli *makes me relax*).

The following are categories of individually experienced needs that can be satisfied by mass communication (O'Sullivan et al. 1996:326):

- **diversion** refers to the need to escape from our daily routines or problems, to release tension and to relax, which are essentially affective needs to be entertained;
- **personal relationships** refer to the social need for companionship, which is fulfilled by getting to know media personalities, as if they were friends and/or by using mass-mediated messages as topics of conversation;
- **personal identity** refers to the need to evaluate and confirm our sense of self, by continually comparing our personal situation and values with those found in the so-called reality conveyed by the mass media; and
- **surveillance** refers to the need for information about issues and events in our social world, which are essentially cognitive needs.

It is expected that gratifications sought and satisfactions obtained will, in future, include comparisons between different delivery channels, such as printed newspapers versus their on-line electronic versions. For example, readers have direct access to on-line electronic versions of certain newspapers at times that suit them, and this delivery channel could be increasingly preferred to waiting for a newspaper to be printed and distributed.

Readership studies and readers' preferences in the case of print media can also be combined with an analysis of visual codes. This type of research is dealt with in the next section.

## 5.3.5 Typography and layout research

Typography and layout research measures the effects of different typefaces and various elements of the page layout of print media (newspapers, brochures, knock-and-drop pamphlets and magazines). In addition to focus-group interviews, motivational research and concept testing, an experimental design can be used in which subjects are assigned to one or more treatment group(s) and exposed to an experimental (independent) stimulus. The latter is usually presented in the form of a mock magazine or newspaper page. The independent variable(s) can include one or more (but is not limited to) different white spaces, headings and column widths; different types of layout; different sizes, faces and styles of font; and different sizes of photographs combined with the text.

The subjects' interest and preference (as dependent variables) can be measured by a **semantic differential scale**, whereas comprehension and recall (as dependent variables) can be measured by **multiple-choice** questions or a series of **true/false** questions. These scales and types of questions were discussed in Unit 3.

**montage:** pieces of pictures and graphics combined on a page

With the advent of computerised pagination, layout and montage, and certain publications becoming available on the World Wide Web, it is anticipated that the effects of graphic and electronic design elements on readers' preferences and understanding, will become an important area of research.

---

### EXECUTIVE SUMMARY:
#### AUDIENCE ANALYSES OF PRINT AND BROADCAST MEDIA

1  Research methods used:
   - field research;
   - survey research;
   - experimental research.

2  Analysing the audiences of the print media:
   - item-selection studies;
   - typography and layout research.

3  Analysing the audiences of print and broadcast media:
   - audience profile (demographics; psychographics; lifestyles);
   - reader/non-reader studies;
   - uses and gratifications studies.

## 5.4 Researching mass-media efficiency

Determining the most effective medium or combination of media, is of interest to media managers and advertisers of a particular service or product. The key terms that are important in such media research are:
- research;
- frequency;
- gross ratings points (GRPs);
- circulation;
- ratings research; and
- non-ratings research.

### 5.4.1 Reach, frequency and gross ratings points (GRPs)

**Reach** can be defined as 'the total number of households or persons that will be exposed to a message in a particular medium at least once over a certain period (usually four weeks)' (Wimmer and Dominick 1997:322). This cumulative audience is usually calculated as a percentage of the total population. For example, if 300 households of a target population of 1 000 households are exposed to a particular television message, the reach is 30%.

**Frequency** can be defined as the number of times the same message has been received by each household. To calculate the average frequency, the following formula is applied:

$$\frac{\text{Total number of exposures for all households}}{\text{Reach}} = \text{Average frequency of exposure}$$

This calculation means that if, in a sample of households, the total number of exposures to the same message, such as an advertisement, is 600 and the reach is 30, then the average frequency of exposure is 20. We can then conclude that the average household was exposed to the message 20 times.

According to this formula, it stands to reason that if the reach were to increase, the average frequency would decrease. For example, if the reach in the example were 75% and not 30%, then the average frequency drops to 8 (calculated as follows: 600 ÷ 75 = 8).

**GRPs:**
**gross ratings points**

**GRPs** are calculated on the basis of both reach and average frequency, when we have to select between two media or two programmes in which to broadcast an advertisement. For example, soap opera A has a reach of 30% and an average frequency of 20, whereas soap opera B has a reach of 30% and an average frequency of 10. The question that arises is: Which soap opera offers a better reach-frequency relationship? This can be answered by calculating the GRPs of each programme using the following formula:

$$\text{GRPs} = \text{Reach} \times \text{Average frequency}$$

The GRPs in the above cases are:
For soap opera A: 30 x 20 = 600
For soap opera B: 30 x 10 = 300

In this example, soap opera A scores better in terms of the gross ratings points and would, in all likelihood, be selected by the advertiser.

In addition to measuring the most effective medium or combination of media, advertising media research includes an analysis of the size and composition of audiences.

**5**

## 5.4.2 Circulation

**circulation:**
print circulation,
exhibition audi-
ences/attendees,
cinema audiences
or Internet hits

A variety of methods are used to collect information about the size and composition of audiences of both print and broadcast media. In the print media, a publication's **circulation** is determined by calculating the number of copies of magazines or newspapers per issue that are delivered to subscribers, and those sold at other outlets. Because magazine and newspaper advertising rates are determined by their circulation figures, institutions such as an Audit Bureau of Circulations usually verify these. In the case of South Africa, circulation figures are independently audited and certified by the Audit Bureau of Circulations of Southern Africa. Circulation figures are often used to measure the advertising efficiency of a particular medium based on the following calculation:

|  | **MAGAZINE A** | **MAGAZINE B** |
|---|---|---|
| Cost of an advertisement for the same size space | R1 000 | R1 300 |
| Circulation | 50 000 | 80 000 |
| Cost per thousand circulated copies | R1 000 ÷ 50 = R20 | R1 300 ÷ 80 = R16,25 |

The above calculation of the cost per thousand circulated copies indicates that magazine B is a more cost-effective advertising medium. In the case of television and radio, the cost-effectiveness is calculated or expressed in cost per thousand households using television, or per thousand persons using radio.

## 5.4.3 Ratings research

Circulation studies are undertaken for newspapers and magazines, whereas **ratings** research is used by television and radio managers, programme producers and advertising agencies. A rating can be defined as an approximation of the percentage of households (or people) in a specified population that watch a specific television station/channel or listen to a specific radio station.

As ratings research cannot investigate total listening or viewing populations, the importance of drawing a representative sample is essential. That is why multistage **area probability sampling** is appropriate (*see* Unit 3). Since ratings are estimates of the size of listening and viewing audiences, these should not be regarded as facts. Ratings must be interpreted keeping the following variables in mind:

- the type and size of the sample drawn;
- the time of day (e.g. fewer people are expected to watch television at 08:00, than during peak time, between 19:00 and 20:00); and
- the number of channels or stations from which audiences can select (with a greater selection of channels, the ratings become more meaningful).

The different methods used during audience rating **surveys** to collect data include telephonic interviews, electronic meters, diaries and so-called people meters. A rating is determined using the following formula:

$$\frac{\text{Households (or people)}}{\text{Population (sampled)}} = \text{Rating}$$

If, out of a sample of 4 000 households, 440 households are tuned to Station-1 at the time of a survey, the rating would be 0,11 or 11% (calculated as 440 ÷ 4 000).

Broadcast managers and advertising agencies are not only interested in the audience rating of one station, but in the combined ratings of all stations that broadcast and compete with one another in a particular geographic area. Combined ratings give an estimate of the total number of HUT – or, in the case of radio broadcasting, PUR.

**HUT:**
households using television

**PUR:**
persons using radio

In the following hypothetical example, the HUT is 1 956 and the combined (or total rating) is 48,9%, which means that approximately 1 956 of the 4 000 households sampled were watching television on one of the three stations at the time of the survey:

**STATION-1** $\dfrac{440}{4\,000}$ = 0,11, or 11%

**STATION-2** $\dfrac{800}{4\,000}$ = 0,20, or 20%

**STATION-3** $\dfrac{716}{4\,000}$ = 0,179, or 17,9%

**HUT = 1 956**        **TOTAL RATING = 48,9%**

**5**

These calculations are made in terms of a sample that represents a target population. This means that the rating for each station can be interpreted as a **share** of the audience using this formula:

**share:** percentage of the sample of HUT or PUR

$$\frac{\text{Households (or people)}}{\text{HUT (or PUR)}} = \text{Share}$$

The share can also be interpreted as an estimated percentage of the target population. In other words, if the sample of 4 000 households were drawn from a population of 9,5 million, a rating of 11% for Station-1 could be projected to represent a rough estimate of 1 045 000 households of the population.

Just as advertising media research considers circulation figures to determine the most cost-effective print medium, in the case of radio and television, such cost effectiveness is calculated or expressed in CPT. The CPT calculations do not indicate the effectiveness of an advertisement, but do offer a monetary estimate of the advertisement's reach. In other words, it provides an estimate of what it would cost an advertiser to reach 1 000 households (television), or persons (radio).

**CPT:** cost per thousand (households or persons)

The following formula is used to calculate the CPT:

$$\frac{\text{Cost of advertisement}}{\text{Audience size (in thousands)}} = \text{CPT}$$

By using the hypothetical survey figures above, if a 30-second advertisement on Station-1 costs R150 000, the CPT would be:

$$\frac{\text{R150 000}}{\text{1 045 (thousand households)}} = \text{R143,54}$$

Although the CPT is an important criterion, advertisers also consider other variables when buying advertising time on radio and television, including the marketing strategy, the audience profile, the time of day and the type of programme during or after which it will be broadcast.

Three American radio consultants introduced a new ratings procedure in 2000 to enable listeners to **rate music** for radio stations and record companies. By visiting the website http://www.ratethemusic.com, listeners can evaluate music in a variety of categories. This service enables record companies to survey listeners' opinion of music before it is distributed commercially, and other marketing variables such as CD cover designs.

Although ratings research is a basic decision-making instrument for programmers and advertisers, it does not measure the quality of radio and television programmes, or the audience's opinions about the programmes. For such additional information, broadcasters, advertisers and consultants turn to different types of **non-ratings research**.

## 5.4.4 Non-ratings research

The objective of non-ratings research can be diverse, depending on, but not limited to, whether the focus is on audience's likes and dislikes of the programme content, scheduling or format, or the appropriateness and popularity of presenters, performers and entertainers. Demographic and lifestyle **profiles** of audiences, and **uses and gratifications** research, are also examples of non-ratings research.

Non-ratings research is appropriate during the different stages of planning, developing and producing a radio or television programme. **Formative** evaluation occurs after the initial idea, plan or purpose of the programme has been formulated, or after a rough edited version or sections of the whole production have been completed. Simulations, such as storyboards, photographs or drawings − in addition to rough cuts − are used because they are inexpensive. Such research can test the general appeal of the storyline, characterisation, relationships among characters and specific audiovisual codes used, as well as aspects such as stereotyping or gender issues. Focus-group interviews, motivational research and especially concept testing are appropriate techniques to use. Based on the research findings, changes can still be made.

**Summative** evaluation takes place after post-production, after which the programme cannot be changed. However, negative findings can result in discontinuing the broadcast or at least avoiding similar problems in future productions. Research can be conducted by means

of **group administration** (and the use of Likert scales and semantic differential scales), or **experiments**, such as the one-group pre-test-post-test design, and/or by means of **surveys** using questionnaires. These research methods and aided-recall and unaided-recall techniques can be applied to evaluate the cognitive, affective and conative dimensions of the effectiveness of a radio or television programme.

Broadcasting organisations, such as the SABC, use a self-administered postal questionnaire as a standard qualitative measuring instrument, known as the **AI**, to measure the general entertainment level of television programmes. The kind of items usually included in such a survey require respondents to answer two questions and respond to a rating question related to each programme broadcast during a week, such as:

**AI:**
Appreciation
Index

- *How much of this programme did you watch?*
- *When you think of the past seven broadcasts, how many did you watch?*

and…

- *Please rate this programme by selecting one of the following options:*
  *Extremely enjoyable* ☐
  *Very enjoyable* ☐
  *Fairly enjoyable* ☐
  *Not very enjoyable* ☐
  *Not at all enjoyable* ☐

As part of summative research, the AI provides a measure of the entertainment gratifications (satisfactions) derived from watching a particular programme. When viewed from a uses and gratifications approach, it means that the viewer becomes the judge of the meaning of 'entertainment'. The rationale behind these surveys is that, although a prime-time programme, such as news, may receive a high rating (many HUTs), its appreciation index (entertainment value or programme appreciation in general) may be low. In other words, although many people watch the news, its appreciation index can be low.

Radio stations often make use of **phone-in** programmes, or invite listeners to communicate by means of faxes, letters and the Internet, as methods to determine listeners' preferences and complaints. A type of non-ratings research that is of particular interest to radio stations is to measure listeners' likes and dislikes of different types of music.

In addition to the methods mentioned above, such as **focus-group** interviews, **group administration** and especially **call-out** research methods are used. These two methods involve playing a number of hooks to sampled respondents, each of which are rated on an evaluation scale (e.g. from *my favourite* to *I can't stand it)*. In a group administration, respondents could meet in a comfortable auditorium, with a quality sound system and in an environment devoid of other distractions. In call-out research, respondents are contacted and hooks played telephonically, which respondents then rate verbally. Because of the fatigue factor, the duration of the rating sessions needs to be considered. If it takes someone five seconds to rate each of the 15-second segments, it means that a one-hour session should be limited to rating 180 hooks (3 600 seconds ÷ [15 seconds + 5 seconds] = 180). If we use the same calculations, then call-out research that consists of 20 hooks will take approximately seven minutes, plus the time it takes to introduce the interview. The objective of applying these two methods need not be limited to listeners' music tastes (in terms of likes and dislikes), but can also be used to research whether a particular type of music is judged appropriate for the particular radio station.

**hooks:** segments of musical recordings, each with a duration of approximately 15 seconds

**fatigue factor:** respondents become tired, for various reasons

Instead of relying only on head counting (ratings research), non-ratings research enables broadcast managers to make informed decisions about altering programming schedules or discontinuing the production of a second series. Non-ratings research can also be undertaken to determine how external publics, such as advertisers and audiences, perceive the image and services of the broadcasting station. As this involves conducting a public relations audit, it is dealt with in Unit 6.

---

## *EXECUTIVE SUMMARY:* RESEARCHING MASS-MEDIA EFFICIENCY

1 Research methods used:
- field research;
- survey research;
- experimental research.

2 Formulas and calculations used:
- reach;
- frequency;
- gross ratings points;
- circulation;
- ratings;
- share;
- cost per thousand;
- ratings via the Internet.

3 Non-ratings research:
- audiences' profiles;
- uses and gratifications studies;
- formative research;
- summative research;
- Appreciation Index;
- call-out research.

---

## Self-evaluation and portfolio tasks

**5.14** What does the following statement mean?

*A radio advertisement broadcast between 08:00 and 08:30 on a particular radio station over a period of one month has a reach of 60%.*

**5.15** Consider the following figures and calculate the average frequency of exposure.
*In a sample of households, the total number of exposures to a television news broadcast is 1 680 and the reach is 8%.*

**5.16** What is the purpose of calculating gross ratings points (GRPs)?

**5.17** Consider the following scenario and decide in which newspaper you would advise a client to place an advertisement:
*Newspaper A has a reach of 45% and an average frequency of 10.*
*Newspaper B has a reach of 50% and an average frequency of 5.*

**5.18** A government department wants to advertise a number of vacancies but, due to budget cuts, it has to ensure that it selects the most efficient newspaper as an advertising medium. Consider the following scenario and indicate which newspaper you would advise the department to select:

| NEWSPAPER | CIRCULATION FIGURES | COST OF ADVERTISEMENT |
|-----------|---------------------|-----------------------|
| A | 1 883 000 | R1 000 |
| B | 1 224 000 | R960 |

**5.19** A community newspaper is distributed free of charge, on a weekly basis, and financed by selling advertising space. Assume that you are the editor of one such newspaper and you want to conduct a readership study. Which research method would you select and which techniques would you apply?

**5.20** Read the scenario below and do the following calculations:
- calculate each television station's share of the audience;
- project the total number of households in the population that are watching each of the three stations.
- calculate the CPT for a R1 000, 30-second advertisement to be broadcast on TV2.

**Scenario**: Assume the local television broadcasting market consists of three stations: TV1, TV2 and TV3. The market consists of 200 000 households with television sets. A research company draws a random sample of 1 200 households and their findings indicate the following:

25% of the sample is watching TV1;

15% of the sample is watching TV2; and

10% of the sample is watching TV3.

**5.21** You have been requested by a local radio station to conduct music call-out research. Perform a pilot study by following these steps:

- compile a seven-point semantic differential scale that you want to use as measuring instrument;
- edit several selections of music recording onto an audio-cassette (of about 15 seconds each); and
- approach 10 people to rate these music selections, by filling in the semantic differential scales.

# 5.5 Summary

Consumers and mass-media audiences are becoming more fragmented and sophisticated in their needs. This, with an increase in competitors, means that research is essential when making content, programming, sales and/or marketing decisions. The discussion in this unit was aimed at dealing with different methods and techniques that can be used in the diverse areas of advertising, print media and broadcasting research.

We started the unit with advertising message research, in which we dealt with understanding consumers' behaviour, message content, structure and effectiveness, including researching the cognitive, affective and conative dimensions of persuasive effects. This was followed by methods and techniques used to analyse audiences of print and broadcast media. The latter included an analysis of audience profiles, item-selection studies, reader/non-reader studies, uses and gratifications studies, as well as typography and layout research. The unit ended with techniques and formulas that are used to research mass-media efficiency, including calculating the reach, frequency, gross ratings points, circulation, ratings, and non-ratings research.

**5**

Before continuing with Unit 6, you are encouraged to evaluate your achievement of the learning outcomes using the following guide.

> ### ASSESSMENT OF LEARNING OUTCOMES
> Ratings for evaluation of performance:
> 5    very high (extremely good)
> 4    high (good)
> 3    medium (average)
> 2    low (poor)
> 1    very low (extremely poor)
> 0    evidence is absent

| Outcomes (knowledge, competence and orientations) *You should be able to demonstrate your understanding and ability to:* | Evidence of performance | Examples of criteria used to evaluate evidence of performance | Evaluation of performance Ratings | | | | | |
|---|---|---|---|---|---|---|---|---|
| | | | 5 | 4 | 3 | 2 | 1 | 0 |
| Conduct advertising message research | by selecting appropriate research methods or techniques. | The selection shows an understanding and meets the requirements and options summarised in the Executive Summary at the end of section 5.2. | | | | | | |
| Undertake audience analyses of print and broadcast media; and research mass-media efficiency | by conducting pilot studies. | The selection is appropriate to the goal and objective of the research, as well as the mass medium (summarised in the Executive Summaries at the end of sections 5.3 and 5.4). | | | | | | |
| | | Each pilot study follows the steps, and reflects consideration having been given to the ratings evaluations, as well as to the issues relevant to each step (*see* Unit 2). | | | | | | |

## Suggested reading

Belch, GE and Belch, MA. 1998. *Advertising and promotion: an integrated marketing communications perspective.* (4th edition). Boston: Irwin/McGraw-Hill.

Berger, AA. 1991. *Media analysis techniques.* Revised edition. Newbury Park, California: Sage.

Bless, C and Higson-Smith, C. 1995. *Fundamentals of social research methods: an African perspective.* (2nd edition). Kenwyn, Cape Town: Juta.

Deacon, D, Pickering, M, Golding, P and Murdock, G. 1999. *Researching communications. A practical guide to methods in media and cultural analysis.* London: Arnold.

Government Communication and Information System (GCIS). 2000/01 (or later edition). *South Africa Yearbook 2000/01.* Pretoria: Government Printer. Also available on Government Online http://www.gov.za

Leedy, LD. 1997. *Practical research: planning and design.* (6th edition). Upper Saddle River, NJ: Prentice-Hall.

Lester, PM. 1995. *Visual communication. Images with messages.* Belmont, California: Wadsworth.

McQuail, D. 1997. *Audience analysis.* Thousand Oaks, California: Sage.

Priest, SH. 1996. *Doing media research: an introduction.* Thousand Oaks, California: Sage.

Riffe, D, Lacey, S and Fico, FG. 1998. *Analyzing media messages.* Mahwah, NJ: Lawrence Erlbaum.

Silverstone, R. 1999. *Why study the media?* London: Sage.

Wimmer, RD and Dominick, JR. 1997. *Mass media research: an introduction.* (5th edition). Belmont, California: Wadsworth.

Winston, B. 1998. *Media, technology and society.* London: Routledge.

# Organisational and development communication research

*If you want one year of prosperity, grow grain.*
*If you want ten years of prosperity, grow a tree.*
*If you want one hundred years of prosperity,*
*grow people.*

CHINESE PROVERB

## Overview

Media and other communication professionals, educators, community leaders, health and social workers, trade unionists, government ministers, leaders and managers in large institutions, and telecommunications policymakers are examples of private and public individuals and institutions that are faced with the realisation that we have entered the era of knowledge management. *Knowledge management,* in brief, means that research data that have been collected need to be turned into information, and information needs to be turned into action.

This unit concentrates on the application of research techniques and methods to investigate communication issues and problems that implicate communities or publics outside of an institutional context, including organisations' social performance in external communities. It also deals with the application of research techniques and methods to investigate communication issues and problems encountered by employees (as internal publics) in a variety of organisations, including organisations' social responsibilities towards their employees. Although this unit deals with diverse settings, the thread that connects these settings is the achievement of national priorities, such as reconstruction and development.

## Learning outcomes

By the end of this unit, you should be able to demonstrate your understanding and ability to undertake pilot research studies, by conducting:

- environmental monitoring research;
- a social audit;
- participation action research;
- a public relations audit; and
- a communication audit.

# 6.1 Introduction

We start this unit by dealing with environmental monitoring research, conducting a social audit of an organisation, and researching participatory strategies in organisational and development contexts. The unit ends with guidelines for conducting participatory action research, a public relations audit and a communication audit. The examples and tasks set in this unit are aimed at enhancing an awareness of the relevance of research related to organisational and development communication. In addition to achieving the learning outcomes, this unit aims to develop learners':

- problem-solving, self-responsibility and environmental literacy skills; and
- awareness of the importance of a cultural and aesthetic understanding of the society in which we live.

Table 6.1 summarises the **contexts** in which the different types of research that are discussed in this unit apply.

**TABLE 6.1:** Contexts of organisational and development research

| ORGANISATIONAL AND DEVELOPMENT RESEARCH | | | |
|---|---|---|---|
| **Environmental monitoring research** usually investigates publics, issues and communication problems that are **external** to organisations | **Social audit** usually investigates publics, issues and communication problems that are **external** and **internal** to organisations | **Public relations audit** usually investigates publics, issues and communication problems that are **external** and internal to organisations | **Communication audit** usually investigates publics, issues and communication problems that are **internal** to organisations |

## 6

## 6.2 Environmental monitoring research

Communication research that is used to monitor a particular socio-economic environment can be of value to public relations campaigns and development projects. The objective is to describe events and changes in public opinion that can have an important influence on the functioning of a particular organisation.

The **first phase** of environmental monitoring research involves three types of monitoring processes.

- Monitoring **social events** that can trigger the public's concern about a topic – for example, a number of serious bus accidents may focus the public's concern on issues such as adequate training of bus drivers and lowering the maximum speed limit. Simultaneously, these events raise questions about the accountability of bus companies and travel agents in terms of safety precautions, and can have serious implications for organisations that function in the tourism and hospitality sectors.

- Monitoring **public opinion**. For example, the 100th commemoration of the Anglo-Boer War (1899–1902) re-opened debates around the following issues. First, whether the war should be called the South African War, the Pre-Union War, the Anglo-South African War, the Three-year War, the Freedom War or the *Boere-oorlog*. Secondly, whether Britain should apologise for its actions and the political implications if such a formal apology were extended.

**corporate strategies:** organisations' long-term goals, planning and policy (changes) necessary to achieve these goals

As public opinion represents views, especially moral views held by people as a whole, these views can contribute to divergence that, in turn, enhances public contention, prejudice and conflict. We therefore argue that the corporate strategies of organisations that function in diverse spheres, such as mass communication, commerce and industry, social welfare, politics, foreign relations, education, environmental management and even religion, will benefit from monitoring public opinion.

**e-trade:** electronic trade via the Internet

- Identifying **new** or emerging **issues** or topics of interest. The growing use of the Internet for a variety of purposes, such as e-trade, has prompted developments and changes in different organisational settings. For example, computer software developers continuously update anti-virus programs. Some financial advisors have started to target their advertisements at home owners who want to sell their own homes, without the aid of an estate agent, on the Internet.

Two research methods that are appropriate during this 'early warning phase' (Wimmer and Dominick 1997:332) of environmental monitoring, are **content analyses** and **surveys**. A cross-sectional content analysis can be undertaken of daily newspapers, of the Internet and of publications that report on new developments, such as journals that deal with trade and industrial or technological matters. In addition, surveys can be conducted among opinion leaders, stockholders or community leaders, or long-standing customers. These individuals are purposively sampled from the sectors within which the organisation functions.

**purposively sampled:** subjects selected because they have specific characteristics; not representative of a target population

A **second phase** of environmental monitoring research consists of a tracking process. To monitor the extent to which past social events have triggered the public's concern about a topic over a period of time, or to monitor changing trends in public opinion, or to monitor whether interest in previously emerging topics of interest has grown or fizzled away, requires longitudinal research (*see* Unit 2). Both content analysis and panel surveys can be used over a specified period. For example, a panel survey can be conducted among people who acted as facilitators during hearings held by the Truth and Reconciliation Commission, held from 16 December 1995 until five volumes of the report were presented to former president Nelson Mandela on 29 October 1998.

**tracking:** monitoring over a period of time

**panel surveys:** longitudinal studies in which the same sample of respondents are repeatedly interviewed

Since the mid-1990s, on-line technologies and databases have emerged as useful additional methods for public relations practitioners and communication specialists, to monitor news events and/or track changing trends. In South Africa, the White Paper on Science and Technology (1996) opened the way for the Department of Arts, Culture, Science and Technology to initiate projects and processes aimed at realising the potential of science and technology and stimulating a climate of innovation. The projects involve various role-players, including the 18 science councils in South Africa, and international agreements on co-operation. One such initiative, which included the creation of an audit database (the National Research and Technology Audit), in 1998, contains information on areas such as science and technology infrastructure, human resources and business surveys.

**6**

Sascon (established in 1999), which aims to improve the dissemination of information on science and technology, is an example of involvement in a worldwide communication network. Another example of expanding communication between government departments and citizens is found in a new demarcation electronic map (or atlas) of South Africa, which was launched by the IEC in October 1999.

The atlas contains an analysis of the geographic support-bases of political parties, using a technique of spatial management to record the population, gender and classes in different areas, as well as trends and graphical illustrations of the 1999 election results. Because this atlas provides more accurate data about the state of affairs, including residence, in geographic areas, it is not only useful in the monitoring of municipal electoral processes, but can enable stakeholders involved with the RDP to make informed decisions.

---

### EXECUTIVE SUMMARY: ENVIRONMENTAL MONITORING RESEARCH

1   Research methods:
  - content analysis; and
  - survey research.

2   Processes:
  - monitoring social events;
  - monitoring public opinion;
  - identifying new issues or topics; and
  - longitudinal tracking.

---

### Self-evaluation and portfolio task

6.1   Select an organisation (e.g. in the sphere of print media, broadcasting, health, education, social welfare or correctional services) and follow these procedures:
  - Analyse the mass media for a period of two weeks as part of 'early warning' (environmental monitoring) research.
  - Identify social events that could trigger the public's concern about a topic (related to the selected organisation).
  - Describe the nature of public opinion about these social events. (For example, do letters addressed to newspaper editors contain debates and conflicting opinions?)
  - Identify new or emerging issues or topics that may be of interest to the selected organisation. Can you predict how these new issues or topics could influence the corporate strategy, future operations or goals of the organisation?

# 6.3 Social audit

**social performance:** processes, capabilities, responsibilities, duties, fulfilments and/or accomplishments concerned with human beings

When undertaking a social audit of an organisation, we measure its **social performance**, which can include company-sponsored educational programmes, programmes that deal with affirmative action, involvement with community-service projects and/or in-house training. A social audit of an organisation can focus on different areas, depending on the reasons or needs that lead to an audit being undertaken. For the purpose of this discussion, three areas are distinguished and discussed in detail: to research the organisational **climate**, the organisational **substantive** nature, and the organisational and management **structures**.

## 6.3.1 Organisational (corporate) climate

**corporate identity:** the distinctiveness of an organisation, usually communicated visually

**corporate image:** impressions that people have of an organisation

**corporate personality:** qualities that are unique to an organisation, including its corporate identity and image

When auditing an organisation's corporate climate, the main aim is not only to identify, but also to evaluate an organisation's philosophy. The concept *philosophy* is used here in its widest sense to include the nature of the organisation and the principles governing its existence. These principles can be related to physical phenomena (e.g. buildings and furniture), human behaviour, sets of beliefs, values and perceptions. Every organisation is visually perceptible and identifies itself in unique ways to its internal and external publics (e.g. by means of buildings, office furniture, letterheads, colour schemes, languages used for purposes of communication and record-keeping, logotypes or uniforms). These variables make up an organisation's **corporate identity**. For example, when visiting larger shopping centres, the security guards may differ from one centre to the next, in terms of their uniforms, shoes and headgear, designed in specific colour schemes, with a logo and name of the firm they represent.

An organisation's corporate identity is relevant to an investigation of the organisational climate depending on whether or not it contributes to its corporate image. The **corporate image** of an organisation consists of the impressions, beliefs and/or feelings that both internal and external publics have of an organisation. These impressions will vary because they are influenced by individuals' knowledge and experience of the organisation as an institution, its services and/or products. All the characteristics that contribute to the uniqueness of an organisation collectively create its **corporate personality**.

An organisation's philosophy is a very abstract construct. Therefore, to identify and evaluate the nature and principles that govern an organisation's existence, we need to conduct a survey among internal and external publics to determine:

- how they view the organisation's corporate identity – and whether changes should be made; and
- how they view the organisation's corporate image (including services and/or products) – and whether changes should be made.

## 6.3.2   Substantive nature of an organisation

The substantive nature of an organisation refers more specifically to the rights and duties of an organisation, that could – for the purpose of doing a social audit – be divided into four broad areas:

- employment policies and conditions of service;
- affirmative action;
- in-service training and mentorship; and
- social investments and services.

### *Employment policies and conditions of service*

A social audit that focuses on the employment policies and conditions of service of a particular organisation can be guided by asking open-ended questions. We would start with a **content analysis** of an organisation's policy documents to determine which policies and procedures have been approved and recorded 'on paper'. While doing the content analysis, the questions that appear in the subsections below can be used as evaluation guidelines. However, a key question is:

*Do any of the policies or procedures imply bias or discrimination against certain groups or individuals?*

Such a content analysis provides us with a conceptual framework that can be used as an evaluation scheme that can be tested by a **group-administered questionnaire survey** of individuals sampled from the organisation's employees, and **in-depth interviews** with both top management and employees. (These data-collection methods were discussed in Unit 3.) The research objectives during these surveys and interviews would be to determine:

- whether employees are aware of the policies and procedures; and

- whether there is a discrepancy between what appears in policy documents and what occurs or is perceived to occur in practice.

Policies that apply to the **appointment of new employees** can be divided into recruitment procedures, appointment procedures and conditions of employment policy.

The following are examples of questions that can guide the analysis of such policies and procedures:

- **Recruitment policy:** Does the organisation first advertise internally? If advertising is addressed to external publics, which organisations are notified and which media are used? Does the organisation actively recruit blacks, women and disabled people?
- **Appointment policy:** What selection criteria are applied when appointing new employees? Are the appointment criteria transparent? Is merit (skills and experience) the only criterion when selecting new employees? Are selection committees sensitised to the possible disadvantages that blacks, women and disabled applicants faced in the past? Does the organisation have a quota system as part of its appointment policy? How do the following variables impact on appointment procedures: determination of operational needs; consultation with employees' unions; terms of employment; recruitment mechanisms; minimum eligibility criteria; searching and selection procedures? What issues (e.g. policies and conditions of service) are contained in the content of letters of appointment? What motivated new employees to join the organisation?
- **Conditions of employment policy:** In addition to the conditions outlined in Table 6.2, the following questions can be used as guidelines. Are employees exposed to unsafe working areas or equipment? What security and safety measures are in place for employees (e.g. wearing protective clothing)? What is the language policy of the organisation? Does it marginalise certain language groups? Does the organisation support the right of employees to associate with employees' unions, to participate in collective bargaining and to strike (e.g. in South Africa, as permitted by the Labour Relations Act, 1995 (Act 66 of 1995), as amended on compliance with the stipulations), without the fear of being dismissed? Are employees well informed of their legal rights in terms of labour relations, discipline and grievance procedures,

**quota system:** the proportion allowed/aimed at as a specified percentage of the total

**collective bargaining:** negotiation by an organised body of employees

and other rights such as sick leave? Does the organisation have proper procedures in place to deal with sexual harassment?

Table 6.2 contains a checklist for a written offer of employment and can be adapted to suit the needs of any particular organisation.

**TABLE 6.2** Checklist for a written offer of employment

**CHECKLIST FOR AN EMPLOYEE'S WRITTEN OFFER OF EMPLOYMENT**

1. Name of organisation and specific department (employer)
2. Name of employee
3. Starting date of employment
4. If a contract appointment, agreed ending date of employment
5. The position (job title or post level)
6. Job description
7. Provisions regarding probation
8. Name of employee's supervisor or head
9. Name of employee's mentor
10. Salary or rate of pay (and how it is calculated)
11. Leave pay; sick pay
12. Payment intervals (weekly or monthly)
13. Additional payments (e.g. commissions) and how they are calculated
14. Minimum hours of work (weekly or monthly)
15. Clauses regarding working overtime
16. Regulations regarding working flexi-hours
17. Public holidays, leave (annual, sick, maternity, paternity, special)
18. Pension or provident schemes
19. Medical aid or medical schemes
20. Disciplinary code and procedures
21. Security regulations (e.g. the right to search individuals)
22. Grievance procedures
23. Discounts and other benefits for employees
24. Any policies that form an integral part of the contract (e.g. agreements with trade unions)
25. The notice period required for the employment/contract to be terminated
26. A statement reflecting any special agreement reached between the employer and the employee regarding conditions of employment
27. A statement in which the employee verifies receipt and acceptance of the offer, with above policies and documentation
28. Space for the signature of the employer and date of offer
29. Space for the signature of the employee and date of acceptance
30. Space for the signature and date of a witness to the acceptance.

Issues related to performance and promotion are usually addressed in policies, such as the remuneration policy, performance appraisal policy, and a promotion, transfer and demotion policy.

The following are examples of questions that can guide an analysis of these policies:

**productivity:** efficiency and valued quality of work or commodities produced

- **Remuneration policy:** What is the income (wage) differential between employers and employees? Are women being paid less than men? Are employees financially rewarded for increased productivity?

**management-by-objectives:** the process of managing or being managed, based on previously formulated targets, goals or aims

- **Performance appraisal policy:** How are jobs graded and classified? How are job and performance appraisals conducted? What criteria are applied and how are improvements and progress monitored? Are management-by-objectives techniques used to establish targets and to evaluate actual performance?

- **Promotion, transfer and demotion policy:** What promotional opportunities are available? Is merit (skills and experience) the only criterion for promoting employees? Are the promotion criteria transparent? Does the organisation have a quota system as part of its promotion policy?

**revolving door syndrome:** people in managerial positions leaving an organisation after one or two years

- **Termination of service:** What motivated employees to leave the organisation (during the past two years)? Is there any evidence of the so-called revolving door syndrome? Are there any so-called hidden barriers that cause people to resign, such as inadequate access and other facilities for the disabled?

In the event of cutbacks, layoffs, retrenchments and/or early retirement packages or retirement incentive schemes, what type of assistance does the organisation provide (e.g. financing retraining or finding alternative employment)?

What provisions are made in retrenchment packages for a housing subsidy, pension and medical aid? Are the legal procedures for dismissing employees covered in employment policies? Are employees aware of these procedures?

In the event of normal retirement, what benefits do pensioners receive? Are these benefits differentiated according to demographic characteristics, such as marital status and gender?

## *Affirmative action*

Since South Africa's first democratic general election in 1994, and especially after the acceptance of the Constitution of the Republic of South Africa (Act 108 of 1996) (South Africa 1996b), organisations in both the public and private spheres have been faced with the challenge of achieving equality of employment (often referred to as affirmative action). This means that organisations may not directly or indirectly discriminate against someone on the basis of variables such as 'race, gender, sex, pregnancy, marital status, family responsibility, ethnic or social origin, colour, sexual orientation, age, disability, religion, HIV status, conscience, belief, political opinion, culture, language and birth' (South Africa 1998a, Employment Equity Act, 1998 (Act 55 of 1998)). Considering the meaning of equality, it can be noted that feminists sometimes draw a distinction between 'sex' (as a biological identity) and 'gender' (as a social identity). In this publication, the terms are used interchangeably.

**affirmative action:** programmes and procedures that proactively address past discrimination (e.g. based on class, gender and race)

Attitudes towards affirmative action have been both supportive and negative. The phrases below illustrate the diverse interpretations of the social implications of affirmative action (or anti-discriminatory) policies:
- it undermines the basis of free enterprise (rewards should be based on merit);
- it is patronising (towards blacks, women or those who are disabled);
- it provides equal opportunities;
- it promotes development and socio-economic upliftment;
- it leads to a lowering of standards;
- it undermines profit growth;
- it can be misused as tokenism;
- it is preferential treatment and reverse discrimination;
- it is a form of strategic resourcing;
- it harmonises; and/or
- it is corrective action.

**tokenism:** a form of window dressing to make an impression on others

During the opening speech of the second session of the democratic parliament of the Republic of South Africa, on 17 February 1995, Nelson Mandela, in his capacity as president, had the following to say about affirmative action:

*This is what we mean when we talk of affirmative action programmes. We speak of a human resource development programme which will*

*ensure that all our people, and not merely some, are given the oppor-*
*tunity to develop their talents and to contribute to the reconstruction*
*and development of society to the best of their ability.*

*I therefore call on all our people to refuse to listen to the false*
*prophets who seek to perpetuate the apartheid divisions and imbal-*
*ances of the past by presenting affirmative action as a programme*
*intended to advantage some and disadvantage others on the basis of*
*race and colour.* (Mandela 1995:70-71)

The realities of South Africa dictate that organisations must continue to
overcome the legacy of apartheid and, simultaneously, become globally
competitive. In terms of South Africa's Employment Equity Act, 1998
(Act 55 of 1998), the first phase of which was promulgated in August
1999, all forms of discrimination in the workplace are prohibited. The
act also requires companies to submit reports to the Department of
Labour indicating how any forms of existing discrimination will be eliminated by 2005, with progress being monitored annually by the
Department of Labour. An affirmative action policy should therefore
feature in every organisation's social policy.

An integral part of a social audit that focuses on researching affirmative action strategies, is the identification of overt and, especially,
covert discrimination.

**overt:**
open and
observable

**Overt discrimination** can be researched by asking and answering the
following questions:
- Does the organisation have an affirmative action policy and plan
  of action?
- What percentage of the assets (private sector) is owned by blacks?
- What percentage of top managerial positions do blacks, women
  and/or disabled people hold?
- Does the organisation have management-labour committees
  that function as forums in which discriminatory issues can be
  addressed?
- Does the organisation have a human resources department
  that facilitates the process of affirmative action and employee
  development?
- What is done to advance (empower) blacks, women and the
  disabled?

- Are blacks, women and/or disabled people mainly appointed to so-called soft jobs (e.g. involving repetitive administrative tasks)?
- Are women given the opportunity to be trained for skilled work that, in the past, was primarily done by men?
- Is the organisation's income dependant on or influenced by its affirmative action strategy (e.g. securing government contracts or obtaining tax rebates)?
- Are there any instances of wage discrimination based on gender, race or disability? Does the organisation's remuneration policy adhere to the principle of equal pay for work of equal value?
- Are regular surveys conducted to assess issues related to affirmative action? (For example, unequal workload for men versus women; monitoring the progress made by blacks and/or measuring employees' perceptions of inequality.) An action-research approach is required when new policies have to be applied in practice, because practices need to be monitored, evaluated and, where necessary, adapted. Participatory action research is discussed in detail in sections 6.4 and 6.5.

**action-research approach:**
participatory research in which the researcher and community are equal partners

- How does the affirmative action (empowerment) programme:
  - link to developing an organisation's human resources;
  - contribute to the overall goals of the organisation (e.g. to increase profits)?
- Are short-, medium- and long-term affirmative action targets or goals formulated? Are these goals realistic? Are these goals linked to skills training and other in-service educational programmes? Are these goals an integral part of an organisation's overall strategic plan? Are the goals also part of individual departments' or sections' strategic plans? Who is responsible for managing and monitoring the progress of affirmative action programmes? Are these managers perceived as token appointments or is their credibility respected?

**strategic plan:**
a plan of action/policy, e.g. in business or politics

- How are affirmative action targets and progress made public (internally and externally)?

**covert:**
disguised or secret

**Covert discrimination** can be researched by asking and answering the following types of questions:
- Are all individuals (top management, line managers and the workforce at lower ranks) aware of the objectives and nature of the organisation's affirmative action plan?
- What are their views and attitudes towards this plan? (For example,

are they committed or do they resent affirmative action?)

Although all overt or formal signs of discrimination (e.g. separate facilities based on racial discrimination) may have been removed, covert or informal discrimination may not be easy to detect, research or address. Covert discrimination may be due to people's subconscious values and beliefs, of which they are not necessarily aware. To investigate people's attitudes and behaviours, with specific reference to discrimination in the workplace, researchers need to:

- investigate the **membership** of committees responsible for aspects such as appointments, performance evaluations, managerial issues, (including remuneration), and whether these committees are represented by all stakeholders;
- observe **interaction** between people, during meetings and on the shop floor;
- conduct in-depth interviews and/or focus-group interviews to determine similarities and differences in employers' and employees' **attitudes** and **perceptions** of issues. The following are examples of (sometimes fallacious) perceptions that can be investigated when researching covert discrimination:
  - blacks, women and disabled employees do not have the same advancement opportunities as other employees;
  - blacks and women have to work harder (than whites or men) to receive the same recognition; and/or
  - blacks, women and the disabled are appointed to so-called soft jobs, such as in the personnel department.

**fallacious:**
based on a faulty or unsound argument

Throughout a social audit that focuses on researching affirmative action strategies, affirmative action could be treated as a **process**, and employment equity as the goal or **outcome**.

## *In-service training and mentorship*

**needs analysis:**
investigating employees' educational, development and work-related requirements

When conducting a social audit of an organisation's in-service training and mentorship programmes, the kind of research questions to be formulated will depend on the type of institutionally based educational programmes that are in place and the mentoring procedures used. As development and educational needs can change, due to, for instance, changes in computer programs, the kind of research questions to be asked can simultaneously function as a needs analysis. Newly appointed employees usually follow an orientation programme in which the vision and mission of the organisation are explained. However, the need for training programmes for middle and top managers, to sensitise them to changes, is often overlooked. Before dealing with examples of questions that can be asked during this part of a social audit, consider the purposes of the South Africa's Skills Development Act, 1998 (Act 97 of 1998), quoted below.

---

**THE PURPOSES OF THIS ACT ARE –**

(a)  to develop the skills of the South African workforce –
    (i)  to improve the quality of life of employees, their prospects of work and labour mobility;
    (ii)  to improve productivity in the workplace and the competitiveness of the employers;
    (iii)  to promote self-employment; and
    (iv)  to improve the delivery of social services;
(b)  to increase the levels of investment in education and training in the labour market and to improve the return on that investment;
(c)  to encourage employers –
    (i)  to use the workplace as an active learning environment;
    (ii)  to provide employees with the opportunities to acquire new skills;
    (iii)  to provide opportunities for new entrants to the labour market to gain work experience; and
    (iv)  to employ persons who find it difficult to be employed;
(d)  to encourage employees to participate in leadership and other training programmed [sic];
(e)  to improve the employment prospects of persons previously disadvantaged by unfair discrimination and to redress those disadvantages through training and education;
(f)  to ensure the quality of education and training in and for the workplace;
(g)  to assist –
    (i)  work-seekers to find work;
    (ii)  retrenched employees to re-enter the labour market;
    (iii)  employers to find qualified employees; and
(h)  to provide and regulate employment services

(South Africa 1998b:8)

---

**sic:** quoted as originally spelt

Against the background of the above framework for skills development and related matters, an **in-service training programme** should deal with the following areas:

- **managerial or supervisory tasks**, such as setting performance standards, monitoring these standards; motivating employees; improving work methods and procedures; and planning ahead;

- **communication skills**, such as induction; counselling; problem-solving; interpersonal and small-group communication; computer literacy skills; and collective bargaining skills;
- **the history of the organisation**, as well as its vision, mission and industrial relations, such as the purpose of unions, disciplinary code, principles of freedom of association; issues around stay-aways; and
- **basic living skills** for semi- and unskilled employees, such as budgeting, bond repayments and basic business principles.

Any of these areas can be reformulated as research questions, to which the following are added as examples:
- What types of company-based educational programmes are in place? Does the organisation enable employees to keep abreast of technical skills required by technological changes in the workplace?
- How are training programmes developed and evaluated? To what extent do the economy's needs and market forces guide training programmes? How are unions, such as COSATU (Congress of South African Trade Unions), involved in the conceptualisation, implementation and monitoring of training programmes? Is the training timeous (in that it can benefit employees' promotion in their career paths)? Is the training relevant (in terms of the skills required)? Does training include life-skills training, that can include the promotion of self-awareness, group interaction and organisational cultures, and an increase in self-confidence and social skills?
- Who has access to in-service training? Does the organisation offer internship programmes (e.g. for college and university students) to obtain on-site and hands-on experience of work environments?
- Is in-service training, once successfully completed, acknowledged by an increase in remuneration and/or promotion?

**mentoring:** being advised by someone who is experienced and trusted

The nature and duration of **mentoring** can vary from one organisation to the next, and even within sections or departments of one organisation, depending on the people involved and the purpose of the mentoring programme.

As interpersonal relations have the potential of future disagreements and conflict, it is important to include the trainee employees' immediate supervisor or manager in the process. It is equally important that a contractual agreement be reached between mentor and trainee, that includes information such as the purpose of the mentoring, how regularly they will meet, communication channels to be used, how performance evaluation will be conducted, and what procedures will be followed should conflict arise. Depending on the nature of the trainee employee's work, it is also advisable to specify the outcomes (in the contractual agreement) that can be measured at certain points during the mentoring period – for example, the independent performance of certain skills by the trainee.

As mentoring takes place in an interpersonal communication setting, its effectiveness will depend on many factors. For example, is the mentor efficient at listening, handling confrontation and giving feedback? Are both parties committed to the programme? Do they agree on the potential benefits and is their relationship one of mutual trust? When researching the nature and effectiveness of mentoring, the first and crucial question is: Why does an organisation have a mentoring programme? In other words, what is the aim or purpose of such a programme?

Additional research questions that can be asked are:

- How are mentors appointed (are they volunteers, nominated and appointed by management, or elected by trainees)?
- Do mentors receive any training?
- **dyadic communication:** communication between two people
- Is only dyadic communication used, or are experiences and problems also discussed in groups consisting of experienced and new employees?
- How are trainees identified and what contractual agreement has been negotiated between them and their mentors?
- What does the actual programme consist of (e.g. does it consist of a mentor giving advice, preparing the trainee for a future promotion, teaching the trainee new skills, or being responsible for the trainee's job and performance appraisal)?
- If trainees do not have a say in the appointment of mentors, what are their opinions in this regard?
- When and how frequently does mentoring take place (after hours or during working hours)?
- If trainees are dissatisfied with their mentors, do they know what procedures to follow?

- How do trainees experience and benefit from the mentoring process?

## Social investments and services

When viewing organisations from a global perspective, managers are challenged to provide for employees in a holistic manner, which includes improving quality of life and fulfilling high-order needs, such as self-fulfilment. The following are areas that can be researched to determine whether or not an organisation makes provision for investments and services for its employees, beyond basic provisions such as remuneration (salary, wages, service bonus), child-care facilities, housing subsidies, pension, medical aid, and allowances for vacation, sick, occasional, maternity and paternity leave.

- **Experience and qualifications:** Do employees have opportunities to obtain international experience? What incentives are used to encourage employees to advance their academic or professional qualifications? Has a re-education programme been undertaken to deal with past (and perhaps present) sexist and racist attitudes?
- **Career paths:** Are career-paths mapped out for individuals, especially newly appointed (black) employees? Does each individual know what knowledge, experience and skills are required for future promotion? Are training programmes linked to the individual's career path(s)? Will the organisation benefit from the individual's increase in competency?
- **Skills development:** Are in-service training courses and opportunities provided to develop skills in addition to those that are work-related, in areas such as production, labour relations, adult basic education, computer literacy, time management, communication and negotiation, assertiveness training, marketing, and basic management principles?
- **Teamwork:** What organisational structures and processes are in place to promote individual development within the collective experiences provided by teamwork? Does the organisation have forums that deal with issues (e.g. remuneration) and the nature of the organisation (e.g. technology or exports)?
- **Financial support:** Does the organisation have a financial support scheme for the education of employees' children? What bursary scheme is available to fund employees' studies? Are employees informed about the organisation's financial position and the effects of wage increases on this position?

- **Holistic support:** Does the organisation have support programmes to assist employees who are experiencing physical, marital or emotional problems, such as stress and burnout; or family problems, such as those experienced by employees who are single parents, or who care for the elderly? How are these programmes communicated to employees and how aware are they of the programmes and the procedures to be followed when experiencing such problems?

## 6.3.3 Organisational and management structures

The management of communication between an organisation's top structure and its internal and external publics is not a linear cause-and-effect process. Organisations are faced with a paradigm shift, to deal with factors such as transformation, diversity, instability, unpredictability and pluralism. The **management of change** requires organisational and management structures to be redesigned, to become more open and levelled horizontally, instead of the conventional linear hierarchies.

**paradigm shift:** a change in social positioning, e.g. from conflict to consensus

**pluralism:** a system that recognises diffused distribution of power

**autocratic:** absolute, inflexible

The latter (classical) managerial structures saw their main function as that of minimising conflict, preventing chaos, maintaining order and avoiding risk. Such management structures measure employee productivity and loyalty, and stability of the organisational system by means of autocratic rules and selective or filtered information that ensure control.

Various authors (e.g. Youngblood 1997:28; McDaniel 1997:23; Ströh 1998:21) argue that new managerial approaches that are open, holistic and flexible are required to deal with the changes that have occurred, such as the globalisation of information, changes and developments in information technology and employees who are better informed. For instance, employees are better informed than they were five years ago about the use and development of technology (computer technology in particular) and the procedures and legal mechanics for the referral of labour disputes.

If the key to organisational cultural change is found in economic democratisation, then democratic, representative **participation of**

**employees** is essential. Khoza (1993:80) argues that the attitudes of (white) middle management (in strategic positions) will consciously or unconsciously influence:

- the entry of previously disadvantaged people to managerial positions;
- the creation of an environment that is conducive and supportive of affirmative action;
- conducting progress evaluations and reviews; and
- daily communication (upward, downward and horizontally) with other stakeholders.

When researching the organisational and management structures of an organisation as part of a social audit, the overriding question is whether there is evidence that the organisation has moved away from the traditional authoritarian management style to a participative and interactive style (also called **consensus management**)?

**consensus management:** collective agreement reached through negotiation

The following are examples of appropriate research questions:

- What assessment procedures are followed to identify employees who have managerial potential, or who are talented and can be assisted to develop?
- Do employees have a say at all levels of corporate decision-making?
- Does management unilaterally introduce the social investment programme, or is it based on consensus having been reached through negotiation between management and employees?
- What is the quality and nature of supervision and management? (For example, is middle management accountable to both top management and to the workforce in lower positions?)
- To what extent do blacks, women and disabled people have managerial and decision-making power in the organisation (e.g. dealing with employment policies)?
- If flexitime is in operation, how does it influence productivity and the achievement of corporate goals?
- How do the organisational and management structures reflect commitment to equality and to the objectives of the affirmative action programme?
- What role do trade unions play in human resources development?
- Is control shared? (Is participatory involvement the basis for delivering products or services?)
- Is there any evidence that management is avoiding (or denying)

problems of racism and sexism? (It is a common procedure to isolate a problem, such as sexual harassment, and to defuse the conflict by making reparation to the person who experienced victimisation or by moving the victim to another section.)

- What type of leadership style(s) is/are characteristic of the organisation's top and middle management?

Conceptually, three **leadership styles** have traditionally been distinguished:

- authoritarian leaders, who are task-oriented, determine an organisation's policy and often make decisions without consulting others;
- democratic leaders, who are people-oriented and act as facilitators by involving everyone concerned with policy or other issues; and
- laissez-faire leaders, who do not usually actively participate in the decision-making procedures, but who may sometimes make inputs.

When doing research, it is difficult to use these three distinctions as an analytical tool, because top and middle management consist of individuals and all three types of leadership styles may be represented in one organisation. As researchers, we may find individuals in managerial positions who have the ability to adapt their preferred leadership style, depending on the circumstances. Therefore, a **strategic** framework, as a conceptual or theoretical framework, should be considered (*see* section 6.4.4).

When focusing specifically on **management** and to determine whether the managers of an organisation function as leaders, facilitators and co-ordinators, our evaluation can be guided by research questions such as:

- Do managers regard organisational change(s) to be their sole responsibility?
- Do managers involve all interested parties, at all levels, in organisational change(s)?
- Do managers recognise the diversity of individual employees' basic values, aspirations, expectations and fears?
- How do managers address these diversities?
- Do managers encourage and create opportunities for self-expression and employee participation at all levels?
- Do managers facilitate an even distribution of an organisation's profits?

- What type of leadership style is used to give participants a sense of purpose and enable them to identify with the goals of participation?
- Are the managers of the organisation or programme equipped to handle the dynamics of individuals' differences and small-group behaviour, including conflict?

**In-depth** interviews and **focus-group** interviews are appropriate techniques to collect data about above management styles. In view of the possibility that managers may say one thing, but do another, it would be appropriate to not only research their views (e.g. by means of self-reporting **questionnaires**) but also to have their styles and actions evaluated by their subordinates.

*EXECUTIVE SUMMARY:*
**SOCIAL AUDIT**

1   Research methods and techniques:
- content analysis;
- field research; and
- survey research.

2   Areas researched:
- organisational (corporate) climate:
  – corporate identity;
  – corporate image;
  – corporate personality.
- Organisational substantive nature:
  – employment policies and conditions of service;
  – affirmative action;
  – in-service training and mentorship; and
  – social investments and services.
- organisational and management structures:
  – management of change; and
  – participative management.

## Self-evaluation and portfolio task

**6.2** Select one of the following areas of research that can be investigated as part of a social audit of the substantive nature of an organisation:
- employment policies and conditions of service;
- affirmative action;
- in-service training and mentorship; or
- social investments and services.

Obtain a copy of the policy documents that deal with the selected area (e.g. affirmative action) of two similar organisations (e.g. two vehicle manufacturers or two educational institutions). If such policies do not exist, obtain a copy of the organisation's human resources development programmes.

The goal of the audit is applied research and the objectives are mainly exploratory. Do a content analysis of the documents by working though and answering the questions in section 6.3.2.

Contact the organisation's corporate communication manager, public relations specialist, or the human resources manager and arrange for a semi-structured interview. The purpose of the interview is twofold:
- to find answers to questions that could not be answered by analysing the policy documents; and
- to establish whether the opportunities, programmes and activities for which the policy documents make provision, take place in practice.

Compare the profiles of the two organisations and compile a list of proposals as to how each organisation can increase its social efficiency.

(If you are a member of a workers' union, the above self-evaluation and portfolio task can be repeated, with the aim of sensitising yourself to provisions and opportunities in your union's human resources policy.)

# 6.4 Researching participatory strategies

This section deals with five strategic frameworks that can be used when public and private organisations, as well as voluntary and other institutions (e.g. involved in development projects), are researched. These five strategies are based on the arguments and discussions by Burke (1975:196-207); Innes, Kentridge and Perold (1993); and Ströh (1998:16-41).

**value premise:** an assumption, based on a judgement associated with an attitude

Participation by all employees in an organisation (or all members of a community) is based on an idealised value premise that it (participation) is the means to a perfect democratic communication process. Put simply, employees should have the opportunity to be part of decisions that affect their lives. In reality, this is not always possible. For example, not everyone has a legal background or technical competency if decisions of a legal or technological nature have to be made. This dilemma contributes to a value conflict between participatory democracy (freedom) and the need for expertise in decision-making (control).

**Participation** by citizens of a particular community does not involve a single or undifferentiated strategy. It is therefore appropriate to consider several strategies, because participation will be guided by the objectives, purposeful action as an outcome, resources, the character of the organisation or community, and the demands of the social environment. Success will clearly depend on the adaptability of the strategies. Participation is dealt with as a basis of five strategies, by considering the **objectives**, **assumptions** and **organisational conditions** or **demands** of each. It must be noted that the concept *citizens*, refers to individuals and subgroups employed in an organisational context, as well as individuals, families and members of subgroups (e.g. youth groups) who are members of a wider social community.

The remainder of this section concentrates on a conceptual framework that can be used while undertaking research in organisational and/or development contexts. As participation by ourselves, individuals and representatives of particular stakeholders, is an essential part of such research, we would use **survey** research (especially face-to-face

interviews) and **field** research (especially focus-group interviews) as research and problem-solving methods and techniques.

## 6.4.1  Educational-therapeutic strategy

### *Objectives*

The objective of this strategy is essentially the development and improvement of participants as individuals. This implies that the type of tasks to be accomplished is irrelevant; that the processes involved are secondary; and that the focus is on participants as so-called clients.

### *Assumptions*

With the emphasis on education, participation takes the form of citizenship training. Although citizens work together – for example, to solve a community problem such as inadequate housing – the educational goals are to enable them to experience:

● how co-operation works as a problem-solving method; and
● how democracy works.

This strategy further assumes that the achievement of these goals will improve local government, and contribute to community identification and development.

In addition to its educational component, this strategy regards participation as a form of therapy. It assumes that, through participation, individuals will develop self-confidence and self-reliance. It is based on the argument that, by working together with our neighbours (and fellow employees), we will inspire one another, we will increase our sense of responsibility, and bring about changes in our environment.

### *Organisational conditions or demands*

The application of this strategy in practice has to meet four organisational conditions or demands. First, the organisation of citizens in participatory groups – for example, to focus on health planning programmes – has to be a formal and deliberate action. Secondly, local government and professional groups – for example, in medical and paramedical professions – must support participation as the overriding objective. (In institutional contexts, such support should come from employers and top management.) Thirdly, provision must be made for longitudinal time frames, such as periods of three or five years, before expecting changes to have taken place. Fourthly, the so-called *voice of the people* must be trusted. In other words, participants must be allowed to make decisions and decide on policies.

Instead of encouraging people to make their own decisions about what is good for them, this strategy treats participation as a process through which co-operative attitudes can be developed, problems solved and tasks effectively undertaken. The organisational demands listed above unfortunately frustrate the application of the strategy in practice, because participants' decisions and policies may not always be wise, and may contribute to controversy and conflict. This is particularly problematic in instances where development programmes are steered by financial rather than educational or therapeutic considerations.

## 6.4.2  Behavioural change strategy

This strategy is also change-oriented, but its objectives and assumptions differ from the educational-therapeutic strategy.

### *Objectives*

The objective of this strategy is to change a group (as a system or subsystem), and through inducing such change, to change the behaviour of individual group members. Although the individual is the indirect target, whether or not he or she develops and improves while participating in the process, is of secondary importance. The objective is primarily focused on a specific development task and enabling the group to achieve the development goal.

### *Assumptions*

The main assumption of this strategy is that individuals will more easily change their behaviour through group membership and group participation, rather than being addressed as individuals. It is assumed that group-made decisions and norms are important influences on individuals' behaviour.

There are two further assumptions. First, that change is brought about by changing the behaviour, group standards, or style of leadership of all the members of a particular group, or influential representatives of the group. Secondly, because decisions imposed from outside a group are likely to be met with resistance, group members will support decisions in which they were involved and participated. In other words, individuals will more likely assist in development programmes if they were part of identifying needs and plans to accommodate those needs. This implies that decisions made during a participatory process can result in commitment to new tasks with new objectives.

## Organisational conditions or demands

The effectiveness of this strategy depends on three organisational conditions or demands being met. First, members of the group must experience an assurance that their participation is meaningful to both the group and to themselves as individuals. Secondly, there must be some form of reward from participating, based on their association with the group or by the accomplishments achieved by the group. Thirdly, individuals must be actively involved in the decisions being made. This condition is based on the premise that active involvement – doing a needs analysis, debating plans for development and change, agreeing on decisions, and taking on the responsibility for the consequences of change – are important dynamics in changing behaviour. To accomplish such a condition therefore requires open dialogue among all members.

Several factors, however, make it difficult to adhere to the three conditions or demands, including:

- one-way communication channels, such as between a local authority and citizens, or between management and employees;
- the demand to submit budget and planning proposals, often by agents who, due to time constraints, have not involved the individuals concerned;

**reference groups:** groups with which individuals have relevant connections, relations and/or correspondence

- the problem of including all members of a particular community during the phases of analysing, planning and executing the programme or project; and
- the members of particular subgroups who are involved are not necessarily in the position to apply the groups' intentions, or may not be acknowledged as representatives of the groups.

Keeping in mind both the conditions and the problematic factors, the key to the effectiveness of this strategy lies in whether or not those participating in the change process can bring about change in their reference groups.

## 6.4.3 Supplementary employees strategy

This strategy involves individuals in two ways. First, doing voluntarily work for organisations that do not have the necessary employees, such as fund-raising agencies. Secondly, where an organisation does not necessarily have expertise, such as welfare organisations, individuals are recruited for their expertise and involved in committees. In both instances, participation is voluntary.

### *Objectives*

The main objective of this strategy is to secure the time, abilities and/or expertise of individuals on a voluntary basis, to achieve a particular goal.

### *Assumptions*

Volunteers are recruited as supplementary employees, based on the assumption that their participation can contribute to achieving a particular goal. In the case of experts, such as criminologists in a programme to combat delinquency, goals could and often do include participation in policy decisions.

### *Organisational conditions or demands*

First, the volunteers must agree with and support the objectives of the organisation for which they volunteer their services. Secondly, although supplementary employees often fulfil auxiliary functions, such as raising funds, an ideal condition would be for them to participate in policy and other organisational decision-making processes. Thirdly, an incentive to secure volunteers to participate willingly is a crucial condition. Depending on the objectives of the organisation and the nature of tasks, a fourth condition can be added – that of compiling actual job descriptions for volunteers' roles, which can be used during both recruitment and when participating.

**auxiliary functions:** to give additional, supportive assistance

The assessment of the effectiveness of this strategy is difficult, because it depends on the objectives of the organisation and the actual nature of volunteers' work. When dealing with issues, such as social welfare, planning and decision-making are often the result of negotiation and compromise. Therefore research into the effectiveness of this strategy would have to take the values into account that are part of such bargaining processes. Questions that would have to be answered, are whether the expert volunteer's inputs are merely treated as yet another opinion; and how the organisation that uses this strategy overcomes the value differences that can arise between the organisation and its volunteers, especially those who are recruited for their expertise.

## 6.4.4    A strategy of co-optation

Co-optation is not a new participatory strategy. Welfare organisations, corporations, tertiary (educational) institutions and even political parties are some organisations that co-opt or elect representatives from specific segments of the community (e.g. representatives from banking institutions) to their management structures, policy-making structures or boards of directors.

### *Objectives*

**preventative measure:** an action, plan or procedure that offers a safeguard and protection

Citizens' participation as a strategy of co-optation has two core objectives. First, as a preventative measure to avert future threats to the stability and existence of the organisation. Secondly, citizens who are of strategic importance to the nature of the organisation are co-opted to sanction procedures and decisions, to enable the organisation to achieve its goals.

**sanction:** *verb*. to approve

### *Assumptions*

By co-opting individuals or representatives from certain interest groups, such as professional groups, women's organisations, labour unions, or from business, religious and legislative sectors, it is assumed that future demands for changes or accusations about irresponsible administration will be nullified. It is assumed that, by applying this strategy, current organisational policy will be met with consent and treated as legitimate.

### Organisational conditions or demands

As this strategy relies on sharing the responsibility of power and organisational decision-making, the organisation that applies this strategy must be willing to deal with inputs made by those who have been co-opted and the likelihood that major changes to organisational policy could result. The advantage of achieving sanction from important interest groups may, therefore, come at the cost of impeding current organisational goals.

Secondly, in order to find compatible goals, it is important that an organisation sets up and maintains communication networks with all stakeholders.

## 6.4.5 A strategy of community empowerment

Empowerment, as used here, refers to giving a group the power and right to exert influence and enforce decisions. Two strategies can be distinguished when using citizen participation to empower people at a community level. The one is to obtain informal co-operation from influential people in the community to participate in an organisation. This strategy is very similar to that of co-operation discussed above, except that co-operation has the specific purpose of realising an organisation's goals. The other strategy involves confrontation between a collection of people who are organised and committed to a particular cause, and those who hold administrative and/or political power. To illustrate the second strategy, let us look at the objectives, assumptions, and organisational conditions or demands.

**confrontation:** a face-to-face comparison of two things, individuals or groups

### Objectives

The main objectives of a confrontational strategy are to secure involvement and commitment of individuals in the community who identify with a particular cause; and to secure citizens' interest for a long enough period to achieve the objectives.

### Assumptions

This strategy assumes that a change of control, from power held by those who control institutions and wealth, can be brought about

because of the number of people involved and their collective dedication. It also assumes that change can be brought about through the creation of conflict and subsequent negotiations. In addition, it assumes that, although individuals may hold personal views with emotional connotations, their involvement in achieving the cause, signifies agreement with goals that may have been defined by community leaders.

## Organisational conditions or demands

**PAC:**
Pan Africanist
Congress

The persons or institutions that hold the power must be willing to negotiate, even if it means that they are forced to do so as a result of tactics such as demonstration, boycotts, sit-ins, picketing and (in South Africa) toy-toy marches. An example in South Africa is that of the PAC, which launched its now well-known 'decisive action' campaign against the South African pass laws on 1 March 1960 (*Sunday World* 1999:12). This culminated in the massive peaceful demonstrations against the pass laws around the country, which, because security forces gunned down people in Sharpeville, achieved global sympathy for the cause of the black majority.

This strategy, with its acknowledgement of the relevance of confrontation, may be regarded in a negative light, unless we consider the organisational conditions or demands on a wider socio-economic scale. It is argued that the empowerment of communities does not lie in conflict and changing power between the 'have's' and the 'have nots'. Empowerment requires involvement from government, the business sector, major trade union formations and the multiplicity of community organisations. Batat, *Masakhane* and Nedlac are briefly described as South African examples:

- The South African Department of Agriculture, renamed Agri-SA in October 1999, adopted a strategy referred to as Broadening Access to Agriculture Thrust (Batat) in 1995, to further the aims of the Reconstruction and Development Programme (RDP). This implementation strategy is aimed at service provision for people who become farmers for the first time. The strategy's focus is on financial services, human resource development, technological development, delivery systems and marketing (Msane 1995:23).
- Boycott actions and the non-payment of municipal services, for example, resulted in the collapse of many local authorities in former black local areas in South Africa. As a result, government

launched the *Masakhane* campaign on 24 February 1995. The aims of the campaign were partly 'to restore legitimacy and dignity to local structures, stabilise local communities for development, engender self-respect and responsibility, and foster a favourable climate for the local government elections ... [and to promote] ... the payment of rent, services charges and bond instalments' (Lombaard 1995:34). An annual President's Award for Community Initiative was introduced in 1998 to promote the spirit of *Masakhane*, of which the first provincial winners included sewing and community educational projects, and projects that involved unemployed mothers, homeless people and retrenched mineworkers.

- Forums and bodies, such as Nedlac (National Economic Development and Labour Council), fulfil an important function in socio-economic transformation and involve all stakeholders in their decision-making processes, because they 'ensure effective coordination and partnership between the [South African] Government, labour, business and community-based organisations' (Mandela 1995:78).

---

*EXECUTIVE SUMMARY:*
**RESEARCHING PARTICIPATORY STRATEGIES IN ORGANISATIONAL AND DEVELOPMENT CONTEXTS**

1 Research methods:
- field research; and
- survey research.

2 Participatory strategies – a conceptual framework:
- educational-therapeutic strategy;
- behavioural change strategy;
- supplementary employees strategy;
- a strategy of co-optation; and
- a strategy of community empowerment.

3 Variables in each strategy:
- objectives;
- assumptions; and
- organisational conditions or demands.

---

## Self-evaluation and portfolio task

**6.3** Identify a community resource that provides a supportive service to the community, or to families or individuals who need rehabilitative care or are facing a crisis (such as Alcoholics Anonymous, Suicides Anonymous, Lifeline, Childline, Gayline, Victims line, Police crisis line, St John's Ambulance, Medic Alert, or the Salvation Army).

Contact the organisation's corporate communication manager, public relations specialist, or the human resource manager and arrange for a semi-structured interview. The goal is applied research and the objectives are exploratory and descriptive. The objective of your interview is two-fold:

1. to explore and describe how the organisation or service functions; and
2. to explore and describe which participative strategy(-ies) is/are used in the organisation or particular service centre.

The interview schedule that you compile for the first objective can be guided by the following headings:

● General information (the name of the organisation/service; the geographic area it serves; where it is situated; physical facilities; and how accessible the facilities and services are).
● Financial support and funding mechanisms.
● Organisational (corporate) climate, including the nature and goal of the organisation or service.

The interview schedule for the second objective can be guided by:

● A description of the participatory strategy(-ies) followed by the organisation.
● A description of the specific (target) external publics for which the organisation/service was established.
● Client admission (or selection) procedures.
● Communication procedures (e.g. how calls/requests are handled and by whom).
● The nature of documentation and record keeping.
● The nature of the relations between care givers and clients, and among clients.
● The treatment of clients – the measures taken to maintain contact with reality and to enable the individual to remain functional in the community. (Are individuals' families involved in any rehabilitation programmes? Are clients referred to other resources?)

● The participatory strategy(-ies) that you would regard appropriate for the effective functioning of this organisation or service as a community resource. (What changes can be made?)

# 6.5 Participatory action research

## 6.5.1 Orientation and research questions

Based on the discussion in section 6.4, it is evident that each of the five participatory strategies discussed, has its own advantages and limitations. When researching the effectiveness of a particular strategy in organisational and development communication, we need to carefully scrutinise these variables and determine whether the strategy currently being implemented is **appropriate**:

- to the nature of the particular organisation or development programme;
- for the particular environmental setting in which the organisation functions or in which the development project is implemented; and
- to achieve the goal(s) that initiated the need for participation.

A question that has to be asked repeatedly is whether a different strategy or a combination of strategies would be more effective in achieving the organisational and/or development goals. For example, government-sponsored development programmes require co-operation and especially co-ordination. A strategy of community empowerment that is confrontational would not be appropriate, but could serve as a useful initial strategy for labour unions to deal with disputes. In the case of community empowerment, it would be more appropriate to apply a behavioural change and a supplementary employees strategy.

Additional examples of **research questions** that can be used to guide an evaluation of the participatory strategy used by a particular organisation or development programme include:

- How has the organisation or community identified participants who represent the sentiments and needs of subgroups or communities?
- Are citizens involved on a voluntary basis?
- Are citizens selected because of their expertise, or because their lives are affected by the problem that has to be solved, and/or because they represent the sentiments of a community?
- What administrative skills and experience do participants have?
- Are various interests accommodated within a free market procedure of competition?
- Are value preferences and differences part of the planning processes and subject to open dialogue?

**free market:** a market in which unrestricted competition determines the price of goods

- How is co-operation gained and how are fears allayed?
- Is participation used to create a culture of mutual trust?
- Is participation only evident in work-related decision-making?
- Is there a discrepancy between what an organisation or community purports to do via citizen participation and what it actually accomplishes?
- If signs of demoralisation are evident, to what can such disillusionment be ascribed? What went wrong?
- Are the voices of citizens treated as tokenism or are they part of planning and policy-making decisions?
- How are participants' needs, aspirations, values, expectations, personal goals and mistrusts addressed?

**voices:**
in this context –
ideas, opinions,
recommendations

These research questions illustrate how diverse the goals and objectives of participatory research can be. Although the emphasis in this section is on **development communication**, the methods and procedures discussed can be adapted and applied to research in other contexts, where the objectives are knowledge development, knowledge utilisation and/or design and development. These three types of research are facets of what is called 'intervention research' (De Vos 1998:11).

## 6.5.2.   RDP and intervention research

Intervention research can be defined as applied research that extends knowledge of human behaviour, while finding solutions (e.g. providing new services or introducing technological developments) for practical problems. A concept that is central to this type of research is **change**, which can occur at a microlevel, where a solution is adopted or rejected – often referred to as diffusion, adoption, modernisation, acculturation, learning or socialisation. Alternatively, it can take place at a macrolevel, where change and modernisation take place at the level of a social system (usually the main aim of development communication research).

**microlevel:**
at the level of an
individual person

**macrolevel:**
at the level of a
community or
society

Effective research aimed at knowledge development involves more than enabling adults to read and write. It should purposively be directed at solving practical problems and, in so doing, improving the quality of life of the community. According to the principle of

**congruence:**
agreement

congruence, the effectiveness of such research will depend on the extent to which researchers can dovetail research goals and objectives with the target behaviour and circumstances of the population or clients concerned. First, as with any research population consisting of individuals and subgroups, we should become familiar with their demographic, psychographic and lifestyle **characteristics** (including, but not limited to gender, age, occupation, educational level, income, living area, activities, interests and opinions), and the target behaviour involved. Secondly, we should identify what kind of **intervention** behaviour will be relevant to solving the problem. Thirdly, we need to identify the relevant **conditions** (social, environmental, political and/or religious).

Economists traditionally distinguish between those who are affluent and those who are poor. But as we find ourselves in an era characterised by advanced information technology, we – from a communication point of view – are still faced with the distinction between those 'who know' and those 'who do not know'. This distinction and the need for knowledge development is particularly applicable in South Africa, where, according to Statistics South Africa (1999:37) 19,3% of the population aged 20 years or older have never received any formal education, and an additional 24,2% of the same age group have completed only some of the grades at the level of primary schooling.

These statistics underline the need for intervention research, especially when linked to achieving the goals of the RDP.

**RDP:**
Reconstruction and Development Programme

The South African government's RDP consists of many proposals, strategies and an integrated socio-economic policy framework, introduced in 1995, to build a non-racial, non-sexist and democratic future. In addition to programmes that centre on the implementation of the RDP, four key policy programmes, which are interlinked, can be identified:
- meeting basic human needs;
- developing human resources;
- democratising the State and society; and
- building the economy.

According to the RDP, the goals for a developmental social welfare programme in South Africa include:

- *attaining basic social welfare rights for all;*
- *redressing inequities of the past, especially with regard to women, children, the youth, the disabled, and people in rural communities and developing areas;*
- *recognising the role of organs of civil society in the welfare system, such as non-governmental development organisations; community-based rehabilitation centres and organisations; the private sector; religious organisations; traditional and other complementary healers; trade unions and individual initiatives, in the establishment of guidelines for mutual co-operation;*
- *empowering individuals, families and communities to participate in the process of deciding on the range of needs and problems to be addressed through local, provincial and national initiatives* (Government Communication and Information System 1999:405).

How can we apply participatory research to achieve social upliftment in terms of the RDP?

Communication specialists work in sectors that vary from education; foreign relations; justice and correctional services; safety, security and defence; economy; finance; health; social welfare; the mass and community media; to posts and telecommunications. Because of the diverse nature of professional and personal experiences, research that aims to contribute to the RDP has to meet certain theoretical and practical **prerequisites**, of which the following are the most important:

1. The first prerequisite represents two ethical issues. First, as researchers, we need to ensure that participants are truly **representative** of the various stakeholders. Secondly, as the research process progresses, we need to establish whether the need for change or the problem to be solved is supported by the **majority** of the community or organisation.

2. **Consensus** needs to be reached among all stakeholders (e.g. local government, representatives of the community, representatives from the business sector, community organisations, community media and local NGOs) that a prior or present programme or system has failed, and needs to be changed.

**NGOs:**
non-governmental
organisations

3. Development communication projects have, during the past four decades, for various reasons, been ineffective. One of the reasons was a lack of understanding on the part of researchers, of what community members perceived their participatory roles to be.

We therefore have to move away from bureaucratic and fixed hierarchical decision-making structures. Instead, **participatory structures** need to be **negotiated** with community members, to reach an agreed demarcation of roles and tasks.

4. A community's (or organisation's) **resources** need to be mobilised. In the words of Nelson Mandela (1998:7) ' ... democratic governance is management of a process whereby people govern themselves. Government is not an employment agency'. Communication researchers can no longer rely on the arguments that they have the monopoly on explaining or solving communication problems in particular social contexts. Instead, it is our duty to enable those who participate in research to 'understand their own situation and solve their own problems, become aware of their own potential, regain their sense of dignity and take collective action for self-development' (De Vos 1998:409).

Against this background of prerequisites, the question asked above can be answered by considering the features of a participatory action research process.

## 6.5.3 Participatory action research process

The research process starts with someone (as a member of a community or as an outsider) **stimulating** an interest in the need for a certain change in a social system or an awareness of a problem. For example, a teacher may become aware of children's drug use. During this initial stage, however, the awareness of the problem, or the need for change, will not necessarily be known or shared by other members of the community (or organisation).

**legitimation:** sanction, approval, justification or licence of an act

Two processes that can occur simultaneously, or chronologically, follow the initial stage: initiation and legitimation. **Initiation**, in the context of collective decision-making, refers to the dissemination of information about the problem, or need for change, either by an individual or a group that has a personal knowledge of the organisational or social system. Initiation usually takes the form of discussions with representatives from a particular community, followed by workshops that involve other community members. During these workshops, subjects not only become participants (as is the case in conducting focus-group interviews), they also become research participants. For example, the

teacher who became aware of children's drug use can approach you as a communication scientist and as a fellow teacher, so you could act as a facilitator by involving other teachers, parents, community members, and the children themselves. **Legitimation** can involve any number of individuals or groups, depending on the size of the community and the nature of collectively decided change(s) to be introduced. Because legitimisers have status and social power (e.g. the town mayor or the president of an organisation), their involvement during the initial stages of participatory action research will increase the chances of securing decision and proposal approval.

**power:**
capacity to influence the decisions and actions of others

Once a **collective decision** has been approved, this intent is translated into **action** or the execution of an action plan. For example, while investigating the children's drug-taking behaviour, the group collectively realises that a lack of parental involvement in children's schooling, an absence of recreation facilities and entrepreneurial opportunities are some of causes for such behaviour.

Legitimation, in this example, points to the involvement of parents and other role-players, such as local businesses, that can be functional in finding solutions (financial support or raw materials) for the lack of recreational and entrepreneurial facilities and opportunities.

**collaboration:**
work in co-operation with one another

The participatory action research process can be **summarised** by stating that participants collectively and in collaboration with the researcher, determine:
- the nature of the problem;
- what research questions need to be asked;
- who should be investigated as respondents;
- how the project can be broken down into smaller tasks;
- what short-, medium- and long-term objectives can be identified;
- what other data need to be collected;
- what methods should be used to collect data;
- which stakeholders should be involved;
- how they as participants will be involved in gathering data;
- how and by whom the data will be interpreted;
- how responsibility for the tasks can be allocated to participants;
- the action plan to be implemented, based on the findings; and
- how and by whom the effectiveness of the action plan will be monitored.

A collective analysis of the problem(s) can also include a **situation analysis** by covering questions, such as:

- What are the imbalances in availability and accessibility of resources (e.g. water) and services (e.g. telephones)?
- How can financial support from government and/or the business sectors be generated?
- What are community members' legal rights?
- What can each participant or subgroup be expected to contribute to the project?
- What can each participant or subgroup expect to gain from the project?
- What skills need to be developed?
- What action programme needs to be implemented and by whom?

Because we (as researchers) and the community are equal partners in the investigation, planning and implementation of a specific project, no fixed procedure or research plan can be prescribed.

Some authors (e.g. Bless and Higson-Smith 1995:58) suggest that it is useful to compile a formal contract in which all participants (after negotiation) specify what their contributions and expectations will be.

Table 6.3 is an example of a simple participatory action research agreement that applies to the example about children's drug use.

**triangulation:** using two or more theories, types of sampling, investigators, sources of data, and/or data-collection methods

Because development projects involve different stakeholders (e.g. nurses, educationalists, NGOs, government departments), they are multidisciplinary and **triangulation** is the most appropriate methodology. In other words, a combination of quantitative and qualitative data-collection methods can be used: in-depth interviews, focus-group interviews, survey questionnaires and field observations. (Because participants are equal partners in the research process, they are equally responsible for identifying and eventually selecting the most appropriate data-collection methods.)

The more popular research methods used in participatory action research are focus-group interviews, in-depth interviews and participant observation, because, in the words of Bless and Higson-Smith (1995: 56), they 'acknowledge the value of the opinions and thoughts of all people'.

During the process, research findings are documented and experiences shared. Participants are encouraged to reflect on research findings and taking action. As an ongoing process, information on which action plans are based can be disseminated not only in the form of printed reports, but also as dramatisations, street plays, musicals and work-shops involving other members of the community (or organisation).

**TABLE 6.3:** An example of a participatory action research agreement

| COMMUNICATION SCIENTIST | STAKEHOLDERS IN THE COMMUNITY OR ORGANISATION |
|---|---|
| *Expected contributions* <ul><li>active participation as change agent;</li><li>communication (academic) knowledge;</li><li>communication research skills (e.g. to guide and evaluate research);</li><li>skills development in interpersonal and small-group communication (negotiation and mediation).</li></ul> | *Expected contributions* <ul><li>active participation as a representative of a subgroup (e.g. parents);</li><li>knowledge of the need for change or problem (e.g. children using drugs);</li><li>raw material and/or financial resources (e.g. for recreational facilities, from local businesses);</li><li>specific skills training (e.g. basic business and marketing skills).</li></ul> |
| *Expected gains* <ul><li>to create an atmosphere of mutual trust and respect;</li><li>to reach meaningful group consensus;</li><li>to promote communication among different stakeholders;</li><li>to understand the problem(s) experienced by a particular community;</li><li>to understand a particular community's problem in relation to other communities, or in a wider social context;</li><li>to empower individuals and subgroups involved;</li><li>to contribute to an ongoing development of theory and participatory action research processes, procedures and methods;</li><li>to disseminate the understanding and information gained to others;</li><li>to enable society (communities or organisations) to benefit from research.</li></ul> | *Expected gains* <ul><li>to solve the identified problem, or initiate the intended change;</li><li>to acquire an awareness of how future similar problems can be resolved;</li><li>to develop participatory action skills to deal with future (community or organisational) problems;</li><li>to obtain access to resources;</li><li>to promote self-development and community empowerment.</li></ul> |

## 6.5.4 Our role(s) as researchers

**change agents:**
professionals
who influence
innovations seen
as desirable by
a community

As researchers in participatory action research, our role(s) are unique as we simultaneously act as change agents, team builders, facilitators or catalysts for change. As facilitators, we should instil into participants' interactions the following communicative practices to reach meaningful group consensus (adapted from Poole and DeSanctis 1992:26; Walther and Burgoon 1992:57-63):

- Participants should approach and argue decisions on the basis of logic, and not on the basis of personal or individualistic judgements.
- Participants should only support solutions with which they agree (even in cases of partial agreement).
- Differences of opinion should be expected and treated as natural, positive and helpful inputs in the decision-making process.
- Everyone should be involved and be given the opportunity to participate in the decision-making process.

**trading:**
exchange,
especially as a
compromise

- Conflict-reducing techniques to reach decisions, such as basing decisions on a majority vote, averaging, or trading, should be avoided.
- A change of mind for the purpose of preventing conflict or simply for the sake of reaching agreement, should also be avoided.

**negotiation:**
communication
to reach an
agreement

We have to purposefully create and maintain an atmosphere of mutual trust and respect among stakeholders. Towards this end, we have to ensure that participants are democratically elected and representative of the subgroups involved. Our role, therefore, is to promote the processes of **negotiation** among participants and **mediation**, especially where there is conflict between two subgroups (e.g. rival gangs).

**mediation:**
to act between
parties to reach
a compromise
or reconciliation

While being open to ideas and information that may differ from previously established problem-solving practices, we − as researchers − become **co-learners** in the research process. As co-learners, we can start by identifying stakeholders' resources (e.g. their skills, experience, knowledge, and their cultural and value orientations). While acknowledging their resources, we can also create opportunities, such as regular, informal community meetings, for them to share the experiences and views they hold as individuals and as members of the subgroups they represent. The premise is that a range of opinions and

information, including disagreement, can create opportunities for groups to eventually reach solutions that are more appropriate.

To effectively contribute to the development of action programmes (and policies) within the framework of the RDP, participatory action research has to be a **cyclical**, never-ending process. As this type of research is fundamentally aimed at empowering the people, our inputs and involvement as researchers should gradually be phased out as the participants take on collective responsibility for:

**cyclical:** decisions and actions recurring in cycles

- the implementation of the action plan;
- the periodical evaluation of the plan; and
- if necessary, the adaptation of the plan.

## 6.5.5 Notes of caution

There is no fixed procedure or research plan for conducting participatory action research. And because we as researchers and the community are equal partners in the investigation, planning and implementation of a specific project, four cautionary notes need to be made when undertaking this type of research:

1. The goal of this kind of research is to solve a specific problem in a particular community or organisation. We therefore have to be careful not to generalise our findings to other communities or organisations. If requirements, such as external validity, are essential to our research, other research procedures and methods (not participatory action research) need to be considered.

**experimenter bias:** errors that support the researcher's hypothesis

2. Given the relationship that develops among participants who become co-researchers, we may become subjectively involved in decision-making processes that influence our observations and interpretation of results – similar to experimenter bias.

3. In addition to selective perception on the part of researchers, participative action research can also suffer from the problem of reactivity on the part of participants. In other words, they do not respond as they would under normal circumstances and their awareness of being part of a research process can have an impact on their behaviour.

**extraneous variables:** any factors (excluding the independent variable) that can influence the (dependent) variable

4. Extraneous variables are difficult, if not impossible, to control. We may incorrectly conclude that the success (or failure) of a project is due to the actions and changes introduced, whereas other factors may have contributed to such results.

## EXECUTIVE SUMMARY: PARTICIPATORY ACTION RESEARCH

1  Research methods and techniques:
   - field research; and
   - survey research.

2  Objectives:
   - RDP;
   - knowledge development;
   - knowledge utilisation; and
   - design and development.

3  Prerequisites:
   - representativeness of stakeholders;
   - majority of the community;
   - group consensus;
   - negotiated participatory structures; and
   - mobilisation of own resources.

4  Research process:
   - stimulation;
   - initiation;
   - legitimation;
   - negotiation and mediation;
   - research agreement;
   - implementation of action plan;
   - evaluation/adaptation of action plan; and
   - researcher's role(s).

5  Notes of caution:
   - lack of external validity;
   - subjectivity;
   - reactivity; and
   - influence of extraneous variables.

## Self-evaluation and portfolio task

6.4  You are asked to research the feasibility of initiating a community project in your area that will improve the quality of life for a specific group in that community (e.g. a feeding scheme, care for street children, the elderly or the homeless, nutritional gardens, literacy training for illiterate adults).

The goal of your research is applied research and the main objective is exploratory.

Describe the procedure that you would follow to research the feasibility of the project by answering the following questions:
- What are the research goal(s) and objective(s)?
- Who would you identify as the stimulator(s), initiator(s) and legitimiser(s) of the project?
- Who or what (units of analysis) would you research to determine the need to implement the project?
- Who are the major role-players? (For example, who would you approach for financial support?)

Based on the previous sections it has become clear that organisations cannot function in isolation from the communities and customers they serve and on which they rely. In the next section, this interdependence is further highlighted by the need for and procedures followed when researching public relations. The research and problem-solving skills discussed in section 6.6 are, however, not only of interest to **public relations** practitioners. These skills can be transferred to other organisational contexts and communication-related occupations, such as those involved in the print, broadcasting and telecommunications sectors.

# 6.6  Public relations audit

The goals of public relations (PR) research can be divided into basic research (to examine models and processes that underlie public relations theory and practices) and applied research (*see* Unit 2). When undertaking a public relations audit, the goal is usually **applied** research to measure:

- how effective communication with various publics are; and how such communication (as a PR campaign) can be improved; and/or
- the effectiveness of the planning, implementation and eventual impact of a PR campaign.

A PR audit is of particular strategic importance to determine an organisation's long-term goals, and the planning and policies necessary to achieve these goals. In organisational communication, the term 'publics' includes everyone who has any interest in a specific organisation. In public relations, a finer distinction is made between internal publics and external publics. **Internal publics** can be defined as groups of individuals who are members of a particular organisation, such as employees, middle management and top management. The nature of subgroups found in an organisation's internal public will differ according to the nature of the organisation. For example, within the South African Revenue Services (SARS) a distinction can be made between Inland Revenue, and Customs and Excise. Within the Customs division, other subgroups can be differentiated on the basis of the core functions of personnel, such as managing the administration and application of matters relating to rules of origin; developing and maintaining a risk analysis strategy, trade agreements, and certification.

The description and demarcation of **external publics** also depends on the nature of the organisation. External publics include individuals, groups, and other organisations that are found outside of the particular organisation and with whom the organisation interacts. For example, a consumer public consists of individuals and groups in society who, by consuming the products produced by an organisation, is involved with and affected by the organisation and/or can actually affect the organisation.

**Focus-group interviews, surveys** via self-administered questionnaires, telephone surveys, personal interviews and **content analyses** are the most popular research methods used, with participant observations being used less frequently.

## 6.6.1 The research process in a PR audit

As with any communication research, the *first phase* of the research process when conducting a PR audit includes identifying the problem, subproblems, assumptions, and research goals and objectives.

### Researching the corporate image

When the goal is to measure how effective communication with various publics is, and how such communication (as a PR campaign) can be improved, research is guided by questions such as:

- What is the organisation's standing in the eyes of its internal publics?
- What are the external publics' opinions of the organisation?

These kind of questions point to the fact that the research objective(s) of this type of PR audit are essentially exploratory and descriptive.

It is important to identify the subgroups in both the internal and external publics that are important to the organisation, and to establish their demographic characteristics, their media preferences, and why they are important for the organisation. This *first phase* of the PR audit can be accomplished by using two research methods. First, a cross-sectional **content analysis** (over a period of a month) can be undertaken of communications by the organisation to both internal and external publics, and of communications about the organisation. Internal communication can include newsletters, memos, messages posted on noticeboards and/or message disseminated via the Intranet. External communication can include brochures, year-books, advertisements, press releases, letters to customers and/or messages distributed via the Internet. Communication about the organisation refer specifically to messages disseminated via the mass media. For example, a quick scan of local newspapers published on the same day revealed a variety of debates about matters relating to the SABC, such as criticising the ANC's endorsement of the nomination of a former minister in the apartheid regime as a member of the SABC board; and a debate about whether more locally produced television talk shows should be produced, instead of broadcasting American ones. From these examples of communication about the SABC as an organisation, we can deduce that important members of the external publics are not only television viewers and licence holders, but also political parties, and television and media employees, including newspaper editors.

The identification of the most important subgroups in an organisation's internal publics can be accomplished by conducting **face-to-face interviews** with representatives from the different departments and sections, and from different hierarchies within the organisation. Employees in lower ranks may have more frequent and direct contact with clients than top management, and can therefore make meaningful contributions to the first phase of this kind of PR audit.

The *second phase* in this kind of PR audit involves a corporate image study. Our objectives would be to determine what the target publics believe or feel towards the organisation, and their knowledge (famil-iarity), impressions and experience of the organisation. The description of a corporate image is usually accomplished by doing a **survey**, using ratings scales and semantic differential scales in a questionnaire (*see*

**Intranet:** a network of computers connected only within a particular institution

**Internet:** telecommunica-tion links among computers

**SABC:** South African Broadcasting Corporation

**ANC:** African National Congress

**target publics:** internal and external publics that are important to an organisation

Unit 3). Such a survey enables us to do several descriptive analyses, such as a comparison:

- between an ideal profile and the real profile;
- between the internal public's views and the external public's views;
- among different subgroups within the internal public (e.g. top management versus employees); and
- among different subgroups within the external public (e.g. young clients versus old clients).

A comparison between an ideal and the real is also one of the characteristics of a **communication audit** (see section 6.7). The following example illustrates how a **semantic differential scale** can be used to rank respondents' perceptions of the ideal public television broadcasting organisation.

**FIGURE 6.1** A semantic differential scale for eliciting perceptions of the ideal public television broadcasting organisation

The purpose of this scale is to measure what the ideal public television broadcasting organisation means to you. Please judge the ideal public television organisation against the following set of descriptive scales by placing a tick ✔ in one of the seven spaces on each line, between the pairs of words. For example, if you feel that the ideal television organisation is always objective, place a tick in the first space next the word 'objective'. If you feel that the ideal television organisation is only slightly described by the word 'objective', place a tick in the second or third space. If the two words in a pair are equally descriptive of the ideal television organisation, or if neither word applies, tick the fourth (middle) space. If you feel that the ideal television organisation is only slightly described by the word 'subjective', place a tick in the fifth or sixth space. If you feel that the ideal television organisation is always subjective, place a tick in the seventh space, next to the word 'subjective'.

The ideal public television broadcasting organisation is ...

| Objective | :....:....:....:....:....:....: | Subjective |
| Dependent | :....:....:....:....:....:....: | Independent |
| Unfair | :....:....:....:....:....:....: | Fair |
| Impartial | :....:....:....:....:....:....: | Biased |
| Unresponsive | :....:....:....:....:....:....: | Responsive |
| Concerned | :....:....:....:....:....:....: | Unconcerned |

After some time (two to six weeks; sufficient to prevent respondents remembering their previous responses), the sample of respondents are given the same scale and asked to rate a specific public television broadcasting organisation. In other words, the inter-correlations of the different scores are calculated. The time between the two measurements is also an important requirement of testing the scale's reliability (*see* Unit 3).

**inter-correlations:** measuring the extent of mutual relations

**FIGURE 6.2** A comparison of an ideal profile and a real profile of a corporate image

The purpose of this scale is to measure what STV, as a public television broadcasting corporation, means to you. Please judge the STV corporation against the following set of descriptive scales by placing a tick ✔ in one of the seven spaces on each line, between the pairs of words. For example, if you feel that the STV corporation is always objective, place a tick in the first space next the word 'objective'. If you feel that the STV corporation is only slightly described by the word 'objective',

place a tick in the second or third space. If the two words in a pair are equally descriptive of the STV corporation, or if neither word applies, place a tick in the fourth (middle) space. If you feel that the STV corporation is only slightly described by the word 'subjective', place a tick in the fifth or sixth space. If you feel that the STV corporation is always subjective, place a tick in the seventh space, next to the word 'subjective'.

The STV as a public television broadcasting corporation is ...

| | | |
|---|---|---|
| Objective | | Subjective |
| Dependent | | Independent |
| Unfair | | Fair |
| Impartial | | Biased |
| Unresponsive | | Responsive |
| Concerned | | Unconcerned |

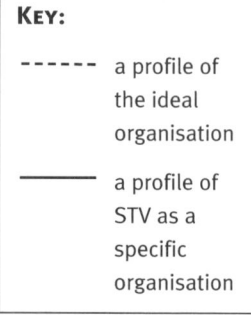

**KEY:**

- - - - - - a profile of the ideal organisation

———— a profile of STV as a specific organisation

The profiles are compiled by calculating the average score of each item and tabulating it on each scale, and by connecting each mean with a line. By comparing the solid line (specific organisation) with that of the broken line (ideal organisation), public relations researchers can identify in which areas the specific organisation falls short of an ideal.

**mean:** an arithmetic average of a set of scores

The **third phase** of this kind of PR audit involves interpreting survey results and determining the nature of themes that future short-term and long-term PR campaigns should emphasise. It may be found that a short-term campaign should emphasise defensive themes, followed by positive image-building themes.

## Researching a PR campaign

When the goal is to measure the effectiveness of the **planning, implementation** and eventual **impact** of a PR campaign, the research process, during each of the three stages discussed above, is guided by different questions.

During the *first phase*, the focus is on measuring the effectiveness of **planning** a PR campaign. The kinds of questions that need to be answered are:
- What are the objectives of the PR campaign?
- Who are the target publics?
- Which communication media would be the most efficient to use?
- What are the estimated costs of the campaign?
- Should a pilot test involving a sample of the target publics be conducted?

**above-the-line:** messages disseminated by print media, radio, television, films and posters (outdoors and on transportation)

**below-the-line:** direct contact with the public (e.g. by pamphlets and point-of-sale displays)

It is important to know what image the PR campaign wants to project about the organisation and to ensure that both above-the-line and below-the-line messages contribute towards this image and that these are not contradictory. The target publics can be researched as part of a pilot study by conducting interviews with a purposive sample of respondents drawn from both internal and external publics, and by analysing their values, lifestyles and motivations, as part of formative research. To evaluate the content of the PR campaign and the media to be used, focus-group interviews, motivational research, concept testing, ratings research and non-ratings research are appropriate methods (*see* Unit 5).

During the *second phase*, the focus is on measuring the effectiveness of the **implementation** of a PR campaign. The kinds of questions that need to be answered are:
- Does the campaign correlate with the initial plans?
- Is the campaign reaching the target publics?

A qualitative **content analysis** of messages that are communicated will reveal whether or not they correlate with the initially planned PR

**gatekeeping:**
the selection, rejection and/or alteration of the form and substance of messages in mass communication

**news releases:**
free information, publicity or a news story supplied to the mass media

**syntax:**
the grammatical way in which words are arranged

programme – for example, to emphasise informative, persuasive and/or defensive themes. A quantitative content analysis of the mass media will determine the number of messages communicated over a specified period. To measure whether the programme is reaching the target publics, methods of audience research can be used, as well as an audit of circulation figures and ratings (*see* Unit 5). Wimmer and Dominick (1997:337) distinguish an area of PR research called **gatekeeping research**, which can be applied during the second phase. This involves two types of content analyses, with the objective of determining what kinds of messages pass through the so-called 'gate' and are disseminated by the mass media. One type of analysis involves a comparison between the original news releases formulated by an organisation and the version that is published or broadcast. The analysis can be guided by asking whether changes are made to the length of sentences and syntax; and whether a trend or pattern of changes can be established over time.

A second type of analysis is a content analysis of news releases in the press, radio and television, to analyse style, thematic topics and visual material (e.g. photographs). Gatekeeping research is useful, not only to determine how many news releases are judged to be sufficiently newsworthy, but also to determine variables such as content and style, which are preferred by the mass media. Although a news release is aimed at benefiting the organisation, its newsworthiness will depend on the extent to which it is of public interest. Subjects frequently included in news releases are announcements (about the development of new products, the introduction of new services, forthcoming events and policy-related matters); changes in managerial appointments; and speeches made by management.

The following are examples of **research questions** that can be used for the analysis of print and broadcast media (radio and television):
- What are the main themes or topics addressed in the content of the news story?
- Is the report balanced – for example, is more than one side of an argument presented, or can opinions be distinguished from fact?
- Is a news story an appropriate genre to use? In other words, would an advertisement, for which the organisation pays, have been more appropriate?
- Is immediacy conveyed by the report using present tense

(e.g. *The organisation's vision involves the …*) or present perfect tense (e.g. *The organisation's vision has involved the …*), rather than past tense (e.g. *The organisation's vision involved the …*)?

- Is mainly active voice (instead of passive voice) used? (The verb shows the relation of the subject to the action and an active relation is more direct and, therefore, preferred.) For example: *This organisation delivers innovative information technology solutions.*
  is preferred to
  *Innovative information technology solutions are delivered by this organisation.*
- Are mainly concrete words used? For example, the statement below is less precise, abstract, vague and potentially ambiguous, because it is difficult to determine the factual nature of words such as 'new', 'global sourcing' and 'mindset':
  *We, as marketing consultants, can develop a new global sourcing mindset in your organisation.*
  Whereas the following statement is more precise, concrete and the factual nature can be verified:
  *We, as marketing consultants, can develop a profitable export business plan for your organisation.*
- Are the majority of the sentences formulated in a declarative form? (A declarative sentence informs or makes something known to the reader, viewer or listener.) For example:
  *We provide opportunities for self-starters from previously disadvantaged groups.*
  Depending on the kind of information that is conveyed, additional communicative functions can be fulfilled by such a statement. In the above example, the statement also conveys the messagethat this organisation is concerned and committed to correct the wrongs of the past.

When analysing the visual codes (in print media and television), additional research questions can be asked:
- If photographs or video inserts are included, what messages do they communicate?
- How do the visuals enhance the main topic of the story?
- What other type of photographs or visual images could have been used to enhance the verbal report?

When printed news releases are analysed, the following additional questions can be asked:

- What is the average Readability Ease of the news reports?
- Do the headlines summarise the stories?
- Will the headlines arouse readers' interest to read the stories?

During the **third phase**, the focus is on measuring the effectiveness of the **impact** of a PR campaign. An important question is:

- How do the costs of the PR campaign translate into benefits for the organisation?

The methods used to measure the effectiveness of messages (*see* section 5.2.4) can also be applied to research the three dimensions of effectiveness of the PR campaign. In the cognitive dimension, we determine how much the target publics have learnt from the campaign by testing their attention, comprehension, awareness, recognition, exposure and recall of the campaign. At the affective level, we measure the target publics' feelings, involvement, the extent to which they like or dislike the organisation, and their attitude change towards the organisation, following exposure to the PR campaign. In the conative dimension of measuring the effectiveness of the PR campaign, we measure the target publics' behaviour – first, by measuring their predisposition towards the organisation and, secondly, their actual behaviour and behavioural changes, for example as clients.

---

### *EXECUTIVE SUMMARY:*
### PUBLIC RELATIONS AUDIT

1 Research methods and techniques:
   - content analysis;
   - gatekeeping research;
   - field research; and
   - survey research.

2 Researching the corporate image:
   - internal publics;
   - external publics;
   - comparing the real with the ideal;
   - planning future short-term PR campaigns; and
   - planning future long-term PR campaigns.

3 Researching a PR campaign:
   - effectiveness of planning;
   - effectiveness of implementation; and
   - effectiveness of impact.

## Self-evaluation and portfolio tasks

**6.5** Assume that you are a public relations practitioner for a major vehicle manufacturer. Describe how you would conduct a PR audit to measure how effective the manufacturer's communications with various publics are, and how such communication (as a PR campaign) can be improved.

**6.6** You have been approached by the Department of Health to assess the effectiveness of the impact of a PR information campaign designed to persuade people to use condoms to prevent the spreading of HIV (Human Immunodeficiency Virus), AIDS (Acquired Immunodeficiency Syndrome) and STDs (Sexually Transmitted Diseases). Describe how you would conduct a PR audit to measure the effectiveness of the impact of this PR campaign.

**6.7** Identify an organisation that is partially or entirely dependent on the goodwill of the community to function (e.g. the SPCA - Society for the Prevention of Cruelty to Animals). Do a gatekeeping research study of your local community newspaper, over a period of a month, by evaluating the content and style of reports that deal with this organisation. Use the research questions formulated in section 6.6.1 as guidelines for the content analysis.

# 6.7 Communication audit

Although a communication audit can be used as part of a social audit, or as part of a public relations audit, its aim is specifically to measure the effectiveness of internal communication.

## 6.7.1 Methods, techniques and measuring instruments

**Readership studies** (*see* Unit 5) are used to determine how many employees read certain messages, such as internal newsletters or official announcements and/or to measure how much they remember of the messages communicated. **Content analyses** are done of the information about and from an organisation that is disseminated via the mass media. Because a communication audit focuses on internal communication, a content analysis of these external messages would usually be undertaken in addition to using one or more of the other measuring instruments and if the organisation is concerned about its corporate image among its external publics. It would, therefore, be more appropriate to do **Readability Ease tests** (*see* Unit 4) as a content analysis of internal publications, to determine the ease with which messages can be read.

The full ICA communication audit procedure, developed and used in the USA and Europe since 1971, involves the following five measuring instruments (Goldhaber et al. 1978; Goldhaber and Rogers 1979), which can be administered in combination or separately.

- A survey is conducted, using a **self-administered questionnaire**. As the questionnaire is constructed in specific sections and therefore differs from other questionnaires used in survey research, it is discussed and illustrated below in section 6.7.2.
- Employees complete a **communication experience form**, over a specified period, in which they record important communication occurrences that they consider effective or ineffective. Other information, such as to what and to whom the experience is primarily related, are included in the examples of communication experiences forms as part of a self-administered questionnaire.
- Two types of **personal interviews** are conducted with a representative sample of employees that is drawn randomly, or with key role-players, such as heads of sections, drawn by means of a purposive sample. One type of interview that can be conducted independently of the other measuring instruments, with the aim of exploring and describing specific communication experiences, is open-ended questions. The second type of interview is used as a follow-up interview, to elaborate and explain the findings of one of the other measuring instruments.
- Employees are requested to keep a **communication diary** of their communication experiences over a specified period. The following information can be recorded: the communication medium used (e.g. e-mail); the topic (e.g. new flexitime regulations); whether the information was sent or received; and by whom.
- **Focus-group interviews** are conducted to do a **network analysis** to describe the communication links and networks that operate in an organisation; to identify the communication roles fulfilled by

specific employees (such as middle management); and to identify gatekeepers that create bottlenecks.

**gatekeepers:** people who control the flow of information and/or the form and substance of messages

**skewed:** biased or distorted

The communication experience form, interviews, the communication diary and a network analysis provide qualitative data about the effectiveness of internal communication and the reasons behind employees' answers, opinions, motivations or behaviours. For example, a network analysis can reveal that important work-related messages are skewed because they reach employees on lower ranks in the form of rumours.

The main **disadvantage** of a communication audit is the question of whether it is cost-effective. This not only refers to the expenses incurred and the time involved, but especially if findings and recommendations are not implemented. Nevertheless, some of the **advantages** of an audit include the following:

- an audit provides data about attitudes, perceptions and actual communication behaviour as they relate to the different components of the communication process (e.g. sources of information);
- an audit is based on a valid framework that investigates the effectiveness of organisational communication during a specified (cross-sectional) time period;
- the selection of one measuring instrument (or the combination of two or more instruments) provides flexibility in the research design and can be guided by the objective of the research, the extent of the problem and the size of the population; and
- an instrument, such as a questionnaire, can be adapted to the nature of the particular organisation and, once standardised, can be used during follow-up audits.

## 6.7.2 Applying a self-administered questionnaire

The self-administered questionnaire developed by the ICA, consists of the following eight sections or domains, which include perceptions, elements, behaviours and processes of organisational communication:

- Receiving information from others (★).
- Sending information to others (★).
- The action on information sent (★).
- Sources of information (★).

- Timeliness of information received from key sources.
- Communication relationships.
- Communication and work satisfaction (★).
- Communication channels (★).

The sections marked (★) include two Likert scales for each item, which measure respondents' perceptions of the ideal (or what they need), versus their perceptions of what occurs in reality. These two scales enable us to compare the ideal with the real, and where large discrepancies between the two are recorded, these are indicative of problem areas that need to be addressed.

For example:
- 12% of the respondents indicate that they currently receive 'none', and 78% of the respondents indicate that they receive 'little' information about how well they are doing their work in their section (**the real**); whereas
- 82% of the same respondents indicate that they need more than average information (**the ideal**) about how well they are doing their work in their section.

This discrepancy indicates that employees need more information about their work performance.

Additional items can be included to record the demographic characteristics of respondents and to measure unique aspects of organisational communication, if they warrant inclusion. A practical example is that of the top management of an organisation using e-mail to disseminate official work-related messages, while not all employees have regular access to a personal computer.

The self-administered questionnaire that follows on pages 322 to 340 was constructed to do a communication audit of the UNISA library. Certain terms were introduced (such as 'head of division') to correspond with the nature of the organisation and the hierarchy of employees. (It is published with the permission of the compilers, RS Rensburg and GM du Plooy, and the Management Committee of UNISA's Department of Library Services.) Each of the eight sections is followed by an **communication experience form.**

## 6.7.3 Findings of communication audits

Once the problem areas have been identified, the written report to the organisation can be prepared using the eight demarcated topic areas. As with any other research project, the report ends with recommendations that the organisation's management can consider.

As the communication audit of the UNISA library was of a confidential nature, the findings were only communicated to its top management and are not necessarily reflected in the following overview of findings of ICA audits that have been conducted in the USA (Kreps 1990:215-216; Goldhaber 1990:365).

- Employees have a need for different procedures during meetings and better upward communication, to enable them to make inputs without feeling threatened.
- Employees need clearer communication of the organisation's goals, objectives and policies, especially if these affect their work.
- Employees need more information about future career opportunities.
- Employees in certain sections feel that middle and top management are ineffective managers of people and need training in communication and managerial skills.
- Employees generally feel a need to receive more information (about work-related matters) than to send information.
- Employees feel a need to receive official information through formal communication channels, rather than via the grapevine.
- Employees feel a need for more frequent interpersonal communication with top management.
- No correlations are generally found between communication variables and demographic characteristics.
- In some instances, the greater the distance between the sources and the recipients of communication, the less information is received; the less are the opportunities to receive more information; the less is the follow-up action; the greater is the use of the grapevine; the poorer is the quality of information and the poorer are the interpersonal relations.

These findings illustrate how regular communication audits can be used to evaluate an organisation's internal communication system, and how recommendations can be made about how communication practices (including content, media and information flow) can be improved.

**6**

*EXECUTIVE SUMMARY:*
**COMMUNICATION AUDIT**

1  Research methods and techniques:
   - readership studies;
   - content analyses:
     – of communication diaries;
     – of field and survey data; and
     – Readability Ease tests.
   - field research:
     – personal interviews;
     – focus-group interviews; and
     – network analyses.
   - survey research:
     – self-administered question-
       naires;
     – communication experience
       forms; and
     – personal interviews.

2  Communication domains
   researched:
   - the effectiveness of internal
     communication;
   - receiving information
     from others;
   - sending information to others;
   - the action on information sent;
   - sources of information;
   - timeliness of information
     received from key sources;
   - communication relationships;
   - communication and work
     satisfaction; and
   - communication channels.

## Self-evaluation and portfolio tasks

**6.8**  You have been requested to research an organisation's communication efforts among its employees, some of whom are semi-literate.
Briefly describe which research methods and techniques you
would consider appropriate and briefly motivate the reason(s) for
your choice.

**6.9**  'Central to the effectiveness of organisational communication is the
acknowledgement of the importance of interpersonal communication between individuals and in small-group settings.' This is the
view held by the management of an organisation that has asked you
to conduct a communication audit.

Instead of compiling a questionnaire to conduct a comprehensive
communication audit, compile a questionnaire consisting of
approximately 20 items (a mini-survey) to evaluate:
- how employees experience interpersonal communication in the
  organisation; and
- how they perceive the ideal (or what they need) in terms of
  interpersonal communication, to do their work effectively.

# 6.8 Summary

This unit concentrated on broadening your knowledge, understanding and ability to apply different communication research methods and techniques in an environmental monitoring research, a social audit, a public relations audit and a communication audit. By situating the research in a southern African environment, we conceptualised the relevance of communication research in diverse settings related to organisational and development communication.

In dealing with research of organisations' corporate culture, including their substantive natures, which (in South Africa) are currently undergoing many changes, the social audit more specifically dealt with researching:

● employment policies and conditions of service;
● affirmative action;
● in-service training and mentorship; and
● social investments and services.

Given the South African government's national priorities, including the RDP and programmes aimed at building the economy and promoting democratisation, this unit also incorporated a conceptual scheme and practical guidelines that can be applied in development communication research involving:

● participatory strategies; and
● participatory action research.

The self-evaluation and portfolio tasks set in this unit were not only formulated to test learners' knowledge and understanding of theoretical concepts, but also to increase an awareness of how communication research can be used to promote the development of problem-solving skills, self-responsibility skills and environmental literacy skills. Doing research in practice also contributes to our awareness of the importance of a cultural and aesthetic understanding of the society in which we live and how we can contribute to achieving national priorities.

Before continuing with Unit 7, you are encouraged to evaluate your achievement of the learning outcomes using the following guide.

**ASSESSMENT OF LEARNING OUTCOMES**

Ratings for evaluation of performance:

5 very high (extremely good)

4 high (good)

3 medium (average)

2 low (poor)

1 very low (extremely poor)

0 evidence is absent

| Outcomes (knowledge, competence and orientations) *You should be able to demonstrate your understanding and ability to:* | Evidence of performance | Examples of criteria used to evaluate evidence of performance | Evaluation of performance | | | | | |
|---|---|---|---|---|---|---|---|---|
| | | | Ratings | | | | | |
| | | | 5 | 4 | 3 | 2 | 1 | 0 |
| Undertake pilot research studies | by conducting: <br> • environmental monitoring research; <br> • a social audit; <br> • participation action research; <br> • a public relations audit; and <br> • a communication audit. | The choices and practical applications made during each step in the research process must be motivated with reference to the criteria discussed in Units 2-6. <br><br> The quality of contributions generated by the information collected and actions taken to solve the research problem or issue, also serve as criteria to determine the success of each pilot study. | | | | | | |

## SUGGESTED READING

Bless, C and Higson-Smith, C. 1995. *Fundamental of social research methods: an African perspective.* (2nd edition). Kenwyn: Juta.

Collins, K. 1999. *Participatory research: a primer.* Cape Town: Prentice Hall.

Davies, CA. 1999. *Reflexive ethnography: a guide to researching selves and others.* London: Routledge.

Government Communication and Information System (GCIS). 2000/01 (or later edition). *South Africa Yearbook 2000/01.* Pretoria: Government Printer. Also available on Government Online http://www.gov.za

GuideStar Communications. 1999. *Human resources surveys – online and dual media.* Available: http://www.guidestarco.com Accessed on 2001/01/18

Innes, D, Kentridge, M and Perold, H (eds). 1993. *Reversing discrimination: affirmative action in the workplace.* Cape Town: Oxford University Press.

Kotler, P. 1997. *Marketing management. Analysis, planning, implementation and control.* (9th edition). New Jersey: Prentice Hall.

Pottier, J (ed). 1993. *Practising development. Social sciences perspectives.* London: Routledge.

Samovar, LA and Porter, RE (eds). 1995. *Communication between cultures.* (2nd ed). Belmont, California: Wadsworth.

Schwandt, DR and Marquardt, MJ. 1999. *Organizational learning from world class theories to global best practices.* MA: Saint Lucie.

Servaes, J (ed). 1996. *Participatory communication for social change.* Thousand Oaks, California: Sage.

Servaes, J. 1999. *Communication for development: one world, multiple cultures.* Cresskill, NJ: Hampton.

Swanepoel, H. 1992. *Community development: putting plans into action.* (2nd edition). Kenwyn: Juta.

# UNISA Library Communication Audit:
## Questionnaire Survey

*Instructions*
Please circle all your answers on the enclosed answer sheet. For example

| Work satisfaction | | Never | Seldom | Sometimes | Most of the time | Always |
|---|---|---|---|---|---|---|
| My salary | 1. | (1) | 2 | 3 | 4 | 5 |

Please use a pencil and carefully erase any stray pencil marks. Please answer all questions/items since each is important for possibly improving the communication in your division and the library in general. **If there are any questions/items which do not apply to you, please draw a line through them.** We appreciate your patience with this important survey.

**PLEASE CIRCLE ONLY ONE ANSWER TO EACH QUESTION/ITEM**

*You may find the following definitions useful as you answer the questions in this survey:*

**Communication:** The exchange of information from one person to another (upward, downward or horizontally) in the hierarchy of a section, division or the library as a whole.

**Communication audit:** A large scale effort to determine the communication effectiveness of an organisation (in this case the library) and to diagnose possible communication problems within the library and its divisions.

**Library policies:** Sets of guidelines determined by management of how things ought to be done in a specific division and the library as a whole.

**Subordinate:** Person lower down than yourself in the hierarchy of the section, division or library.

**Co-worker:** Person on the same level as yourself in the hierarchy of the section, division or library.

**Immediate supervisor:** Person higher up than yourself in the hierarchy of the section, division or library.

**Head of section:** The head of your specific section, for example the head of the Lending section or the head of the Audiovisual section.

**Head of division:** The head of your specific division, for example the head of the Subject Reference division or the head of the Acquisitions division.

**Library management:** The top structure of the library, for example the Chief Director, Directors and Senior Deputy Directors.

**Grapevine:** Informal communication structure not prescribed by the library in general or a specific section or division. Also used for the spreading of rumours.

# Section 1: Receiving information from others

*Instructions for items 1 through 30*

You can receive information about various topics in your section, division or the library. For each topic listed below, circle the number that best indicates:

(1)  the amount of information you receive on that topic *now* and

(2)  the amount of information you *need* to receive on that topic, that is, the amount you *have to have* in order to do your work effectively.

| Topic area | | This is the amount of information I receive now | | | | | | This is the amount of information I need to receive | | | | | Office use only |
|---|---|---|---|---|---|---|---|---|---|---|---|---|---|
| | | None | Little | Average | More than average | Enough | | None | Little | Average | More than average | Enough | |
| About how well I am doing my work in my section | 1. | 1 | 2 | 3 | 4 | 5 | 2. | 1 | 2 | 3 | 4 | 5 | 5–6 |
| About my work duties (functions) in my section | 3. | 1 | 2 | 3 | 4 | 5 | 4. | 1 | 2 | 3 | 4 | 5 | 7–8 |
| About library policies | 5. | 1 | 2 | 3 | 4 | 5 | 6. | 1 | 2 | 3 | 4 | 5 | 9–10 |
| About salary and benefits | 7. | 1 | 2 | 3 | 4 | 5 | 8. | 1 | 2 | 3 | 4 | 5 | 11–12 |
| About how technological changes in the library affect my work | 9. | 1 | 2 | 3 | 4 | 5 | 10. | 1 | 2 | 3 | 4 | 5 | 13–14 |
| About mistakes and failures in my section | 11. | 1 | 2 | 3 | 4 | 5 | 12. | 1 | 2 | 3 | 4 | 5 | 15–16 |
| About how I am being judged as an individual in my section | 13. | 1 | 2 | 3 | 4 | 5 | 14. | 1 | 2 | 3 | 4 | 5 | 17–18 |

| Topic area | | This is the amount of information I receive now | | | | | | This is the amount of information I need to receive | | | | | Office use only |
|---|---|---|---|---|---|---|---|---|---|---|---|---|---|---|
| | | None | Little | Average | More than average | Enough | | None | Little | Average | More than average | Enough | |
| About how my work-related problems are being handled in the library | 15. | 1 | 2 | 3 | 4 | 5 | 16. | 1 | 2 | 3 | 4 | 5 | 19–20 |
| About how divisional decisions are made that affect my work in my section | 17. | 1 | 2 | 3 | 4 | 5 | 18. | 1 | 2 | 3 | 4 | 5 | 21–22 |
| About promotion opportunities in my division | 19. | 1 | 2 | 3 | 4 | 5 | 20. | 1 | 2 | 3 | 4 | 5 | 23–24 |
| About important new services or developments in the library | 21. | 1 | 2 | 3 | 4 | 5 | 22. | 1 | 2 | 3 | 4 | 5 | 25–26 |
| About how my work relates to the total operation of the library | 23. | 1 | 2 | 3 | 4 | 5 | 24. | 1 | 2 | 3 | 4 | 5 | 27–28 |
| About specific problems experienced by the head of my section | 25. | 1 | 2 | 3 | 4 | 5 | 26. | 1 | 2 | 3 | 4 | 5 | 29–30 |
| About specific problems experienced by the head of my division | 27. | 1 | 2 | 3 | 4 | 5 | 28. | 1 | 2 | 3 | 4 | 5 | 31–32 |
| About specific problems experienced by library management | 29. | 1 | 2 | 3 | 4 | 5 | 30. | 1 | 2 | 3 | 4 | 5 | 33–34 |

# SECTION 1: RECEIVING INFORMATION FROM OTHERS: YOUR COMMUNICATION EXPERIENCE

While you were filling out Section 1, the items (1-30) may have brought to mind a recent work-related experience of yours in which *communication* was particularly ineffective or effective. Please answer the questions below and give a summary of that experience (in Section D below).

**A.** To whom does this experience primarily relate (circle *one*):
1. Subordinate
2. Co-worker
3. Immediate supervisor
4. Head of section
5. Head of division
6. Library management

35

**B.** Please rate the quality of communication described in the experience below (circle *one*):
1. Effective
2. Ineffective

36

**C.** To what item (1-30) in Section 1 does this experience primarily relate? ...............
(Write in the item number.)

37–38

**D.** Describe the communication experience, the circumstances leading up to it, what the person did that made him/her an effective or ineffective communicator, and the results (outcome). PLEASE PRINT.

...............................................................................................................

...............................................................................................................

...............................................................................................................

...............................................................................................................

...............................................................................................................

...............................................................................................................

...............................................................................................................

# Section 2: Sending information to others

*Instructions for items 31 through 44*

In addition to receiving information, there are topics on which you can send information to others. For each topic listed below, circle the number that best indicates:

(1) the amount of information you send on that topic *now* and
(2) the amount of information you *need* to send on that topic in order to do your work effectively.

| Topic area | This is the amount of information I send now | | | | | This is the amount of information I need to send | | | | | |
|---|---|---|---|---|---|---|---|---|---|---|---|
| | None | Little | Average | More than average | Enough | | None | Little | Average | More than average | Enough |
| About reporting what I am doing in my work | **31.** 1 | 2 | 3 | 4 | 5 | **32.** 1 | 2 | 3 | 4 | 5 | 39–40 |
| About reporting what I think my work requires of me | **33.** 1 | 2 | 3 | 4 | 5 | **34.** 1 | 2 | 3 | 4 | 5 | 41–42 |
| About reporting my work-related problems | **35.** 1 | 2 | 3 | 4 | 5 | **36.** 1 | 2 | 3 | 4 | 5 | 43–44 |
| About my complaints regarding my work and/or working conditions | **37.** 1 | 2 | 3 | 4 | 5 | **38.** 1 | 2 | 3 | 4 | 5 | 45–46 |
| About my requesting information necessary to do my work | **39.** 1 | 2 | 3 | 4 | 5 | **40.** 1 | 2 | 3 | 4 | 5 | 47–48 |
| About my evaluating the work performance of my immediate supervisor | **41.** 1 | 2 | 3 | 4 | 5 | **42.** 1 | 2 | 3 | 4 | 5 | 49–50 |
| About my asking for clearer work instructions | **43.** 1 | 2 | 3 | 4 | 5 | **44.** 1 | 2 | 3 | 4 | 5 | 51–52 |

## Section 2: Sending information to others: Your communication experience

While you were filling out Section 2, the items (31-44) may have brought to mind a recent work-related experience of yours in which *communication* was particularly ineffective or effective. Please answer the questions below and give a summary of that experience (in Section D below).

A.   To whom does this experience primarily relate (circle *one*):
   1.   Subordinate
   2.   Co-worker
   3.   Immediate supervisor
   4.   Head of section
   5.   Head of division
   6.   Library management

53

B.   Please rate the quality of communication described in the experience below (circle *one*):
   1.   Effective
   2.   Ineffective

54

C.   To what item (31-44) in Section 2 does this experience primarily relate? ...........
   (Write in the item number.)

55–56

D.   Describe the communication experience, the circumstances leading up to it, what the person did that made him/her an effective or ineffective communicator, and the results (outcome). PLEASE PRINT.

.................................................................................................................

.................................................................................................................

.................................................................................................................

.................................................................................................................

.................................................................................................................

.................................................................................................................

.................................................................................................................

.................................................................................................................

# Q

## SECTION 3: ACTION ON INFORMATION SENT

*Instructions for items 45 through 54*

Indicate the amount of action that *is* and *needs* to be taken on information you sent to the following people. For each person listed below, circle the number that best indicates:

(1)  the amount of action *now* and

(2)  the amount of action *needed*

| People | | THIS IS THE AMOUNT OF ACTION NOW | | | | | | THIS IS THE AMOUNT OF ACTION NEEDED | | | | | | |
|---|---|---|---|---|---|---|---|---|---|---|---|---|---|---|
| | | Never | Seldom | Sometimes | Most of the time | Always | | Never | Seldom | Sometimes | Most of the time | Always | |
| By my subordinates | 45. | 1 | 2 | 3 | 4 | 5 | 46. | 1 | 2 | 3 | 4 | 5 | 57–58 |
| By my co-workers | 47. | 1 | 2 | 3 | 4 | 5 | 48. | 1 | 2 | 3 | 4 | 5 | 59–60 |
| By the head of my section | 49. | 1 | 2 | 3 | 4 | 5 | 50. | 1 | 2 | 3 | 4 | 5 | 61–62 |
| By the head of my division | 51. | 1 | 2 | 3 | 4 | 5 | 52. | 1 | 2 | 3 | 4 | 5 | 63–64 |
| By the library management | 53. | 1 | 2 | 3 | 4 | 5 | 54. | 1 | 2 | 3 | 4 | 5 | 65–66 |

# Section 3: Action on information sent
## Your communication experience

While you were filling out Section 3, the items (45-54) may have brought to mind a recent work-related experience of yours in which *communication* was particularly ineffective or effective. Please answer the questions below and give a summary of that experience (in Section D below).

**A.** To whom does this experience primarily relate (circle *one*):
  1. Subordinate
  2. Co-worker
  3. Immediate supervisor
  4. Head of section
  5. Head of division
  6. Library management

67

**B.** Please rate the quality of communication described in the experience below (circle *one*):
  1. Effective
  2. Ineffective

68

**C.** To what item (45–54) in Section 3 does this experience primarily relate? .........
(Write in the item number.)

69–70

**D.** Describe the communication experience, the circumstances leading up to it, what the person did that made him/her an effective or ineffective communicator, and the results (outcome). PLEASE PRINT.

-------------------------------------------------------------------

-------------------------------------------------------------------

-------------------------------------------------------------------

-------------------------------------------------------------------

-------------------------------------------------------------------

-------------------------------------------------------------------

-------------------------------------------------------------------

# Q

## Section 4: Sources of information

*Instructions for items 55 through 74*

You receive information from *various sources* within the library, your division and/or your section. For each source listed below, circle the number that best indicates:

(1) the amount of information you receive from that source *now* and

(2) the amount of information you *need* to receive from that source in order to do your work effectively.

| Information | THIS IS THE AMOUNT OF INFORMATION I RECEIVE NOW | | | | | | | THIS IS THE AMOUNT OF INFORMATION I NEED TO RECEIVE | | | | | | | |
|---|---|---|---|---|---|---|---|---|---|---|---|---|---|---|---|
| | | None | Little | Average | More than average | Enough | | | None | Little | Average | More than average | Enough | | |
| From my subordinates | **55.** | 1 | 2 | 3 | 4 | 5 | | **56.** | 1 | 2 | 3 | 4 | 5 | | 5–6 |
| From my co-workers | **57.** | 1 | 2 | 3 | 4 | 5 | | **58.** | 1 | 2 | 3 | 4 | 5 | | 7–8 |
| From individuals in other divisions in the library | **59.** | 1 | 2 | 3 | 4 | 5 | | **60.** | 1 | 2 | 3 | 4 | 5 | | 9–10 |
| From the head of my section | **61.** | 1 | 2 | 3 | 4 | 5 | | **62.** | 1 | 2 | 3 | 4 | 5 | | 11–12 |
| From the head of my division | **63.** | 1 | 2 | 3 | 4 | 5 | | **64.** | 1 | 2 | 3 | 4 | 5 | | 13–14 |
| From library management | **65.** | 1 | 2 | 3 | 4 | 5 | | **66.** | 1 | 2 | 3 | 4 | 5 | | 15–16 |
| From meetings between sections | **67.** | 1 | 2 | 3 | 4 | 5 | | **68.** | 1 | 2 | 3 | 4 | 5 | | 17–18 |
| From meetings between divisions | **69.** | 1 | 2 | 3 | 4 | 5 | | **70.** | 1 | 2 | 3 | 4 | 5 | | 19–20 |
| From formal management presentations | **71.** | 1 | 2 | 3 | 4 | 5 | | **72.** | 1 | 2 | 3 | 4 | 5 | | 21–22 |
| From the grapevine | **73.** | 1 | 2 | 3 | 4 | 5 | | **74.** | 1 | 2 | 3 | 4 | 5 | | 23–24 |

# Section 4: Sources of information: Your communication experience

While you were filling out Section 4, the items (55-74) may have brought to mind a recent work-related experience of yours in which *communication* was particularly ineffective or effective. Please answer the questions below and give a summary of that experience (in Section D below).

**A.** To whom does this experience primarily relate (circle *one*):
1. Subordinate
2. Co-worker
3. Immediate supervisor
4. Head of section
5. Head of division
6. Library management
7. Grapevine

25

**B.** Please rate the quality of communication described in the experience below (circle *one*):
1. Effective
2. Ineffective

26

**C.** To what item (55-74) in Section 4 does this experience primarily relate? ............. (Write in the item number.)

27–28

**D.** Describe the communication experience, the circumstances leading up to it, what the person did that made him/her an effective or ineffective communicator, and the results (outcome). PLEASE PRINT.

.................................................................................................

.................................................................................................

.................................................................................................

.................................................................................................

.................................................................................................

.................................................................................................

# Q

## SECTION 5: TIMELINESS OF INFORMATION RECEIVED FROM KEY SOURCES

*Instructions for items 75 through 80*

Indicate the extent to which information from the following sources is usually *timely*. For each source listed below, circle the number that best indicates the timeliness of information received.

| | | Never | Seldom | Sometimes | Most of the time | Always | |
|---|---|---|---|---|---|---|---|
| From my subordinates | 75. | 1 | 2 | 3 | 4 | 5 | 29 |
| From my co-workers | 76. | 1 | 2 | 3 | 4 | 5 | 30 |
| From the head of my section | 77. | 1 | 2 | 3 | 4 | 5 | 31 |
| From the head of my division | 78. | 1 | 2 | 3 | 4 | 5 | 32 |
| From library management | 79. | 1 | 2 | 3 | 4 | 5 | 33 |
| From the grapevine | 80. | 1 | 2 | 3 | 4 | 5 | 34. |

## Section 5: Timeliness of information received from key sources: Your communication experience

While you were filling out Section 5, the items (75-80) may have brought to mind a recent work-related experience of yours in which *communication* was particularly ineffective or effective. Please answer the questions below and give a summary of that experience (in Section D below).

**A.** To whom does this experience primarily relate (circle *one*):
1. Subordinate
2. Co-worker
3. Immediate supervisor
4. Head of section
5. Head of division
6. Library management

35

**B.** Please rate the quality of communication described in the experience below (circle *one*):
1. Effective
2. Ineffective

36

**C.** To what item (75-80) in Section 5 does this experience primarily relate? ..........
(Write in the item number.)

37-38

**D.** Describe the communication experience, the circumstances leading up to it, what the person did that made him/her an effective or ineffective communicator, and the results (outcome). PLEASE PRINT.

_____

_____

_____

_____

_____

_____

_____

# Q

## SECTION 6: COMMUNICATION RELATIONSHIPS

*Instructions for items 81 through 102*

A variety of communication relationships exist in the library. Personnel exchange messages regularly with one another. Considering your relationship with others in the library, circle the number that best describes the relationship in each item.

| Relationship | | Never | Seldom | Sometimes | Most of the time | Always | |
|---|---|---|---|---|---|---|---|
| I trust my co-workers | 81. | 1 | 2 | 3 | 4 | 5 | 39 |
| My co-workers get along with each other | 82. | 1 | 2 | 3 | 4 | 5 | 40 |
| My relationship with my co-workers is satisfactory | 83. | 1 | 2 | 3 | 4 | 5 | 41 |
| I trust my immediate supervisor | 84. | 1 | 2 | 3 | 4 | 5 | 42 |
| My immediate supervisor is honest with me | 85. | 1 | 2 | 3 | 4 | 5 | 43 |
| My immediate supervisor listens to me | 86. | 1 | 2 | 3 | 4 | 5 | 44 |
| I am free to disagree with my immediate supervisor | 87. | 1 | 2 | 3 | 4 | 5 | 45 |
| I may tell my immediate supervisor when things are going wrong | 88. | 1 | 2 | 3 | 4 | 5 | 46 |
| My immediate supervisor acknowledges my good work | 89. | 1 | 2 | 3 | 4 | 5 | 47 |
| My immediate supervisor is friendly with his/her other subordinates | 90. | 1 | 2 | 3 | 4 | 5 | 48 |
| My immediate supervisor understands my work needs | 91. | 1 | 2 | 3 | 4 | 5 | 49 |

| Relationship | | Never | Seldom | Sometimes | Most of the time | Always | |
|---|---|---|---|---|---|---|---|
| My relationship with my immediate supervisor is satisfactory | 92. | 1 | 2 | 3 | 4 | 5 | 50 |
| I trust the library management | 93. | 1 | 2 | 3 | 4 | 5 | 51 |
| The library management is sincere in its efforts to communicate with personnel | 94. | 1 | 2 | 3 | 4 | 5 | 52 |
| My relationship with the library management is satisfactory | 95. | 1 | 2 | 3 | 4 | 5 | 53 |
| I get along with personnel that belong to other cultural groups | 96. | 1 | 2 | 3 | 4 | 5 | 54 |
| Library management encourages differences of opinion | 97. | 1 | 2 | 3 | 4 | 5 | 55 |
| I have a say in decisions that affect my work | 98. | 1 | 2 | 3 | 4 | 5 | 56 |
| I influence operations in my section | 99. | 1 | 2 | 3 | 4 | 5 | 57 |
| I influence operations in my division | 100. | 1 | 2 | 3 | 4 | 5 | 58 |
| I influence operations in the library | 101. | 1 | 2 | 3 | 4 | 5 | 59 |
| I contribute to the accomplishment of the library's objectives | 102. | 1 | 2 | 3 | 4 | 5 | 60 |

# Q

## Section 6: Communication relationships
## Your communication experience

While you were filling out Section 6, the items (81-102) may have brought to mind a recent work-related experience of yours in which *communication* was particularly ineffective or effective. Please answer the questions below and give a summary of that experience (in Section D below).

**A.** To whom does this experience primarily relate (circle *one*):
1. Subordinate
2. Co-worker
3. Immediate supervisor
4. Head of section
5. Head of division
6. Library management

61

**B.** Please rate the quality of communication described in the experience below (circle *one*):
1. Effective
2. Ineffective

62

**C.** To what item (81-102) in Section 6 does this experience primarily relate? ..........
(Write in the item number.)

63–65

**D.** Describe the communication experience, the circumstances leading up to it, what the person did that made him/her an effective or ineffective communicator, and the results (outcome). PLEASE PRINT.

.................................................................................................

.................................................................................................

.................................................................................................

.................................................................................................

.................................................................................................

.................................................................................................

.................................................................................................

# Section 7: Communication and work satisfaction

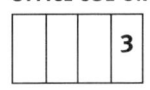

*Instructions for items 103 through 115*

Work satisfaction or lack thereof can relate to the work itself, one's co-workers, immediate supervisor, etcetera, or the library as a whole. Circle the number that best indicates the extent to which you are *satisfied* with:

| Satisfaction | | Never | Seldom | Sometimes | Most of the time | Always | |
|---|---|---|---|---|---|---|---|
| My work | **103.** | 1 | 2 | 3 | 4 | 5 | 5 |
| My salary | **104.** | 1 | 2 | 3 | 4 | 5 | 6 |
| My promotion possibilities in my division | **105.** | 1 | 2 | 3 | 4 | 5 | 7 |
| My promotion possibilities in the library | **106.** | 1 | 2 | 3 | 4 | 5 | 8 |
| Opportunities available for my contributing to the overall success of the library | **107.** | 1 | 2 | 3 | 4 | 5 | 9 |
| This library's recognition and reward for outstanding performance | **108.** | 1 | 2 | 3 | 4 | 5 | 10 |
| This library's concern for its personnel's welfare | **109.** | 1 | 2 | 3 | 4 | 5 | 11 |
| This library's communicative efforts in general | **110.** | 1 | 2 | 3 | 4 | 5 | 12 |
| Working in this library | **111.** | 1 | 2 | 3 | 4 | 5 | 13 |
| This library as compared to other libraries | **112.** | 1 | 2 | 3 | 4 | 5 | 14 |
| This library's efficiency in general | **113.** | 1 | 2 | 3 | 4 | 5 | 15 |
| The quality of this library's service in general | **114.** | 1 | 2 | 3 | 4 | 5 | 16 |
| This library's achievement of its objective | **115.** | 1 | 2 | 3 | 4 | 5 | 17 |

## SECTION 7: COMMUNICATION AND WORK SATISFACTION
## YOUR COMMUNICATION EXPERIENCE

While you were filling out Section 7, the items (103-115) may have brought to mind a recent work-related experience of yours in which *communication* was particularly ineffective or effective. Please answer the questions below and give a summary of that experience (in Section D below).

**A.**  To whom does this experience primarily relate (circle *one*):
1.  Subordinate
2.  Co-worker
3.  Immediate supervisor
4.  Head of section
5.  Head of division
6.  Library management

18

**B.**  Please rate the quality of communication described in the experience below (circle *one*):
1.  Effective
2.  Ineffective

19

**C.**  To what item (103-115) in Section 7 does this experience primarily relate? ....... (Write in the item number.)

20–22

**D.**  Describe the communication experience, the circumstances leading up to it, what the person did that made him/her an effective or ineffective communicator, and the results (outcome). PLEASE PRINT.

.................................................................................................

.................................................................................................

.................................................................................................

.................................................................................................

.................................................................................................

.................................................................................................

.................................................................................................

# Section 8: Channels of Communication

*Instructions for items 116 through 133*

The following is a list of channels through which information is transmitted to personnel. Circle the number that best indicates:

(1) the amount of information you receive through that channel *now* and

(2) the amount of information you *need* to receive through that channel.

| Channel | This is the amount of information I receive now | | | | | This is the amount of information I need to receive | | | | | Office use only |
| | None | Little | Average | More than average | Enough | None | Little | Average | More than average | Enough | |
|---|---|---|---|---|---|---|---|---|---|---|---|
| Face-to-face contact between two people | **116.** 1 | 2 | 3 | 4 | 5 | **117.** 1 | 2 | 3 | 4 | 5 | 23–24 |
| Face-to-face contact among more than two people (groups) | **118.** 1 | 2 | 3 | 4 | 5 | **119.** 1 | 2 | 3 | 4 | 5 | 25–26 |
| Telephone | **120.** 1 | 2 | 3 | 4 | 5 | **121.** 1 | 2 | 3 | 4 | 5 | 27–28 |
| Written (memo's, letters) | **122.** 1 | 2 | 3 | 4 | 5 | **123.** 1 | 2 | 3 | 4 | 5 | 29–30 |
| Bulletin boards | **124.** 1 | 2 | 3 | 4 | 5 | **125.** 1 | 2 | 3 | 4 | 5 | 31–32 |
| Internal publications (Nota Bene, Bibliovaria) | **126.** 1 | 2 | 3 | 4 | 5 | **127.** 1 | 2 | 3 | 4 | 5 | 33–34 |
| Internal (UNISA) electronic mail | **128.** 1 | 2 | 3 | 4 | 5 | **129.** 1 | 2 | 3 | 4 | 5 | 35–36 |
| UNISA publications (Bulletin, News) | **130.** 1 | 2 | 3 | 4 | 5 | **131.** 1 | 2 | 3 | 4 | 5 | 37–38 |
| External media (television, radio, newspapers) | **132.** 1 | 2 | 3 | 4 | 5 | **133.** 1 | 2 | 3 | 4 | 5 | 39–40 |

# Q

## SECTION 8: CHANNELS OF COMMUNICATION: YOUR COMMUNICATION EXPERIENCE

While you were filling out Section 8, the items (116-133) may have brought to mind a recent work-related experience of yours in which *communication* was particularly ineffective or effective. Please answer the questions below and give a summary of that experience (in Section D below).

**A.** To whom does this experience primarily relate (circle *one*):
1. Subordinate
2. Co-worker
3. Immediate supervisor
4. Head of section
5. Head of division
6. Library management

41

**B.** Please rate the quality of communication described in the experience below (circle *one*):
1. Effective
2. Ineffective

42

**C.** To what item (116-133) in Section 8 does this experience primarily relate? .......... (Write in the item number.)

43-45

**D.** Describe the communication experience, the circumstances leading up to it, what the person did that made him/her an effective or ineffective communicator, and the results (outcome). PLEASE PRINT.

---------

---------

---------

---------

---------

---------

---------

# The research report

*The most carefully designed and executed research will be worthless, unless we communicate the details, the research findings and their implications to others.*

ANONYMOUS

## Overview

This unit provides a framework of criteria and guidelines that can be used when planning, writing and evaluating research reports. This unit also functions as a synthesis of the previous units in this book and, by combining separate units into a connected whole, its presentation differs stylistically. The framework of criteria is presented in the form of questions, similar to a checklist of questions that guide our critical evaluation. These are grouped into four broad components: thematic evaluation, methodological evaluation, contextual evaluation, and an evaluation of the presentation and credibility of the report.

## Learning outcomes

By the end of this unit, you should be able to demonstrate your understanding and ability to:

- analyse and evaluate a research report or article (by applying scientific criteria and guidelines).

## 7.1 Introduction

Developing basic skills to evaluate a single report (e.g. an article published in an academic journal) and to compare several reports (e.g. when doing a literature review), alerts us to the criteria that are important when we conduct and report on our own research. Developing skills to evaluate other research reports is an integral part of our development as researchers. Such skills enable us to

assess information – for example, to determine whether it is new, important, credible and useful. The framework of criteria presented in this unit – as a form of evaluating completed research – can also be used as a guide while planning, conducting and reporting research.

**vetting:**
evaluating,
verifying,
approving

Editorial committees apply specific criteria when vetting research articles to be published in accredited journals, such as whether the research is original, if it promotes the science of communication and if it meets theoretical, methodological and technical requirements, such as using the Harvard method of referencing. The framework of criteria presented in this unit incorporates these aspects, and is grouped in four broad components:

- thematic evaluation;
- methodological evaluation;
- contextual evaluation; and
- an evaluation of presentation and credibility.

These components are not mutually exclusive. For example, the goal and objectives of the research are considered part of the thematic evaluation and the methodological evaluation. Throughout this book we support a pluralistic methodology instead of a quantitative (positivist) or qualitative (naturalist) approach, which is why the criteria and guidelines can be applied to both approaches.

**pluralistic:**
multiple
alternative
paradigms

## 7.2 Thematic evaluation

Communication research is undertaken in diverse areas of specialisation, such as development and intercultural communication, media studies, organisational communication, advertising and marketing communication, health communication, or international telecommunications research. A thematic evaluation would be aimed at determining the subject area, topic or essence of the research. When doing such an evaluation, it is particularly useful to critique the following aspects, especially when we have to evaluate many reports, as a part of a literature review:

- problem criteria;
- literature review; and
- theoretical aspects.

## 7.2.1 Problem criteria

Unit 2 contained a discussion of the different sources of research problems. Although a research report may not necessarily identify the source(s) of problems, it should provide answers to the following questions:

- Was the problem or issue clearly stated?
- Why was the problem or issue selected?
- How does the research problem or issue relate to communication as a science?
- Was the problem divided into subproblems?
- Were the goal and objective(s) of the study specified?
- Were the formulations of the research hypothesis (or research questions) clearly stated?
- How were the main problem, subproblems and/or assumptions reflected in the hypothesis (or research question)?

**assumptions:**
ideas taken for granted without proof

When considering the **assumptions** on which a problem was based, we are not only concerned with conceptual arguments, but also considering methodological aspects. For example, if a researcher assumes that focus-group interviews generally follow a predictable and standardised procedure, irrespective of the moderator, this assumption is questionable. Variables such as the moderator's age, gender, language ability and previous experience as a moderator may affect the procedure followed in the group interview. Similarly, a researcher who decides to use postal self-administered questionnaires to ensure that respondents remain anonymous, may find this an inappropriate measuring instrument, because the problem being investigated (e.g. of a personal and sensitive nature) may have required in-depth interviews.

**anonymous:**
unknown or nameless

The above arguments often give rise to the following questions:

- On what conceptual and methodological assumptions was the study based?
- Were these assumptions reasonable?
- How did the assumptions relate to the subproblems?
- How did the hypotheses (research questions) relate to the assumptions?
- If hypotheses were formulated, what kinds of predictions were proposed?
- How were the assumptions measured or tested?

The questions asked about the problem statement and assumptions represent finer details that are often not reflected in research reports, especially those published as articles or as a collection of conference proceedings. The latter is usually due to limitations that are placed on authors by editorial or conference committees. However, just as we have obligations to research participants to respect their anonymity and confidentiality, we also have obligations to the research community. When planning and writing research reports, the above two sets of questions can guide and enable us to give a complete account of the problem criteria.

Two further aspects that should be considered when conducting a thematic evaluation are to critique the literature review in the report and other theoretical aspects that are elaborated on below.

## 7.2.2 Literature review and theoretical aspects

Many communication research studies are based on established theoretical concepts or are guided by methods and techniques used in previous studies. This cumulative process gives rise to questions that apply to the **literature review** contained in a published report:

**conceptually:** of mental comprehension or understanding

- Does the report demonstrate adequate coverage, conceptually, of literature relevant to the problem area?
- How was the methodology related to existing literature that is relevant to the problem?
- Was the formulation of the research question(s) or hypothesis(-es) related to the literature?
- Were primary or secondary sources of data consulted and how relevant are these sources?

By answering these questions, we should be able to establish and indicate how a particular study differs from previous studies that have dealt with a similar problem area.

When evaluating the **theoretical aspects** that apply to problem criteria, the following questions arise:

**philosophical:** logical, reasoned or rational

- On which theoretical approach or philosophical perspective was the study based?
- Was the researcher's orientation clarified?

- Were the most important theoretical constructs (key concepts) clearly defined, and were these constructs clarified by means of operational definitions?

**bias:**
prejudice

- Does the conceptualisation of the study contain any bias on the part of the researcher?
- Did the researcher follow a deductive or inductive form of reasoning, and was this appropriate?

**motives:**
examples are
self-interest and
professional
advancement

A thematic evaluation enables us to determine the originality and relevance of the research problem, goal and objectives; the depth and extent of the study; and whether current research findings and theories are accommodated, critically appraised and synthesised. Such an evaluation simultaneously makes us aware of the researcher's motives.

## 7.3 Methodological evaluation

A methodological evaluation is mainly concerned with the scientific merit of applying a certain research design in a specific subject area. Scientific requirements were dealt with mainly in Units 1, 2 and 3, and include sampling, measurement, internal and external validity and reliability. We consider these criteria in three categories: the overall research design, the collection of data, and the analysis of data.

### 7.3.1 Research design

The following questions can be used to guide the critical evaluation of the **research design** and to assess whether these aspects are **objectively** reported:

- Was the quantitative/qualitative nature of the research design appropriate for studying the problem (e.g. the measuring instruments used, the characteristics and number of the population, the type of sample drawn)?
- What were the goal and objectives of the study?
- Was the objective of the research exploratory, descriptive and/or explanatory?

**validity:**
a quality
indicating
accurate
measures

- Were the procedures used in conducting the research reported?
- Was the research problem formulated in an unbiased manner?
- Were any threats of internal validity (of the research design)

**statistical regression:** a tendency of initial high and low measures to move to the mean in subsequent measurements

applicable – such as the effects of history, mortality, testing, instrumentation, maturation, statistical regression, differential selection, interactional effects, temporal bias, integrity of the treatment and the ability to identify and control the independent variable, which alone causes change in the dependent variable?

- How were threats to internal validity controlled?
- Were threats of external validity (of the research design) applicable, such as the extent to which the findings can be generalised to other individuals, groups, organisations, socio-economic conditions or measures not involved in a particular study?

To assess external validity, consideration must be given to the representativeness of the sample, the internal validity of the design, and replication. In the case of experimental research, the threats to external validity include pre-test treatment interaction, selection-treatment interaction, how variables were specified, reactive effects, researcher bias, and multiple-treatment interference.

**replication:** repetition

- Was the research design appropriate to accomplish the goal of the study?
- Were rival hypotheses discussed or ignored in the design?
- Did the researcher have to make any compromises or changes to the research design due to organisational, political, financial or personal constraints?

**rival hypotheses:** alternative hypotheses to examine different aspects of relationships between or among variables

As indicated in section 7.1, certain criteria can be included in more than one evaluation category. Although the formulation of the research problem is evaluated as part of the thematic evaluation (to establish whether the problem was clearly stated) the formulation of the problem is again considered part of the methodological evaluation (to ensure that it is unbiased).

## 7.3.2  Collection of data

Data collection is concerned with who, what, how, when and where data was collected. The following questions could be asked to determine the procedures used when collecting data.

### *Who (what) were the sources of data?*

- Was a target or accessible population selected? What population parameters were applicable? How did these parameters influence the selection of the data-collection method? (For example, a self-administered questionnaire cannot be used if the population consists of illiterate individuals.)

**population parameters:**
characteristics of the population

- What were the units of analysis? Why were these units selected (sampled)?

**accuracy:**
degree of correspondence between the sample and the population

- Which type of sample was drawn? Why was this type of sample drawn? How appropriate was the sampling to the nature of the population parameters? What was the size of the sample? What sampling error was tolerated? Were sampling requirements, such as accuracy and level of confidence, met?
- What type of data was collected (primary, secondary or tertiary)?

**level of confidence:**
the probability that the size of the sample drawn is adequate

## When and how was the data collected?

- What time-dimension applied to the research (cross-sectional versus longitudinal)? How relevant was the time-dimension to the goal and objective(s) of the research?
- Was the method (e.g. a survey) appropriate for investigating the problem?
- What measuring instruments (e.g. a self-administered postal questionnaire or an interview schedule) were used? Was the measuring instrument appropriate considering the goal, the nature of the problem and the population parameters? (For example, a questionnaire in English may not be understood by inhabitants of a rural settlement whose preferred choice of language is Zulu. Or, to take another example, it is not feasible to undertake a face-to-face interview when surveying 10 000 people.) Do the test items (e.g. questions and statements in a questionnaire) relate to and actually investigate the stated hypothesis(-es) or research question(s)? Do these items meet ethical and scientific requirements? (For example, do these items contain mistakes such as double-barrelled statements or leading questions?)
- Were reliability and validity tests conducted of the measuring instrument? If such tests were not undertaken, what are the ethical implications?
- How did the researcher obtain access to the units of analysis (e.g. subjects or respondents)?
- How were errors, which could have been caused by the researcher's lack of objectivity or the sources' lack of reliability, avoided?

- How was interviewer bias and judgement controlled?
- If research assistants (e.g. a team of interviewers) were used, how were they trained?

If a research study investigates **independent** and **dependent** variables, the following questions can be used to guide evaluation:
- Were the dependent and independent variables clarified?
- Was the relationship between the independent and dependent variable reasonable?
- How many independent variables were tested?
- Were independent variables in rival hypotheses specified? Were the independent variables in rival hypotheses adequately controlled?
- What type of outcome measure was used to indicate change in the dependent variable?
- Could the researcher control the independent variables?
- Was the independent variable specified clearly enough (identifiable and observable) to facilitate replication?
- Were any extraneous or intervening variables identified?

Communication research studies often involve people as subjects. We are continuously reminded that one of our most important ethical responsibilities towards the people whom we evaluate, question or observe, is that they be protected from harm. However, publications of research studies very often fail to report on how the researcher adhered to **ethical requirements** while dealing with subjects, respondents or participants. Towards this end, the following questions should be considered:
- Was the principle of *do no harm* adhered to (with no harm occurring, whether emotionally, physically, or due to embarrassment or humiliation)?
- Was informed consent obtained (did respondents have the legal competency to give consent; was participation voluntary; were subjects properly informed about what the research would entail)?
- Were respondents' privacy and anonymity respected?

## 7.3.3　Analysis of data

As researchers, we have an ethical obligation to the research community to give an accurate account of how the analysis of data was undertaken. In the absence of such information, future readers and researchers can neither evaluate the validity of the research, nor can they replicate it.

The following are useful questions to ask when evaluating the **analysis of data**, as reported:

- Was the cause of change to the dependent variable clear?
- How were respondents' responses coded? What kinds of categories were used?
- What reliability and validity tests were applied during the analysis of data? (If these tests were not undertaken, what were the implications for the reliability and validity of the findings?)
- Could the findings be generalised to other individuals or groups, settings and across different times – the scientific requirement of external validity?
- What was the suitability of the statistical analyses that were used? (In other words, were appropriate statistical techniques used?)
- Was statistical information, such as the accuracy and levels of confidence of sample sizes, reported?

In the case of **experimental** research, we need to question the following criteria (and whether they were reported):

- Was the time between pre-tests and post-test adequate? (If the time between a pre-test and post-test is brief, the results of the post-test can be affected by the pre-test, because participants may not be as interested, motivated or as anxious as they were during the pre-test. Or participants may remember their answers and responses during the pre-test.)
- Were any signs of sampling error present? (Where control groups or comparison groups are used, a method such as random assignment is one way in which to avoid sampling error. It is therefore important to exclude alternative explanations for the independent variables.)
- Can it be anticipated that a meaningful difference would take place if independent variables were applied in a (non-controlled) practical communication situation?

If a study is mainly based on a **qualitative** design, these additional questions can be asked:

- Was the rationale for analytical procedures explicitly stated?
- How were the findings and conclusions substantiated?
- Are there any signs that the researcher's gender and/or cultural and social background skewed the formulation of research questions and/or the interpretation of results?
- Was internal validity promoted by using one or more of the triangulation strategies (e.g. of theories, data, methods, sampling, or investigators collecting and interpreting the data)?
- Was external validity promoted by investigating different kinds of people (population validity), found in different settings (ecological validity) and/or at different time periods (temporal validity)?
- Can it be anticipated that the findings will differ if the study were replicated using different people, different settings and/or different time frames?

**skewed:**
slanted or distorted

When doing a methodological evaluation of the research study, on the basis of what is reported, it is clear that different questions will be asked when the study was mainly quantitative (e.g. how data was collected) versus a study that was mainly qualitative (e.g. the procedures followed when analysing the data). Applying the above questions also raises a point of criticism that applies to many research articles – that as reports, they are incomplete.

## 7.4 Contextual evaluation

Communication research takes place in a social environment and it therefore has to be critiqued in this context. The following questions are examples of information that should be reported and (when evaluating a report) should be asked of every study:

- Was the person or institution that initiated and funded the study acknowledged?
- Was the problem researchable?
- Are any political or institutional constraints evident? (For example, is the research apolitical and objective when initiated by governmental institutions or political parties?)
- Were descriptions given of the socio-economic and political conditions of the place and at the time when the study was conducted?

- Was the problem of relevance at the time it was researched and was it still relevant at the time of publication?
- Does the report represent an understanding of current thinking on the particular research problem?
- Was the study cost-effective? Did the problem merit scientific research, time, money, energy and the people involved?
- Was the research biased because of one or more of the following characteristics of the researcher: age, gender, culture, language ability and/or personal interests, such as promotion in a work situation?
- How were the findings used and by whom?
- Could any of the above variables have influenced the research design and how the findings were reported?

A contextual evaluation is concerned with the contribution that the research makes in a particular subject area, by adding to existing knowledge, by presenting new points of view on the basis of particular findings, and/or by investigating a problem that is of local, national or international value. Although the technical and presentation aspects of the research article or report are dealt with in section 7.5, a contextual evaluation includes aspects that are considered solely on the basis of what appears in such a report. Therefore, we should question whether the research (as reported) complies with the following requirements:

- **Utility:** Can the research, as reported, solve practical communication problems or contribute to information needs in a particular communication field?
- **Feasibility:** Are the findings realistic and can they be applied in practice?
- **Propriety:** Does the research, as reported, take legal and human welfare into consideration?
- **Generalisability:** Can the findings be generalised or are they idiosyncratic?

Traditionally, communication research was considered a neutral and moral striving for objectivity. Today, however, we realise that this much-vaunted 'objectivity' is value-laden and that researchers are often subject to non-scientific influences, such as moral assumptions, personal interests, intellectual climate and political considerations. Consequently, instead of striving for objectivity in isolation, we try to reconcile the requirements of the different interest groups with those of science. Objectivity entails satisfying scientific epistemological requirements, while simultaneously taking cognisance of the individuals and institutions participating in or functioning as sponsors of the research.

This dilemma is one of the main reasons why the means and procedures used during the research process and the consequences of the research findings must be specified and evaluated as part of a contextual evaluation.

Methods that are based on case studies, focus-group interviews or unstructured interviews, especially those conducted in the subjects' natural environment, minimise researchers' control over unknown variables. To eliminate errors or inaccuracies, and to ensure that reports are complete and honest, brings us to the last component: the evaluation of presentation criteria and the credibility of the report.

## 7.5 Evaluation based on presentation criteria and credibility

Scientific research should be made public and enable future researchers to cumulatively build on present findings. This requires that the report is written in an objective and explicit manner. The way in which a research report is structured and presented depends on the reason why and for whom the research was undertaken. Academic and research institutions usually have specific guidelines to follow (as indicated in Unit 2).

In other instances, a report could consist of a brief motivation for the need to undertake the research, a brief literature review and an equally brief overview of the methods used. The major part of the report could consist of the findings and recommendations. The points raised and the questions that follow, may not apply in all instances.

### Title

Does the title adequately summarise the problem and the nature of the study? Does it identify the variables, the problem, the research method, the intervention or action, and/or the anticipated outcome?

## Introduction

Does the introduction deal with the background nature of the problem, including the need for, and the importance and scope of the research study?

## Cohesiveness of the organisation of the report

When evaluating the way in which separate parts of the report were combined, the following questions can be asked:

- Is the report structured or organised in a logical manner or does it contain unconnected fragments?
- Does the literature review provide a link between the problem being investigated and the research design used?
- Is the literature review conceptually integrated using both inductive and deductive approaches?
- Are previously reported studies documented and critiqued?
- Are any gaps in the existing literature identified?

**inductive:** reasoning that begins with a particular instance and infers general conclusions

**deductive:** reasoning that begins with a general assumption and derives a conclusion about particular instances within the initial generalisation

## Register

The writing style and vocabulary used in academic discourse is formal, objective and impersonal. Three types of narratives that can be distinguished when reporting (especially qualitative) research were discussed in Unit 4.

Writing a research report using formal register means that the author has to **avoid** using:

- passive voice (such as *30% of the questionnaires were returned by respondents*); instead of active voice (such as *30% of the respondents returned the questionnaires*);
- abbreviations in the text (such as ANC, etc. viz.);
- shortened words (such as *ads* instead of *advertisements*);
- contractions (such as *can't,* instead of *cannot;* or *don't* instead of *do not);*
- exclamation marks (!) – because they introduce an emotive and subjective element to the statements being made;
- slang or informal words (such as *kids,* instead of *children*);
- personal types of address (such as *I, me, my, we, us*).

When evaluating the register of a report, we would question whether the information is presented in an objective, formal and impersonal style. In studies that include a qualitative approach, the validity can be promoted by using low inference descriptors.

**low inference descriptors:** direct quotations of subjects' exact words

## *Technical requirements*

Does the report comply with the following technical requirements?
- If the report contains a table of contents, does the table correspond with the subheadings used in the text?
- Are all sources consulted and mentioned in the text cited in the reference list?
- Are these citations accurate, complete and presented in a uniform style?
- Are there any signs of plagiarism?
- Are the styles (typography and layout) used for tables, charts, graphs and section headings consistent?
- Are the tables and figures clear and understandable?
- Do the labels used for each table, graph, chart or figure accurately describe the information presented?
- Do accompanying explanations or interpretations correspond with the information contained in tabulated summaries?

**plagiarism:** using the thoughts and writings of another, pretending that they are our own

## *Graphs and tables*

Different types of graphs can be used in research reports.

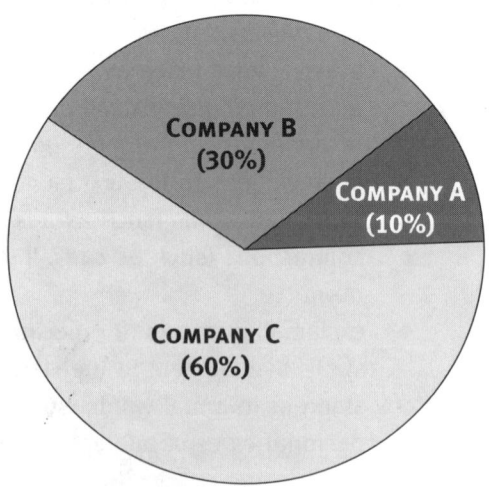

**FIGURE 7.1:** Example of a circle graph (or pie chart) depicting computer sales

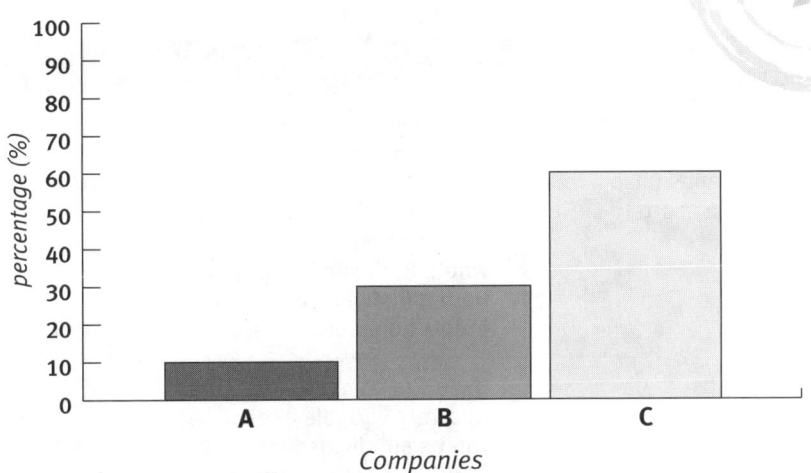

**FIGURE 7.2:** Example of a bar graph depicting computer sales

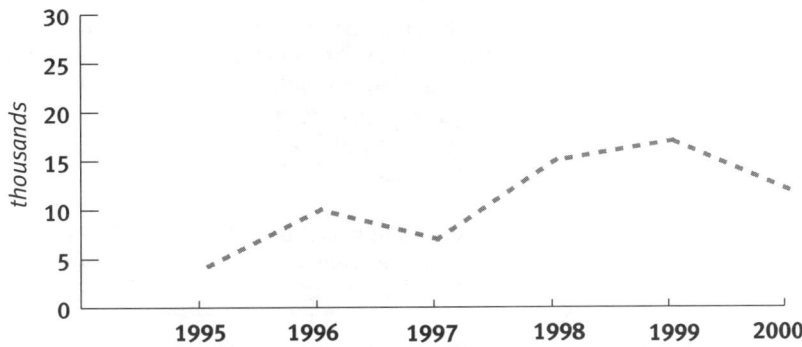

**FIGURE 7.3:** Example of a line graph depicting computer sales

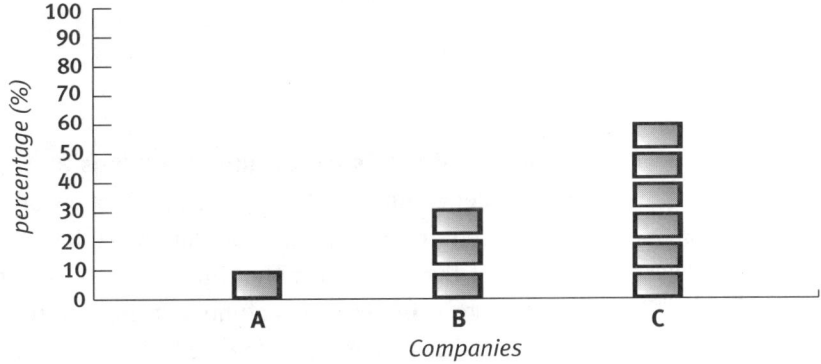

**FIGURE 7.4:** Example of a pictogram depicting computer sales

Figure 2.1 in Unit 2 contains an example of a flow chart depicting the steps in the research process.

**TABLE 7.1:** Advantages and limitations of different graphs

| Type of graph | Advantages | Limitations |
|---|---|---|
| Circle graphs (also called pie charts) | Useful to visualise cyclical processes (for example, time). The circle represents the whole (for example, population) and divisions show the proportional divisions. | Not visually precise or exact. |
| Bar graphs | Useful to compare quantities (discrete variables); each bar can be subdivided into sub-parts (e.g. for percentages). | Difficult to use when variables in the data are numerous and complex. Not appropriate to use when a continuous relationship between data is important. |
| Line graphs | Useful to summarise a relationship between the independent variable (horizontal axis) and the dependent variable (vertical axis). | Accuracy of information depends on the scales used on the two axes and the horizontal-vertical grid. |
| Pictograms | Figures and icons, used to summarise statistical data are visually attractive. | The least exact of all the types of graphs. |
| Flow charts (also called tree charts) | With connecting lines, can depict sequences (in time) or progressions (arranged hierarchically). | Not suitable to summarise or compare data. |

**stub:**
left-hand column of a table

The design of **tables** (consisting of columns and rows) can be adapted depending on the type of information or data that is being summarised and the number of categories. In Table 7.1, the stub consists of five categories The three column headings describe the information in the vertical columns. If the nature of the data includes frequencies or percentages, the units of measurement should be included in the column headings. Tables are especially useful to summarise large amounts of data in minimum space.

## Objectivity and accuracy

The requirement that research reports have to be written in an objective and accurate manner has been repeatedly stated in this unit. Towards this end, the following questions could be asked:

- Is the information presented in an objective style or are there signs of bias and one-sidedness?
- Does the report comply with accuracy as a scientific requirement? (Is the report an accurate account and/or summary of the research design, the methodological procedures followed and the interpretation of the findings?)
- Are any signs of misrepresentation, concealment, distortion or fabrication evident in the way in which the findings are reported?
- Are primary sources of data used? (If secondary or tertiary sources of data were used, how was the authenticity and credibility of existing data verified?)

## Statistics

A report of a research study in which statistical calculations have been used, should also include a description of the statistical formulas.

The following are questions that guide our evaluation:

- Are the inferences drawn about causality based on statistically significant results?
- Are the statistical tests used appropriate to the level(s) of measurement?

## Limitations

We undertake communication research for various reasons. One such reason is to contribute to information that can be used to solve real-world problems. However, irrespective of the objective of a particular research study, problems beyond a researcher's control can sometimes cause the study to be limited in terms of time-dimension, the sample size, etcetera. Such limitations should be reported if a report is to be treated as objective, accurate and truthful.

The following questions can be used as guidelines when considering limitations:

- Are any limitations in the research design recorded?

- Are any shortcomings of the execution of the study acknowledged?
- How are unexpected changes to the research design (e.g. the method used for data collection) reported?
- Does the operationalisation of theoretical constructs represent valid tests of the phenomena being studied (thus evaluating construct or conceptual validity)?

## The presentation of findings

The way in which the findings of a study are presented is important for two reasons. First, the findings determine whether the study contributes to existing knowledge, or can be applied in new policies, and whether it has relevance in practice, and/or in the further development of research methods. Secondly, the presentation of the findings contributes to the cohesiveness of the organisation of the report. Therefore, when evaluating the presentation of reported findings based on our own research, the following questions should be considered:
- Are the findings related to previous findings reported in the literature survey?
- To what extent do the findings support the hypothesis(-es) (or answer the research questions)?
- Are the implications and significance of findings substantiated by the results obtained in the study?
- Does the study accomplish its goal and objectives?
- Do the findings contain answers to the research questions and/or hypotheses?
- What are the social and practical implications of the findings?
- What are the implications of the findings for the norms and standards of a professional communicator (e.g. a public relations practitioner)?

## The presentation of conclusions

Conclusions contain deductions and inferences, and in some reports, suggestions for future research. The way in which conclusions are presented should logically be linked to other steps in the research process. Therefore, the following questions should be considered when evaluating conclusions:
- Are the conclusions consistent with and supported by the data?
- Can conclusions be generalised beyond the data collected?

- Are conclusions, proposals and implications of the study reasonable?
- Are the conclusions valid? Are they data based or are they based on reasoning?
- Can the conclusions be used to change future methods, theoretical approaches or communication practice?
- Do the conclusions contain suggestions or recommendations for future research?
- Do the conclusions contain a logical synthesis of the main points?
- Do the conclusions relate to the original research problem(s), hypothesis(-es) and/or research question(s)?

Based on the points raised in above subsections, it should become clear that there are no fixed guidelines for evaluating the presentation and credibility of a research report. Nevertheless, just as the presentation of research findings and conclusions have to be justified, when writing a research report, when doing a critique, our evaluation has to be justified by the evidence found in the report.

## EXECUTIVE SUMMARY:
### THE RESEARCH REPORT – EVALUATION CRITERIA

1 Thematic evaluation:
- problem criteria;
- assumptions;
- literature review; and
- theoretical aspects.

2 Methodological evaluation:
- research design;
- collection of data; and
- analysis of data.

3 Contextual evaluation:
- utility;
- feasibility;
- propriety; and
- generalisability.

4 Evaluation based on presentation criteria and credibility:
- title;
- introduction;
- cohesiveness of the organisation of the report;
- register;
- technical requirements;
- graphs and tables;
- objectiveness and accuracy;
- statistics;
- limitations;
- the presentation of findings; and
- the presentation of conclusions.

# 7.6 Summary

This unit was not intended to be comprehensive, but instead served as an overview of the guidelines and framework of scientific criteria that can be used when we critique published research and compile our own research reports. This unit should also sensitise us as communication scholars, or even as ordinary citizens, not to accept everything that is published as accurate, factual or the truth.

Finally, as an evaluator (and author) of a research report, the usefulness of a research study can be determined by answering these questions:

- What kind of communication profession or situation is being researched?
- Working with what kind of products, services or clients?
- In which practical situations?
- Involving what kind of problems?
- Based on what theoretical approach?
- Using which methods to collect and analyse the data?
- Produced what kind of results?
- That can be applied in what future practices?

## Self-evaluation and portfolio task

**7.1** Select a research article that has been published in an accredited journal, such as *Communicare* or *Communicatio*. Analyse and evaluate the article according to the criteria discussed in this unit. Write your evaluation by using the headings in the executive summary.

Assume that you are a member of the editorial committee of the journal. If you find that the article is publishable, your evaluation should support this decision. If, however, you decide that the article should be revised, your evaluation should contain specific recommendations about what the author should add or change. If you are able to do this evaluation with a fellow-learner or in a group, do your peers agree with your evaluation?

You are encouraged to evaluate your achievement of the learning outcomes using the following guide.

## ASSESSMENT OF LEARNING OUTCOMES

Ratings for evaluation of performance:

5   very high (extremely good)

4   high (good)

3   medium (average)

2   low (poor)

1   very low (extremely poor)

0   evidence is absent

| Outcomes (knowledge, competence and orientations) *You should be able to demonstrate your understanding and ability to:* | Evidence of performance | Examples of criteria used to evaluate evidence of performance | Evaluation of performance | | | | | |
|---|---|---|---|---|---|---|---|---|
| | | | Ratings | | | | | |
| | | | 5 | 4 | 3 | 2 | 1 | 0 |
| Analyse and evaluate a research report or article | by applying scientific criteria and guidelines. | Thematic evaluation: problem criteria; assumptions; literature review; theoretical aspects. | | | | | | |
| | | Methodological evaluation: research design; collection of data; analysis of data. | | | | | | |
| | | Contextual evaluation: utility; feasibility; propriety; generalisability. | | | | | | |
| | | Evaluation of presentation criteria and credibility: title; introduction; cohesiveness of the organisation of the report; register; technical requirements; graphs and tables; objectiveness and accuracy; statistics; limitations; presentation of findings; and of conclusions. | | | | | | |

## SUGGESTED READING

Arnaudet, ML and Barrett, ME. 1984. *Approaches to academic reading & writing*. Englewood Cliffs, NJ: Prentice Hall.

Babbie, ER. 1995. *The practice of social research*. (7th edition). Belmont, California: Wadsworth.

Borcherds, MM, English, PJ, Fielding, ML, Honikman, KS, Jacobs, GA, Kurgan, AZ, Pickering-Dunn, EK, Steyn, ME and Van der Merwe, NM. 1991. *Handbook. A guide to effective spoken and written communication*. Cape Town: Arrow.

Du Toit, P, Heese, M and Orr, M. 1995. *Practical guide to reading, thinking and writing skills*. Halfway House: Southern.

Hammersley, M. 1998. *Reading ethnographic research: a critical guide*. London: Longman.

Henson, KT. 1995. *The art of writing for publication*. Needham Heights, Massachusetts: Allyn & Bacon.

Hult, CA. 1996. *Researching and writing in the social sciences*. Needham Heights, Massachusetts: Allyn & Bacon.

Leedy, PD. 1997. *Practical research: planning and design*. (6th edition). Upper Saddle River, NJ: Merrill, an imprint of Prentice Hall.

Morris, D. 1994. *Guidelines for writing a qualitative research report*. Chicago: American Marketing Association.

Smit, GJ. 1995. *Research: guidelines for planning and documentation*. Halfway House: Southern.

Strunk, W and White, EB. 1995. *The elements of style*. Neeham Heights, Massachusetts: Allyn & Bacon.

Westmeyer, PM. 1994. *A guide for use in planning, conducting, and reporting research projects*. (2nd edition). Springfield, Illinois: Charles C Thomas.

# Addendum A:
## Useful electronic addresses

The .za domain space has been assigned to South Africa, and (at the time of writing) the following secondary domain spaces have been assigned to individuals, institutions and organisations:

| | |
|---|---|
| .ac.za | research and academic institutions |
| .co.za | commercial establishments |
| .edu.za | distance educational institutions |
| .gov.za | government departments |
| .law.za | legal professions |
| .mil.za | military establishments |
| .net.za | ports on the networks |
| .ngo.za | non-governmental organisations (NGOs) |
| .nom.za | individuals |
| .org.za | non-commercial establishments |
| .school.za | schools |
| .tm.za | owners of legally registered trademarks |
| .web.za | Web servers |

Following is an alphabetical list of electronic addresses (fax, e-mail or the Internet) that apply mainly to South Africa, and which are useful for scholars, researchers and communication practitioners in retrieving up-to-date information.

Since April 2001, South Africans can also obtain direct access to institutions that have registered their names, provided for by *Keywords of RealNames*, such as Honda, Virgin, Shell, Hewlett Packard, Andersen Consulting, Nintendo and Ernst & Young. In other words, users can obtain access to the Internet addresses of institutions once registered, by typing in the name of the institution, without the http://www. prefix and without the domain suffix (such as .co.za).

# A

AC NIELSEN – MRA (Market Research Africa Ltd)
E-mail: mra@mra.acnielsen.co.za
All Academic (International) – *see* Search Engines
All Media and Products Survey (AMPS), http://www.saarf.co.za
Ananzi (South Africa) – *see* Search Engines
ANC Internet newspaper, http://www.anc.co.za
Argus Clearinghouse – *see* Search Engines
Audit Bureau of Circulation of Southern Africa, Johannesburg
E-mail: abc@printmedia.org.za

# B

Broadcasting Research Unit, South African Broadcasting Corporation,
Auckland Park (*See also* South African Broadcasting Corporation)
E-mail: vvuurend@sabc.co.za
Bureau for Market Research (BMR), University of South Africa
http://www.unisa.ac.za/dept/bmr
Bureau for Statistical and Survey Methodology (STATOMET),
University of Pretoria, E-mail: statomet@hakuna.up.ac.za
Business Intelligence Live by Satellite – SIYANDA, http://www.siyanda.co.za

# C

Centre for African Research and Transformation (CART),
University of Natal, E-mail: cart@innov.und.ac.za
Centre for Health Systems Research and Development; Sentrum vir
Gesondheidsisteemnavorsing en Ontwikkeling (CHSR&D; SGSN&O),
University of the Free State, E-mail: svr@rs.uovs.ac.za
Centre for Higher Education Transformation (CHET), Pretoria
http://chet.hsrc.ac.za
Centre for Interdisciplinary Studies; Sentrum vir Interdissiplinêre Studie
(CENIS; SENIS), University of Stellenbosch, E-mail: jm6@akad.sun.ac.za
Centre for the Study of Violence and Reconciliation, University of
Witwatersrand, http://www.wits.ac.za
**Citing Internet Resources:**
Citing Internet and Electronic Resources
http://www.mlb.ilstu.edu/ressubj/subject/intrnt/citeweb.htm
Citing URLs in a Bibliography
http://www.nrlssc.navy.mil/meta/bibliography.html
Columbia Guide to Online Style
http://www.columbia.edu/cu/cup/cgos/idx_basic.html
Guide for Citing Electronic Information
http://www.wpunj.edu/wpcpages/library/citing.htm

Commission for Conciliation, Mediation and Arbitration (CCMA), Marshalltown, http://www.ccma.org.za

Commission on Gender Equality (CGE), Braamfontein, http://www.cge.org.za

Community Press Association (CPA), Johannesburg
E-mail: cpa@printmedia.org.za

Co-operative for Research and Education (CORE), Fordsburg
E-mail: corejhb@wn.apc.org

Council for Black Education and Research (COBERT), Langa
Fax number: (021) 695-4197

Curriculum 2005, government policy and discussion documents
http://www.polity.org.za/govdocs/discuss/curric1.html

**D** Delta Environmental Centre
http://www.deltaenviro.org.za/coursesprogrammes/index.html

Development Planning and Research (DPR), Johannesburg
E-mail: dpr@iafrica.com

Development Policy Research Unit; Industrial Strategy Project; Science and Technology Policy Research Centre (DPRU; ISP; STPRC), University of Cape Town, http://www.uct.ac.za/depts/dpru

Dogpile (Multisearch International) – *see* Search Engines

**E** Eastern Seaboard Association of Tertiary Institutions (esATI), Durban
http://www.esati.org.za

E-Data, http://www.edata.co.za

Education and training in South Africa http://www.cohsssa.co.za/SAQA.html

Energy and Development Research Centre (EDRC), University of Cape Town, http://www.edr.uct.ac.za, E-mail: edrc@engfac.uct.ac.za

Energy Research Institute (ERI), University of Cape Town
http://www.eri.uct.ac.za/eri.html

**F** Film and Publication Board (FPB), Cape Town, http://www.fpb.gov.za

FutureFact (a South African marketing and business-related research project),
http://www.unileverinstitute.co.za

**G** General resources for research – *see* Search Engines

Govan Mbeki Research Resource Centre (University of Fort Hare, Alice)
E-mail: sean.m@ufhcc.ufh.ac.za

Government Departments – *see* SOUTH AFRICA

GuideStar Communications (Human resources surveys – online and
        dual media), http://www.guidestarco.com
Guides to specialised Search Engines – *see* Search Engines

**H**     Human Resources Surveys – Online and Dual-media http://www.guidestarco.com
Human Sciences Research Council (HSRC), Pretoria http://www.hsrc.ac.za

**I**     Independent Communications Authority of South Africa (ICA),
        previously: Independent Broadcasting Authority and South African
        Telecommunications Regulatory Authority, Sandton, http://www.iba.org.za
Industrial Health Research Group (IHRG), University of Cape Town
        E-mail: ihjud@protem.uct.ac.za
I-Net Bridge, http://www.inet.co.za
Institute for Black Research (IBR), Durban, E-mail: harcharaur@mtb.und.ac.za
Institute for Communication Research (ICR); Instituut vir Kommunikasienavorsing
        (IKN), Potchefstroom University for CHE
        E-mail: komasdeb@puknet.puk.ac.za
Institute for Development Planning and Research (IDPR);
        Instituut vir Ontwikkelingsbeplanning en Navorsing (IOBN),
        University of Port Elizabeth, E-mail: piaclc@upe.ac.za
Institute for Futures Research (IFR); Instituut vir Toekomsnavorsing
        (ITN), University of Stellenbosch), E-mail: futures@maties.sun.ac.za
Institute of Social and Economic Research (ISER), Rhodes University
        http://www.ru.ac.za, E-mail: issec@warthog.ru.ac.za
International Development Research Centre (IDRC), Johannesburg
        http://www.idrc.org.za
International Journalism Organisations
        http://poynter.org/research/jsites/je_jsites1.htm
Internet Resources – *see* Citing Internet Resources
ITWeb, http://www.itweb.co.za

**J**     Johannesburg Stock Exchange (JSE), http://www.jse.co.za

**L**     Labour Research Service (LRS), Woodstock, Cape Town, E-mail: lrs@iafrica.com
Law, Race and Gender Research Unit (LRG), University of Cape Town
        http://www.uct.ac.za
Lifelong learning for the 21st century, curriculum 2005, government policy and
        discussion documents, http://www.polity.org.za/govdocs/misc/curr2005.html

**M**  Magazine Publishers' Association (MPA), Johannesburg
E-mail: mpa@printmedia.org.za
MagPortal (magazine articles international) – *see* Search Engines
**Mailing Lists/Newsgroups:**
Liszt's Mailing list Directory, http://www.liszt.com
Liszt's Usenet Newsgroups Directory, http://www.liszt.com/news
Mamma (Multisearch International) – *see* Search Engines
Market Research Africa Ltd (MRA) – *see* AC NIELSEN
Max (South Africa) – *see* Search Engines
Mbendi: Information for Africa (South Africa) – *see* Search Engines
Medical Research Council (MRC), Tygerberg, http://www.mrc.ac.za
Mobile Telephone Network (MTN), E-mail: webmaster@mtn.co.za

**N**  National Archives, Pretoria, E-mail: arg02@dacst4.pwv.gov.za
National Arts Council of South Africa, Newtown, E-mail: info@nac.org.za
National Association of Distance Education Organisations in South Africa
(NADEOSA) – *see also* South African Institute for Distance Education,
http://www.saide.org.za/nadeosa
National Research Foundation (NRF), Pretoria, http://www.nrf.ac.za
National Urbanisation and Health Research Programme (UHP), Tygerberg,
http://www.mrc.ac.za/urbanheal/urban.htm
News groups – *see* Mailing Lists
Newspaper Association of South Africa, E-mail: na@printmedia.org.za
NOKIA, http://www.rf.nokia.co.za
Northern Light – *see* Search Engines

**O**  Online newspapers, http://www.onlinenewspapers.com
OPTION International (Mobile Data Communications), http://www.option.co.za

**P**  Pan South African Language Board, Arcadia, http://www.pansalb.org.za
Press Ombudsman, E-mail: ombudsman@ombudsman.org.za
Print Media in Education, E-mail: pmie@printmedia.org.za
Print Media SA, E-mail: printmediasa@printmedia.org.za
Profile Media, http://www.profile.co.za

**R**  Research-It (International) – *see* Search Engines

**S**

SABTIN (South Africa) – *see* Search Engines

SAIDE Resource Centre – *see* South African Institute for Distance Education

**Search Engines/Subject Directories**
**(general resources for research):**

All Academic (International), http://www.zebra.co.za

Ananzi (South African), http://www.ananzi.co.za

Argus Clearinghouse, http://www.clearinghouse.net/index.html

Dogpile (Multisearch International), http://www.dogpile.com

Guides to specialised Search Engines, http://www.searchability.com

MagPortal (magazine articles international), http://MagPortal.com

Mamma (Multisearch International), http://www.mamma.com

Max (South African), http://www.max.co.za

Mbendi: Information for Africa (South African), http://www.mbendi.co.za

Northern Light, http://www.northernlight.com

Research-It (International), http://www.itools.com/research-it/research-it.html

SABTIN (South African), http://www.sabtin.co.za

Yahoo (International), http://www.yahoo.com

Zebra (South African), http://www.zebra.co.za

Shoma Education Foundation, http://www.shoma.org.za

Siemens Telecommunications, http://www.siemens.co.za

SISA Information Centre, E-mail: ltempleh@csir.co.za

SIYANDA – *see* Business Intelligence Live by Satellite

Social Sciences and the Humanities Research Networking Database
http://www.nrf.ac.za/nexus

Social Sciences Research Development Forum (SOSRDEF)
http://sosrdef.org.za/index.html

Social Sciences WWW Virtual Library,
http://www.clas.ufl.edu/users/gthursby/socsci/index.htm

**South Africa – Government Departments:**

Arts, Culture, Science and Technology, http://www.dacst.gov.za

Communications, http://docweb.pwv.gov.za

Education, http://education.pwv.gov.za

Environmental Affairs and Tourism, http://www.environment.gov.za

Government Communication and Information System (GCIS),
http://www.gcis.gov.za

Health, http://www.health.gov.za

Labour, http://www.labour.gov.za

Social development, http://www.welfare.gov.za

South African Police Service, http://www.saps.gov.za

Statistics South Africa, http://www.statssa.gov.za
E-mail: info@statssa.pwv.gov.za

South African Advertising Research Foundation (SAARF), http://www/saarf.co.za

South African Broadcasting Corporation (SABC), http://www/sabc.co.za

South African Certification Agency (SACA), http://www.saca.net.za

Southern African Global Distance Education Network
http://www.saide.org.za/worldbank/Default.htm

South African Government Information, http://www.polity.org.za

South African Human Rights Commission, Houghton, http://www.sahrc.or.za

South African Institute for Distance Education (SAIDE), http://www.saide.org.za

South African Law Commission, Pretoria http://www.law.wits.ac.za/salc/salc.htm

South African Local Government Association, Pretoria
http://www.local.gov.za/SALGA/salindex.html

South African National Editors' Forum, E-mail: saeditor@iafrica.com

South African Post Office Ltd, Pretoria, http://www.sapo.co.za

South African Tourism, Pretoria, http://www.satour.co.za

Southern African Marketing Research Association (SAMRA),
http://www.samra.co.za

Specialist Press Association, E-mail: spa@printmedia.org.za

State Information Technology Agency (Pty) Ltd., Monument Park
http://www.sita.co.za

STATOMET – *see* Bureau for Statistical and Survey Methodology

**T** Telecom Information Resources on the Internet
http://china.si.umich.edu/telecom/telecom-info.html

Telematics for African Development (TAD) Consortium, Johannesburg
Fax (011) 403-2814

Telkom SA Ltd, Pretoria, http://www.telkom.co.za

**U** UHP – *see* National Urbanisation and Health Research Programme

United Nations Development Programme, E-mail: undpsa@lia.co.za

**V** Vodacom, http://www.vodacom.co.za

**W** WWF South Africa and The Green Trust, Fax (021) 887-7517

**Y** Yahoo (International) – *see* Search Engines

**Z** Zebra (South Africa) – *see* Search Engines

# Bibliography

Anderson, JA. 1987. *Communication research: issues and methods.* New York: McGraw-Hill.

Arnaudet, ML and Barrett, ME. 1984. *Approaches to academic reading & writing.* Englewood Cliffs, New Jersey: Prentice Hall.

Babbie, E. 1983. *The practice of social research.* (3rd edition). Belmont, California: Wadsworth.

Babbie, E. 1990. *Survey research methods.* (2nd edition.) Belmont, California: Wadsworth.

Babbie, ER. 1995. *The practice of social research.* (7th edition). Belmont, California: Wadsworth.

Baily, A. 1996. *A guide to field research.* Thousand Oaks, California: Pine Forge.

Bales, RF and Cohen, SP. 1979. *SYMLOG: A system for the multilevel observation of groups.* New York: Free.

*Beeld* 1999a. Beroepskeuse, *Bylae tot Beeld.* 4 Augustus:7.

*Beeld* 1999b. Vigsprogram "n klaaglike mislukking'; HI-virus 'lei tot die volgende verlore geslag'. 5 November:9.

Belch, GE and Belch, MA. 1998. *Advertising and promotion: an integrated marketing communications perspective.* (4th edition). Boston: Irwin/McGraw-Hill.

Bennett, T. 1985. Theories of the media, theories of society, in *Culture, society and the media,* edited by M Gurevitch, T Bennett, J Curran and J Woollacott. New York: Methuen.

Berger, AA. 1991. *Media analysis techniques.* (Revised edition). Newbury Park, California: Sage.

Blalock, H. 1979. *Social statistics.* New York: McGraw-Hill.

Bless, C and Higson-Smith, C. 1995. *Fundamentals of social research methods: an African perspective.* (2nd edition). Kenwyn: Juta.

Bless, C and Kathuria, R. 1993. *Fundamentals of social statistics: an African perspective.* Wetton: Juta.

Bloom, M. 1986. *The experience of research.* New York: Macmillan.

Blumer, H. 1939. The mass, the public and public opinion, in *New outlines of the principles of sociology,* edited by AM Lee. New York: Barnes & Noble.

Borcherds, MM, English, PJ, Fielding, ML, Honikman, KS, Jacobs, GA, Kurgan, AZ, Pickering-Dunn, EK, Steyn, ME and Van der Merwe, NM. 1991. *Handbook. A guide to effective spoken and written communication.* Cape Town: Arrow.

Brink, PJ. 1976 (reissued 1990). *Transcultural nursing. A book of readings.* Prospect Heights, Ill: Waveland.

Bulmer, M (ed). 1982. *Social research ethics.* London: Macmillan.

Burger, M. 1998. Information campaigns and local authorities: a DSC case study. *Communicare* 17(1):143–159.

Burger, M. 1999. Participatory small-group communication as a medium for information campaigns in KwaZulu-Natal. *Communicatio* 25 (1&2):88–94.

Burke, EM. 1975. Citizen participation strategies, in *Readings in community organization practice*. (2nd edition), edited by RM Kramer and H Specht. Englewood Cliffs, New Jersey: Prentice Hall.

Buys R (ed). 2000. *Cyberlaw. The law of the Internet in South Africa*. Pretoria: Van Schaik.

Carmines, EG and Zeller, RA. 1979. *Reliability and validity assessment*. Beverly Hills, California: Sage.

Cohen, J. 1960. A coefficient of agreement for nominal scales. *Educational and Psychological Measurements*. 20:37–46.

Collins, K. 1999. *Participatory research: a primer*. Cape Town: Prentice Hall.

Cook, TD and Campbell, DT. 1979. *Quasi-experimentation*. Boston: Houghton Mifflin.

Cozby, PC. 1989. *Methods in behavioral research*. (4th edition). Mountain View, California: Mayfield.

Cronbach, LJ. 1970. *Essentials of psychological testing*. (3rd edition). New York: Harper & Row.

Dadzie, S. 1993. *Working with black adult learners. A practical guide*. Leicester: National Institute of Adult Continuing Education.

Davies, CA 1999. *Reflexive ethnography: a guide to researching selves and others*. London: Routledge.

Deacon, D, Pickering, M, Golding, P and Murdock, G. 1999. *Researching communications. A practical guide to methods in media and cultural analysis*. London: Arnold.

DeFleur, ML and Ball-Rokeach, SJ. 1989. *Theories of mass communication*. (5th edition). New York: Longman.

Denzin, NK and Lincoln, YS (eds). 1994. *Handbook of qualitative research*. Thousand Oaks: Sage.

DePoy, E and Gitlin, LN. 1998. *Introduction to research: understanding and applying multiple strategies*. (2nd edition). St Louis, Mo: Mosby.

DeVito, JA. 1992. *The interpersonal communication book*. (6th edition). New York, NY: HarperCollins.

De Vos, AS (ed). 1998. *Research at grass roots. A primer for the caring professions*. Pretoria: Van Schaik.

Douglas, JD. 1976. *Investigative social research: Individual and team field research*. Beverly Hills, California: Sage.

Drew, CJ, Hardman, ML and Hart, AW. 1996. *Designing and conducting research; inquiry in education and social science*. (2nd edition). Needham Heights, Massachusetts: Allyn & Bacon.

Du Plooy, GM. 1991. *500 Communication concepts*. English/Afrikaans. Wetton: Juta.

Du Plooy, GM (ed). 1995. *Introduction to communication: course book 2 – communication research*. Kenwyn: Juta.

Du Plooy, GM (ed). 1996. *Introduction to communication – course book 2: communication research.* (Reprinted edition). Kenwyn: Juta.

Du Plooy, GM. 2000. Communication science in the context of higher/distance education: changes and challenges (inaugural lecture). Pretoria: GM du Plooy & University of South Africa.

Du Toit, P, Heese, M and Orr, M. 1995. *Practical guide to reading, thinking and writing skills.* Halfway House: Southern.

Ecolar (Employer Confederation of Labour Relations). 1999. Draft employment policy (seminar).

Elliot, P. 1974. Uses and gratifications: a critique and a sociological alternative, in *The uses of mass communication,* edited by E Katz, JG Blumer and M Gurevitch. Beverly Hills, Sage.

Emmert, P and Brooks, WD (eds). 1970. *Methods of research in communication.* Boston: Houghton Mifflin.

Ferguson, GA. 1971. *Statistical analysis in psychology and education.* (3rd edition). London: McGraw-Hill.

Fisher, BA and Drexel, GL. 1983. A cyclical model of developing relationships. A study of relational control interaction. *Communication Monographs* 44:231–240.

Fleiss, JL. 1981. *Statistical methods for rates and proportions.* New York: Wiley.

Fowler, F. 1984. *Survey research methods.* Beverly Hills, California: Sage.

Fraenkel, JR and Wallen, NE. 1993. *How to design and evaluate research in education.* (2nd edition). New York: McGraw-Hill.

Frey, JH. 1983. *Survey research by telephone.* Beverly Hills, California: Sage.

Frey, LR, Botan, CH, Friedman, PG and Kreps, GL 1992. *Interpreting communication research. A case study approach.* Englewood Cliffs, New Jersey: Prentice Hall.

Fuhr, I. 1993. Addressing diversity in the workplace, in *Reversing discrimination: affirmative action in the workplace,* edited by D Innes, M Kentridge and H Perold, Cape Town: Oxford University Press.

Gatherer, J and Erickson, J. 1993. Affirmative action in Zimbabwe: a private sector case-study, in *Reversing discrimination: affirmative action in the workplace,* edited by D Innes, M Kentridge and H Perold, Cape Town: Oxford University Press.

Gerbner, G, Gross, P and Melody, P. 1973. *Communications technology and social policy: understanding the new 'cultural revolution'.* New York: Wiley.

Gitlin, T. 1978. Media sociology: the dominant paradigm. *Theory and Society* 6:205–253.

Glynn, CJ, Herbst, S, O'Keefe, GJ and Shapiro, RY. 1999. *Public opinion.* Boulder, CO: Westview.

Goduka, IN. 1999. Indigenous epistemologies – ways of knowing: affirming a legacy. *South African Journal of Higher Education* 13(3):26–35.

Goldhaber, GM. 1990. *Organizational communication.* (5th edition). Dubuque, Iowa: Wm C Brown.

Goldhaber, GM and Rogers, DP. 1979. *Auditing organizational communication systems; the ICA communication audit.* Dubuque, Iowa: Kendall/Hunt.

Goldhaber, GM, Yates, MP, Porter, DT and Lesniak, R. 1978. Organizational communication. *HCR* 5:76–96.

Government Communication and Information System (GCIS). 1999. *South Africa Yearbook 1999.* Pretoria: Government Printer.

Government Communication and Information System (GCIS). 2000/01. *South Africa Yearbook 2000/01.* Pretoria: Government Printer.

Grinnell, RM. 1993. *Social work research and evaluation.* (4th edition). Itasca, Illinois: FE Peacock.

Grovers, RM and Kahn, RL. 1979. *Survey by telephone: A national comparison with personal interviews.* New York: Academic.

GuideStar Communications. 1999. Human resources surveys – online and dual media. Available: http://www.guidestarco.com (accessed 2001/01/18)

Hale, JL, Boster, FJ and Mongeau, PA. 1991. The validity of choice dilemma response scales. *Communication Reports* 4:30–34.

Hammersley, M. 1998. *Reading ethnographic research: a critical guide.* London: Longman.

Hanekom, MJ. 1990. Television audience ratings and programme appreciation in South Africa. Unpublished MA dissertation. University of South Africa: Pretoria.

Hardt, H. 1991. *Critical communication studies.* London & New York: Routledge.

Hawes, L. 1972. Development and application of an interview coding system. *Central States Speech Journal* 23:92–99.

Henkel, RE. 1976. *Tests of significance.* Beverly Hills, Calfornia: Sage.

Henson, KT. 1995. *The art of writing for publication.* Needham Heights, Massachusetts: Allyn & Bacon.

Homan, R. 1991. *The ethics of social research.* London: Longman.

Howell, DC. 1995. *Fundamental statistics for the behavioural sciences.* (3rd edition). Belmont, California: Duxbury.

Hsia, HJ. 1988. *Mass communications research methods: a step-by-step approach.* Hillsdale, New Jersey: Lawrence Erlbaum.

Hult, CA. 1995. *Researching and writing in sciences and technology.* Needham Heights, Massachusetts: Allyn & Bacon.

Hult, CA. 1996. *Researching and writing in the social sciences.* Needham Heights, Massachusetts: Allyn & Bacon.

Inayatullah, S. 1998. Deconstructing the information era. *Futures* 30:2/3:235–247.

Innes, D, Kentridge, M and Perold, H (eds). 1993. *Reversing discrimination: affirmative action in the workplace.* Cape Town: Oxford University Press.

Jendrek, MP. 1985. *Through the maze: statistics with computer applications.* Belmont, California: Wadsworth.

Johnson, RB. 1997. Examining the validity structure of qualitative research. *Education* 118(2):282–292.

Kalton, G. 1983. *Introduction to survey sampling.* Beverly Hills, California: Sage.

Katz, E and Lazarsfeld, PF. 1964. *Personal influence.* Glencoe: Free.

Khoza, H. 1993. Affirmative action: a personal view, in *Reversing discrimination: affirmative action in the workplace,* edited by D Innes, M Kentridge and H Perold, Cape Town: Oxford University Press.

Kotler, P. 1997. *Marketing management. Analysis, planning, implementation and control.* (9th edition). New Jersey: Prentice Hall.

Kreps, GL. 1990. *Organizational communication: theory and practice.* (2nd edition). New York: Longman.

Krueger, RA. 1994. *Focus groups: a practical guide for applied research.* (2nd edition). Thousand Oaks, London: Sage.

Lasswell, H. 1948. The structure and function of communication in society, in *The communication of ideas,* edited by L Bryson. New York: Harper.

Lavrakas, PJ. 1987. *Telephone survey methods: sampling, selection, and supervision.* Beverly Hills, California: Sage.

Lazarsfeld, PF and Merton, RK. 1971. Mass communication, popular taste and organised social action, in *The processes and effects of mass communication,* edited by W Schramm and DF Roberts. Champaign: University of Illinois Press.

Leahy, M and Voice P. 1992. *The media book 1991/92.* Bryanston: WTM.

Leckenby, J and Wedding, N. 1982. *Advertising management.* Columbus, Ohio: Grid.

Leedy, PD. 1989. *Practical research: planning and design.* (4th edition). New York: Macmillan.

Leedy, PD. 1997. *Practical research: planning and design.* (6th edition). Upper Saddle River, New Jersey: Merrill, an imprint of Prentice Hall.

Leigh, JH and Martin, CR (eds). 1982. *Current issues & research in advertising.* Ann Arbor, Michigan: University of Michigan Press.

Lester, PM. 1995. *Visual communication. Images with messages.* Belmont, California: Wadsworth.

Lofland, J. 1971. *Analyzing social settings: a guide to qualitative observation and analysis.* Belmont, California: Wadsworth.

Lombaard, S. 1995. All set for the first democratic local elections. *RSA Review* 8(3):26–34.

Mandela, N. 1995. Collective responsibility for a human society. *RSA Review* 8(2):64–82.

Mandela, N. 1998. The state of the nation. Address by President Nelson Mandela to Parliament, 6 February 1998. *The building has begun! Government's report to the nation '98.* Pretoria: Government Communication and Information System.

Marcuse, H. 1964. *One-dimensional man.* London: Routledge & Kegan Paul.

Marshall, C and Rossman, GB. 1989. *Designing qualitative research.* Newbury Park, California: Sage.

McCroskey, JC. 1982. *An introduction to rhetorical communication.* (4th edition). Englewood Cliffs, New Jersey: Prentice Hall.

McDaniel, RRJ. 1997. Leadership: a view from quantum and chaos theory. *Health Care Management Review* 22(1):21–37.

McQuail, D. 1996. *Mass communication theory: an introduction.* (3rd edition), reprinted. London/Thousand Oaks, California: Sage.

McQuail, D. 1997. *Audience analysis.* Thousand Oaks, California: Sage.

McQuail, D. 2000. *McQuail's mass communication theory.* (4th edition). London: Sage.

Merton, RK. 1957. *Social theory and social structure.* New York: Free.

Meyer, P. 1973. *Precision journalism.* Bloomington, Indiana: University Press.

Mielke, KW and Chen, M. 1983. *Learning from television. Psychological and educational research.* London: Academic.

Milavsky, JR, Kessler, RC, Stipp, HH and Rubens, WS. 1982. *Television and aggression: a panel study.* New York: Academic.

Mills, CW. 1951. *White collar.* New York: Oxford University Press.

Mills, CW. 1956. *The power elite.* New York: Oxford University Press.

Mona, V. 2000. Teach the poor how to fish. *City Press* 5 March:10.

Morley, D. 1980. *The 'nationwide' audience.* London: BFI.

Morris, D. 1994. *Guidelines for writing a qualitative research report.* Chicago: American Marketing Association.

Morrison, D and Henkel, RE (eds). 1970. *The significance test controversy: a reader.* Chicago: Aldine-Atherton.

Mouton, J. 1996. *Understanding social research.* Pretoria: Van Schaik.

Mouton, J and Marais, HC. 1989. Metodologie van die geesteswetenskappe: Basiese begrippe. Pretoria: Raad vir Geesteswetenskaplike Navorsing.

Mowrey, ME. 1995. Feminist ethics and the 'postmodernist debate'. *The Annals of the Society of Christian Ethics.* 275–284.

Msane, T. 1995. Working towards a diverse agricultural sector. *RSA Review* 8(5):18–25

Neuman, WL. 1997. *Social research methods: qualitative and quantitative approaches.* (3rd edition). Boston, Mass: Allyn & Bacon.

Oosthuizen, LM. 1996. A brief history of communication research, in *Introduction to communication – course book 2: communication research* (reprinted edition), edited by GM du Plooy. Kenwyn: Juta.

Osgood, CE, Suci, GJ and Tannenbaum, PH. 1957. *The measurement of meaning.* Urbana: University of Illinois Press.

O'Sullivan, T, Hartley, J, Saunders, D, Montgomery, M and Fiske, J. 1996. *Key concepts in communication and cultural studies.* (2nd, reprinted edition). New York, NY: Routledge.

Patti, CH and Moriarty, SE. 1990. *The making of effective advertising.* Englewood Cliffs, New Jersey: Prentice Hall.

Pitfield, DJ and Naude, CMB. 1999. Public opinion on crime seriousness and sentencing. *South African Journal of Criminal Justice/Suid-Afrikaanse Tydskrif vir Strafregspleging* 12(1):22–40.

Pitout, M. 1996. Televisie en resepsiestudie: 'n analise van kykersinterpretasie van die seep-opera *Egoli – Plek van Goud*. DLitt et Phil, Universiteit van Suid-Afrika: Pretoria.

Plug, C, Louw, DAP, Gouws, LA and Meyer, WF. 1997. *Verklarende en vertalende sielkundewoordeboek*. Johannesburg: Heinemann.

Poole, MS and DeSanctis, G. 1992. Microlevel structuration in computer-supported group decision making. *Human Communication Research* 19(1):5–49.

Pottier, J (ed). 1993. *Practising development. Social sciences perspectives.* London: Routledge.

Priest, SH. 1996. *Doing media research: an introduction.* Thousand Oaks, California: Sage.

Real, M. 1989. *Supermedia.* London/Newbury Park, Calif: Sage.

Reinard, JC. 1994. *Introduction to communication research.* Dubuque, Iowa: Wm C Brown.

Rensburg, RS (ed). 1996. *Introduction to communication: course book 4 – communication planning and management.* Kenwyn: Juta.

Rensburg, RS and Angelopulo, GC. 1996. *Effective communication campaigns.* Halfway House: International Thomson.

Riffe, D, Lacey, S and Fico, FG. 1998. *Analyzing media messages.* Mahwah, New Jersey: Lawrence Erlbaum.

Robinson, J and Shaver, P. 1973. *Measures of social psychological attitudes.* (2nd edition). Ann Arbor, MI: Institute for Social Research.

Rogers, EM. 1962. *Diffusion of innovations.* New York: Free.

Rogers, EM. 1986. *Communication technology.* New York: Free.

Rogers, EM. 1993. Looking back, looking forward: a century of communication research, in *Beyond agendas; new directions in communication research,* edited by P Gaunt. Newhaven, CT: Greenwood.

Rogers, EM and Shoemaker, FF. 1971. *Communication of innovations.* London: Collier Macmillan.

Roscoe, J. 1975. *Fundamental research statistics for the behavioral sciences.* New York: Holt, Rinehart & Winston.

Rosnow, RL and Rosenthal, R. 1999. *Beginning behavioral research. A conceptual primer.* (3rd edition). Upper Sadle River, New Jersey: Prentice Hall.

Rossouw, J. 1999. Inligting word nie sommer net kennis. Perspektief, *Rapport* 21 November: 3.

Rothman, J and Thomas EJ. 1994. *Intervention research: design and development for human service.* New York: Haworth.

Rubin, A and Babbie, A. 1993. *Research methods for social work.* (2nd edition). Pacific Grove, California: Brooks/Cole.

Russell, T and Verrill, G. 1986. *Otto Kleppner's advertising procedure.* (9th edition). Englewood Cliffs, New Jersey: Prentice Hall.

Samovar, LA and Porter, RE (eds). 1995. *Communication between cultures.* (2nd edition). Belmont, California: Wadsworth.

Schiffman, SS, Reynolds, ML and Young, FW. 1981. *Introduction to multidimensional scaling: theory, methods, and applications.* New York: Academic.

Schwandt, DR and Marquardt, MJ. 1999. *Organizational learning from world class theories to global best practices.* MA: Saint Lucie.

Scott, W. 1955. Reliability of content analysis: the case of nominal scale coding. *Public Opinion Quarterly* 321–325.

Seaman, CHC. 1987. *Research methods: principles, practice, and theory nursing.* (3rd edition). Los Alton, California: Prentice Hall.

Servaes, J. 1989. *One world, multiple cultures: a new paradigm on communication for development.* Leuven: Acco.

Servaes, J (ed). 1996. *Participatory communication for social change.* Thousand Oaks, California: Sage.

Servaes, J. 1999. *Communication for development: one world, multiple cultures.* Cresskill, New Jersey: Hampton.

Shannon, C and Weaver, W (eds). 1949. *The mathematical theory of communication.* Urbana, Illinois: University of Illinois Press.

Shapiro, MJ. 1970. Discovering interviewer bias in open-ended survey responses. *Public Opinion Quarterly* 34(3): 412–415.

Shaw, ME and Wright, JM. 1967. *Scales for the measurement of attitudes.* New York: McGraw-Hill.

Silverstone, R. 1999. *Why study the media?* London: Sage.

Singer, E and Presser, S (eds). 1989. *Survey research methods: a reader.* Chicago: University of Chicago Press.

Singh, JP. 1998. Unravelling 'the missing link': the provision of telecommunications services in select developing countries. *Communicatio* 24(1):48–58.

Smit, GJ. 1995. *Research: guidelines for planning and documentation.* Halfway House: Southern.

Smith, MJ. 1988. *Contemporary communication research methods.* Belmont, California: Wadsworth.

South Africa. 1995. Labour Relations Act 66 of 1995. Pretoria: Government Printer.

South Africa. 1996a. Films and Publications Act 65 of 1996. Pretoria: Government Printer.

South Africa. 1996b. The Constitution of the Republic of South Africa Act 108 of 1996. Pretoria: Government Printer.

South Africa. 1997. Green Paper – Broadcasting Policy. Pretoria: The Ministry for Posts, Telecommunications & Broadcasting.

South Africa. 1998a. Employment Equity Act 55 of 1998. Pretoria: Government Printer.

South Africa. 1998b. Skills Development Act 97 of 1998. Pretoria: Government Printer.

Stacks, DW and Hocking, JE. 1992. *Essentials of communication research.* New York, NY: HarperCollins.

Statistics South Africa (Stats SA) – previously Central Statistical Service (CSS). 1999. *The people of South Africa population census, 1996.* Report no. 03–01–11 (1996). Pretoria: Statistics South Africa.

Steinberg, S. 1999. *Communication studies: an introduction.* Kenwyn: Juta.

Steinberg, S and Du Plooy GM. 1999. *Introduction to communication studies.* Only study guide for COM101–X. Pretoria: University of South Africa.

Stewart, CJ and Cash, WB. 1982. *Interviewing: principles and practices.* (3rd edition). Dubuque, Iowa: Wm C Brown.

Stewart, DW and Shamdasani, PN. 1990. *Focus groups. Theory and practice.* Newbury Park, California: Sage.

Strauss, A and Corbin, J. 1990. *Basics of qualitative research: grounded theory procedures and techniques.* Newbury Park, California: Sage.

Ströh, U. 1998. Communication management in a millennium of chaos and change. *Communicare* 17(2):16–41.

Strunk, W and White, EB. 1995. *The elements of style.* Neeham Heights, Massachusetts: Allyn & Bacon.

Sudman, S and Bradburn, NM. 1982. *Asking questions: a practical guide to questionnaire design.* San Francisco: Jossey-Bass.

*Sunday Times.* 1999. *Sunday Times Magazine* (an advertisement for *Sunday Times Magazine*) 31 October:29.

*Sunday World.* 1999. Black icons of the millennium 3 October:12

Swanepoel, H. 1992. *Community development: putting plans into action.* (2nd edition). Kenwyn: Juta.

Tagiuri, R and Petrullo, L (eds). 1958. *Person perception and interpersonal behavior.* Stanford: Stanford University Press.

Tannenbaum, PH (ed). 1980. *The entertainment functions of television.* Hillsdale, New Jersey: Lawrence Erlbaum.

Terre Blanche, M and Durrheim, K (eds). 1999. *Research in practice: applied methods for the social sciences.* Cape Town: UCT Press.

Thomas, EJ. 1984. *Designing intervention for the helping professions.* Beverly Hills: Sage.

Traugott, MW and Katosh, JP. 1979. Response validity in surveys of voting behavior. *Public Opinion Quarterly* 43:359–377.

Tuckman, BW. 1975. *Measuring educational outcomes: fundamentals of testing.* New York: Harcourt Brace Jovanovich.

Tuckman, BW. 1978. *Conducting educational research.* (2nd edition). New York: Harcourt Brace Jovanovich.

Turner, AG. 1982. What subjects of survey research believe about confidentiality, in *The ethics of social research: surveys and experiments,* edited by JE Sieber. New York: Springer.

University of South Africa. Department of Communication. 1995. *Introduction to communication research. Only study guide for CMN211–W.* Pretoria.

University of South Africa. Faculty of Arts. 2000. *Research in the social sciences. Only study guide for RSC201–H.* Pretoria.

Van Niekerk, MH. 1998. Putting a portfolio together – some guidelines. *Progressio* 20(2):81–101.

Walther, JB and Burgoon JK. 1992. Relational communication in computer-mediated interaction. *Human Communication Research* 19(1):50–88.

Watt, JH and Van den Berg, SA. 1995. *Research methods for communication science.* Needham Heights, Massachusetts: Allyn & Bacon.

Webster, JG. and Phalen, PF. 1997. *The mass audience: rediscovering the dominant model.* Mahawa, New Jersey: Lawrence Erlbaum.

Weeks, MF and Moore, RP. 1981. Ethnicity-of-interviewer effects on ethnic respondents. *Public Opinion Quarterly* 45:245–249.

Westmeyer, PM. 1994. *A guide for use in planning, conducting, and reporting research projects.* (2nd edition). Springfield, Ilinois: Charles C Thomas.

Whithers, JR. 1994. *Conceptual dictionary.* Kenwyn: Juta & TTT Programme, University of Natal.

Wildman, RC. 1977. Effects of anonymity and social setting on survey responses. *Public Opinion Quarterly* 41(1):74–79.

Wimmer, RD and Dominick, JR. 1994. *Mass media research: an introduction.* (4th edition). Belmont, California: Wadsworth.

Wimmer, RD and Dominick, JR. 1997. *Mass media research: an introduction.* (5th edition). Belmont, California: Wadsworth.

Winston, B. 1998. *Media, technology and society.* London: Routledge.

Wolf, FM (ed). 1986. *Meta-analysis: quantitative methods for research synthesis.* Beverly Hills, California: Sage.

Wyatt, D and Campbell, D. 1950. A study of interviewer bias as related to interviewer expectations and own opinions. *International Journal of Opinion and Attitude Research* 4:77–83.

Youngblood, MD. 1997. *Life at the edge of chaos: creating the quantum organization.* Dallas: Perceval.

# Index

advertising message research 217, 218–40
  advertising goals 231, 232, 233
  characteristic elements of advertisements 226
  cognitive, affective and conative dimensions of persuasive effects 217, 233, 237, 254
  consumers' behaviours, values and lifestyles 217, 218–24
  content analysis 218, 225, 230, 235
  experimental research 217, 218
  field research 218
  longitudinal research 223, 224
  market segmentation 219
  marketing research 222
  mass market 219, 220
  message content 224–30
  motivational intervention 223
  opinion leaders 221, 222
  self-reporting techniques 222
  survey research 218, 221, 223, 233, 234, 236, 245
analysis
  audience (*see* audience analyses)
  data 93
  content 159, 160, 161, 181, 185, 191–7, 199, 201, 206
  units of 54, 55, 81, 85, 89
  verbal (spoken) communication 197–200
applied research 27, 28, 48, 159–340
  assumptions, conceptual model 20–1
  epistemological 20, 21, 27, 32, 35
  methodological 21, 27, 32
  ontological 20, 21, 22, 24, 30, 35, 40
  theoretical 20, 21, 24, 25, 26, 27, 28, 31, 32, 39
audience analyses (print and broadcast media)
  aided-recall techniques 172, 234, 242, 244
  audience profiles 241–2, 245, 252
  item-selection studies 242–3, 245
  masked recall 244
  reader/non-reader studies 235, 243–5
  survey research 233, 234, 236, 245
  typography and lay-out research 247
  unaided-recall techniques 235, 244, 254
  uses and gratifications studies 245–6, 253, 254
audience analysis techniques 172
audit
  communication 261, 307, 313–8
  public relations (PR) 261, 304–13
  social 261, 265–82, 313
basic research 19, 28, 48
bias 86, 101, 106, 108, 110–13, 115, 117, 124, 130
coding categories (*see also* observations)
  absolute zero 120
  exhaustive 119, 150, 151
  mutually exclusive 119, 140, 142, 150
  rank order 119
communication, verbal (spoken) 197–200
communication audit 261, 307, 313–8

communication diary 314, 315
communication experience forms 314, 315, 316
content analysis 263, 266, 306, 309, 310, 314
focus-group interviews 273, 279, 284, 297, 299, 305, 309, 314
methods, techniques, measuring instruments 313–5
network analyses 314, 315
personal interviews 305, 314
Readability Ease tests 312, 314
readership studies 313
self-administered questionnaires 305, 314, 315, 316
conceptual model, assumptions 20–1
content analysis 159, 160, 161, 181, 185, 191–7, 199, 201, 206
  coder training 197
  coding or tallying the data 193–7, 198, 213
  contiguous analysis 198, 199, 200
  contingency table 194, 195
  post-coded categories 196
  pre-coded categories 196
  proportion 192, 195, 196
  ratio 194, 195, 196, 203
  sampling 161, 167, 170, 183, 186, 187, 189, 193
  scale scoring 195
  scientific requirements 192
cross-sectional designs 85
data
  analysing 93
  interpreting 93
  self-report 134
  sources (*see* sources of data)
data collection 93, 99–158
  devices and techniques 147–8
  interview schedule 143, 147
  items in self-administered questionnaire 137–43
  measuring 117–33
  observing 147–54
  questioning 134–46
  sampling 100–16
  self-administered questionnaire 105, 134, 137–43, 147, 155
  types of interview questions 143–4
definitions 60, 61, 62, 64, 65, 70
  operational 62, 64, 66, 67, 70, 72, 82, 88
  theoretical 62, 66, 67, 70, 72, 79
dimension of persuasive effects 217, 231, 233
  affective 230, 235
  cognitive 230, 233, 234
  conative 217, 237, 254
elementary descriptive statistics 159, 160, 191, 200–6, 208
  basic statistical notations 202
  central tendency 189, 203, 204, 205
  data array 204
  frequency distribution 194, 205

mean 203, 204, 205, 308
    median 203, 204
    mode 203, 205
    standard deviation 205, 206
    total range 205, 206
environmental monitoring research 261, 262–4
    content analysis 263, 266, 306, 309, 310, 314
    longitudinal tracking 263
    monitoring public opinion 262
    monitoring social events 262
    survey research 283, 314
error (sources of) 181–82, 189–90
    compliance 182
    contrast error 189
    deviation 182, 205, 206
    error of central tendency 189
    error of leniency 189
    error of severity 189
    halo effect 189
    Hawthorne effect 188
    minimising (see minimising sources of error)
    personal style 181-2
    situational factors 181
    social factors 181, 182
ethical implications (of research proposal) 90–1
ethical issues 91, 159, 173, 182, 188, 211–2
    collecting data 160, 161, 172, 173, 186
    interpreting data 159, 211, 213
ethnography 29, 30, 99, 148, 151–3
evaluation 44, 45, 50, 52, 58, 62, 65, 79
    peer 62
feasibility (of research proposal) 51, 90–1
field observations 162, 186–90
    complete observer (covert) 186, 187
    complete participant (overt/covert) 187, 188
    covert observations 186, 187
    observer-as-participant (overt) 187
    participant-as-observer (overt) 187
    roles fulfilled by observer 187
    sources of error (see error) 189–90
focus groups 178–84
    implementation procedures 182–4
    informed consent 173, 180, 188
    moderator 179, 180, 181, 182, 183, 184, 197
    pre-group questionnaire 180
    procedures followed in 179–81
    realised sample 180
    screener 180
    sources of error 181–2
group research designs
    control 162, 163, 164, 165, 166, 167, 168, 205
    control over the research environment 167–8
    experimental 162, 164, 165, 166, 167, 168, 205
    factorial designs 164, 166, 167, 212
    notation for experimental designs 164
    post-test-only control-group 164, 165, 166, 186, 212
    pre-test-posttest control-group 164, 212
    randomisation 164, 168

hypotheses 28, 44, 48, 64, 66, 71, 72, 73–5, 76,
    82, 83, 84, 88, 91, 92, 93
    concepts 48, 60, 61, 62, 64, 65, 66–70,
    77, 78, 82, 84, 85
    constructs 66–70, 72, 73, 82, 88
    criteria for formulation 51, 64, 73
    formulating 66–81
    types of hypotheses 74, 75–7
    variables 47, 50, 52, 53, 54, 55, 61, 62, 66, 70–2,
    73, 75, 76, 77, 78, 81, 82, 87
industrialisation 22, 24, 30
interviews 175–8
    debriefing 188
    inter-interviewers variability 183
    interview schedule 161, 175, 176, 177, 183
    partially structured 176, 177
    projective techniques 178
    questions, types of 143–4
    standardised 176–7
    structured 176–7, 178
    unstructured 176, 177–8, 183
items
    abbreviations 137
    ambiguous 136
    complex 137
    double-barrelled 134, 135
    incomplete 136
    lengthy 136
    loaded language 135
    negative 128, 130, 131, 135
    one logical answer 135
    presumptive 135
    problems with wording 145
    questionable assumption 134, 135
    throw-away questions 176, 182
    vague agents of action 136
levels of measurement
    interval 120, 121
    nominal 118–9
    ordinal 119–20, 131
    ratio 120–1
literature review 44, 49, 57, 65, 66, 82, 87, 93, 95,
    57–65
    critical 58, 60, 61, 60–5
    getting started 58
    recording and summarising 63–5
longitudinal designs
    cohort study 85, 86, 263
    panel study 85, 86
    trend study 85
mass-media efficiency 248
    circulation 73, 217, 246, 248, 250, 252
    CPT (cost per thousand) 250, 252
    formulas and calculations 249, 251, 252
    frequency 217, 248, 249
    gross ratings points 217, 248, 249
    HUT (households using television) 251, 254, 252
    PUR (persons using radio) 251, 252

ratings 217, 230, 246, 248, 250, 251, 253, 254, 255
reach 28, 248, 249, 252
research 217, 218, 233, 234, 236, 245, 248–57
share 231, 252
meanings 48, 54, 61, 62, 63, 66, 73
connotative 66, 67, 84
denotative 66, 70
measurement 67, 68, 70, 71, 85, 86, 92, 99–158, 99
indirect 68, 69
levels of 117–21
measuring instrument 65, 67, 69, 85, 86, 90, 92,
principles of 117–21
reliability 121–4
scales 127–32 (*see also* scaling)
validity 124–7
message content 224
elements of advertisements 226
focus-group interviews 224, 225, 226, 233, 247, 253, 255
motivational research 224, 247, 253
testing 224, 226, 247, 253
message effectiveness 231–8, 244
advertising goals 231–3
AIDA 232
aided-recall techniques 234, 242, 244, 254
blind test 235
marketing mix 233
PEAC 236
tests 234, 237
unaided-recall techniques 235, 244, 254
message structure 230–1
pilot tests 231
Readability Ease tests, 206–9, 230
research 217, 230, 248, 250–3, 254
storyboard 230, 253
minimising sources of error
coder training 197
pilot tests 174, 189
reliability tests 174, 197
respondent validation 190
triangulation 190
validity tests 189
modernisation 24
narratives
confessional 201
impressionistic 202
realist 202
nonprobability samples
convenience 105, 114
dipstick 114
known-group 114
purposive 114, 263
quota 114, 115
snowball 114, 115
volunteer 115
non-ratings research 217, 248, 253–5
Appreciation Index 75, 254
audiences profiles 245, 252, 241, 217, 242

call-out 255
formative 220, 221, 230, 253
summative 230, 253, 254
uses and gratifications studies 217, 245, 253, 254
observations
data 100, 148, 149
data-collection devices and techniques 147–8
ethnographic 99, 148, 151–3
field 162, 186–90
indexing communication 152
observation schedule 100, 148, 149, 150, 151
systematic 148–51
operationalisation 67, 69, 85 (*see also* definitions)
paradigm 19, 20, 21, 24, 31, 33, 38, 39, 40
participatory action research 261, 272, 293–304
field research 284, 282
notes of caution 302–3
prerequisites 296, 297
research process 296, 297–300, 301, 302, 305, 309
survey research 283, 284
participatory strategies
behavioural change 285–7, 293
community empowerment 289–91, 293, 300
co-optation 288–289
educational-therapeutic 284–5
organisational conditions or demands 283, 284, 286, 287, 289, 290
researching 283–92, 314
supplementary employees 287–8, 293
pilot test 48, 93, 189
population 49, 53, 54, 62, 75, 82, 83, 85, 89
accessible 85, 86, 101
parameters 53, 54, 55, 91, 100
target 53, 85, 101
units of analysis 53, 54, 55, 78, 81
postmodernisation 24
presentational criteria and credibility
cohesiveness 353, 358
graphs and tables 354–6
introduction 353
limitations 357–8
objectiveness and accuracy 357
presentation of conclusions 358–9
presentation of findings 358
register 353–4
statistics 357
technical requirements 352, 354
title 352
principles of measurement 117–21
reality isomorphism principle 118
rule of correspondence 118
probability samples
known quotas 107, 108
simple random 102, 107, 111, 104, 105
strata 108, 109
stratified random 108, 109
public relations (PR) audit 261, 304–13
content analysis 263, 266, 306, 309, 310, 314
corporate image 265, 266, 305–9, 314

external publics 265, 266, 267, 278, 304, 305, 306, 307, 309, 314
    field research 284, 282
    gatekeeping research 310
    internal publics 305, 307
    PR campaign 304, 305, 309–12
    survey research 283, 284
qualitative approach 15, 16, 19, 21, 29, 32, 34, 37, 38, 39
    application of 34–8
qualitative design, characteristics of 83–4
qualitative research approach 29–34
quantitative approach 21–9, 32, 34–8
quantitative design, characteristics of 82–3
quasi-probability samples
    area 111
    cluster random 110, 112, 113
    multistage random 110, 111, 112
    systematic random 103, 110, 111
questions
    closed-ended 138, 139, 140, 142, 143
    direct 138
    general 138
    indirect 138
    open-ended 138, 139, 140, 143, 144
    problems experiences in wording 134–7
    specific 138, 151
    unstructured 143, 144, 152, 155
questions/statements (*see* items)
RDP 8, 14, 47, 264, 294–7
Readability Ease tests 159, 160, 191, 193, 206–9
reasoning 54
    deductive 27, 82
    inductive 32, 82, 83
    subjective 83
relationship, types of 77–9
reliability 60, 61, 64, 81, 86, 92, 93, 121–4
    computer programs 123–4
    equivalency 122, 123, 124
    intercoder 123, 196
    internal consistency 122, 123, 124
    item-to-total 123, 155
    measurement 121, 132
    random errors 121
    stability 122, 124
    unobtrusiveness 85
replication 47, 49
research
    advertising message 217, 218–40
    applied 27, 28, 159–340
    basic 19, 28
    environmental monitoring 261, 262–4
    historical 160, 185
    in controlled environments 161–9
    in natural environments 185–91
    future 38–40
    of advertising, mass-media audiences and mass-

    media efficiency 216–59
    nonratings 217, 248, 253–5
    participatory action 261, 272, 293–304
    process 44–98
research data, interpreting 159–215
research design 44, 49, 62, 65, 81, 84, 85, 87, 89, 90, 91, 93, 95, 162–7
    content analysis 159–215
    cross-sectional 82, 85
    experimental 50, 52, 79, 83, 86, 91, 159, 160, 163, 164, 205
    field research 159, 160, 161, 178, 185, 186
    group 163–7
    longitudinal 82, 85–7
    pre-testing 93
    qualitative 72, 81, 65, 69, 83, 84, 88, 92, 95
    quantitative 81, 49, 65, 69, 81, 82, 83, 84, 88, 91, 93, 95
    quasi-experimental 50, 52, 91
    selecting or developing the 81–7
    single-system 162–3
    survey research 160, 183, 160, 183
    threats to the validity of 84–7
research goals 48, 51
research objectives 48, 49, 50, 82–3, 88, 89, 179
research problem 44, 64, 79, 90
    assumptions 48, 79, 44, 49, 51–57, 60, 61, 62, 75, 79, 83, 88, 89, 95
    formulating the 44, 50, 51–57, 87, 95
    identifying and analysing 45–57
    subproblems 48, 53, 79, 44, 51–57, 61, 72, 75, 88, 95
research proposal
    feasibility 51, 90–1
    writing a 88–92
research questions 44, 66–81, 84, 88, 91, 93, 72–3, 293–4 (*see also* hypotheses)
research report 94–5, 341–62
    analysis of data 93, 345, 349–50
    assumptions 343, 344, 351
    collection of data 93, 345, 346–8
    contextual evaluation 350–2
    ethical requirements 348
    evaluation criteria 369
    feasibility 351
    generalisability 351
    literature review 341, 342, 344–5, 352, 353
    methodological evaluation 345–50
    methodology 342, 344
    presentational criteria and credibility 341, 342, 351, 352, 357, 359
    problem criteria 342, 343–4
    propriety 351
    research design 345–6, 351, 353, 357, 358
    thematic evaluation 341, 342–5, 346
    theoretical aspects 342, 344–5
    utility 351

research setting 163, 168
   controlled 159, 161, 163, 186
   natural 159, 185
   semi-controlled 159, 169
samples 105, 106, 107, 110, 112, 113, 180
sampling 61, 90, 91, 81, 99–158, 193
   accessible population 101, 102, 115
   accuracy of the sample drawn 101–3, 111
   availability 89
   calculation of the standard error 102, 103
   ecological fallacy 106
   error related to the degree of confidence 104–6
   level of confidence 101
   periodicity 111
   population parameters 101, 102, 103, 108, 114, 115
   replication 47, 49, 113
   representativeness 109, 115
   sample rate 110
   sampling interval 110
   table of random numbers 107, 112
   target population 101, 108, 113, 114, 115
   types of 99, 106–15
   validity 105, 113, 124
scaling 127–32
   comparing 127
   counting 127
   Likert scale 117, 127, 128–9, 137, 141, 155
   ranking 127, 139, 140, 154
   semantic differential 117, 127, 129–32
scientific method, characteristics or requirements 18–9
self-administered questionnaire
   applying a 315–6
   closed-ended questions 138, 139, 140, 142, 143
   compiling the 172–5
   contingency questions 139
   filter questions 139
   formatting the 173–4
   inventory questions 140, 143
   items in 137–43
   matrix questions 140, 141
   multiple-choice questions 142
   open-ended questions 123, 138, 140, 143, 144
   paired-comparison questions 139
   precoding 175
   ranking questions 139, 140, 154
social audit 261, 265–82, 313
   affirmative action 265, 266, 270–3, 279
   content analysis 263, 266, 306, 309, 310, 314
   corporate identity 265–6, 305, 306, 314
   corporate image 265–6, 305, 306, 314
   corporate personality 265
   employment policies and conditions of service 266–9, 279
   field research 284, 282
   in-service training and mentorship 266, 273–7
   management of change 278
   organisational and management structures 265–6, 278–81

participative management 279
   social investments and services 266, 277–8, 279
   substantive nature of an organisation 265, 266–78
   survey research 283, 314
sources of data 59, 60, 82, 93
statistics 159, 160, 191, 200–6, 208
surveys 170–2
   computer-administered 170
   DBM 170, 183
   group-administered 170–2
   mail 170–2, 178
   personal 172
   telephone 170, 172
theories
   agenda-setting 26
   cultivation 26
   grounded 32
   information theory 24
   stimulus-response 25, 28
   two-step flow 25
   uses and gratifications 26
triangulation 39, 81, 190, 299
units of analysis 54, 55, 81, 85, 89, 191, 197, 198
unstructured questions 143–4, 152, 155
urbanisation 22, 24
uses and gratifications 216, 217, 245, 246, 253, 254
validity 61, 64, 81, 93, 60, 70
   construct 126–7, 155
   content 125
   criterion-based 125–6
   expert-jury 125, 155
   external 84, 85, 87, 105, 113, 124, 108, 111
   face 70, 125, 155
   internal 84, 85, 86, 105
   measurement 70, 124
   threats to 84, 85, 84–7
variables 49, 50, 52, 53, 54, 55, 61, 62, 66, 70–2, 73, 75, 76, 77, 78, 81, 82, 87
   characteristic 71
   continuous 70, 71, 118 120
   dependent 50, 52, 71, 72, 85
   dichotomous 70
   discrete 70, 71, 117, 118
   extraneous (confounding) 71, 72
   extraneous (intervening) 71, 72
   independent 50, 52, 71, 72, 78, 85, 86
   polytomic 70
ways of knowing 16, 17–19, 33
   a priori method 17, 18
   method of authority 17
   method of reasonableness 17, 18
   method of tenacity 17
   mystical method 17
   scientific method 17, 18, 19, 27
WWW (World Wide Web) 58, 59, 247, 253